downstream

ENVIRONMENTAL
HUMANITIES

Environmental Humanities Series

Environmental thought pursues with renewed urgency the grand concerns of the humanities: who we think we are, how we relate to others, and how we live in the world. Scholarship in the environmental humanities explores these questions by crossing the lines that separate human from animal, social from material, and objects and bodies from techno-ecological networks. Humanistic accounts of political representation and ethical recognition are re-examined in consideration of other species. Social identities are studied in relation to conceptions of the natural, the animal, the bodily, place, space, landscape, risk, and technology, and in relation to the material distribution and contestation of environmental hazards and pleasures.

The Environmental Humanities Series features research that adopts and adapts the methods of the humanities to clarify the cultural meanings associated with environmental debate. The scope of the series is broad. Film, literature, television, Web-based media, visual art, and physical landscape—all are crucial sites for exploring how ecological relationships and identities are lived and imagined. The Environmental Humanities Series publishes scholarly monographs and essay collections in environmental cultural studies, including popular culture, film, media, and visual cultures; environmental literary criticism; cultural geography; environmental philosophy, ethics, and religious studies; and other cross-disciplinary research that probes what it means to be human, animal, and technological in an ecological world.

Gathering research and writing in environmental philosophy, ethics, cultural studies, and literature under a single umbrella, the series aims to make visible the contributions of humanities research to environmental studies, and to foster discussion that challenges and reconceptualizes the humanities.

Series Editor:
Cheryl Lousley, English and Interdisciplinary Studies, Lakehead University

Editorial Committee:
Brett Buchanan, Philosophy, Laurentian University
Adrian J. Ivakhiv, Environmental Studies, University of Vermont
Cate Sandilands, CRC in Sustainability and Culture, Environmental Studies,
    York University
Susie O'Brien, English and Cultural Studies, McMaster University
Laurie Ricou, English, University of British Columbia
Rob Shields, Henry Marshall Tory Chair and Professor, Department of Sociology,
    University of Alberta

downstream
reimagining water

Dorothy Christian
and Rita Wong
editors

**WILFRID LAURIER
UNIVERSITY PRESS**

Wilfrid Laurier University Press acknowledges the support of the Canada Council for the Arts for our publishing program. We acknowledge the financial support of the Government of Canada through the Canada Book Fund for our publishing activities. This work was supported by the Research Support Fund. This book has been published with the help of a grant from the Canadian Federation for the Humanities and Social Sciences, through the Awards to Scholarly Publications Program, using funds provided by the Social Sciences and Humanities Research Council of Canada.

Library and Archives Canada Cataloguing in Publication

downstream : reimagining water / Dorothy Christian and Rita Wong, editors.

(Environmental humanities)
Includes bibliographical references and index.
Issued in print and electronic formats.
ISBN 978-1-77112-213-9 (paperback).—ISBN 978-1-77112-214-6 (pdf).—ISBN 978-1-77112-215-3 (epub)

1. Water—Social aspects. I. Wong, Rita, [date], editor II. Christian, Dorothy, [date], editor III. Series: Environmental humanities

GB665.D69 2016   553.7   C2016-905178-1
                                       C2016-905179-X

Cover design by Lara Minja, Lime Design, Inc. Cover photo: *Adams River Salmon Run*, by Michael D. Blackstock. Text design by Angela Booth Malleau, designbooth.ca.

© 2017 Wilfrid Laurier University Press
Waterloo, Ontario, Canada
www.wlupress.wlu.ca

This book is printed on FSC® certified paper and is certified Ecologo. It contains post-consumer fibre, is processed chlorine free, and is manufactured using biogas energy.

Printed in Canada

Dedicated to
Violet Caibaiosai
(October 26, 1952–August 13, 2016)

Noodinnasemegabowet (Woman Facing into the Wind),
water guardian, and *Downstream* contributor. Violet passed into the
spirit world while this publication was in process. She was a beautiful
Water Walker and one of the original Grandmothers who began with
Josephine Mandamin. Violet dedicated her life to Nibi (Water), the
Minaaweyweygaan Midewiwin Lodge, her family, and
to the Anishinabe people.

and to
Paul Harrison

downstream contributor who passed away suddenly and
tragically on December 17, 2016,while on a ship giving a series
of oceanography talks. Humble mentor to many, Paul loved learning and
spending time in nature. He was Professor Emeritus at the University
of British Columbia, an outstanding international scientist who
contributed tremendously to oceanography.

and to the
Peace River

the spirit of water, and life downstream
all the way to the Arctic Ocean

Contents

Acknowledgements   ix

Introduction: Re-storying Waters, Re-storying Relations   1
Rita Wong and Dorothy Christian

Part I: Contexts for Knowing and Unknowing Water

1   Planetary Distress Signals   29
Alanna Mitchell

2   Water   33
Lee Maracle

3   Interweaving Water: The Incremental Transformation of   39
Sovereign Knowledge into Collaborative Knowledge
Michael D. Blackstock

4   Water and Knowledge   51
Astrida Neimanis

5   Excerpts from "a child's fable"   69
Baco Ohama

Part II: Water Testimonies: Witness, Worry, and Work

6   Water: The First Foundation of Life   75
Mona Polacca

7   From Our Homelands to the Tar Sands   81
Melina Laboucan Massimo

8   Keepers of the Water: Nishnaabe-kwewag Speaking   89
for the Water
Renée Elizabeth Mzinegiizhigo-kwe Bédard

9   Water Walk Pedagogy   107
     Violet Caibaiosai

10   A Response to Pascua Lama   113
     Cecilia Vicuña

Part III: Shared Ethical and Embodied Practices

11   Moving with Water: Relationships and Responsibilities   117
     Alannah Young Leon and Denise Marie Nadeau

12   Bodies of Water: Meaning in Movement   139
     Seonagh Odhiambo Horne

13   Upstream: A Conversation with Water   161
     Cathy Stubington

14   Ice Receding/Books Reseeding   181
     Basia Irland

15   Tsunami Chant   193
     Wang Ping

Part IV: A Respectful Coexistence in Common:
Water Perspectives

16   Listening to the Elders at the Keepers of the Water Gathering   197
     Radha D'Souza

17   Coastal Waters in Distress from Excessive Nutrients   207
     Paul J. Harrison

18   Bodies of Water: Asian Canadians In/Action with Water   217
     Janey Lew

19   Permeable Toronto: A Hydro-Eutopia   241
     Janine MacLeod

20   Saturate/Dissolve: Water for Itself, Un-Settler Responsibilities,   259
     and Radical Humility
     Larissa Lai

21   Bring Me Back   271
     Janet Rogers

About the Contributors   275

Index   281

Acknowledgements

Waters, we thank you! The *Downstream* anthology comes from many streams that have flowed together. We would like to thank all the contributors, as well as the many participants and helpers whose efforts helped to make the Downstream gathering happen in a good way in March 2012, including but not limited to Florence James, Larry Grant, Chief Bill Williams, Amy (Marie) George, Jeff Bear, Art Leon, Cecilia Chen, Matthew Evenden, Karen Bakker, Leila Harris, Marissa Munoz, Shahira Sakiyama, Janey Lew, Asava Dance, Sandra Semchuk, Naomi Steinberg, Celia Brauer, Jeneen Frei Njootli, Samantha (Lefort) Welsh, Chookien Kua, Vanessa Brown, Elisa Yon, Elisa Ferrari, Marten Sims, Heather Lippold, Rocio Graham, Carol Tsang, Hiromi Goto, Beth Carruthers, Bryson Robertson, and more. Thank you to the Aboriginal Gathering Place at Emily Carr University of Art and Design for hosting this originating gathering—Brenda Crabtree and Michelle Sound, you rock! We would also like to thank all the artists who participated in the Downstream exhibition: Sheinagh Anderson, Michaela Baer, Neil Chung, Caitlyn Connors, Alyssa Dusevic, Jennifer Hagel, Maegan Harbbridge, Peter Holmes, Julia Hong, Basia Irland, Maria Lantin and Leila Sujir, Nathalie Lavoie, Jennifer Martin, Caroline Mousseau, Fabiola Nabil Naguib, Alex Phillips, William Phong-Ly, David Roth, Emile Rubino, Diana Lynn Thompson, Marika Swan, Gu Xiong. Special thanks to Alannah Young Leon and Denise Nadeau for guidance early on, and to Lee Maracle for introducing us to each other.

We gratefully acknowledge the Social Sciences and Humanities Research Council of Canada for the Research-Creation and Workshop grants that made this anthology possible, as well as the Network in Canadian History and Environment Water (NiCHE) History Project, UBC's Program of Water Governance, and the President's Research Fund of Emily Carr University.

We thank our families and friends, whose support and love makes our water work possible, and we acknowledge the deeply inspiring work of the Vancouver Women's Water Collective, the Peace River protectors, Standing Rock, Keepers of the Water, the Tar Sands Healing Walk, the Mother Earth Water Walkers, and the Unist'ot'en Camp, whose guardianship of the Wedzin Kwah has taught us so much. Thank you, water protectors everywhere. For each and every day we live and work on the unceded Coast Salish territories of the Tsleil-Waututh First Nation, the Squamish First Nation, the Musqueam First Nation, the Sto:lo Nation, thank you.

Introduction
Re-storying Waters, Re-storying Relations
Rita Wong and Dorothy Christian

In March 2002, we the co-editors, Rita Wong and Dorothy Christian, met at a conference organized by Lee Maracle, called Imagining Asian and Native Women: Deconstructing from Contact to Modern Times at Western Washington University. This conference brought together Indigenous and Asian Canadian women writers for some critical dialogues. Since that fortuitous meeting over a decade ago, we have both come to live as guests on unceded Coast Salish territories, the homelands of the Musqueam, the Squamish, and the Tsleil-Waututh, also known as Vancouver. During this time, we have also come to articulate more consciously that water is a bond that brings us together. This is a connection that we share with each and every reader who encounters this anthology. Building from the Downstream gathering in Vancouver in 2012 that brought together artists, scientists, writers, Elders, environmentalists, scholars, and activists to discuss our work with water, this anthology focuses on cultivating peaceful and creative cultures that foreground water as a builder of relationships.

Dorothy carries three tribal names from the land: Cucw-la7 from Splatsin (her Secwepemc community), Kwash Kay from the Syilx (her grandmother's people), and Animkibinesikwe from the Anishinabe people, who adopted her into the Otter clan when she lived on their territories. As a child she spent her summers swimming in the Shuswap River and helping out when it was time to pick berries and catch salmon for winter food supplies. Shuswap, Okanagan, and Kalamalka lakes, all freshwater lakes, are also a big part of her childhood water memories. She now lives on the shores of a great body of salt water known as the Pacific Ocean.

The backstory of her alliance building work started after the so-called Oka Crisis in 1990. Following this life-altering event, which left her with a post-traumatic stress disorder that took years to recover from, she questioned how Indigenous peoples were to live a peaceful coexistence with the settler populations. This quest started by examining her relationships with white settler people, which is documented in a chapter she co-wrote with Victoria Freeman, "The History of a Friendship, or Some Thoughts on Becoming Allies" in 2010.[1] Then she expanded her discussion to look at other settler populations, which resulted in a chapter, "Reconciling with the People and the Land" (2011).[2] It is within a memory of Canada mobilizing its military against Indigenous peoples who were protecting their ancestral lands and from a consciousness of the diversity of Canada's population that she does her alliance building and intercultural work with Rita Wong.

Rita carries the Cantonese name 黃錦兒, and grew up in the Bow River watershed on Treaty 7 territories, where the Tsuu Tina, Siksika, and Stoney First Nations meet and intersect, also known as Calgary, after her family emigrated from the Pearl River watershed (Toisan, Guangdong, China) to Turtle Island. Educated in a colonial school system that was largely devoid of Indigenous perspectives, she would like to thank the Lubicon Cree for speaking up during the 1988 Winter Olympics in Calgary, and raising her awareness of the violence inflicted upon the land through resource extraction in northern Alberta. From that moment, she has gradually and steadily worked to educate herself about the impact of colonization upon Indigenous peoples and to address her responsibilities as a settler (or unsettler) on Turtle Island. She would also like to acknowledge the influence of Lee Maracle, who offered a workshop for the Women of Colour Collective in Calgary in 1993 that was formative in guiding her toward her life's work. She is grateful for the wonderful teachers and storytellers who have so generously shared their insight and wisdom.

When we acknowledge our ancestral and gifted names, we are asserting the continuance of cultural heritages that predate and survive through the imposition of colonial paradigms and naming practices. When we go back far enough in our familial lines, we find ancestors who lived in relationship with the lands and waters that they relied upon for sustenance; indeed, countless generations intimately understood the importance of water. None of us would be here today if our ancestors had not chosen to live in close proximity with rivers, wells, sources of fresh water that are not only practical, but sacred to the continuance of life.

In June 2010, we were invited to be a part of the Thinking with Water workshop at Concordia University in Montreal, on the shores of the St. Lawrence River, a major waterway of the Mohawk peoples. At this gathering, we co-presented from an Indigenous perspective and from a settler-ally perspective.[3] Dorothy discussed the differences in Indigenous and Euro-Western knowledge systems of thought and how that affects the cultural interface when Indigenous and non-Indigenous cultures meet. Most importantly, ·how do those differences manifest when discussing the extraction of natural resources from the land, including the current approaches to water? Dorothy gave specific examples of her intimate, personal, and spiritual experiences with water. She talked about how difficult it is to be "the only Indian in the room" at such gatherings. Her motivation for comparing these two ways of knowing is to comprehend a lifetime of invalidation in a society that does not seem to accept the original peoples of the land.

This invalidation needs to be addressed and stopped if Indigenous and settler cultures are to live together peacefully. Comparing Indigenous and Euro-Western systems of thought is not new to Dorothy; it started during her undergraduate studies and continues to this day in her doctoral studies. Land, she has come to see, is the core issue between Indigenous peoples and settler populations in Canada. The Indigenous relationship to land includes all the seen and unseen beings—that is, not just the physical but also the spirits of the land, the waters, animals, birds, trees, plants, insects, and rocks. Each Indigenous group has cultural stories that tell them how they came to be on their ancestral homelands. Also embedded in those cultural stories is how we are to conduct our relationships with each other and with all the other beings on the land. We believe the conundrum for Euro-Western thinkers is the spiritual relationship that Indigenous peoples have with those beings and the land.

For Dorothy to understand Euro-Western ways of knowing, she needed to understand their stories. To do that, she turned to those often referred to as the "fathers of Enlightenment," namely, John Locke (1632–1704),[4] Jeremy Bentham (1748–1832),[5] John Stuart Mill (1806–73), and Jean-Jacques Rousseau (1712–78).[6] She compared how these philosophers of the sixteenth, seventeenth, and eighteenth centuries approached their relationship with land. It became clear to her that individualism, land ownership, and utilitarianism are the central concepts that surround Euro-Western thinkers' approach to land, and it is time to creatively transform these old theories, given the critical state of industrially induced climate change in the environment. Furthermore, when Euro-Western social and political theory is coupled with Christian religious beliefs that empower human domination over all things, it becomes apparent that this is antithetical to the Indigenous ways of seeing, doing, acting, and listening on the land. Most Indigenous cultures are guided by principles of respect, reciprocity, responsibility, and reverence,[7] while coexisting with all the other beings on the land.

While considering these central political and social theorists of Euro-Western knowledge, Dorothy also turned to the work of Indigenous social and political philosophers. Vine Deloria Jr.'s *God Is Red* (1973) had a profound effect on her academic studies. Deloria Jr. was a philosopher, a theologian, a lawyer, an activist, and an outstanding scholar who published prolifically. This was the first text she encountered that validated how Indigenous peoples know and see in the world. His work continues to be the foundation for her quest of examining Indigenous and Euro-Western ways of knowing because he articulated the differences in values, and most importantly for her, he explained the spiritual relationship that Indigenous peoples have with the land and their environment. In addition, George Manuel and Michael Posluns's *The Fourth World: An Indian Reality* and John Mohawk's work, specifically his article, "How the Conquest of Indigenous Peoples Parallels the Conquest of Nature," influenced her philosophical stance. More recently, the book *Thinking in Indian: A John Mohawk Reader* has substantiated her conclusion that the two systems of knowing are diametrically opposed ways of seeing the world.

In Dorothy's pursuit for a physical peaceful coexistence, she seeks ways and means to intellectually coexist with Euro-Western ways of knowing. Thus she adopted Martin Nakata's concept of "cultural interface" in her graduate work. Nakata describes the cultural interface as a dialectical space where Indigenous systems of knowledge are accepted as legitimate. It is a space where Indigenous scholars are not paralyzed in the ever pervasive colonial binaries of how Indigenous peoples only seem to exist in relation to their settlers, within the hegemony of colonialism. It is a place where Indigenous peoples have agency and can express their Indigenous world views.[8] Dorothy continues to be cognizant of the differences between Indigenous and Euro-Western ways of knowing and how that impedes Indigenous knowledge production in the academy. Her doctoral research centres Indigenous systems of knowledge and gives priority to contemporary Indigenous scholars like Glen Coulthard (Dene), Leanne Simpson (Anishinabe), and Alannah Young Leon (Anishinabe-Cree), who have developed place-based critical Indigenous theories on how people relate to their territories, including the water systems. To bring some understanding of how cultural stories inform Indigenous peoples' relationship with their ancestral lands, she turns to Secwepemc and Syilx scholarship[9] from her home territories. These culturally specific stories provide integral principles of how to perpetuate life on the land in a sustainable way that ensures a continuance of Indigenous cultures. It is within this context that Dorothy approaches the co-editing of this anthology, which brings together presentations and conversations that happened in March 2012 at the Downstream gathering on unceded Coast Salish territories.

To open a window into how Indigenous peoples see, do, act, and listen on their homeland, we quote Rueben George, Sundance chief and spiritual leader from the territories where we live. At a Defend Our Coast Rally on October 22, 2012, he stated:

> The sacredness of what we have—there is no price that we can put down on those things—our Earth, our Water, our Lands. There is no price you can put on it because of our sacred connection that we have to it. The lineage that I come from is directly from the water. We are the Tsleil-Waututh people, that means the People of the Inlet—that's where our lineage comes from, that's where the creation of the first human being comes from, that is what we believe. We can't put a price on that.[10]

In front of the Chinese Consulate in Vancouver on January 8, 2012, Elder Amy (Marie) George (Tsleil-Waututh) gave further insight into the Indigenous way of seeing the notion of progress and development when she said:

> […] when we were standing up for the trees, when the trees were coming down, we would go and block it [the logging]. They would always send the older women, the Elders out first. And, they said, "there goes the Indians stopping progress again!" And, yet it's not stopping progress, it's just the top 1% who are filling up their bank accounts. How many more billions do they want? My Dad[11] used to say, when you go in the ground, they're not going to say, "Did you have a big house, did you have a big car, did you have a big bank account?" They're going to say, "Did you love?" Not just your intimate family but everything, everything that lives. Mother Earth is alive. And Mother Earth is being abused. Her water is being abused.[12]

At the Downstream gathering at Emily Carr University of Art and Design we were fortunate to hear the original peoples of this land open each day of the gathering. Amy George (Tsleil-Waututh), Larry Grant (Musqueam), and Chief Bill Williams (Squamish Nation) shared with us what the waters of these lands mean to them. It was critical for participants to hear these points of view. In addition, it is important for readers to understand that the diversity of Indigenous peoples represents various outlooks; however, there are shared "commonalities in those ontologies and epistemologies,"[13] and the differences are usually directly related to the land the Indigenous group has lived on for generations.

Clearly, Dorothy is not the only Indigenous person who is thinking about how these two systems of thought can interface, given Michael Blackstock's Blue Ecology approach in this volume, which seeks to interweave Indigenous and Euro-Western knowledge(s) as two autonomous ways of knowing. What Dorothy calls the "cultural interface"[14] is also explored in Cathy Stubington's piece, which is about building relationship between the town of Enderby and

Splatsin, Dorothy's home community, through the arts. Cathy worked with Rosalind Williams of Splatsin to co-write a historical play from an Indigenous and settler perspective. As well, we note Larissa Lai's "engagement in epistemologies" as she thoughtfully deconstructs her understandings of what she has seen, heard, and read about the differences in the two philosophical approaches. Larissa searches for workable strategies, given what she calls "neo-colonial capitalism" while at the same time grappling with the Indigenous concept of respect. She is engaged in building an intellectual relationship from her particular Asian Canadian perspective. In addition, Astrida Neimanis thoughtfully addresses "epistemic violence" in her piece while she brilliantly looks at different theoretical approaches that affect how we relate to water.

It's about building *relationships*.

In approaching water together as a way to build relationships between Indigenous and Euro-Westernized systems of knowledge, how do we learn from each other? That's what this volume is about for us—learning about how others see and perceive and learn. How do we negotiate ourselves as humanity, given the dire circumstances of the Earth and its waters? It is urgent that we begin by first taking responsibility for our inherited cultures—what they enable and disable through their values. As Dorothy has mentioned, there is a very obvious cultural dissonance between Indigenous and settler world views, something that Rita navigates as a Canadian-born Chinese woman working to be a respectful guest on Indigenous homelands. Having inherited centuries of colonization, including the attempted genocide of Indigenous peoples through the residential school system and the ongoing attempts at dispossession through resource extraction from Indigenous homelands, Rita is well aware that the historical devastation she was born into will take many generations to address. One crucial way to do the work of building better relations is to proceed with water as a shared bond. Rita began working with water in 2007 as a response to Dorothy and Denise Nadeau's forum calling for people to protect our sacred waters. Over the years, she has worked to learn from and with water itself, paying attention to watersheds, to what is often taken for granted, yet necessary to our survival and well-being.

In the midst of the many stresses facing us in contemporary urban settings, which often distract us from being mindful of basic physical realities, it is still the shared commonalities that keep us alive: the air we breathe, the water we drink, the ocean that regulates our climate and enables biodiversity, the range of relationships we have with one another as people who experience some precious and transitory time together on this Earth. There is enough for everyone's need, but not everyone's greed, as the saying goes. These necessities are priceless even though many may take them for granted or act as though such details are not worth their attention. Just see how long our bodies, which are roughly two-thirds water, can go without fluid replenishment. If we are holding out for clean, unpolluted air, how long can we hold our breaths?

What does it mean for two women living in a city on the edge of the Pacific Ocean to understand ourselves as part of this larger watershed? It is insufficient to only talk about water as a substance that is outside and separate from us, for water is always making us up from within. Water reconstitutes us on a perpetual basis. When we are thirsty, we gulp it up eagerly, and thankfully, water replenishes our throats, blood, skin, and even our eyes. Water continually remakes us, whether we notice it or not. The root of the word "poetry" is found in "poiesis," in making, in creation, which water does par excellence, necessary as it is for the generation of all life. We might call this its spiritual aspect, as well as its physical directive, and in so doing, we may reconnect to all the larger water bodies that we have a relationship with, whether we've been trained or educated to see this or not. The challenge to reimagine ourselves beyond our skins, as a living part of a larger watershed, can hold both frustration and promise. A complex gift carries many lessons, two of which are interdependency with one another as well as dependency on fresh source waters, whose energies we need every day.

When we tell the stories of ourselves, we are also telling the story of the specific waters that move through us at a particular moment, albeit more often than not unconsciously. As Janine Macleod phrases it in this anthology, "wishes for water are never only wishes for water. It is a substance much too thoroughly mixed with everything." When we tell a story of water, we are also telling stories of ourselves, our societies. The dominant stories given to us by colonization have been violent, painful, hateful, anchored more often in fear and attempted control of Indigenous peoples and their homelands than in respect for others. We need and deserve better stories, ones that will restore our relations with one another and ourselves, somehow, despite the immense burden of history that we have inherited. The burden exists regardless of whether we choose to address it or not; it is the poison in the room that must be transformed into a cure, or it will kill us all, systematically and insidiously. These better stories have always existed, regardless of political agendas that sought to eradicate or marginalize them, and are recorded, for instance, in the wampum belts of the Haudenosaunee. As legal scholar John Borrows points out in the CBC series, *Eighth Fire*, "Canada wasn't just formed through British law alone. It was an intermingling of British law with Indigenous people's law and putting those two sources of law together, with the wampum belts, with the [1764 Treaty of Niagara] agreement, is the foundation of our country, founded on peace, friendship and respect. It's a story I think we'd love to celebrate."[15]

In that episode of *Eighth Fire*, Howie Miller also says, "I'm not going to get over it [colonization] because it's not fixed yet."[16] It is in the work of addressing and healing the broken relationships that are colonization's legacy, through decolonizing ourselves, that we will also deepen and invigorate our familiarity and relationships with the watersheds of Turtle Island. In educating ourselves about the histories of First Nations such as the Cheslatta, the TseKehNay, the Athabasca Chipewyan, and many more, we learn that these are also water stories involving displacement and dispossession through industrial-scale dam flooding and redirection of water that devastated Indigenous peoples' ability to live on the land. While there are many paths toward deepening and invigorating our relationships with watersheds, one crucial path we propose is to decolonize and work toward respect for and restitution of Indigenous cultures' long-standing relations with the waters of the lands of Turtle Island. This is one of the keystones that bring us together as we turn our attention to the urgent challenges our societies face with water, giver of life. In addressing a major source of the problems—the waves of violence, inequity, and dehumanization that is left in the wake of colonization—we propose that solutions arise with a paradigm shift that puts Indigenous core values of the four R's of "respect, relevance, reciprocity, responsibility" that Barnhard and Kirkness have articulated, along with "reverence" offered by Archibald, at the centre, not the margins, of the dialogue regarding how we coordinate and co-operate through our perceptions of and practices with water—a radical approach to ensure everyone's well-being. How we govern ourselves, as equal partners in an egalitarian-striving society, determines our impact on the watersheds; as such, water always has political implications, as well as the cultural dimensions that are the focus of this anthology.

What does it mean to take an intercultural approach to water in these post–residential school apology times? Setting aside the question of how seriously one takes an apology in 2008 that is then followed by a statement at the 2009 G20 by the prime minister that Canada has no history of colonialism,[17] it could mean telling a better story than the one divide-and-conquer narrative that settler colonialism inflicted on the Indigenous peoples of this land, a narrative that exalted newcomers at the expense of the First Peoples here.[18] The systemic violence of residential schools, the Sixties Scoop,[19] state agencies' ongoing apprehension of Indigenous children from their families, the deplorable numbers of suicides in Indigenous communities, and the high rates of unprosecuted murders of Indigenous women are not only symptoms of a society that has elevated normative whiteness by debasing brown people, but they are also part of a long historical effort to eliminate Indigenous peoples from their traditional homelands. In the face of ongoing injustices and violence, those of us who have come to live on Turtle Island as visitors, settlers, or unsettlers[20] have a responsibility to learn and respect the perspectives of Indigenous peoples. This is not only a matter of justice and principle, though it is certainly that, but it is also a practical matter of developing the cultural fluencies, actions, and philosophies needed to navigate together in a spirit of peace, friendship, and respect through an increasingly precarious future of climate instability and anthropogenic global warming.

This anthology comes at a critical time, a time when the Canadian government has recently gutted environmental protection legislation, even to the point of removing water from the Navigable Waters Protection Act, now tellingly named the Navigation Protection Act, signalling the prioritization of industry at the expense of the waters that make it possible. These are short-sighted, ecologically illiterate, and dangerous moves, distressing for scientists,[21] citizens who believe in the public good, and anyone who understands how deeply society's well-being depends on the health of the lands and waters that sustain our living capacity. As of February 2016, eighty-five First Nations communities were under 134 drinking water advisories, meaning that they did not and do not have safe, clean drinking water.[22] Furthermore, there is less information than before as Health Canada has stopped publishing a complete list of which communities are under such advisories.[23] This decrease in reliable public information falls within a political agenda that has included destroying science libraries, gutting the information available through the national census, and muzzling public servants in Canada. Whether there are adequate records or not, the fact remains that many Indigenous communities that used to be able to drink clean fresh water right out of the lakes and rivers can no longer do so because of pollution, the effects of resource extraction, and other colonial impositions. In the wake of attempted genocide, systemic violence, legislative irresponsibility,[24] and colonial oppression, it is still somehow possible to witness cultural resilience by and for Indigenous peoples, who have a prophecy or a warning that now is the time of the eighth fire,[25] the time when people from all four directions can come together for our common well-being for peace or face the dire consequences of not achieving this potential. In Canada, we are witnessing Indigenous-led movements like Idle No More, which are open to all people. As a number of people, including Sylvia McAdam, one of the founders of Idle No More, have asserted, "if you drink water, this is your issue."[26] Idle No More, which has sown the seeds for the Indigenous Nationhood Movement (http://nationsrising.org/), mobilized in direct response to the 2012 omnibus Bill C-45, which gutted the Fisheries Act, the Navigable Waters Protection Act, the Canadian Environmental Assessment Act, and much more that was basic to caring for the watersheds we all have a responsibility to protect.[27] In order to recognize and work with the leadership of First Nations peoples, settlers or unsettlers of Canadian citizenship need to examine our own assumptions very carefully. We have inherited a legacy of systemic racism and white supremacy that needs to be named and dismantled so that we can build honest, healthy relationships based on mutual respect, reciprocity, and strength in diversity. Paradoxically, we build an understanding of each creature's right to autonomous being by acknowledging our responsibilities to maintain and support a shared, vital, living ecology. This begins with recognizing that the historical and continuing dispossession of Indigenous peoples from the land needs to be addressed, so that Indigenous peoples' practices and relationships with lands and waters can continue today (or be re-established where they were violently stopped) in ways that are culturally meaningful and self-determined.[28]

In her contribution to this anthology, Lee Maracle writes, "We do not own the land, the water, the sky, the plant world, the animal world. They own themselves. The water owns itself." She asserts the intrinsic autonomy of life, articulating a value system that recognizes how humans are guests, not bosses, of this Earth, and reminds us that the pollution and desecration of her family's homelands happened without their consent. In identifying the destructiveness that comes with colonial arrogance, she offers a better alternative: to humble ourselves to water, to care for it, to maturely engage in meaningful relationships. The obligation to water, which she identifies as a Salish tradition, is also a call to all people capable of opening their hearts and minds wide enough to think seven generations before and seven generations ahead.

While humbling ourselves to water is an Indigenous teaching, it can be approached through Western epistemologies as well, as Astrida Neimanis discusses in her essay. She writes, "[b]ecause each body has a different relation to water *as a matter of survival*, nobody can do what Donna Haraway calls the God Trick. Nobody can ever fully know water. For me, this underlines questions of incursion, hubris, and humility, as a necessary consideration for any epistemology, or system of knowledge."[29] The shift from presumptuously "knowing about" water to humbly learning with and through water opens possibilities that would be foreclosed by a colonial mindset. This is also demonstrated by Janine MacLeod's imagining of what Toronto could someday be if enough people embraced and respected water as an intimate partner in our lives, not merely a substance to be controlled and used. In order to do this, she needs to stretch forward four generations, writing that "Ancestors and descendants are present—as memory or as virtuality—in the water that is always with us. A feeling for our intimacy with the dead and the unborn, and with a multitude of other creatures, may help to fend off the crippling influences of isolation and despair."[30]

Clever, tricky, and powerful, Western technology has the capacity to both massively astound and massively demoralize or destroy; it needs the wisdom and values of contributors like Mona Polacca and Lee Maracle to ground it in a long-term ethics, guiding humans to not merely be a short-term burst and bust in the planet's evolutionary history. When we track water's paths and relationships, our sense of time and place expands to elucidate a much longer now, a much wider here. No longer (if ever) would one see a northern boreal forest, the home of Melina Laboucan Massimo's community, as an allowable sacrifice zone for the sake of urban dwellers in the global economy; instead, one would understand that the entire planet is becoming the sacrifice zone when poor decisions are made to briefly profit from the rampant destruction of the millennial-old moist forests and commons that absorb and filter our carbon emissions. Such a long-term, large-scale view is necessary as Janine MacLeod points out: "It seems to me that transformative collective action is unlikely to emerge from our stories of past abundance unless we conceive of our love for the world in multi-generational terms."[31] Today we have more tools to examine the large scale both temporally and spatially; these tools come with the responsibility to use them well.

While each of us hails from specific watersheds and specific histories, we simultaneously share a reliance on the global ocean, the enormous body of water that covers two-thirds of the Earth's surface. Contemplating the ocean offers us a way to scale up to the larger collective questions of humanity's future, which is intimately dependent on how we navigate our relationship with water in generations to come. For Rita, the Pacific Ocean is an enormous mystery that connects where she lives now, Turtle Island, with her family's ancestral villages in China. In Chinese, the character for ocean (*hai*) consists of the radical for water paired with the ideogram for "every," which includes within it the character for "mother," an etymology that reminds us of life's origins. Not only is the ocean deeply significant historically, but it is also the holder of the planet's future as we rely on the ocean's plankton, which produces the oxygen for every second breath we take. As journalist Alanna Mitchell emphasizes, the ocean is the primary life support system of our planet, one we cannot afford to ignore in this time of increasing climate instability. Having interviewed marine scientists around the world to produce her book, *Sea Sick: The Global Ocean in Crisis*, she elucidates how our biology relies on basic chemistry. Our lives depend on a particular equilibrium of the ocean, an equilibrium that is threatened by acidification from increased greenhouse gases. Our daily actions, and those large-scale ones of industry, accumulate. The challenge that faces us now is to reorganize our communities and societies so as to accumulate differently, in ways that contribute to shared resilience rather than mass extinction. Clever as humans may be, we cannot outwit the chemistry upon which our biological bodies rely. Hopefully, we are living in a moment when humanity's intelligence recognizes and responds to the physical limits we are reaching thanks to climate change. Perhaps this era will be one where our species matures enough to more widely and humbly dedicate ourselves to improving the conditions of life for future generations as well as our non-human neighbours, though this remains to be seen. Mitchell's contribution to this anthology, a revised transcript of her oral presentation at the Downstream gathering, summarizes some of the key points from her book *Sea Sick*, which she has since transformed into a one-woman play that was produced by Toronto's Theatre Centre in 2014, and nominated for a Dora Award for outstanding new play. This is a surprising and welcome turn in how science and art may strengthen one another.

Today, Western science is confirming that we are interdependent and interconnected in ways we have not previously understood, but which have long been embodied in Indigenous perspectives. Michael Blackstock suggests that Western science and Indigenous ways of knowing are both sovereign entities that need to be interwoven so that we have better ways of facing the complex environmental problems that global warming poses to us at an unprecedented pace. He outlines four steps toward collaborative knowledge: humility, transcending of boundaries, interweaving of worlds, and transformation of attitudes. The climate crisis facing humanity is a complex problem that we will either adapt to or not. Part of adaptation is the transcendence of boundaries that Blackstock identifies.

Healthy water is crucial for our lives. Whether this is spoken with the evidence-based language of science or the Indigenous science that is grounded in generations of observing and listening to the land, we as readers have the capacity and responsibility to draw such connections across different disciplines, cultural traditions, and discourses. The anthology's first section—entitled "Contexts for Knowing and Unknowing Water"—asks us if we are paying attention to what we need to know, as well as acknowledging how much we don't know through the contributions of Alanna Mitchell, Lee Maracle, Michael Blackstock, Astrida Neimanis, and Baco Ohama. Ohama's poem offers glimpses into the "unsteady question[s]" animated by a turn to water. While this may appear to be an unusual grouping, it emphasizes how our shared need to protect and respect water brings new conversations and connections into being, gradually wearing away the colonial mindsets and disciplinary barriers that would normalize separation and compartmentalization of what is actually a very fluid *umwelt*.[32] In so doing, humbly approaching water together opens up new possibilities for democracy, peace, and relationship.

When we look for contemporary stories that respect water, that remind us of its immeasurable value, we come across films like *Land of Oil and Water*; *White Water, Black Gold*; *H_2Oil*; *Flow: For Love of Water*; *Water on the Table*; *Samaqan*; *Downstream*, and many more documentaries that show how water is being threatened by oil expansion and pollution. These stories are crucial to listen to, as Melina Laboucan Massimo reminds us with regard to the Athabasca Rivershed. As a member of the Lubicon Cree First Nation in northern

Alberta, she has experienced and witnessed the effects of massive resource extraction on her community's ability to sustain itself on its watersheds, which have been devastated by more than 2,600 oil and gas wells[33] and a large pipeline rupture in 2011. While the extractive violence that has been inflicted on Laboucan Massimo's community is documented and discussed in earlier books such as John Goddard's *Last Stand of the Lubicon Cree*, and in Kevin Thomas's interview of Chief Bernard Ominayak, entitled "These Are Lubicon Lands" in *Speaking for Ourselves: Environmental Justice in Canada*, we feel it is crucial to hear directly from young women like Laboucan Massimo about the impacts on her community. The anthology's second section—entitled "Water Testimonies: Witness, Worry, and Work"—draws our attention to both the extreme dangers posed to water today, vividly outlined by Laboucan Massimo, as well as examples of the dedication and courage of Indigenous commitments to protect water in the face of immense adversity and ongoing colonial injustices.

Reciprocity beats in the heart of Violet Caibaiosai's and Mona Polacca's pieces, bringing into focus the power of personal practices and oratory. Polacca is a Hopi-Havasupai/Tewa Elder whose community is threatened by uranium mining near the Grand Canyon. As a member of the International Council of 13 Indigenous Grandmothers, she is guided by a larger purpose to protect the Earth for future generations. Caibaiosai shared her experiences as one of the original Mother Earth Water Walkers, who have collectively walked around the perimeter of all the Great Lakes, to acknowledge the sacredness of water in the face of threats posed by pollution and social disregard. Cognizant of how generous Mother Earth has been to us, they understand that we are living through a time of imbalance, when too much has been taken from the Earth and not enough returned in gratitude. Through ceremony and the sharing of their stories, they seek to return balance to this planet. They are humble women warriors, in a sense guardians of humanity. While many of us live in a world where the simple is more easily said than done, they demonstrate the beautiful necessity of the simple as a desirable way to live, to be in right relations with other beings, to have the courage to face ugly industrial realities with Indigenous values as a way to guide us through the dangers that humans face together as a species.

In this section, Renée Elizabeth Mzinegiizhigo-kwe Bédard's essay, "Keepers of the Water,"[34] offers a compelling articulation of Nishnaabeg women's responsibilities to water, which contextualizes Caibaiosai's narrative. Cecilia Vicuña's poem, "A Response to Pascua Lama," juxtaposes the tension between the glacier waters that are sacred to the Indigenous Diaguita people in Chile and the long-proposed Pascua Lama gold mine planned by the Canadian mining company Barrick Gold, suspended in 2013 due to the valiant efforts of the locals in Chile. As host to 70–80 percent of the world's mining companies,

Canada has had a largely negative impact on many of the waters wherever its companies have mined, to the extent that where Canadians were once widely welcomed abroad just a couple decades ago, today this is often no longer the case.

In raising the alarm about the state of water, we need to cultivate our ability to respond to dire situations, which is our collective responsibility. There are many excellent books that offer guidance in terms of public policy and governance, such as *Eau Canada*, edited by Karen Bakker; *Ethical Water* by Robert Sandford and Merrell-Ann Phare; Maude Barlow's *Blue Future*, and countless more. There are also wonderful books that unpack and encourage us to re-examine our cultural assumptions around water, such as Jamie Linton's *What Is Water?* and the anthology, *Thinking with Water*, edited by Cecilia Chen, Janine MacLeod, and Astrida Neimanis, to which the co-editors of this anthology contributed. We observe many powerful Indigenous thinkers raising their concerns and perspectives on water, such as Ardith Walkem (in *Eau Canada*), Kim Anderson (whose paper, "Aboriginal Women, Water and Health," is referenced in this anthology by Michael Blackstock, Alannah Young Leon, and Denise Nadeau), Darlene Sanderson (whose dissertation was entitled "Nipiy Wasekimew/Clear Water: The Meaning of Water, from the Words of the Elders"), and Jeannette Armstrong in the report for the Third World Water Forum, for instance. Large-scale political, economic, and systemic solutions are required, as are cultural engagement and individual responsibility. What we contribute to this large and growing body of literature is a lively engagement with personal, creative, and intercultural dialogues that are brought together in one place, rather than sitting in two solitudes, as often happens. The challenge in bringing often disparate voices together is to find connections yet to also respect and make space for differences to continue to exist.

The third section—called "Shared Ethical and Embodied Practices"—consists of arts-based responses to the question of water that make space for both individual reflection and community building through attention to physical, experiential learning. Enacting an interdependent approach to how one acts in concert with others to fulfill one's responsibilities to water, Alannah Young Leon and Denise Marie Nadeau collaborate to work with ethics, protocols, spiritual responsibilities, and embodied knowledge through movement and dance, focusing on what can be learned from attending to the body's fluid composition. Similarly, dancer and choreographer Seonagh Odhiambo Horne also turns our attention to the implications of embracing and performing embodied experiences of water as central, not peripheral, to human consciousness, whether these be through an openness to Yemaya, the Orisha of the ocean and "the owner of all waters" in the Yoruba tradition, or to the Los Angeles River. Two contributors, Basia Irland and Cathy Stubington, then discuss how their community-based artistic practices have cultivated human relationships with significant rivers. Wang Ping's poem, "Tsunami Chant," draws important connections between water, peace, and social justice.

Many things that are not possible alone become possible together. This is borne out by the community art projects described by Cathy Stubington and Basia Irland, wherein hundreds of people creatively animate their site-specific relationships with their watersheds, and community resilience is fostered, relationship by relationship, in rhythms that are both age-old and contemporary. Direct experience of our local rivers is crucial, as is a spirit of gratitude, curiosity, play, and generosity. As Irland notes, "gifting is an important part of a community-based ethic."[35] In the face of industrial disasters, we need both large-scale systems responses as well as personal commitment, acts of giving back, and restoring balance, honouring the waters that keep us alive.

We are part of the stories that we renew through retelling, and we forget this at our peril. An assumption of separation from the larger stories that we're part of can breed denial or disassociation in the face of global climate change. Such enormous problems are daunting, but rather than shrinking into fear, despair, and paralysis, cultural workers have a key role in helping our communities work through these challenges together. In these times, it remains important to take care of our collective health as best we can, and to foster and tap into whatever creative energies we can access. This anthology makes a strong case for the roles that culture, arts, and the humanities play in supporting a healthy, water-based ecology while simultaneously cultivating courageous, democratic practices that foster solidarity and respectful relations through understanding how the creative commons as a whole is dynamically greater than all the pieces constituting it. Bringing together local, global, and Indigenous perspectives on water, the collection offers readers many ways to consider what is both spatially and temporally downstream in an era of global warming. Artists, writers, environmentalists, and scholars situated in different communities discuss the creative and critical approaches they are taking to reimagine water, building dynamic, engaged relationships with the waters where they live, work, struggle, and play.

Direct experience of the perpetual connection between the waters outside and the waters inside is cultivated through bodily awareness, as seen in the collaboration between Denise Nadeau and Alannah Young Leon, as well as in Seonagh Odhiambo's piece. In her discussion of Asava Dance, Odhiambo writes, "Like lines carved by water on the mountain, lines are defined and drawn by water in our bodies." Cognizant of the subtle power of how we perform our culture through everyday life, Nadeau and Young Leon emphasize the importance of "daily acts of renewal." Where colonial practices have disrupted the care and knowledge of water that was historically critical to

Indigenous communities, they work in service of Indigenous resurgence by addressing colonial upheaval and re-engaging Indigenous knowledge principles. Incorporating life-art process and modelling reciprocity, Nadeau and Young Leon cultivate bodily wisdom.

The fourth section—entitled "A Respectful Coexistence in Common: Water Perspectives"—offers narratives that range from practical to visionary in tone, spanning from relatively remote areas (the ocean, the North) to urban centres. What might appear to be an eclectic mix is simultaneously a strategy to remind ourselves of water's ubiquity, of the intrinsic value of differences in discipline and culture that exist, and of the relations between places that are relatively sparsely populated by humans to those that are denser. Legal scholar Radha D'Souza, based in the United Kingdom, offers a compelling international perspective of a Keepers of the Water gathering that occurred in northern Manitoba, where Elders reiterate what Lee Maracle states in this volume—that "no one can own water or land," and that we all have a responsibility to abide by our covenant with nature. Composed of First Nations, Métis, and Inuit peoples, environmental groups, concerned citizens, and communities working for the protection of air, water, and land, the Keepers are a grassroots organization striving to protect the Arctic Ocean watershed (http://keepersofthewater.ca/). Writer Janine MacLeod shares a creative and reflective narrative as to how a desirable watery future might look and feel in the future. Such a future will rely upon the kind of practical and ecologically literate contributions of eminent scientists like Paul Harrison. While it may seem unusual to invite a marine scientist of Paul Harrison's stature and experience to an arts-based and creative group of thinkers and makers mostly working with freshwater ways, we recognize that unusual times call for unusual tactics, unprecedented conversations, and a large-scale systems context for our individual contributions. In a sense, his work in the Pacific Ocean returns us full circle to what Alanna Mitchell introduced. In reading Harrison's account of why our nitrogen pollution poses a serious threat to the ocean's health, we may transcend disciplinary boundaries and realize that different stories share certain underlying themes, such as voluntary simplicity as a desirable virtue. The changes that are within individual reach that Harrison identifies—such as a reduction in energy consumption and meat consumption—echo, from a different angle, with Maracle's and Neimanis's earlier call for humbleness.

Through reflection and movement toward a participatory water ethic, Janey Lew confronts a mediated sense of despair, or helplessness, in the face of stories transmitted through news media: the oil spill in the Gulf of Mexico, three earthquakes in the Pacific region, including the tsunami with its nuclear fallout in Japan. While such an ethic requires the physical and spiritual engagement evidenced in Violet Caibaiosai's, Mona Polacca's, Basia Irland's,

Cathy Stubington's, and Denise Nadeau and Alannah Young-Leon's pieces, it also involves the writerly process that Lew shares with us. The importance of reflection is further witnessed in Larissa Lai's piece, which functions as an afterword for the anthology.

With a nod to the precautionary principle, we use the term "commons" with some reservations, as well as with hope for its possibilities. On the one hand, the commons offers a way to describe all that evades or resists the relentless drive toward commodification and privatization under capitalism; as such, it does important work in keeping alive the concept of the collective, the communal.[36] That said, the commons cannot be used to yet again ignore the very real cultural differences and power imbalances that restrict some people's access to it, as well as the historical violence that threatens to erase Indigenous naming and protocols with the land. As such, a tentative approach to the commons would be one that resists the tired and culturally biased assumptions of Garrett Hardin's "Tragedy of the Commons," which assumes short-sighted selfishness at the expense of the common good, and instead acknowledges how protocols held in common have historically and effectively worked in many cultures across the world for very long periods of time, as gestured to by conferences like The Tragedy of the Market: From Crisis to Commons (2012). The dangers of using the commons in such a way that leaves colonialism uninterrogated have been pointed out by Indigenous scholars like Glen Coulthard,[37] whose warnings we heed seriously; we do not use the term in the way that the state has misappropriated it, nor do we use it as a free pass for avoiding the protocols of Indigenous peoples. Rather, the commons is a contingent settler term that could exist as a complement or supplement to Indigenous ways of naming and doing, supporting Indigenous leadership if practised respectfully and in dialogue with Indigenous peoples' protocols and laws. The term cannot be used to elide histories or evade responsibilities, and so we close with a poem by Janet Rogers, a praise poem in the voice of poet Pauline Johnson for the Grand River, a significant waterway that flows through the Six Nations of the Iroquois Confederacy territories in what is known as Ontario. A use of the commons as a term needs to articulate how the specificity of local knowledges matter, starting first and foremost with the names, stories, and places that Indigenous communities have long cultivated through oral and now written traditions.

The necessary path is clear in some ways—in the way that water follows gravity, follows the contours of the land—and unpredictable in other ways, in that surprise and creativity are needed to shake us out of the status quo, out of the regime of profit, numbers, and corporate control. Capitalism has been very adept at manipulating and channeling some elements of surprise and creativity; the challenge for us is to reconnect those elements to ethics, to relationship, to long-term thinking, ecological literacy, to the careful commons and to Indigenous nationhood and sovereignty.

In the spirit of strengthening coordination across differences, awareness of one another's knowledge and practices, and living the changes that we hope for, this anthology contributes to a large and robust water conversation that is happening globally. We hope it fuels your spirit in the watery times to come. Gary Paul Nabhan writes, "To restore any place ... we must also begin to re-story it, to make it the lesson of our legends, festivals, and seasonal rites. Story is the way we encode deep-seated values within our culture."[38] May the stories we share and tell together help us to move forward with wisdom and determination with water. Cultural narratives are social constructions that can help us rearticulate and reimagine our relationships with waters that are always both local (temporarily) and global (in their ongoing circulation). One of the many lessons water teaches us, if we are open to it, is continual transformation as it moves through watersheds and cycles, connecting fresh water to salt water, and earthling communities through its circulation.

In short, this book contributes to the formation of an intergenerational, interdisciplinary, culturally inclusive, participatory water ethic. Such an ethic arises from spiritual responsibilities, from a deep appreciation for human dependence on water for a meaningful quality of life, and from an ecologically grounded realization that individual well-being is predicated upon interdependence with other humans and living creatures, all of whom need healthy water to coexist together on and with Earth. That is, the anthology's contributors advance many ways to demonstrate a water ethic wherein one participates in learning about one's watershed and lovingly engages with the fluid flows that make up our homelands and our bodies, out of a deep relationship of humbleness, respect, and necessity.

The organizing principle for the chapters is to start with a global perspective and acknowledgement of what Indigenous perspectives have to contribute as guidance and values to our thinking through of water. This entails listening to Indigenous voices and offering samples of practice-based engagement with the realm of water in the contact zone where Indigenous and settler (or unsettler) voices work toward creative co-existence with and acknowledgement of water's key role in our imaginations and lives. While grappling with the urgent matters of pollution, climate change, and commodification recurs in many chapters, the chapters are not separated out by topic so much as flowing from questions of knowing (epistemology) to examples of doing (through testimony, community art, embodied movement/dance practices, creative writing, science). The diversity of these practices emphasizes how water is central to so much of our lives and society whether or not we realize it. The contributors offer their perspectives in this spirit, and we hope you, as interlocutors, will contribute to this rising tide.[39]

We see this anthology as part of a necessary trilogy. We began our work with *Thinking with Water*, asking for more inclusion of Indigenous voices in an anthology that would have inadvertently omitted such voices as authors. This anthology works in the messy interface where cultures meet and mingle, akin to an estuary where fresh water and salt water mix. We also see the need for an all-Indigenous anthology for water, one encompassing the breadth and depth of Indigenous approaches with water throughout Turtle Island. Such a scope is beyond us at this moment, but we would like to invite you to read *Indigenous Message on Water*,[40] issued by the Indigenous World Forum on Water and Peace in 2014 as part of the ongoing process of decolonization and re-indigenization that is the hope for humanity's future on this Earth. Given the breadth and scope of Indigenous water actions, we see the need for more anthologies and gatherings that respect and centre on Indigenous perspectives. In the songs of Takaiya Blaney,[41] the courageous work of the Unist'ot'en Camp, the inspiring work of Dechinta University, the many Healing Walks and Water Walks[42] led and undertaken by Indigenous peoples, and the Keepers of the Water who aim to protect the Arctic Ocean watershed, to name just a few examples, there are more necessary and urgent stories we need to nourish and guide us in order to truly build peace, diversity, and resilience through Indigenous resurgence.

Notes

1 Dorothy Christian, with Victoria Freeman, "History of a Friendship or Some Thoughts on Becoming Allies," in *Alliances: Re/Envisioning Indigenous and non-Indigenous Relationships*, ed. Lynne Davis (Toronto: University of Toronto Press, 2010), 376–90.

2 Dorothy Christian, "Reconciling with the People and the Land," in *Cultivating Canada: Reconciliation Through the Lens of Cultural Diversity*, vol. 3, ed. Ashok Mathur, Jonathan Dewar, Mike DeGagné (Ottawa: Aboriginal Healing Foundation, 2011).

3 Dorothy Christian and Rita Wong, "Untapping Watershed Mind," in *Thinking with Water*, ed. Cecilia Chen, Janine MacLeod, and Astrida Neimanis (Montreal: McGill-Queen's University Press, 2013), 232–53.

4 John Locke's brief biography is available at the Internet Encyclopedia of Philosophy—A Peer-Reviewed Academic Resource, http://www.iep.utm.edu/locke-po/.

5 "The History of Utilitarianism" is available from the Stanford Encyclopedia of Philosophy, http://plato.stanford.edu/entries/utilitarianism-history/.

6 Biography available at the European Graduate School website, http://www.egs.edu/library/jean-jacques-rousseau/biography/.

7 See R. Barnhardt and V. Kirkness, "First Nations and Higher Education: The Four R's—Respect, Relevance, Reciprocity, Responsibility," *Journal of American Indian Education* 30, no. 3 (1991): 1–15. See also: Jo-ann Archibald, *Indigenous Storywork: Educating the Heart, Mind, Body and Spirit* (Vancouver: UBC Press, 2008).

8 See Nakata in the bibliography. His body of work (1997, 1998, 2002 2006, 2007, and 2008) informs my thinking.

9 Jeannette Christine Armstrong, "Constructing Indigeneity: Syilx Okanagan Oraliture- and _tmix^w centrism" (PhD diss., University of Greifswald, Germany, 2010); Janice Billy, "Back From the Brink: Decolonizing Through The Restoration of Secwepemc Language, Culture, and Identity" (PhD diss., Simon Fraser University, 2009); W. A. Cohen, "School Failed Coyote, So Fox Made a New School: Indigenous Okanagan Knowledge Transforms Educational Pedagogy" (PhD diss., University of British Columbia, 2010); R. E. Ignace, "Our Stories Are Our Corner Posts: Secewepemc Stories and Historical Consciousness" (PhD diss., Simon Fraser University, 2008); K. A. Michel, "Trickster's Path to Language Transformation: Stories of Secwepemc Immersion from Chief Atahm School" (PhD diss., University of British Columbia, 2012); Marlowe Sam, "Oral Narratives, Customary Laws and Indigenous Water Rights in Canada" (PhD diss., University of British Columbia–Okanagan, 2013).

10 Rueben George, Defend Our Coast Rally, October 22, 2012, http://www.youtube.com/watch?v=mCi0odDrtOc.

11 Amy (Marie) George's father is well-known actor and activist Chief Dan George.

12 Amy George, "Tsleil-Waututh Elder Amy George Speaks About Oil Tanker Concerns at the Chinese Consulate," The Four Worlds International Institute, January 8, 2012, http://www.fwii.net/video/tsleil-waututh-elder-amy-george-speaks-about-oil-tanker-concerns.

13 Bryan McKinley Jones Brayboy, "Toward a Tribal Critical Race Theory in Education," The Urban Review 37, no. 5 (December 2005): 427. Also see MargaretKovach, Indigenous Methodologies: Characteristics, Conversations and Contexts (Toronto: University of Toronto Press, 2009).

14 This concept is put forward by Nakata, a Torres Strait-Islander in the education discourse.

15 CBC, Eighth Fire: Aboriginal Peoples, Canada and the Way Forward, 2011, http://www.cbc.ca/8thfire/2011/11/its-time.html.

16 Ibid.

17 David Ljunggren. "Every G20 Nation Wants to Be Canada, Insists PM," September 25, 2009, http://www.reuters.com/article/2009/09/26/columns-us-g20-canada-advantages-idUSTRE58P05Z20090926.

18 See Sunera Thobani, Exalted Subjects (Toronto: University of Toronto Press, 2007).

19 For more information about the Sixties Scoop, see "Sixties Scoop," http://indigenousfoundations.arts.ubc.ca/home/government-policy/sixties-scoop.html.

20 As Ted Chamberlin points out in his book If This Is Your Land, Where Are Your Stories?, it is odd and arguably inaccurate to name those who are relatively new to a place "settlers," when there are people who have already been living in this place for thousands of years, who are much more settled than the newcomers. As such, we may need to question or "unsettle" the concept of the "settlers," as the title of Paulette Regan's book, Unsettling the Settler Within, also reminds us.

21 See Chris Turner, The War on Science (Vancouver: Greystone Books, 2013), or the organization Evidence for Democracy, https://evidencefordemocracy.ca/.

22 "Drinking Water Advisories in First Nations Communities," http://www.hc-sc.gc.ca/fniah-spnia/promotion/public-publique/water-dwa-eau-aqep-eng.php.

23 The Health Canada website states, "As part of the British Columbia Tripartite Framework Agreement on First Nation Health Governance, on October 1st 2013, Health Canada transferred its role in the design, management, and delivery of First Nations health programming in British Columbia to the new First Nations Health Authority (FNHA). Therefore, Health Canada no longer reports DWAs in BC First Nations." Health Canada, "Drinking Water and Wastewater," http://www.hc-sc.gc.ca/fniah-spnia/promotion/public-publique/water-eau-eng.php#s2a.

24 Consider, for example, the Natural Resources Transfer Act of 1930, which happened unilaterally when the Government of Canada transferred authority for handling natural

resources to the provinces of Alberta, Saskatchewan, and Manitoba without consulting First Nations who were affected by this.

25 See Leanne Simpson, ed., *Lighting the Eighth Fire: The Liberation, Resurgence and Protection of Indigenous Nations* (Winnipeg: ARP Books, 2008), for instance.

26 Quoted from a panel at the Native American and Indigenous Studies Association (NAISA) conference, University of Saskatchewan, June 15, 2013.

27 For more on Bill C45, see Grace Visconti, "Jessica Clogg explains Bill C-45, First Nations Rights, FIPA," West Coast Environmental Law, http://wcel.org/resources/environmental-law-alert/jessica-clogg-explains-bill-c-45-first-nations-rights-fipa.

28 See Leanne Simpson, "Restoring Nationhood: Addressing Land Dispossession in the Canadian Reconciliation Discourse," November 13, 2013, http://www.sfu.ca/tlcvan/clients/sfu_woodwards/2013-11-13_Woodwards_VOCE_Restoring_Nationhood_12308/.

29 Astrida Neimanis, this volume, page 57.

30 Janine Macleod, this volume, page 247.

31 Ibid., page 246.

32 By *umwelt*, we mean the perceptual world of a being. What makes it on the radar or the filters of an Idle No More activist may be very different from what a Conservative senator perceives or that of a beaver or grizzly bear, for that matter, yet all need water, whatever their attitudes or levels of consciousness toward it may be.

33 See Amnesty International, "From Homeland to Oil Sands," for a map of the oil wells, http://www.amnesty.ca/sites/amnesty/files/amr200022010enhomelandsoilsands.pdf.

34 "Keepers of the Water: Nishnaabe-kwewag Speaking for the Water" was first published in Simpson, *Lighting the Eight Fire*.

35 Basia Irland, this volume, page 187.

36 See, for example, Heather Menzies, *Reclaiming the Commons for the Common Good* (Gabriola Island, BC: New Society, 2014), and Max Haiven, *Crises of Imagination, Crises of Power: Capitalism, Creativity and the Commons* (Halifax: Fernwood Books, 2014).

37 Glen Coulthard, interview by Andrew Bard Epstein, "The Colonialism of the Present," https://www.jacobinmag.com/2015/01/indigenous-left-glen-coulthard-interview/.

38 Gary Nabhan, *Cultures of Habitat* (Washington, DC: Counterpoint, 1997), 319.

39 We acknowledge and appreciate Rising Tide, the group of allies that are organizing in different cities around the world in solidarity with the Unist'ot'en Camp, which is blocking the black snake (pipelines) from crossing the unceded traditional homelands of the Gitxsan Wet'suwet'en people.

40 Juan Guillermo Sanchez Martinez and Felipe Quetzalcoatl Quintanilla, eds., *Indigenous Message on Water* (London, ON: Indigenous World Forum on Water and Peace, 2014).

41 We encourage you to listen to Ta'Kaiya Blaney's beautiful song, "Shallow Waters," on YouTube, if you haven't already heard it, https://www.youtube.com/watch?v=LkjIkuC_eWM.

42 The Healing Walk for the Tar Sands from 2010 to 2014 is a crucial example of ceremonial action, http://www.healingwalk.org. In October 2013, members of Cold Lake First Nation conducted a three-day ceremonial walk to draw attention to a nine-month-long oil spill caused by CNRL, http://www.cbc.ca/news/canada/edmonton/3-day-ceremonial-walk-underway-to-protest-cold-lake-spill-1.2253076. Another walk to mobilize against proposed pipelines, People for Mother Earth, began on May 10, 2014, in Quebec, and continued to Kanehsatake by June 14, 2014, and then reorganized as a Walk for Mother Earth that concluded in Ottawa, June 22, 2014. For an article on the Healing Walk for the Tar Sands, also see Rita Wong, "Ethical Waters," *Feminist Review* 103 (2012): 133–39. The Mother Earth Water Walk is discussed in this anthology, but there are many more Indigenous-led walks that merit attention. The cross-continental Peace and Dignity Journey focused on the sacred element of water in 2012.

Bibliography

Amnesty International. "From Homeland to Oil Sands: The Impact of Oil and Gas Development on the Lubicon Cree." 2010. http://www.amnesty.ca/sites/amnesty/files/amr 200022010enhomelandsoilsands.pdf.

Anderson, Kim. "Aboriginal Women, Water and Health: Reflections from Eleven First Nations, Inuit, and Métis Grandmothers." Winnipeg: Prairie Women's Health Centre of Excellence, 2010. http://www.pwhce.ca/womenAndWater.htm.

Archibald, Jo-ann. *Indigenous Storywork: Educating the Heart, Mind, Body and Spirit.* Vancouver: UBC Press, 2008.

Armstrong, Jeannette. "Water Is Siwlkw." In *Water and Indigenous Peoples*, edited by R. Boelens, M. Chiba, and D. Nakashima, 18–19. Paris: UNESCO, 2006.

Bakker, Karen, ed. *Eau Canada: The Future of Canada's Water.* Vancouver: UBC Press, 2007.

Barlow, Maude. *Blue Future.* Toronto: House of Anansi Press, 2013.

Barnhardt, R., and V. Kirkness, "First Nations and Higher Education: The Four R's— Respect, Relevance, Reciprocity, Responsibility." *Journal of American Indian Education* 30, no. 3 (1991): 1–15.

Billy, Janice. "Back from the Brink: Decolonizing Through the Restoration of Secwepemc Language, Culture, and Identity." PhD diss., Simon Fraser University, 2009.

Blaney, Ta'Kaiya. "Shallow Waters." YouTube. https://www.youtube.com/watch?v =LkjIkuC_eWM.

Brayboy, Bryan McKinley Jones. "Toward a Tribal Critical Race Theory in Education." *The Urban Review* 37, no. 5 (December 2005): 425–46.

CBC. *Eighth Fire: Aboriginal Peoples, Canada and the Way Forward.* 2011. http://www .cbc.ca/8thfire/2011/11/its-time.html.

Chamberlin, J. Edward. *If This Is Your Land, Where Are Your Stories?* Toronto: Alfred A. Knopf, 2003.

Chen, Cecilia, Janine MacLeod, and Astrida Neimanis, eds. *Thinking with Water.* Montreal: McGill-Queen's University Press, 2013.

Christian, Dorothy. *A "Cinema of Sovereignty": Working in the Cultural Interface to Create a Model for Fourth World Film Pre-Production and Aesthetics.* Burnaby, BC: Simon Fraser University, 2010.

———. "Reconciling with the People and the Land." In *Cultivating Canada: Reconciliation Through the Lens of Cultural Diversity*, vol. 3, ed. Ashok Mathur, Jonathan Dewar, and Mike DeGagné, 69–90. Ottawa: Aboriginal Healing Foundation, 2011.

Christian, Dorothy, with Victoria Freeman. "History of a Friendship or Some Thoughts on Becoming Allies." In *Alliances: Re/Envisioning Indigenous and Non-Indigenous Relationships*, ed. Lynne Davis, 376–90. Toronto: University of Toronto Press, 2010.

Christian, Dorothy, and Rita Wong. "Untapping Watershed Mind." In *Thinking with Water*, edited by Cecilia Chen, Janine MacLeod, and Astrida Neimanis, 232–53. Montreal: McGill-Queen's University Press, 2013.

Cohen, W.A. "School Failed Coyote, So Fox Made a New School: Indigenous Okanagan Knowledge Transforms Educational Pedagogy." PhD diss., University of British Columbia, 2010.

Coulthard, Glen. "The Colonialism of the Present." Interview by Andrew Bard Epstein. January 13, 2015. https://www.jacobinmag.com/2015/01/indigenous -left-glen-coulthard-interview/.

Deloria, Vine. *God Is Red: A Native View of Religion*. 3rd ed. Golden, CO: Fulcrum Publishing, 2003.

"Drinking Water and Wastewater." Health Canada. http://www.hc-sc.gc.ca/fniah-spnia/promotion/public-publique/water-eau-eng.php#s2a.

Driver, Julia. "The History of Utilitarianism." Stanford Encyclopedia of Philosophy. March 27, 2009. http://plato.stanford.edu/entries/utilitarianism-history/.

European Graduate School. "Jean-Jacques Rousseau." http://www.egs.edu/library/jean-jacques-rousseau/biography/.

Evidence for Democracy. https://evidencefordemocracy.ca/.

George, Amy. "Tsleil-Waututh Elder Amy George Speaks About Oil Tanker Concerns at the Chinese Consulate." Four Worlds International Institute. January 8, 2012. http://www.fwii.net/video/tsleil-waututh-elder-amy-george-speaks-about-oil -tanker-concerns.

George, Rueben. Defend Our Coast Rally. October 22, 2012. http://www.youtube.com/watch?v=mCi0odDrtOc.

Goddard, John. *Last Stand of the Lubicon Cree*. Vancouver: Douglas and McIntyre, 1991.

Haiven, Max. *Crises of Imagination, Crises of Power: Capitalism, Creativity and the Commons*. Halifax: Fernwood Books, 2014.

Health Canada. "Drinking Water Advisories in First Nations Communities." http://www.hc-sc.gc.ca/fniah-spnia/promotion/public-publique/water-dwa-eau-aqep-eng.php.

———. "Drinking Water and Wastewater." http://www.hc-sc.gc.ca/fniah-spnia/promotion/public-publique/water-eau-eng.php#s2a.

Ignace, R. E. *Our Stories Are Our Corner Posts: Secewepemc Stories and Historical Consciousness*. PhD diss., Simon Fraser University, 2008.

Indigenous Foundations. "Sixties Scoop." http://indigenousfoundations.arts.ubc.ca/home/government-policy/sixties-scoop.html.

Internet Encyclopedia of Philosophy—A Peer-Reviewed Academic Resource. "John Locke: Political Philosophy." http://www.iep.utm.edu/locke-po/.

"Jean-Jacques Rousseau—Biography." European Graduate School. http://www.egs.edu/library/jean-jacques-rousseau/biography/.

Kovach, Margaret. *Indigenous Methodologies: Characteristics, Conversations and Contexts*. Toronto: University of Toronto Press, 2009.

Linton, Jamie. "What Is Water?" In *The History of a Modern Abstraction*. Vancouver: UBC Press, 2010.

Ljunggren, David. "Every G20 Nation Wants to Be Canada, Insists PM." Reuters, September 25, 2009. http://www.reuters.com/article/2009/09/26/columns -us-g20-canada-advantages-idUSTRE58P05Z20090926.

Manuel, George, and Michael Posluns. *The Fourth World: An Indian Reality*. Toronto: Collier-Macmillan, 1974.

Martinez, Juan Guillermo Sanchez Martinez, and Felipe Quetzalcoatl Quintanilla, eds. *Indigenous Message on Water*. London, ON: Indigenous World Forum on Water and Peace, 2014.

McAdam, Sylvia. Idle No More: The Movement. Panel at the Native American and Indigenous Studies Association (NAISA) conference, University of Saskatchewan, June 15, 2013.

Menzies, Heather. *Reclaiming the Commons for the Common Good*. Gabriola Island, BC: New Society, 2014.

Michel, K. A. "Trickster's Path to Language Transformation: Stories of Secwepemc Immersion from Chief Atahm School." PhD diss., University of British Columbia, 2012.

Mohawk, John. "How the Conquest of Indigenous Peoples Parallels the Conquest of Nature." Lecture. *Schumacher Center for a New Economics* (October 1997): 1–8. http://www.centerforneweconomics.org/publications/lectures/Mohawk/John/How-the-Conquest-of-Indigenous-Peoples-Parallels-the-Conquest-of-Nature.

———. *Thinking in Indian: A John Mohawk Reader.* Edited by Jose Barreiro. Golden, CO: Fulcrum Publishing, 2010.

Mosely, Alexander. "John Locke: Political Philosophy." Internet Encyclopedia of Philosophy. http://www.iep.utm.edu/locke-po/.

Nabhan, Gary. *Cultures of Habitat.* Washington, DC: Counterpoint, 1997.

Nakata, M. "Anthropological Texts and Indigenous Standpoints." *Australian Aboriginal Studies* no. 2 (1998): 3–12.

———. "Australian Indigenous Studies: A Question of Discipline." *Australian Journal of Anthropology* 17, no. 3 (2006): 265–75.

———. "The Cultural Interface." *Australian Journal of Indigenous Education,* Supplement 36 (2007): 7–14.

———. "The Cultural Interface: An Exploration of the Intersection of Western Knowledge Systems and Torres Strait Islanders Positions and Experiences." PhD diss., James Cook University of North Queensland, 1997.

———. *Disciplining the Savages: Savaging the Disciplines.* Canberra, Australia: Aboriginal Studies Press, 2007.

———. "Indigenous Knowledge and the Cultural Interface: Underlying Issues at the Intersection of Knowledge and Information Systems." *International Federation of Library Associations Journal* 28, no. 5/6 (2002): 281–91.

———. "Introduction: Special Supplementary Issue on Indigenous Studies-Indigenous Knowledge: Navigating the Interface." *Australian Journal of Indigenous Education* 37 (2008): 1–4.

Ominayak, Chief Bernard, with Kevin Thomas. "These Are Lubicon Lands: A First Nation Forced to Step into the Regulatory Gap." *Speaking for Ourselves: Environmental Justice in Canada,* 111–22. Vancouver: UBC Press, 2009.

Porsanger, J. "An Essay about Indigenous Methodology." *Nordlit: Working Papers in Literature* (Special Issue on Northern Minorities) 15 (2004): 105–20.

Rising Tide Vancouver Coast Salish Territories. Home page. http://risingtide604.ca/.

Sam, Marlowe. "Oral Narratives, Customary Laws and Indigenous Water Rights in Canada." PhD diss., University of British Columbia–Okanagan, 2013.

Sanderson, Darlene. "Nipiy Wasekimew/Clear Water: The Meaning of Water, from the Words of the Elders." PhD diss., Simon Fraser University, 2008.

Sandford, Robert, and Merrell-Ann Phare. *Ethical Water: Learning to Value What Matters Most.* Calgary: Rocky Mountain Books, 2011.

Simpson, Leanne, ed. *Lighting the Eighth Fire: The Liberation, Resurgence and Protection of Indigenous Nations.* Winnipeg: ARP Books, 2008.

———. "Restoring Nationhood: Addressing Land Dispossession in the Canadian Reconciliation Discourse." November 13, 2013. http://www.sfu.ca/tlcvan/clients/sfu_woodwards/2013-11-13_Woodwards_VOCE_Restoring_Nationhood_12308/.

Stanford Encyclopedia of Philosophy. "The History of Utilitarianism." http://plato.stanford.edu/entries/utilitarianism-history/.

Thobani, Sunera. *Exalted Subjects*. Toronto: University of Toronto Press, 2007.

Turner, Chris. *The War on Science*. Vancouver: Greystone Books, 2013.

Unist'ot'en Camp. Home page. http://unistotencamp.com/.

Visconti, Grace. "Jessica Clogg Explains Bill C-45, First Nations Rights, FIPA." West Coast Environmental Law. http://wcel.org/resources/environmental-law-alert/jessica-clogg-explains-bill-c-45-first-nations-rights-fipa.

Wong, Rita. "Ethical Waters." *Feminist Review* 103 (2012): 133–39.

part i

contexts for knowing and unknowing water

Planetary Distress Signals

Alanna Mitchell

When I started to write *Sea Sick: The Global Ocean in Crisis*, I knew nothing about the ocean. I saw it only as a place where the beach was, and I played on the beaches at Gibson's Landing, B.C., when I was a child. My father was born in Vancouver, and we went to the sea every summer. I was at the end of writing my first book, *Dancing at the Dead Sea*, when I realized that the ocean was much more than that—biologically and spiritually. I wanted to understand how the ocean worked chemically and biologically because that's what I do. I try to find out what scientists are finding out because these are great, hidden, fascinating stories. I have come to think of scientists as the heroes in many of these stories, and they often have difficulty telling these stories themselves. So I think of myself as a democratizer of information that scientists uncover, often on the public dime, and that doesn't get disseminated into the public discourse. Philosophically, my work is to democratize information, and because I'm a storyteller, I am going to tell you some stories about it.

Those stories centre on the three indicators of the ocean's functions that scientists seem most worried about. At least that's what they told me in my journeys with them. These indicators matter because, as one scientist put it to me, if everything that lives in the air were to die tomorrow, everything in the ocean would still be fine, but if everything in the ocean were to die tomorrow, everything on land would also die. So we're fully dependent on the functions of the global ocean for our own survival—and this is the part that I didn't understand before I wrote *Sea Sick*.

Humans are changing the basic chemistry of the global ocean. It's not just the Pacific and the Atlantic. The oceans and seas are all connected; they are all part of the lifeblood of the planet. So I started to think about the ocean as if it were a patient that I sent to the doctor. What would a doctor say if the doctor were to look at the vital signs of the global ocean today and tell us what is going on?

The ocean's health matters. It helps to control the carbon cycle of the planet. It helps to control the oxygen cycle of the planet. Every second breath that you are breathing is oxygen produced by plankton in the ocean. The nitrogen cycle is partly controlled by the ocean. For the vast majority of time that there has been life on our planet, there has been life only in the ocean. We land-dwellers are latecomers to the planet. Life on land first appeared only 400 million years ago. Most of our body blueprints evolved in the ocean. We're fully dependent on the ocean. This was the shocking revelation to me when I went on these voyages with the scientists.

The scientists talk about three major chemical changes to the ocean that are caused by people. First, the pH of the ocean is changing. That is, the acidity of the ocean is increasing. Second, the temperature of the ocean is changing. Third, the dissolved oxygen content is changing, as Paul Harrison discusses in this anthology, so the ocean is becoming sour, warm, and breathless. Each of those changes on its own is really devastating. When you combine them, they become the evil troika. These are the three things that should never be combined, but they are all connected to the increased carbon load in the atmosphere, which is sickening our global ocean. And life on the planet depends on the ocean.

Life has collapsed catastrophically five times in the whole history of life on the planet. There have been five mass extinctions, and the last one was when the dinosaurs became extinct. The ocean was involved somehow in each of these mass extinctions.

During the biggest of them all, the Permian extinction, which was about 252 million years ago, 95 percent of the species on the planet were extinct. Scientists have been able to reconstruct what happened. The ocean became acidic, warmer, and lost its dissolved oxygen. Today paleontologists say, "We're setting the table for a mass extinction." They say that they can track how fast that carbon load went into the atmosphere during the Permian extinction and prompted those three chemical changes in the ocean. They realize that 252 million years ago, all those species were killed by an immense carbon load that exploded into the atmosphere from the development of the Siberian Traps, a geological formation created by volcanoes. This turned the ocean acidic, made it warmer, and prompted it to lose its dissolved oxygen.

Recently, a paper in *Science* explained that today our burning of fossil fuels is putting carbon into the air at ten times the rate of those ancient Siberian Traps volcanoes.[1] We still have a bit of time to withdraw some of that carbon from the atmosphere, but at this point we're on a trajectory that would catapult us into another mass extinction, so that's why scientists are concerned. That's why they talk about these three things: acidity, temperature, and dissolved oxygen levels.

I travelled around the world with scientists, making thirteen journeys in two and a half years, following their research. I would say to them, "Jeez, I just found out this ..." and they would say, "Oh really?" They weren't necessarily looking at the big picture, which is one of the things that a journalist can do. A journalist can synthesize a lot of this research, which is what I hope *Sea Sick* does. I tried to put all these ideas together and make a whole picture of it.

After I found out all this stuff, after I went on all those journeys, I became very depressed. I think "clinical depression" is the medical term for it. I actually went to bed for about a month, deciding that I would never write this book. It just wasn't worth the trees it would be printed on. I thought we were all doomed. But I ended up having a powerful epiphany at the bottom of the ocean in a tiny submersible 915 metres below the surface. I was in a little chamber at the back of the submersible, lying there terrified that I would die.

But at this very great depth—when you are absolutely pushed to the limits—something happens and you begin to see the world in a different way. I was pushed right past my limits and achieved a whole different way of understanding. Before, I was focused on my own despair, my despair for the planet. Then when I descended 915 metres, I focused on dying. It wasn't the planetary stuff, not the big picture anymore; it was just all about me. I was going to die. Right then. Right there. I would not make it back to the surface. The despair vanished in the teeth of the personal terror, and then I came out of it into this totally different place, which is what I hope I can leave you with. I arrived at a magical place, and it has never fully gone away. I decided to choose hope rather than despair.

What that means is you honour the incredible complexity of this journey and everything that other people have done, including all the things that you have done. And you decide to write a new ending to the story. That's what the participants in Downstream are talking about. Instead of "Oh, boy we're going to mess everything up. We're all going to die and we're going to go right into the mass extinction and this is the end of the story." Instead of writing that ending, you write an ending that says, "This is where we have triumphed. We have come back from the brink, pulled together on a cellular level. All of us, somehow, are doing what we need to do to try to pull us back from the brink." And that is incredibly powerful. That's what people who are trying to put through the pipelines don't expect. They don't expect us all to pull together and say, "Wait a sec. We're going to write a different story. We're going to write a different ending to this story." And that's where we have power.

It will happen in different ways. It will happen in different places. It happened when we were singing on the shore in False Creek with Cathy Stubington.[2] What we did reminded me of a term from the choir I sing in: descant. This when the sopranos at the very end, at the very final verse, take this music that we have been singing for four or five verses into a whole other place. What I've heard at the Downstream workshop, and what I see in other parts of the world, is a descant. The old song is almost over, and we're starting a new one. That's what keeps me going now, so I will leave you with that.

Notes

1 B. Hoenisch et al., "The Geological Record of Ocean Acidification," *Science* 335, no. 6072 (2012): 1058–63, doi: 10.1126/science.1208277.
2 During the Downstream workshop, March 22, 2012.

Bibliography

Hoenisch, B., et al. "The Geological Record of Ocean Acidification." *Science* 335, no. 6072 (2012): 1058–63. doi: 10.1126/science.1208277.

Water

Lee Maracle

In his book, *The Hollow Tree*, Herb Nabigon talks about humbling ourselves to water. I had struggled with the Ojibway concept of humility—humbling ourselves to water—until this moment. *I understand this. I understood myself so much more completely than at any other moment in my life.* So much of my work has been focused on water, but it never occurred to me that I should humble myself to it. I have always cherished the memory of water, the ocean, the life-giving force, and I have tried to be respectful, but until you truly humble yourself to water, you cannot appreciate its magnificence, nor respect life itself. I have not been able to stop thinking about it, feeling it, awakening to it. I was born and raised on the edges of the Pacific Ocean—the Salish Sea—its rhythms, its depths informing my work. The moment I read "humble ourselves to water," I could actually feel, see, and in some psychic and spiritual way experience the depth of the water in my life. I could feel my smallness, my inconsequentiality, my imposition on water. All day, I kept watching myself in my relation to water—don't run the tap so long, the water doesn't have to abide by your wishes. It doesn't have to be that cold that you should run the tap for minutes. I don't need to stand luxuriating for minutes under the shower. I even went out to purchase an ecofriendly tap and shower head. I walked to the edge of the lake here at the bottom of Spadina and just looked at the water. This lake began as a single drop of water from a sheet of ice seven thousand kilometres long and ten kilometres high at its starting point. It rested here, exhausted, unable to go any further. The sun came and began to melt it drop by drop. As the water melted, it gained strength, the drops became *Hayaluq* (a big wave), and the wave gouged out the earth, shoving some of it into the sea. Somehow it formed these lakes.

I am familiar with the water in my body. My eyes have shed tears, drop by drop; my womb has gushed a torrent of water prior to the birth of each of my children. I have bled drops of blood, month by month, as a woman. I understand water and how each drop is so hard won; each drop is so fought for, so essential to my being. Without it, I am dead. Without it, I am a wrinkled old prune, an empty shell.

I humble myself to the *Stólō* (river), to the sea, to the waves that have carried us from place to place and even to those *Hayaluq* that have buried us. I understand the ocean. She is our mother, our food source; she is both loving and dangerous. We depend on her, we cherish her, and we respect her.

When I think of water, I picture each river and its beginning. A single raindrop joins other raindrops, joins with Earth dust, and forms a rivulet that swells to a river cascading to the ocean. The water does her duty by us, sending ever more drops to the sky world to cling to the Earth world dust our mother has sent and returning to us as sweet rain. I understand the struggle of each drop to lift off, to find the dust that will carry it; these unseen tiny drops find their way to cloud formations. They cling together; they aggregate in the clouds like we do in the longhouse. They join one another, gain strength in their unity, until finally, big enough, heavy enough, they fall on the land. They are doing their duty by all the living beings. To cleanse the water, it needs to rise, fall, leech through the soil, find another rivulet, join a stream, which joins a river, which joins the ocean, which joins the sky, and the process begins again. I conduct ceremonies of endless thanks.

The area now called False Creek and Kitsilano in Vancouver was the location of Khatsahlano's village. Khatsahlano came from an era when nobody had gone to residential school, and for the first nineteen years of my life, I was privileged to be alive when he was still alive, of sound mind and telling stories. He explained that the West Coast is Salish Territory. It's also a country. When you come to another country, you naturally adopt the customs, the laws, and the practices of that country. Well, people came here and adopted the laws and practices of Britain. *This is not Britain. You're in Coast Salish territory.* The Squamish people simply called it Squamish. But it didn't end at Snauq'w.[1] It didn't end over there on the other side of False Creek. It started way below Musqueam, and it went way above Vancouver and North Vancouver into actual Squamish, where Whistler Mountain and all those beautiful mountains are.

I return to the Snauq'w, put my feet in the water like so many thousands of my ancestors have done, sing songs to her, recognize her, honour her, and offer up my respect.

only through clear water can we see wolf etchings
carved on cave walls
my eyes obscured by old tears blind
I tip my face
a tear drop falls
and returns to the creek
the tears roll past
grateful to be going home
to be useful again

I cannot talk about Snauq'w without talking about the deliberate destruction of the water. The destruction of the water was accompanied by occupation and desecration of the land, and the wanton slaughter of the animals. The goal was the elimination of my people. The desecration of the land led to the destruction of the plant world. The slaughter of the animals and the destruction of the water led to the starvation of my people and the disconnection from all that empowered us. If someone had said to my ancestors that you could destroy the waters, they would likely have laughed—it turns out that this is in the realm of the possible. The waters of Snauq'w are gone. Housing, docks, businesses, apartments, roads, and the railway station have replaced it, and the garden that Snauq'w was is now destroyed. There is no shoreline left, so the plants that sustained the life of the water are gone as well. There are thousands of people living on top of the destroyed water. This destruction severely weakened all Salish people, and it surely rendered the water impotent.

Khatsahlano's villagers were not the only people who depended on the camas, berries, oysters, clams, and seaweed that grew there; the shell beings, the fish, the medicines, were all needed by Salish to be who we are and who we will always be. The elk, too, were killed; the seals, whales, and great spring salmons are gone. Just above Snauq'w the largest trees in the world grew and now the mountains are bare. The sockeye have been struggling to survive without the care and management of Salish people. There are no big trees left in this area. We fed each other, took care of one another through the caretaking and the sharing of the wealth.

Canada is a guest who moved into our house, tossed us out, and then destroyed everything in the house. The longhouses were outlawed and dismantled, and now we hardly remember the taste of the seals we ate, we can hardly identify the plants that sustained us, and no one remembers how the gardens of False Creek were maintained. We have reserves but no territory; without territory we are homeless.

So much of our territories became little more than garbage dumps. There are over four thousand toxic waste dumps in this country and over three thousand of them are in our backyards. We, too, have been treated like so much garbage. That is what happened to our beautiful gardens. Once the toxic waste was dumped, of course we moved. But the move hurt. The responsibility for Snauq'w was abrogated by our removal. We ache for those gardens; our bodies cannot sustain themselves without the food Snauq'w provided.

We also ache to know how it is that anyone could find the destruction of great amounts of water and gardens acceptable. Please don't tell me it is capitalism or colonialism. I know the system that keeps us all in line. I also know that I and my family have never accepted it. We objected. We objected then and we continue to object now. Ordinary people did not object to our destruction or the destruction of our foods and lands. Ordinary people did the work of destruction. How did it come to pass that ordinary people were so alienated from the land that they would destroy what their grandchildren would come to rely upon? How does one leave their home, arrive at a new place, and destroy that place? How does one come to find the killing of inhabitants of that place acceptable?

Now it is filled with newcomers, and we are not entitled to deny them a place in our world. Everyone has a place here. We welcome you despite everything. I wouldn't mind, but for the most part, the newcomers besmirched our ways, made us invisible, and destroyed our plants, animals, and fish. The murder of us continues unabated. The deprivation of our people is treated as though it is all we deserve.

In the besmirching of our ways, we were severed from the water, land, culture, and ceremonial ways that kept us healthy and alive. We went from citizens of a Salish confederacy to beggars in a landscape we cannot recognize, grubbing for food our bodies don't recognize. Hungry and desperate, we still yearn for the restoration of Snauq'w.

> They changed everything, even the way we eat—they even changed the way Chinese people eat. If we eat like them, we will live like them and die like them. (Khatsahlano)

This is happening now. We are hungry. We are desperate. We are maligned. We are a country-less people. I have heard people say, "I thank the Salish people for allowing me to be here." In the beginning, we did allow you to be here, but I am wondering now if we all still feel that way after the history that has been visited upon us. By our own law, we are not entitled to deny women the right to construct a home, but your society persecutes the very people who entitled you to a home, and it does so with impunity. We are being forced by poverty into making concessions again to the country that was created on our losses. We are being asked to make a treaty, not as a Salish nation, but as tiny little reserves, isolated from each other and impoverished and maligned by those around us. We are being asked not to share the wealth of our land but to give it up. Let Snauq'w go. It is history, water under the bridge.

But the water under the bridge has dried up, it is gone—destroyed. Even as a child I saw the water under the Georgia Viaduct. I watched as they dredged it and put in a new road. Like the water, we are so dispensable. Like camas, cedar, shellfish, sockeye, whales, seals, and elk, we are just so much unnecessary wildlife.

I want to say that I will always be looking for Salish landscapes. I will always yearn for the water that was False Creek, the marshes that were Richmond, the marshes and berry fields that were at John Hendry Park and all over the territory. I will always yearn for how the abundance was considered everyone's. We have been denied so much that we are terrified of sharing with each other. The waters of the inlet (Tsleil waututh) still want to be water; they don't want to be covered in cement and docking facilities. Covering them with cement is not progress to us, nor is it progress for the water. I will always want our trees; I will always hunger for our foods. And I will always want sovereignty. Like the water, I will never give it up. And I have children and grandchildren who feel exactly like me.

We do not own the water, the water owns itself. We are responsible for ensuring that we do not damage the water. We do not have an absolute right to use and abuse the water; we must take care of the water and ensure that we have a good relationship with it. This relationship is based on mutual respect.

A friend forwarded an email that someone else sent her: "The water belongs to everyone." I have been saying this for over forty years: *NO. The water belongs to itself.* We have to ask it to accept us, to work with us, to permit us to consume it, ride it, and harvest the beings from it. We do not *own* the land, the water, the sky, the plant world, the animal world. They own themselves. The water owns itself. I had said that three times at the water gathering and yet there was this email: "The water belongs to everyone." It was sent to educate me, inspire me, or some such thing, but it deflated me. It feels like so few people listen and accept what I say. My lips are weary of repeating themselves. We can never move the conversation to any new place, so long as the first line that comes out of my mouth is unacceptable: The water belongs to itself. We are responsible for taking care of it. In exchange we get to use it—sparingly. In the Salish tradition, we have an obligation to the water.

From encroachment to invasion to destruction is a long journey, but it begins with a single step, like all journeys. But even before we take that step, we must entitle ourselves to travel in the direction we wish to go. We must entitle ourselves to do so. To entitle ourselves to own the water is to put ourselves ahead of it, in front of it, and on top of it—that is invasion. We are entitled to overuse what we own, to destroy what we own—burn it should we choose— but if we don't own it, then we can only engage it in relationship. We have to seek permission from it and to use it, we must care for it.

THE WATER OWNS ITSELF.

Note

1 Snauq'w is also known as False Creek in Vancouver.

Interweaving Water
The Incremental Transformation of Sovereign Knowledge into Collaborative Knowledge
Michael D. Blackstock

A common plot sequence in First Nations oral history is where the main character first transcends a world boundary and then quickly transforms from human to animal or vice versa to adjust to the new world. This sequence is a helpful analogy that modern ontology could take notice of as a prerequisite to tackling anthropogenic ecological consequences,[1] literally piling up before our children's eyes.

The Tsimshian oral history entitled "Myth of Niaslaws"[2] is an excellent example of how a supernatural water being transcended the boundary between the water world and the human world. It starts out with two Tsimshian hunters casting their stone anchor from their boat to moor at an island for the night. Their anchor lands on a supernatural being's roof, so he (Spanaxnox) sends a slave woman to see what is going on, and this is where we join in:

> She saw this big stone anchor and she returned and said to [... Spanaxnox], "There is a big rock on top of the house with a rope on it." The chief [Spanaxnox] said, "Go and see where it comes from." The slave woman went out and swam around the canoe and Txagetk caught it and cut off its fins. He threw it into the water again and the little fish went back into the house of the supernatural being [Spanaxnox] and again changed into a human being but without arms and she was crying. [...] Spanaxnox was sitting at the back of the house and he saw the slave woman crying who said, "There is a huge monster [canoe] on top of the water and it is full of human beings and one took me and cut my hands off," and she cried again. The supernatural being was mad and he said, "I will bring them down and take them into my house." When he said this, there was a strong current, which made a whirlpool, and this brought the men into the house of the supernatural being.[3]

Slave woman transforms into a little codfish in the hunters' world, even though she is human in her water world. The hunters' perception is that slave woman is an annoying little codfish. Additionally, transcending boundaries between the two worlds allows the hunters to see, with new eyes, how this human was maimed by their actions in their world. The hunters' assumption about the ocean just being a place to use and to drop anchor was challenged, and with their newfound empathy they adopted a new attitude of respect, which is a crucial part of transformation.

I have hope in our ability to transcend boundaries, as we see that a Gitxsan Halait (i.e., healing shaman) can when moving between worlds, or as Dvorak's Rusalka can when she, a fish-woman who lived on the bottom of a river, awkwardly emerged from a waterway. This seemingly impossible transcendence offers hope, opens up new paths, and liquefies the "either/or" narrative about traditional boundaries between art and science, Indigenous and Western, living and non-living, biotic and abiotic, salt water and fresh water, and sentient and inanimate. I will examine one more modern narrative in my conclusion: jobs and the environment.

This chapter outlines four steps toward transforming sovereign knowledge into collaborative knowledge: (1) humility, (2) transcending, (3) interweaving, and finally (4) transformation. I illustrate this process using the theory of Blue Ecology, which I developed in collaboration with Indigenous Elders. It interweaves Indigenous and Western science's perspectives on water.[4]

We are borrowing fresh water from future generations. Our children's children will be faced with daunting, complex, and urgent environmental problems that will surge social and economic changes at an unprecedented pace. This impending crisis requires us, the source of this crisis, to transcend and transform, to begin to lay a foundation for our children's children to have something to work with, a starting point, and some options to grasp in the urgent moment. We owe it to future generations as a form of apology. We owe them hope.

Humility

The hunters' arrogance blinded them as they threw their anchor on top of the chief's house. Not one epistemology—whether it is Western science, Indigenous science, art, business, or theology—by itself is fully equipped to deal with the highly complex problems that our children's children will face. Thus, the first incremental step of transcendence is for the knowledge keepers and creators, scientists and philosophers of each epistemology to feel humility. Basia Irland is a water and eco-artist who embodies the idea of humility and courage because she creates ephemeral ice art that is meant to melt away as she sends it on a journey down a river of inspiration; her art moves beyond the walls of the gallery into more contextual and humble spaces. For instance, she spends days creating an ice book in situ, embedded with "riparian text" made of local plant seeds, and then in a moment of courage she floats the ice sculpture down the river from which the ice was made in the first place.[5] The embedded text of humility is courage.

I view Western science and Indigenous ways of knowing as *sovereign* entities. A great deal of energy goes into rationalizing, promoting, and protecting an epistemology. However, now we need to acknowledge that we don't have all the answers. We can build a collaborative epistemological framework if we transcend sovereign contemporary narrative's boundaries, and literally mine each epistemology for gems that can be interwoven in a collaborative manner. Embracing humility will release the energy used to protect and rationalize current academic and political sovereignty and redirect it to the intensive next step: interweaving. Identifying the strong threads—and there are many—of Western science with those of Indigenous traditional knowledge will form a new collaborative fabric of knowledge. Lee Maracle speaks eloquently about the Indigenous concept of humility, which means humbling ourselves *to* water. Additionally, Astrida Neimanis invites us in a humble way, to open up a new imaginative space by paying attention to water and thinking *with* water. Both of these authors view humility as a key ingredient for collaboration; thus the corollary is that arrogance can lead to unnecessary conflict.

Transcendence

In this chapter, transcendence takes on the literal Latin origins of *going beyond* the perceived boundaries of our world, like the hunters entering the underwater world of the supernatural being. In 2002 I appealed for humility and challenged Western science to re-examine its assumption that water is abiotic.[6]

Transcendence looks like *genuine* curiosity. Curiosity about other cultures draws us into a better understanding, and allows us to contrast and compare two worlds. The product of curiosity is an analysis whereby comparison and contrast enable the interweaving process. I have invited Western scientists to transcend the boundary that was built in the sixteenth and seventeenth century, and to be curious about the Indigenous perspective that water is alive (biotic).[7] Once I understood the strengths and contrasts of each perspective on water, I was ready for the interweaving process and published papers that showed how interweaving could happen.

Interweaving

It is difficult to tell which world is which, and who is who in the Tsimshian oral history; the worlds are interwoven. Interweaving is about creating a new form of knowledge through collaboration by interweaving useful threads from each way of knowing into a more robust way. It looks like artists, scientists, theologians, Elders, and poets weaving around the same table. Interweaving is not integration, just as equality is not about assimilation and creativity is not empirical. Mircea Eliade says the coming together of the spirit and matter or sacred and profane "produces a kind of breakthrough of the various levels of existence ... a coexistence of contradictory essences."[8] Interweaving is a collaborative process where apparently contradictory epistemologies are brought together as coexisting threads of information and theory to produce a new entity called collaborative knowledge. Interweaving is an incremental rather than a revolutionary process whereby collaborators identify packets of knowledge that benefit from the interweaving process.

Artist Berndnaut Smilde's indoor cloud installation (see Figure 3.1), entitled *Nimbus D'Aspremont, 2012, Cloud in room*, provides an elegant and amorphous exemplar of interweaving art with science. Using science, he has placed nature within the human domain; this juxtaposition highlights the artistic natural beauty of a cloud.

Figure 3.1 *Nimbus D'Aspremont, 2012, Cloud in room.* (*Source:* Berndnaut Smilde; reproduced with the permission of the artist)

Figure 3.2 *Blue Ecology.* (*Source:* Michael D. Blackstock and Annerose Georgeson)

My expression of Blue Ecology theory came in multiple media, including academic writing, eco-poetics, and visual arts (see Figure 3.2 for an example of a painting entitled *Blue Ecology* or the poem "Blue Ecology" in my book *Salmon Run*).[9] Each form of media expressed the Blue Ecology in a new way to new audiences. This theory was developed over ten years.[10] Our children's children will not have this luxury of research time to solve their immediate crisis.

I defined Blue Ecology as "an ecological philosophy, which emerged from interweaving First Nations and Western thought that acknowledges fresh and salt water's essential rhythmical life spirit and central functional role in generating, sustaining, receiving and ultimately unifying life" on Earth Mother.[11] Many cultures, and in particular Indigenous peoples, believe that water has a spirit and it is commonly characterized as the lifeblood of the planet.[12] Indigenous peoples often use the descriptor "water is lifeblood" since water is seen as the blood flowing through the terrestrial veins of Earth Mother.[13] Blue Ecology does not jettison the great work of modern ecology; however, it does reshape its foundation and opens up new paths of inquiry. This new theory is meant to be a companion because it augments existing Western science hydrology rather than displacing this knowledge. Blue Ecology has, however, identified and challenged some key assumptions of hydrology, while at the same time honouring the wealth of knowledge Western science has produced. The Blue

Ecology vision is collaborative, not competitive. Blue Ecology is a compact or product of interweaving that blends Indigenous knowledge and Western science.

Transformation

Transformation is like the hunters' epiphany that the little codfish is actually a human woman. In short, transformation can mean a shift away from the attitude of sovereign knowledge to collaborative knowledge. The main axiom of transformation is: *It costs you nothing to change your attitude.* A new collaborative knowledge attitude will open up new worlds of possibility. What do you see? Is it a little codfish or a human woman? Is she a water nymph or Rusalka? Is it a wriggling nudibranch (i.e., sea slug) or an elegant First Nations dancer?[14] Is water a non-living fluid or a living and life-giving being? The beholder's transformation can be from one state of mind to another.

Hope

A product of the transformation will be a societal-wide reverence for water. Nasrid poet Ibn Zamrak (AD 1333–93) poignantly expressed reverence in his epigraphic poem inscribed on the Daraxa's water fountain in the Alhambra palace, Granada, Spain. His use of prosopopeia,[15] in poetic form, speaks "*for* the walls of the Alhambra, engages the beholders and guides them beyond visual perception to imaginative comprehension. The beholder is enjoined to ponder."[16]

I am a water orb that appears before the creatures limpid and transparent
a great Ocean, the shores of which are select pieces of work made of special marble
and the waters of which, shaped like pearls, flow on an enormous sheet of ice that has
been delicately carved. In occasions I am overflowed with water, but I, from time to time,
part with the transparent veil that covers me.
     Then I and that part of the water that comes from the borders of the fountain,
appear like a piece of ice, part of which melts and the rest does not …[17]

In the last verse of the poem Zamrak writes about how Nasr, the Sultan of Granada, "has granted me the highest degree of beauty, so that my shape causes the admiration of the sages."[18] The beholder is asked to share the same reverence for the water fountain. This imaginative comprehension or reverence has faded in Western science and does not manifest in the twenty-first century's reverence-less *jobs versus the environment* false conundrum, which has obvious and fundamental flaws: it assumes that jobs, rather than Earth Mother, sustain us.[19] Water is life, not jobs. A job is an abstraction that can disappear in a moment and leave families destitute. A job is, furthermore, a political abstraction used to pit the employed against the unemployed, and the "irrational *greens*" against the "rational" family provider. This abstraction and distraction separates us from each other and from Earth Mother, who is the ultimate provider. Fear over losing our jobs distracts us from having a debate about how this destructive abstraction creates boundaries used by some politicians and those *jobs-riddlers* who lobby politicians. It is a warning sign if you detect the construction of boundaries.[20]

Underlying this lobbying is the notion that "our environmental policy is based on sound (Western) science and it sustains jobs." Western science has provided many wonderful technical and medical inventions to society, and will continue to do so. Artelle et al. are concerned that politicians and resource managers are not held to the same level of independent oversight that research scientists are when they claim that their policies are "science-based."[21] This is a valid concern since commonly used political rhetoric defends controversial resource management statutory decisions like pipeline or mine approvals, for example. Artelle et al. suggest that there should be a peer-review process to ensure scientific research is properly interpreted and incorporated by politicians into "science-based management." Assuming this oversight is put in place in the future, there is still a cultural bias in Western science that needs to be addressed.

"Biocultural diversity," a term that emerged this millennium, inextricably links cultural and biological diversity, focusing on correlations between biodiversity and linguistic diversity. Most importantly, the notion of "linked" implies that biological diversity and cultural diversity have co-evolved, are interdependent, and mutually reinforcing. Cultural groups interact and influence the biological diversity of their environment, and vice versa. Biocultural diversity is the "sum total of the diversity of life in nature and culture."[22]

In 2007 UNESCO launched an international dialogue on biocultural diversity, which is a very valuable resource for policy-makers.[23] They concluded there is a danger in addressing biodiversity independent of cultural diversity, and vice versa. When considering the process of change, like climate change, it is important to understand time scale and historical context. Indigenous peoples around the world are acknowledged to be custodians of biodiversity and proponents of cultural diversity.

Using a biocultural diversity lens, I contend that Western ecological science has a fundamental and repairable cultural bias.[24] Environmental policy-makers and politicians are assuming that Western science has "got it right" when they say our policy is "science-based." However, when it comes to how science and *science-based* environmental policy treats water as a non-living component of the ecosystem, I argue the contrary: Indigenous peoples around the world believe that water is alive and water is life. If the sovereign ecological science of the West is potentially flawed, then its environmental policy derivative is also flawed.

And now I cast doubt on another rhetorical boundary between jobs and the environment. Politicians give voters a false and difficult choice between protecting the environment or creating new jobs. Jacobs argues, however, that we can achieve the "double dividend" of environmental protection and economic growth if there is a policy shift toward placing a tax burden onto environmental impact and creating deep-green jobs.[25]

A job offers us purpose and dignity, which is not to be underestimated; however, the survival of our children and Earth Mother must come first. Morris Berman argues we are now at the end of the capitalist arc, and maybe even at the end of the modernity arc.[26] So now what? We can expect collaborative knowledge to be part of the emergence in a new era when resource managers acknowledge and interweave world views to achieve *sustainable survival with dignity*. To enable hope, we need to act now. We have responsibilities associated with borrowing fresh water from future generations, for instance, which include respecting and responding to Elders' concerns that some of our lakes, springs, and creeks are drying up. Climate change is about water and its transformation from one state to another (e.g., permafrost to water to vapour), and its dramatic movement from one place to another (e.g., from glaciers to rivers to oceans to clouds). In parts of the world, climate change will result in water being the most valued "commodity" produced from forested lands,[27] necessitating a change in our management priorities and approaches. With reverence, the first question asked when contemplating resource management impacts should be: *How does it affect the water?* The highest environmental assessment test for development planning is the paramount water-first principle: *planned development (e.g., real estate, urban planning, hydro power, architecture, forestry, agriculture, fishing, aquaculture, mining, oil and gas extraction) cannot impede the functional delivery of quality water to ecosystems in a healthy rhythm.*[28]

The collaborative vision and operational guiding principles of Blue Ecology, which interweaves cultural perspectives on water in a sustainable and survivable manner, are ready to be implemented now. Hope is not a passive desire but an active attitude. An Elder shared her deep cultural understanding of water and her concern for how humans were disrespecting water, and then she looked into my eyes and said, "What are you going to do about it?"[29] At that moment I knew I had to do more than ethnography. I would try and mediate between two cultural perspectives and develop a new way of looking at water that respected both the Indigenous and Western science perspectives. I moved beyond a strictly "neutral observer's" ethnographic role. Claude Levi-Strauss, in *Structural Anthropology*, describes the trickster's role in mythology as a mediator between two worlds: "The trickster is a mediator. Since his mediating function occupies a position halfway between two polar terms, he must retain something of that duality—namely an ambiguous and equivocal character."[30]

I am a professional chartered mediator, forester, a member of the Gitxsan First Nation, and also of Euro-Canadian descent. I really see the value of each culture being genuinely curious about each other and willing to interweave to resolve disputes: *This is my action.*

It costs you nothing to change your corporate or personal attitude. Now is the time to act on the belief that if we interweave our strengths as traditional knowledge keepers, scientists, poets, artists, and architects in a collaborative manner, we can make a difference. Blue Ecology is an incremental example of how we can interweave cultural perspectives on water, but that is just a starting point in this new era of *interweaving*.

Notes

1 Tom Curtis, *Climate Change Cluedo: Anthropogenic CO2*, 2012. http://www.skeptical science.com/anthrocarbon-brief.html. NASA, *Climate Change, How Do We Know?* 2012, http://climate.nasa.gov/evidence/.

2 J. J. Cove and G. F. Macdonald. *Tsimshian Narratives I: Tricksters, Shamans and Heroes* (Ottawa: Canadian Museum of Civilization, 1987).

3 Ibid., 317.

4 Michael Blackstock, "Blue Ecology: A Cross-cultural Ecological Approach to Reconciling Forest-Related Conflicts," *BC Journal of Ecosystems and Management* 6, no. 2 (2005): 39–54.

5 Basia Irland, *Ice Books*, 2012, http://www.basiairland.com/recent-projects/ice-books.htm.

6 Michael Blackstock, "Water-Based Ecology: A First Nations Proposal to Repair the Definition of an Ecosystem," *BC Journal of Ecosystems and Management* 2, no. 1 (2002): 7–12.

7 Keith Thomas, *Religion and the Decline of Magic: Studies in Popular Beliefs in the Sixteenth and Seventeenth-Century England* (Toronto: Penguin Books, 1971).

8 Mircea Eliade, *Patterns in Comparative Religion* (New York: Sheed and Ward, 1958), 29.

9 Michael Blackstock, *Salmon Run: A Florilegium of Aboriginal Ecological Poetry* (Kamloops, BC: Wyget Books, 2005), 24.

10 See Blackstock 2001, 2002, 2005, 2005, 2008, 2009, 2010, and 2012.

11 Michael Blackstock, "Blue Ecology and Climate Change: Interweaving Cultural Perspectives on Water: an Indigenous Case Study," in *The Role of Hydrology in Water Resources Management*, ed. Hans-Juergen Liebscher, Robin Clarke, John Rodda, Gert Schultz, Andreas Schumann, and Lucio Ub (Proceedings of a symposium held on the island of Capri, Italy, October 2008), IAHS Publ. 327 (2009), 308–9.

   Dr. Marcus Barber describes the Yolngu's (Australian Aborigine) cosmology. They have very little delineation between salt water and fresh water. In Blue Ecology, water is viewed as a spectrum of salinity.

12 I am a member of the UNESCO-IHP expert advisory group on water and cultural diversity. Michael Blackstock, "Blue Ecology, What Is Water? An Indigenous Perspective," in *Water and Culture* (Proceedings of a session at the 5th World Water Forum hosted by TURKKAD [Turkish Women's Cultural Organization] and ISKI [Istanbul Water and Sewage Administration], March 2009), 28–30. UNESCO, *Links Between Biological and Cultural Diversity*, Report of the international workshop organized by UNESCO, 2007, http://unesdoc.unesco.org/images/0015/001592/159255E.pdf.

13 Interestingly, Leonardo Da Vinci's water theory centred on his comparison of the movement of water on Earth to the flow of blood in the human body. Pfister et al., *Leonardo
da Vinci's Water Theory*, 85.

14 Karole Wall and Florence James,'*Imush Q'uyatl'un*, film, 2008, http://blogs.eciad.ca/
karollewall/imush/.

15 Prosopopeia is the use of "I," or the first-person voice, as the writer's voice projected
onto an atypical character, which in this case is the water fountain's voice. Olga Bush
calls it "the deliberate fiction of the 'I'" (55). I prefer to think of it from the Indigenous
perspective of giving voice to the spirit of water and marble, which we call a fountain.
Our Gitxsan tradition is to give our sacred springs a name through a naming ceremony,
for instance, as they are considered a living member of our House.
    Kim Anderson says women have a special spiritual connection to water because
of their ability to carry the waters of new life in their womb. Kim Anderson, "Aboriginal Women, Water and Health: Reflections from Eleven First Nations, Inuit and Metis
Grandmothers," unpublished paper, Atlantic Centre of Excellence for Women's Health
and Prairie Women's Health Centre of Excellence, 2010, http://www.pwhce.ca/women
AndWater.htm.
    The Sultan has asked Zamrak the poet to inspire the imaginative comprehension of
the beholder to transcend the artificial boundary of architecture/sense of place, and to
revere the pearls on ice (water). The poet, sculpture, and architect have interwoven their
talents, under the Sultan's decree, to instil reverence in the beholder.

16 Olga Bush, "When My Beholder Ponders: Poetic Epigraphy in the Alhambra," *Artibus
Asiae* 66, no. 2 (2006): 55.

17 Ibn Zamrak, *Poem of the Fountain of Daraxa's Garden*, circa 14th century, http://www
.alhambradegranada.org/en/info/epigraphicpoems.asp.

18 Ibid.

19 Eban Goodstein, *The Trade-off Myth: Fact and Fiction about Jobs and the Environment*
(Washington, DC: Island Press, 1999).

20 There is a secondary theoretical and practical challenge that Eliade highlights, which is "as
soon as you try and fix the limits to the notion of the sacred you come upon difficulties."
Eliade, *Patterns in Comparative Religion*, 1. Essentially it is not only risky but difficult to
accurately build the boundary or "limits."

21 Kyle Artelle, John D. Reynolds, Paul C. Paquet, and Chris T. Darimont, "When
Science-Based Management Isn't," *Science* 343 (2014): 1311.

22 B. R. Johnston, L. Hiwasaki, I. Klaver, A. Ramos, and V. Strang, "Glossary," in *Water, Cultural Diversity and Global Environmental Change: Emerging Trends, Sustainable Futures*,
ed. B. R. Johnston, L. Hiwasaki, I. Klaver, A. Ramos, and V. Strang (Dordrecht, The
Netherlands: UNESCO and Springer SBM, 2012), 538.

23 UNESCO, *Links Between Biological and Cultural Diversity*, Report of the international workshop organized by UNESCO, 2007, http://unesdoc.unesco.org/images/
0015/001592/159255E.pdf.

24 Blackstock, "Water-Based Ecology: A First Nations Proposal to Repair the Definition of
an Ecosystem."

25 M. Jacobs, *Green Jobs: the Employment Implications of Environmental Policy* (Brussels:
World Wildlife Fund for Nature, 1994).

26 Morris Berman, "The Waning of the Modern Ages," CounterPunch.org, September 20,
2012, http://www.counterpunch.org/2012/09/20/the-waning-of-the-modern-ages/.

27 J. Thompson, "Running Dry: Where Will the West Get Its Water?" *Science Findings*
(2007), http://www.fs.fed.us/.

28 Michael Blackstock, "Blue Ecology: A Cross-cultural Ecological Vision for Freshwater,"
in *Aboriginal People and Forests Lands in Canada*, ed. D. B. Tindall, Ronald L. Trosper,
and Pamela Perrault (Vancouver, BC: UBC Press, 2013), 180–204.

29 See Michael Blackstock, "Water: A First Nations Spiritual and Ecological Perspective," *BC Journal of Ecosystems and Management* 1, no. 1(2001): 54–66, and Blackstock, "Blue Ecology: A Cross-cultural Ecological Approach" for the details of this story.
30 Claude Levi-Strauss, *Structural Anthropology* (Chicago: University of Chicago Press, 1976), 208.

Bibliography

Anderson, Kim. "Aboriginal Women, Water and Health: Reflections from Eleven First Nations, Inuit and Metis Grandmothers." Unpublished paper. Atlantic Centre of Excellence for Women's Health and Prairie Women's Health Centre of Excellence, 2010. http://www.pwhce.ca/womenAndWater.htm.

Artelle, Kyle, John D. Reynolds, Paul C. Paquet, and Chris T. Darimont. "When Science-Based Management Isn't." In *Science* 343 (March 12, 2014): 1311.

Barber, Marcus. "River, Sea, and Sky: Indigenous Water Cosmology and Coastal Ownership Amongst the Yolngu People in Australia." In *Water, Cultural Diversity and Environmental Change*, edited by B. R. Johnston, L. Hiwasaki, I. Klaver, A. Ramos, and V. Strang, 124–25. Dordrecht, The Netherlands: UNESCO and Springer SBM, 2012.

Berman, Morris. "The Waning of the Modern Ages." CounterPunch.org. September 20, 2012. http://www.counterpunch.org/2012/09/20/the-waning-of-the-modern-ages/.

Blackstock, Michael. "Blue Ecology: A Cross-cultural Ecological Approach to Reconciling Forest-Related Conflicts." *BC Journal of Ecosystems and Management* 6, no. 2 (2005): 39–54.

———. "Blue Ecology: A Cross-cultural Ecological Vision for Freshwater." In *Aboriginal People and Forests Lands in Canada*, edited by D. B. Tindall, Ronald L. Trosper, and Pamela Perrault, 180–204. Vancouver, BC: UBC Press, 2013.

———. "Blue Ecology and Climate Change." *BC Journal of Ecosystems and Management* 9, no. 1 (2008): 12–16.

———. "Blue Ecology and Climate Change: Interweaving Cultural Perspectives on Water: An Indigenous Case Study." In *The Role of Hydrology in Water Resources Management*, edited by Hans-Juergen Liebscher, Robin Clarke, John Rodda, Gert Schultz, Andreas Schumann, Lucio Ub, 306–13. Proceedings of a symposium held on the island of Capri, Italy, October 2008. IAHS Publ. 327. Wallingford, UK: IAHS Press, 2009. http://iahs.info/redbooks/a327/iahs_327_0306.pdf.

———. "Blue Ecology and the Unifying Potential of Water." In *Water, Cultural Diversity and Global Environmental Change: Emerging Trends, Sustainable Futures*, edited by B. R. Johnston, L. Hiwasaki, I. Klaver, A. Ramos, and V. Strang, 132–33. Dordrecht, The Netherlands: UNESCO and Springer SBM, 2012.

———. "Blue Ecology: What Is Water? An Indigenous Perspective." *Water and Culture*, 28–30. Proceedings of a session at the 5th World Water Forum hosted by TURKKAD (Turkish Women's Cultural Organization) and ISKI (Istanbul Water and Sewage Administration), Istanbul: TURKKAD, March 2009.

———. *Oceaness*. Kamloops, BC: Wyget Books, 2010.

———. *Salmon Run: A Florilegium of Aboriginal Ecological Poetry*. Kamloops, BC: Wyget Books, 2005.

———. "Water: A First Nations Spiritual and Ecological Perspective." *BC Journal of Ecosystems and Management* 1, no. 1(2001): 54–66.

———. "Water-Based Ecology: A First Nations Proposal to Repair the Definition of an Ecosystem." *BC Journal of Ecosystems and Management* 2, no. 1 (2002): 7–12.

Bush, Olga. "When My Beholder Ponders: Poetic Epigraphy in the Alhambra." *Artibus Asiae* 66, no. 2 (2006): 55–67.

Cove, J. J., and G. F. Macdonald. *Tsimshian Narratives I: Tricksters, Shamans and Heroes.* Ottawa: Canadian Museum of Civilization, 1987.

Curtis, Tom. *Climate Change Cluedo: Anthropogenic CO_2.* 2012. http://www.skeptical science.com/anthrocarbon-brief.html.

Eliade, Mircea. *Patterns in Comparative Religion.* New York: Sheed and Ward, 1958.

Goodstein, Eban S. *The Trade-off Myth: Fact and Fiction about Jobs and the Environment.* Washington, DC: Island Press, 1999.

Irland, Basia. *Ice Books.* 2012. http://www.basiairland.com/recent-projects/ice-books .html.

Jacobs, M. *Green Jobs: the Employment Implications of Environmental Policy.* Brussels: World Wildlife Fund for Nature, 1994.

Johnston, B. R., L. Hiwasaki, I. Klaver, A. Ramos, and V. Strang. "Glossary." In *Water, Cultural Diversity and Global Environmental Change: Emerging Trends, Sustainable Futures,* edited by B. R. Johnston, L. Hiwasaki, I. Klaver, A. Ramos, and V. Strang, 53–56. Dordrecht, The Netherlands: UNESCO and Springer SBM, 2012.

Levi-Strauss, Claude. *Structural Anthropology.* Chicago: University of Chicago Press, 1976.

NASA. *Climate Change, How Do We Know?* 2012. http://climate.nasa.gov/evidence/.

Thomas, Keith. *Religion and the Decline of Magic: Studies in Popular Beliefs in the Sixteenth and Seventeenth-Century England.* Toronto: Penguin Books, 1971.

Thompson, J. "Running Dry: Where Will the West Get Its Water?" *Science Findings* (2007). http://www.fs.fed.us/.

Pfister, Laurent, Hubert H. G. Savenije, and F. Fenicia. *Leonardo da Vinci's Water Theory: On the Origin and Fate of Water.* Oxfordshire, UK: IAHS Press, 2009.

UNESCO. *Links Between Biological and Cultural Diversity: Report of the International Workshop Organized by UNESCO.* 2007. http://unesdoc.unesco.org/images/ 0015/001592/159255E.pdf.

Wall, Karole, and Florence James. *'Imush Q'uyatl'un.* Film. 2008. http://blogs.eciad.ca/ karollewall/imush/.

Zamrak, Ibn. *Poem of the Fountain of Daraxa's Garden.* Circa 14th century. http://www .alhambradegranada.org/en/info/epigraphicpoems.asp.

Water and Knowledge

Astrida Neimanis

This offering is about what we can learn from water about what it means to know. My name is printed below the title, but among the other things that water has taught me, I have learned that knowledge is always a partial and collaborative project. The lines on these pages emerge from entanglements with many (sometimes unwitting) co-authors and interlocutors: Cecilia Chen and Janine MacLeod, who are the other two parts of the three-headed hydra with whom I have been "thinking with water" for several years;[1] Jennifer Spiegel, whose work on water contamination in Bhopal invited me to consider the theory of Gayatri Spivak in new ways;[2] Stacy Alaimo's work in Bodily Natures, *which explores how bodies can be materially invested by something that seeps beyond the limits of our knowledge;[3] Lee Maracle, who, at the Downstream gathering in March 2012 on the traditional unceded Coast Salish territories also known as Vancouver, remarked to me that in many Native languages, there is no word for "knowledge";[4] Rita Wong for insisting that "water has a syntax I am still trying to learn."[5] Other collaborators in this writing include: a thermal hot spring in Iceland, a puddle, a ferry boat, my childhood swimming pool, and an irrational fear of sharks.[6] This list is short and inadequate; it attests to troubling omissions as much as to acknowledged inclusions. Such attempts at accounting, however, are salient in relation to a conversation that has been unfolding in various entanglements, in various places,[7] but often contextualized in rooms in buildings in institutions in a system of Western scholarship that encourages us to treat our ideas as singly authored property to which we must lay claim.*

Thinking with Water (An Aqueous Imaginary)

A simple proposition: "The way we live in the world is bound to what we imagine the world to be."[8]

How we treat the world is bound to how we think the world. Theory—that is, ways, patterns, and frameworks of and for thinking—is a kind of imagination. Through its imaginative choreography of ideas, theory organizes the world, bringing some parts of that world into focus, leaving other parts of it in relief. Theory involves the creative audacity to see connections and contradictions where others might see none. Theory, then, isn't just a way of seeing the world; it tells us what's important, what to value, what's disposable or insignificant. Without a theory of sorts, neither ethics nor politics would be possible.

My work as a feminist writer and theorist in the past decade has been largely focused on one question: How might paying attention to water—really paying attention to it, its movements and relations, its vulnerabilities and gifts, what it does, and how it organizes itself and other bodies—open up a different sort of imaginative space, perhaps interrupting some of the foundational concepts and beliefs in dominant Western systems of thought that I have inherited? In other words, I have been wondering if I think *with* water rather than *about* it, and if I invite water to be a collaborator or an interlocutor in how I imagine or theorize the world, might I also treat water better? Might the concepts and theories I develop also help bring water out of the mute, passive background to which it is too often relegated? For it is no secret that we haven't been paying the right kind of attention to water lately. Water issues have become the most ecologically fraught question of the twentieth-first century. Water serves as the seemingly silent receptacle of the toxins we pass into the sewage system, the plastics we throw into our oceans. And just as we imagine that its uncanny flows will clean up all of our messes, we also somehow imagine it as quantitatively inexhaustible, pumping it through deserts, hauling it up out of ancient aquifers, bottling it in little plastic disposable cylinders, using three barrels of fresh water to extract one barrel of oil. According to the UN's Food and Agriculture Organization, water use has been growing at more than twice the rate of population increase in the last century. Intimately linked to climate change, and ineluctably affected by petropolitics and our dependency on fossil fuel, water seems to be at the short end of all our planetary sticks.

Clearly, then, this desire to "think with water" is guided by a sense of environmental concern and ecological urgency. For me, this is also a resolutely feminist inquiry, and not only because the harm done to water is also harm done to human, sexually different bodies, who bear this harm in gender-disaggregated ways.[9] Thinking with water also demands that we think about power and subordination, master models, binary oppositions, nature, and culture—about who or what gets listened to, and who or what is relegated to an unacknowledged supporting role—and these are all deeply feminist questions.[10] To address the conceptual bifurcations with which feminist thought has concerned itself, where female/natural/fleshy/black/Indigenous/spiritual bodies are subordinated to male/cultural/cerebral/white/colonizer/rational ones, cannot be a simple question of reversing these power-laden hierarchies. Such reversals keep the hierarchies themselves intact, while still begging the question of who or what remains outside of the valued position as the definition of its limit. This is hardly a sustainable solution. Instead, we need to undercut this logic of binary oppositions altogether, and find ways of valuing difference rather than subordinating it. If I am a feminist, opposed to injustice on the basis of a faulty binary and hierarchized system of thought, then looking at what we do to water, "nature," and the conceptual apparatuses that sanction these doings must also matter to me.

Undercutting this logic is then part of the imaginative theoretical work I have already invoked. I am in part inspired by feminist theorists, such as Karen Barad, who demands a more "robust account of the materialization of all bodies—'human' and 'nonhuman'—and the material-discursive practices by which their differential constitutions are marked," and Donna Haraway, who claims that we must cultivate relations in which "all the partners in the potent conversations that constitute nature [can] find a new ground for making meanings together."[11] In other words, I am guided by calls for imagining a different logic that does not subscribe to binaristic thinking. I feel compelled to be curious and critical about how material bodies come to be invested with different meanings—for the conceptual hierarchies of Western patriarchal thinking are neither "natural" nor the only way in which the world might be imagined. My task in the following pages is to consider what water can teach me about both the denigration of the so-called natural, and the incitement to know, which is an integral part of keeping this Western patriarchal logic in place.

Hydro-logics

Water, as thinkers such as Gaston Bachelard and Janine MacLeod have argued, already saturates our concepts and theories. Indeed, flow and fluidity have become ubiquitous in many contemporary Western theoretical apparatuses. If we really pay attention to water, however, we see that fluidity is a rather impoverished way of understanding the logics of water. The idea of flows is certainly helpful for thinking about pathways of connection between bodies and the fallacy of radical independence at all sorts of levels. Indeed, as soon as we consider that our own bodies are mostly water, continuously transformed through water, and continuously giving back to other bodies of water, for better of worse (drinking, urinating, sweating, transfusing, ejaculating, siphoning, breastfeeding, sponging, weeping), it becomes quite clear that human bodies are hardly separate from the myriad other watery bodies (freshwater mussel, water filtration plant, seagrass, sunflower, raincloud, grandmother) with which we coexist, now and across other times.[12] But the liquid is only one of water's phase states, and flowing is just one of the things it does. Water has other manners of being and becoming, other movements and ways of organizing bodies, from which we might also learn. We might refer to these various modes of the aqueous as our planetary hydro-logics, as a way of naming the myriad ways in which water enacts relations with other bodies. These are the logics according to which bodies of water make themselves sensible and intelligible; they are the patterns of existence according to which certain bodies come to affect other bodies. Bodies transform, and transform each other, through these different hydro-logics.

For example, *gestationality* as a hydro-logic describes water's life-giving aspects. It refers to a sort of watery sexuality, where water is figured as a fecund milieu for the proliferation of life. Gestationality is water's capacity to bathe plural life into being in myriad ways, and thus is never limited to human, heteronormative reproductive sexuality. Watery sexuality emphasizes not the reproduction of the same, but the capacity to gestate difference. *Dissolution* is a different kind of logic that figures water's capacity to wash away life in its current forms. On a quotidian view, this could refer to practices of rinsing and renewal, while in the language of meteorology, water's logic of solubility also refers to tsunami, flood, and hurricane. Dissolution reminds us that water's logics are neither benign nor benevolent toward all bodies. Sometimes erroneously referred to as a "universal solvent," water still can affect many other bodies by dissolving them altogether—or perhaps more accurately, by recycling them into new figures and forms. In this sense, water can teach us about a certain closeness between gestationality and dissolution. (To be gestational, bodies of water must partially dissolve themselves to allow new iterations and manifestations of watery life.)[13]

Other hydro-logics include *communication* (as water, in its various mixtures, articulates sounds, temperatures, and others matters between and across bodies) or *conduit* (as water conveys islands of plastic or streams of climate refugees upon ocean currents, or toxic industrial remainders through meteorological systems). Hydro-logics also include water's role as *memory-keeper* or *archive* (storing flotsam, chemicals, detritus, sunken treasure, culture, stories, histories),[14] and *sculptor* (referring to water's terraforming properties and its ability to reshape geological bodies). *Differentiation* is another key hydro-logic that tempers the romantic overtones of water's relational logics. As a differentiator, water also separates bodies, even as it holds them in relation—currents, whorls, eddies, weather fronts are just some of these manifestations. Bodies of water do not all flow into one amorphous puddle, but are always iterated as bodies, in ever new forms, and discerned by various thresholds and membranes. The hydro-logic of differentiation also reminds us that water is never "pure," but is always a hybrid or a mixture, with each iteration engendering its own membranes of difference. According to this logic, water bodies constantly enter into new intracorporeal relations, transforming according to various speeds and slownesses.[15] Just as dissolution is a necessary flip side to gestationality, differentiation balances water's capacity for confluence.

Each of these hydro-logics (and this list could be longer—is not water also lover, scribe, alibi, genealogist, saboteur …?) takes up the specific material, physical, biological, and chemical dimensions of water. When attended to with curiosity and care, these logics evidence a "hydrological cycle" with a far more complex and multivalent choreography of qualities and modalities than rudimentary science textbooks would have us believe. These cycles are, moreover, *lived* by us; hydro-logics seep through every aspect of our material existence. We experience them viscerally, in the superabundance, acute paucity, or mere banality of the rain, sleet, and snow that dominate our daily weather reports, but also in our multivalent interactions and communications with bodies of all kinds. And, if we accept that we are all bodies of water (gestated in and sustained by the aqueous element), then attention to these watery logics might also provide some lessons in living—perhaps in living otherwise with watery bodies that are both like us and different from us. In other words, although I realize that water will always ultimately escape such taxonomic efforts (and elsewhere, I explore this provisionally schematized inventory in more detail),[16] such categorizations can give us imaginative footholds for explaining our everyday lives, and their relation to broader political and ethical questions. Close attention to these properties might open up new ways of respecting and attending to the various water bodies in which we are immersed, and *as* which we ourselves exist.

In light of this, I would like to use these pages to pay even closer attention to another one of water's logics, namely *unknowability*. Somewhat ironically, unknowability refers to water's capacity to elude our efforts to contain it with any apparatus of knowledge. Unknowability is both the logic of refusal and an invitation to humility—about which Lee Maracle and Michael Blackstock both eloquently write in their contributions to this volume. Or, put otherwise, despite all of our dam-building, mega-irrigation schemes, and cloud-seeding efforts, water will always elude our total control and our efforts to fully "know" it. As such, water's unknowability may have much to teach us—both about our efforts to know this aqueous element, *which we also are*, and about knowledge more generally.

Water and the Incitement to Know

What does it mean to want knowledge? What is the goal of knowledge? What is the relationship between the knower and what she knows, or the obligation of the knower to what she knows? Is everything meant to be known? What do we need to know urgently, and what knowledge is better left unknown? What might water teach me about these questions?

In that increasing proportion of contexts where such knowledge-making is funded by corporate interests, these questions are particularly urgent. In part, I am interested in the question of knowledge because my professional life is contextualized within the Western university system—that is, within a knowledge machine. Within this knowledge machine, employees are paid to know—to create knowledge and impart it to our students. We are ranked by our peers on how much knowledge we make. Knowledge must be "excellent." The general assumption prevails that knowledge is unquestionably a good thing. Where knowledge is commodified, where knowledge is seen as a means to an end (which is profit), where for many people in many ways knowledge equals capital, and where *more* knowledge is actively promoted, we need to be exceptionally vigilant about the conditions and uses of knowledge production.[17] Might water teach me to know not necessarily more or more "excellently," but instead more carefully or more responsively?

When I begin to think knowledge with water, feminist and anti-colonial concerns about power and responsibility swim to the surface. Urgent questions circulate where knowledge and water collide: on the one hand, it seems crucial to know more about what we are doing to water, and to ourselves, as bodies of water, in light of water's ecological precarity as noted above. In this volume, the chapters by Alanna Mitchell, Melina Laboucan Massimo, and Paul Harrison are examples of urgent calls for more and better knowledge about water's distressing state in various contexts. In short, we *do* need more knowledge about the causes and effects of the Pacific garbage patches, and about the catastrophic damage being done by the Tar Sands megaprojects to the Athabasca watershed and the many bodies nourished by it, and by other extraction industries in the Amazon and the Niger Delta. We *do* need more knowledge about the levels of poison in our drinking water, and about the levels of water in our aquifers, which we are draining far too rapidly. And again, while these are ecological questions, they are also feminist and anti-colonial. The harm that we do to water is never equally distributed across human bodies. The flows of bio-matter also chart the flows of global power.

But how far should our quests for knowledge reach? The Census of Marine Life promises to document every single species of life in the seas; exploratory vessels are increasingly penetrating our oceans' benthic zones to document these mysterious ecosystems. "More" knowledge—in some of its versions—is also telling me that climate change is natural and no cause for alarm, and that mega-dams are necessary and beneficial—despite the documented loss of human life, culture, and livelihood, and the massive ecological upheaval that major hydroelectric projects have brought in the Three Gorges region of China, the Narmada Valley in India, or the James Bay region of northern Quebec. The relationship between knowledge and water, in other words, is not that simple. Understanding this relationship seems also to be a question of distinguishing between kinds of knowledge—knowledge that commoditizes and colonizes, knowledge that generates necessary anger and action, knowledge that heals. Knowledge that builds communities or knowledge that fractures them. Knowledge that responds or knowledge that masters.[18]

A closer examination of water's hydro-logic of unknowability brings into focus some of the tensions that accompany the incitement to know in relation to water. In the first place, water's unknowability is a geographical question connected to the question of what is livable. Because of varying abilities to live *in* water and *with* water, different bodies (human, sunflower, toad, jellyfish) also have varying capacities to *know* water. In other words, bodies are oriented in and toward water in species- or being-specific ways; humans, it follows, are situated in relation to water in a very human-specific way.[19] This human specificity certainly differs from that of fish, but also from that of other mammals. For example, while our kinship with air-breathing whales is well documented and routinely mythologized, we eventually have to let go of the dorsal fin: the whale will always outswim us, while our own lungs inevitably give out. Cetaceans can dive to depths our human bodies could not fathom. Even the most sophisticated deep-water submersibles and assisted breathing apparatuses will only ever take us so far, for so long. Just as a fish out of water suffocates and dies, we too can only be fully immersed in water temporarily. The seas are teeming with events that humans will only ever glimpse. Any body's orientation to water as material substance, and as geographical location, serves as a *limit* that determines which milieus are habitable, withstand-able, and thus knowable. Water remains one step ahead of, and beyond, the limits of any body (regardless of their watery orientation). In this way (and in resonance with other feminist epistemological projects of "situated knowledges"),[20] the grammar of water necessarily rejects total knowledge by any body. Because each body has a different relation to water *as a matter of survival*, no body can do what Donna Haraway calls "the God Trick." No body can ever fully know water. For me, this underlines questions of incursion, hubris, and humility as a necessary consideration for any epistemology or system of knowledge.

This unknowability is also connected to water's gestational capacity and its insistence on differentiation. Gestationality, as described above, is a hydro-logic of life-giving milieu. Water is always bathing new life into existence, facilitating plurality. This plurality, and the bodies and forms that water takes up, are always part of a future still to come, and as of yet unknown. Water returns, and repeats—but always differently. We see this, for example, in evolutionary processes that continuously engender new and unexpected life forms. Despite all the harm we do to it, in one sense water *is* inexhaustible—the things that it does and the bodies it proliferates cannot ultimately be predicted. Again, water is one step ahead of any body. Water evidences the impossibility of complete knowledge; as feminist theorist Karen Barad would say, it reminds us that the world is "not a secret to be revealed" by us humans.[21] It is rather in a constant process of emergence. As a gestational engine of life, growth, and change, water ultimately defies epistemological capture and containment.

Thinking with water, then, might help me imagine and cultivate a much-needed *epistemology of unknowability*. Such an orientation toward knowledge would be put into necessary conversation with dominant Western paradigms of knowledge. (And, while I write these suggestions from my own perspective as steeped within such Western paradigms, it might also enter into productive collaboration with Indigenous epistemologies that have long cultivated different kinds of relations to what is "knowable" than those stressed by Western positivist science. Elsewhere in this volume, Michael Blackstock addresses these sorts of epistemological collaborations in more depth.) It would be, at its most basic, an understanding of and respect for what human beings do not and cannot know, as a necessary counter to our contemporary techno-capitalized drive toward mastery. To explore this proposition further, I engage in a theoretical experiment of sorts. I want to bring together my explorations of the hydro-logics of water with the work of feminist and post-colonial critic Gayatri Spivak. Spivak is well known for her challenging thinking on the subaltern. In a landmark essay published in 1988, Spivak asks whether or not the "subaltern can speak."[22] The subaltern refers to the most disenfranchised and marginalized populations of the so-called Third World. Spivak expresses skepticism about Western intellectual claims to "speak for" these populations because, as she points out, in a (post-)colonial context such "giving voice" is impossible; the conditions of being heard have already been set by those who construct the dominating discourse. The subaltern could therefore only ever speak in the terms decided by the dominant elite. As with all theoretical experiments, the one I attempt here is fraught with pitfalls and dangers—bad translations, appropriations, infelicitous associations. In particular, I run the risk of suggesting that colonized, subaltern human bodies are to be equated with natural, non-human ones—which is part of the very problem of conceptually binaristic and hierarchized Western systems of thought that I hope to challenge. I also risk suggesting a too simple symmetry between questions of ecological and anti-colonial justice, which, despite their intimate connections, demand their own strategies of resistance. And, in writing about the actors in the story of the Bangladeshi Flood Action Plan below rather than with them, I undeniably engage in silencings of my own.[23] I remain curious about how my own thinking with water might resonate with Spivak's post-colonial thinking, and, even where these projects do not fit together perfectly, I wonder what they might illuminate about each other, and how both, together, might inform an epistemological project. And I hope they might also help me to listen better.

"The Moving Weave of the Water": Unknowability and Planetarity

My engagement with Spivak begins with an essay called "Responsibility," which she published in the late 1990s. The second half of that essay in particular takes up the circumstances around the drafting of a major, foreign donor–funded project for a Flood Action Plan (FAP) in Bangladesh. Because of the perceived hardship and costs sustained by Bangladeshis (and foreign investments, no doubt) caused by massive flooding of the deltaic lands where the country's major rivers feed into the sea, a major joint development initiative was planned that would involve a major rerouting of deltaic watercourses in Bangladesh in an effort to mitigate those flood hazards. This Flood Action Plan became the subject of major contestation and discussion within communities in Bangladesh, government authorities, and the international development and donor apparatuses.[24] Of interest to Spivak in the essay in question is a specific conference, organized by the Green Party and held at the European Parliament in 1993, where "project opponents [had] the opportunity to present their case directly to many of the governments funding the scheme."[25] In Spivak's assessment, the FAP and associated processes exemplify the sort of silencing of the subaltern voices that attempted to speak out against them, which she writes about elsewhere. Forced to speak in the language of the World Bank and global development, the subaltern's concerns for the ways that they themselves and the land-water would be impacted by the FAP could not be heard.

Here, the subaltern certainly refers to specific human voices—"the fisher and the grass-roots peasant"[26] whose basis of livelihood is to be destroyed by the FAP. It also refers to Sattar Khan, an aging leader of the rural Bangladeshi peasant movement, who was, in Spivak's words, "staged as a slice of the authentic."[27] But Sattar Khan's "silence" or his "inability to be heard" bears some further contemplation. As Spivak tells us, this "staging of a slice of the authentic" went slightly awry. Sattar Khan did not follow protocol. He did not "stick to his time allotment." He did not speak in the technocratic language of those in charge. In fact, he did not speak English at all—and no one had thought to have a translator on hand. After a bumbling out-of-sync and ad-hoc translation broke down as Khan began (under pressure to "keep time") to read his speech at breakneck speed, Spivak notes that "'European' discipline," too, "[broke] down."[28]

This story illustrates precisely what, on my reading, is the key point of Spivak's question in "Can the Subaltern Speak?" Khan's speech demonstrates how Spivak's question is perhaps better interpreted in terms of the ability to listen. For, of course, Sattar Khan is speaking—at breakneck speed and at considerable length, we are told! The subaltern—those marginalized populations to which the educated elite endeavour to "give voice"—is speaking all the time. To frame this question from the perspective of listening interrupts the power dynamics whereby speech would be the index of power, and silence the sign of oppression or marginality. On such a view, voice—being heard and understood—could only ever be available to the empowered, and as such must be the sought-after prize for the disempowered. But being heard—"speaking" speech—is not the only way to interrupt a system of power and control. Close attention to the "breaking down" of "'European' discipline" noted by Spivak begins to reveal alternatives to this view of power/speech. Here, Sattar Khan's words, although unintelligible to those in the room, at the same time serve as a silent (but still speaking) interruption to the paradigm of knowing-speaking that the FAP conference attempts to instate. Attention to the silence-speech (silence that nonetheless makes noise; speech that is not comprehended) shows up a different sort of relationship to power. It is this different configuration of power around questions of speech and silence I propose that can lead me toward thinking a relationship to knowledge that provides an alternative to the one presumed both by the power dynamics of the FAP conference, and contemporary Western epistemologies more generally.

The reconfigured relationship between power, speech/silence, and knowledge becomes clearer when we consider how this silence-speech functions elsewhere in Spivak's account of the floods in Bangladesh. In this same essay on "Responsibility," Spivak also discusses other interventions, alongside the FAP, that were used by the "superior civilization" to bring order to the unruly floodplain. She describes, for example, the West's "benevolent gift" to the landless Bangladeshi farmers in the form of a more modern ("better") rice seed to sow. She also describes the context in which this gift was taken up and thwarted by those farmers:

> Living in the rhythm of water, the Bangladeshi peasant long sowed two types of rice paddy seed. One of them survived submerged in water, the other came to full growth after the season of rain and flood. In 1971, agri-cultural reformers introduced a different variety of rice for a single high-yield crop. In the intervening years, the peasant has quietly and gradually shifted the time of sowing of this modern crop to Phalgun-Chaitro (February-March). As was their established custom, accommodating the play of land and water, they now sow pulses and vegetables before this. And now, at the reaping time of the new crop, the old flood-seed is sown, so that in the rain and flood-time, the fields are once again full of that submersible paddy. (By contrast, the land "protected" from water by the embankments loses the fertilizing algae, thus providing an opportunity for

the enhancement of the debt trap and the destruction of the ecobiome by the peddling of chemical fertilizers.) I hesitate to call this silent interruption "flood management."[29]

What Spivak describes here is twofold: on the one hand, this "mis-use" of the "superior civilization's" gift (i.e., the "modern seed") is again a "silent interruption" of the power that (here) the development industry has over the subaltern. We begin, then, to see an alignment or an association here, in Spivak's account, between Sattar Khan's interruption to the FAP knowledge machine of European power and the farmer's planting practices: just as Sattar Khan disrupts the knowledge-power machine by speaking (silently) out of turn, here the farmers (silently) interrupt the power-knowledge of the "superior civilization" by planting the seed according to a different logic than intended. I wonder: Could this "silent interruption" also be an appropriate response to water's logic of unknowability? Here, this silence (the planting), which is also speech, interrupts the control-oriented knowledge of the land-water, and instead engages in a more humble learning-with-the-water, learning-with-the-land. The deltaic floodplain is a crucial collaborator here in the generation of knowledge—the farmer "accommodates the play of the land and water." In this way of knowing, more speech (read: more control) does not generate better knowledge. Speech domination does not equal more wisdom.

Here, the landless farmer engages in what Spivak describes as a "space of intimate learning, of human-animal-watery ground" that "is, after all, an ongoing response to the weave of land and river by the landless and on common waters."[30] This "intimate learning" understands that "flood management" is a language that an epistemology of unknowability does not speak. Such learning is rather an "ongoing response," a response-ability to water's refusal of capture by our systems of knowledge control.

Crucially, for Spivak, not only are Sattar Khan and the landless farmer the objects of the (attempted) silencing. The very land-water itself is subjected to the violence of colonial knowledge control. The FAP, after all, plans to straighten the tangles of the watery deltaic threads with a logic literally built from concrete: "To impose upon the changeful riverscape the straight lines of massive 'pharaonic' embankments is the plan."[31] In her essay, Spivak provides a reproduction of the FAP's proposed cartography: thick, straight lines with hard-angled joints literally overwrite the lineaments of the rivers. One might ask here whether the rivers—water itself—can be read as akin to the subaltern (that is, as a strange, more-than-human kin). I am not invested in insisting that water is a subaltern, for I am cautious about such loose applications of this term (as Spivak herself encourages her readers to be). And just as we shouldn't apply "the subaltern" to any marginalized or oppressed body we choose—it has a specificity and a history that Spivak insists on—nor should we try too hard to fit water, in all of its unruliness, and in all of the logics I've begun to sketch out above, into this human-oriented theoretical terminology. But perhaps there is something to be learned by thinking water with subalternity, in terms of how we might think the question of water, knowledge, and unknowability.

Spivak refers to these riparian re-choreographies—this straightening out of the river—as themselves another violence, against a more profound knowledge that is beyond our grasp: "Let us think of these stupendous drains," she writes, "driving the continually shifting text-ile waters by the violence of reason into the shortest route to the sea as the violence of Reason itself, driving the continually differentiating text-ile of meanings into the shortest route to Truth."[32] In other words, the proposed concrete channels of the FAP drive water to the Sea in the same way colonial Reason drives meaning to the Truth. The "management" of the river here is tellingly linked directly to epistemic violence, and the violence of Reason—an imposition of the logic of order and control. Reducing the rivers, or the planet into "whatever can be fed into Geographical Information Systems"[33] (one of Reason's tools of mastery), is an arrogance, Spivak warns us—a colonial conquest of another kind. Or perhaps of the same kind in a different guise. And the water of the rivers (there is more than one river here: the delta in question is fed by the Ganges, the Brahmaputra, and the Meghna) resists these containments. The deltaic terrain is no terra firma of certainty that can be known and mastered. Tellingly, the environmental scientists describe this "land" as behaving more "like viscous fluids rather than soils."[34] Water quite literally disturbs the solidity of the certain ground beneath one's feet. Even as the FAP "crosses out" the land on which the Bangladeshi deltaic inhabitants depend, this groundedness was already precarious—it "has been already, and is being crossed out, by the moving weave of water."[35] Attempting to live with such precarity, rather than "containing" it, was the point.

Spivak describes the farmers' response to a watery world that resists us as much as we comprise it. Importantly, under the colonial-development industry management of this land-water, not only the river, but this way of responsive knowing, is, too, subjected to "straightening." These comments are meant neither to wash away the many injustices and hardships endured by the inhabitants of the Bangladeshi deltaic lands, nor to romanticize these lives from the perspective of a theoretical observer. I hope they might instead underline the continuity between some Western approaches to the land-water and a more general epistemology of mastery.

Like the speech-silence of Khan, the "silent interruption" of the rice-planting farmers is a sort of silent speech that interrupts a certain logic of power.

And, if this interruption by the farmers can be read as a negotiation with the logic of unknowability that water teaches us, then in the building of the FAP's concrete walls, we bear witness to the site of this teaching. The river delta is "not heard" through these concrete incursions, but surely she continues to speak. The river gurgles, and sometimes roars, and sometimes just swishes by. And the river speaks in anger and frustration or, in less anthropocentric terms, in plain old river-y refusal to be contained: every levee, we know, breaks. Every dam busts. Water remains always one step ahead of our knowledge control.[36] The river's refusal to be silent points us toward the need to cultivate a relationship to knowledge that does not always presume mastery, and that instead comes from an "ongoing response" to water itself. This is closely linked to what Lee Maracle and Larrisa Lai discuss in the pages of this volume as water's resistance to mastery, and to our own human "response abilities." Water babbles in languages we do not fully comprehend, but instead of the violence of translation—into concrete embankments—we might do better just to learn to listen.

Elsewhere, Spivak introduces us to another concept: planetarity. The third chapter of her book *Death of a Discipline* critiques the logic of globalization that tries to introduce a knowable, plot-able uniformity to the globe. She argues that instead of being global, we should strive to be planetary: "The globe is on our computers," she writes. "No one lives there. It ["the global"] allows us to think we can aim to control it."[37] But, she continues, "The planet is in the species of alterity, belonging to another system; and yet we inhabit it, on loan."[38] To put it otherwise, the language of "globalization" for Spivak is strongly linked to what I have been calling the logic of knowability and knowledge control. It presumes a world that can be laid out, grid-like, plotted on our GPSes and ultimately comprehended-conquered. Spivak counters the image of the globe ("even though it is not really amenable to a neat contrast with the globe") with planetarity: "Planet-thought opens us up to embrace an inexhaustible taxonomy of the names [of radical alterity]."[39] Planetarity is "(im)possible" to represent because of this very inexhaustibility. It is always more than it is. But key for Spivak is the fact that this "beyond" is also lived, it is also of us, with us, through us, alongside us (hence the -*im* of the possible is couched only in a parenthetical signpost). This alterity—what is "above and beyond our reach"[40]—is "not continuous with us, as it is not, indeed, specifically discontinuous." Formulaic, codified, categorizable access to planetarity is not possible—there is no overarching knowledge that could contain it because by definition it is in us *and* beyond us.

This is the species to which water, in its logic of unknowability, belongs as well. Perhaps rather than including water in the humanist concept of subalterneity, we can instead think of it as part of this planetarity. This "of me yet beyond me" is the unknowability to which water asks that I attend. Water as planetarity also suggests to me an epistemology that is engaged, embedded, embodied; a way of knowing that is somewhere, situated, implicated—but this is also a form of knowledge in which that location will always exceed my bounds (as even this "my" leaks out of my watery body beyond the realms of any knowability). The water that we are is first of all planetary. We are its curious custodians rather than its masters.

Conclusions and Other Soundings

If you want to learn, be quiet and pay attention. (Smith 134)

1. Water—like all of the more-than-human world—is a collaborator in what we know and how we know.
2. To colonize water is to colonize certain forms of knowledge, and the ability to know differently than Western paradigms of knowledge insist we must.
3. Understanding what we don't or can't know opens up space for knowing differently.

And if, as I claimed in my introduction, how I think with (/as) water might change how I act with (/as) it, I can only hope that this rethinking of knowledge, as illuminated through this watery foray into Spivak's (post-)colonial criticism can help me approach this planetary lifeblood with more humility, generosity, and curiosity. My thinking (writing, theorizing) can guide my actions, but these theories require a complement in the other ways in which I live my life, entangled with watery bodies of all kinds.

After all, as Spivak closes her essay on "Responsibility," "these words, too many, can only point you toward such silences"—silences, that are also, I have argued, spoken loudly, asking to be heard, even if they are in a language we cannot—indeed, should not—ever master.

Notes

1 See thinkingwithwater.net and Cecilia Chen, Janine MacLeod, and Astrida Neimanis, eds., *Thinking with Water* (Montreal: McGill-Queen's University Press 2013). On the question of unknowability, I am also particularly inspired by Chen's work on the unintelligibility of waters, otherwise known as their "babble" (Chen, "Mapping Waters").

2 See Jennifer Spiegel, "Subterranean Flows: Water Contamination and the Politics of Visibility after the Bhopal Disaster," in *Thinking with Water*, ed. Cecilia Chen, Janine MacLeod, and Astrida Neimanis (Montreal: McGill-Queen's University Press, 2013), 84–103.

3 Stacy Alaimo, *Bodily Natures* (Bloomington: Indiana University Press, 2010).

4 See www.downstream.ecuad.ca.

5 See D. Christian and R. Wong, "Watershed Mind," in *Thinking with Water*, ed. Cecilia Chen, Janine MacLeod, and Astrida Neimanis (Montreal: McGill-Queen's University Press, 2013), 232–53.

6 See Astrida Neimanis, "On Collaboration (for Barbara Godard)," *Nordic Journal of Feminist and Gender Research* 20, no. 3 (2012): 215–21.

7 Versions of this chapter have been presented at the Downstream gathering in March 2012, a research seminar at the Gender Institute of the London School of Economics in May 2012, and as a keynote address at the Entanglements of New Materialisms conference in Linkoping, Sweden, in May 2012. I would like to acknowledge and thank the people of the traditional unceded Coast Salish territories upon which the Downstream workshop took place and to which I was invited by Rita Wong and Dorothy Christian to share and listen.

8 Jenna Tiitsman, "Planetary Subjects after the Death of Geography," in *Planetary Loves: Spivak, Postcoloniality and Theology*, ed. Stephen Moore et al. (Bronx, NY: Fordham University Press, 2011), 150.

9 See, for example, Anne Coles and Tina Wallace, eds., *Gender, Water and Development* (Oxford: Berg, 2005), for discussions on how sexually different bodies bear the effects of water pollution, scarcity, disaster, and commodification in different ways.

10 For further discussions of these debates, see Stacy Alaimo, *Undomesticated Ground: Recasting Nature as Feminist Space* (Ithaca, NY: Cornell University Press, 2000); Catriona Sandilands, *The Good-Natured Feminist: Ecofeminism and the Quest for Democracy* (Minneapolis: University of Minnesota Press, 1999); Val Plumwood, *Feminism and the Mastery of Nature* (New York: Routledge, 1993); Greta Gaard, "Women, Water and Energy: An Ecofeminist Approach," *Organization and Environment* 14, no. 2 (2001): 157–72, among others.

11 Karen Barad, *Meeting the Universe Halfway: Quantum Physics and the Entanglement of Matter and Meaning* (Durham: Duke University Press, 2007), 66; and Donna Haraway, *The Haraway Reader* (London: Routledge, 2004), 158.

12 See Astrida Neimanis, "We Are All Bodies of Water," *Alphabet City: Water* (Cambridge, MA: MIT Press, 2009).

13 See Mielle Chandler and Astrida Neimanis, "Water and Gestationality: What Flows Beneath Ethics," in *Thinking with Water*, ed. Cecilia Chen, Janine MacLeod, and Astrida Neimanis (Montreal: McGill-Queen's University Press, 2013), 61–83.

14 See Christian and Wong, "Untapping Watershed Mind"; Jody Berland, "Walkerton: The Matter of Memory," *TOPIA: Canadian Journal for Cultural Studies* 14 (2005): 93–108; Janine MacLeod, "Water, Memory and the Material Imagination," in *Thinking with Water*, ed. Cecilia Chen, Janine MacLeod, and Astrida Neimanis (Montreal: McGill-Queen's University Press, 2013), 40–60; and Peter C. van Wyck, "Footbridge at Atwater," in *Thinking with Water*, ed. Cecilia Chen, Janine MacLeod, and Astrida Neimanis (Montreal: McGill-Queen's University Press, 2013), 256–73.

15 See Astrida Neimanis, "Bodies of Water, Human Rights and the Hydrocommons," in *TOPIA: Canadian Journal of Cultural Studies* 21 (2009): 161–82.

16 See Astrida Neimanis, "Feminist Subjectivity, Watered," *Feminist Review* 103 (2013): 23–41.

17 In case there is any doubt about the commodification of knowledge in university systems, I note that when I worked for the London School of Economics (LSE)—a formidable and excellent institution in many respects—students could purchase T-shirts at the campus bookstore that declared their allegiance to LSE. These were simply emblazoned with the symbols for the pound sterling, the dollar, and the Euro: £$€.

18 For additional explorations of this question, see Lee Maracle and Michael Blackstock (this volume). The relationship between epistemology and the quest for mastery is

foregrounded in the work of many additional scholars, for example, Lorraine Code, *Ecological Thinking: The Politics of Epistemic Location* (Oxford: Oxford University Press, 2006); Linda Tuhiwai Smith, *Decolonizing Methodologies* (London: Zed Boos, 1999); Donna Haraway, "Situated Knowledges: The Science Question in Feminism and the Privilege of Partial Perspective," *Feminist Studies* 14, no. 3 (1988): 581–607. Discerning between objectives and outcomes of different kinds of knowledge projects is also a key aim of Shawn Wilson, *Research Is Ceremony* (Toronto: Fernwood Books, 2008).

19 I am thinking here of Sara Ahmed's excellent discussion of orientations in *Queer Phenomenology* (Durham: Duke University Press, 2006), rehearsed as well in her essay "Orientations Matter," in *New Materialisms*, ed. D. Coole and S. Frost (Durham: Duke University Press, 2010), 234–57.

20 See, for example, Haraway, "Situated Knowledges."

21 Karen Barad, "Living in a Posthumanis Materialist World: Lessons from Schroedinger's Cat," in *Bits of Life: Feminism at the Intersections of Media, Bioscience and Technology*, ed. A. Smelik and N. Lykke (Seattle: University of Washington Press, 2008), 174.

22 G. S. Spivak, "Can the Subaltern Speak?" in *Marxism and the Interpretation of Culture*, ed. C. Nelson and L. Grossberg (Urbana: University of Chicago Press, 1988), 271–313.

23 Here, my caution is particularly inspired by Gayatri Spivak's work. See, for example, "The Politics of Translation," in *Outside the Teaching Machine* (New York: Routledge, 1993), 179–200.

24 See Farhana Sultana, "Fluid Lives: Subjectivity, Gender and Water Management in Bangladesh," *Gender, Place, and Culture* 16, no. 4 (2009): 427–44; and Farhana Sultana, "Water, Culture and Gender: An Analysis from Bangladesh," in *Water, Cultural Diversity & Global Environmental Change: Emerging Trends, Sustainable Futures?*, ed. B. R. Johnston (The Netherlands: Springer, 2011), 237–52.

25 Quoted in G. S. Spivak, "Responsibility," *Boundary 2* 21, no. 3 (1994): 46.

26 Ibid., 55.

27 Ibid.

28 Ibid., 61.

29 Ibid., 55–56.

30 Ibid., 58.

31 Ibid., 49.

32 Ibid., 62.

33 Ibid., 54.

34 Quoted in Spivak, "Responsibility," 47.

35 Ibid.

36 See Chen, "Mapping Waters" for a discussion of "the babble of waters" in relation to intelligibility.

37 G. S. Spivak, *Death of a Discipline* (New York: Columbia University Press, 2003), 72.

38 Ibid.

39 Ibid., 73.

40 Ibid.

Bibliography

Ahmed, Sara. "Orientations Matter." In *New Materialisms*, edited by D. Coole and S. Frost, 234–57. Durham: Duke University Press, 2010.

———. *Queer Phenomenology*. Durham: Duke University Press, 2006.

Alaimo, Stacy. *Bodily Natures*. Bloomington: Indiana University Press, 2010.

———. *Undomesticated Ground: Recasting Nature as Feminist Space*. Ithaca, NY: Cornell University Press, 2000.

Barad, Karen. "Living in a Posthumanist Materialist World: Lessons from Schroedinger's Cat." In *Bits of Life: Feminism at the Intersections of Media, Bioscience and Technology*, edited by A. Smelik and N. Lykke, 165–76. Seattle: University of Washington Press, 2008.

———. *Meeting the Universe Halfway: Quantum Physics and the Entanglement of Matter and Meaning.* Durham: Duke University Press, 2007.

Berland, Jody. "Walkerton: The Matter of Memory." *TOPIA: Canadian Journal for Cultural Studies* 14 (2005): 93–108.

Chandler, Mielle, and Astrida Neimanis. "Water and Gestationality: What Flows Beneath Ethics." In Chen, MacLeod, and Neimanis 2013, 61–83.

Chen, Cecilia. "Mapping Waters." In Chen, MacLeod, and Neimanis 2013, 274–98.

Chen, Cecilia, Janine MacLeod, and Astrida Neimanis, eds. *Thinking with Water.* Montreal: McGill-Queen's University Press, 2013.

Christian, D., and Wong, R. "Untapping Watershed Mind." In Chen, MacLeod, and Neimanis 2013, 232–51.

Code, Lorraine. *Ecological Thinking: The Politics of Epistemic Location.* Oxford: Oxford University Press, 2006.

Coles, Anne, and Tina Wallace, eds. *Gender, Water and Development.* Oxford: Berg, 2005.

Gaard, Greta. "Women, Water and Energy: An Ecofeminist Approach." *Organization and Environment* 14, no. 2 (2001): 157–72.

Haraway, Donna. *The Haraway Reader.* London: Routledge, 2004.

———. "Situated Knowledges: The Science Question in Feminism and the Privilege of Partial Perspective." *Feminist Studies* 14, no. 3 (1988): 581–607.

MacLeod, J. "Water, Memory and the Material Imagination." In Chen, MacLeod, and Neimanis 2013, 40–60.

Neimanis, Astrida. "Bodies of Water, Human Rights and the Hydrocommons." *Topia: Canadian Journal of Cultural Studies* 21 (2008): 161–82.

———. "Feminist Subjectivity, Watered." *Feminist Review* 103 (2013): 23–41.

———. "On Collaboration (for Barbara Godard)." *Nordic Journal of Feminist and Gender Research* 20, no. 3 (2012): 215–21.

———. "We Are All Bodies of Water." In *Alphabet City: Water*, edited by John Knechtel, 82–91. Cambridge: MA: MIT Press, 2009.

Plumwood, Val. *Feminism and the Mastery of Nature.* New York: Routledge, 1993.

Sandilands, Catriona. *The Good-Natured Feminist: Ecofeminism and the Quest for Democracy.* Minneapolis: University of Minnesota Press, 1999.

Smith, Andrea. *Conquest.* Cambridge, MA: South End Press, 2005.

Spiegel, Jennifer. "Subterranean Flows: Water Contamination and the Politics of Visibility after the Bhopal Disaster." In Chen, MacLeod, and Neimanis 2013, 84–103.

Spivak, G. S. "Can the Subaltern Speak?" In *Marxism and the Interpretation of Culture*, edited by C. Nelson and L. Grossberg, 271–313. Urbana: University of Chicago Press, 1988.

———. *Death of a Discipline.* New York: Columbia University Press, 2003.

———. "The Politics of Translation." In *Outside the Teaching Machine*, 179–200. New York: Routledge, 1993.

———. "Responsibility." *Boundary 2* 21, no. 3 (1994): 19–64.

Sultana, Farhana. "Fluid Lives: Subjectivity, Gender and Water Management in Bangladesh." *Gender, Place, and Culture* 16, no. 4 (2009): 427–44.

———. "Water, Culture and Gender: An Analysis from Bangladesh." In *Water, Cultural Diversity & Global Environmental Change: Emerging Trends, Sustainable Futures?*, edited by B. R. Johnston, 237–52. The Netherlands: Springer, 2011.

Tiitsman, Jenna. "Planetary Subjects after the Death of Geography." In *Planetary Loves: Spivak, Postcoloniality and Theology*, edited by Stephen Moore et al., 149–67. Bronx, NY: Fordham University Press, 2011.

Tuhiwai Smith, Linda. *Decolonizing Methodologies*. London: Zed Books, 1999.

van Wyck, Peter C. "Footbridge at Atwater." In Chen, MacLeod, and Neimanis 2013, 256–73.

Wilson, Shawn. *Research Is Ceremony*. Toronto: Fernwood Books, 2008.

Excerpts from "a child's fable"

Baco Ohama

1.
a child's fable
seemed to emerge from the water
cracked at the spine

a tale
of rising oceans
now threatening the islands
themselves abandoned
eroded past
protecting the failed

everything beginning
with inhabitants' luck
rising in the bulges
created by glaciers
Now slowly
sinking
a ragged line
reassembled offshore

the place became an obsession
stumbled upon
a recalled voice
breaking memory

a ghostly outline of a girl
trying to save the island by hand
wasn't enough

waves rolled last winter
pushed held out hope
in a near-deadly drop
a struggle
now
still vulnerable
standing against water
damage obvious
broken in the wind
evidence half-submerged
it hit me
a sad end of an era
just a few inches above
the waves

4.
home
an obsession
stumbled upon
a ghostly outline of chance
remaining pieces
though shorter
standing out
against the obvious

the unsteady question
left

9.
an isolated section
of water
of erased tide
protecting the failed
Historians say
a team traveled to luck
scientists say
some reason
ancient
has created a see-saw sinking

These two factors eroding the reading

14.
strange spine of ocean
the last structure
left

part ii
water testimonies: witness, worry, and work

Water
The First Foundation of Life
Mona Polacca

[Editors' note: Part of respecting Indigenous knowledge systems involves valuing oral cultures as much as written discourses, so what follows is a transcription of Mona Polacca's presentation at the Downstream workshop, supplemented by excerpts from presentations that she has made in Japan and Sweden. Readers are invited to consider what is gained, lost, or shifted in the movement from oral to written word.]

I am of the Hopi-Havasupai people of the southwest in Arizona, North America. One of the concerns that we are dealing with right now is the uranium mining occurring above the Grand Canyon. The Havasupai people are called the people of the blue water, and they live at the bottom of the Grand Canyon. The Grand Canyon is said to have been formed by the mighty Colorado River, and the Havasupai live in what they call a cataract canyon of the Grand Canyon. There is a stream, a creek that goes through there, the Havasu Creek.

We are very concerned with the location of this mining that is on top above the canyon. If there should be a breach of the tailing ponds, up there on top, the waters will run down into the canyon and contaminate the waters. The Colorado River is not just a source of water that the tribes along the Colorado River depend on, but also provides water to California. Southern California draws its water off the Colorado River, and so if the Colorado River becomes contaminated, this affects everyone, not just the tribes.

The tribal community at the bottom of the canyon is very small. The area of land that they live on is one mile wide and three miles long. This is their traditional homeland. They have lived there from time immemorial. They haven't relocated, they haven't left that place. We believe the creator is the one who put the people in that place. So they are the Indigenous peoples of that canyon, and they haven't chosen to move. But should this uranium mining continue, if there is a catastrophe involving that uranium mining, then where are these people going to go? This is the situation that faces many Indigenous peoples throughout the world who are now being impacted by many of these various multinational corporations' industries for oil, for uranium, for the waters and other minerals that are being extracted out of Mother Earth. It is in places where the Indigenous peoples have been able to live, and some have chosen to live in isolation from the rest of modern society. They have chosen to live that way, but these corporations look at these lands and see them as undeveloped. They even call these parts of the world "Undeveloped Countries." When you put that kind of label to that piece of land, it is like putting a tag on it to say that this land needs to be used. Whereas on the other side of it, the Indigenous peoples are using it, they are taking care of it and keeping it in its natural state. But when it is termed "undeveloped," that means that there is this value system that is being imposed on this land to be "developed."

We are living in very challenging times. Indigenous peoples are faced with a challenge: What from our traditions are we going to move forward with and what from Western contemporary society are we going to embrace in order for us to move forward and to exist in this world?

Indigenous peoples from time immemorial have recognized themselves as the people being the foundation of nations, and as part of that understanding their foundation begins with the place where they live and the diversity that supports them in being there. We understand that there were others here in the world before us, that we have followed, and that those before us are the ones who established ways of being and ways of survival, ways of taking care of our environment and how we are going to live, and how we are going to relate with one another, as well as all of the other being or creatures of the Earth.

I'm a member of the International Council of 13 Indigenous Grandmothers.[1] We're an organization of Indigenous women from all over the world, who came together in October 2004. We found, when we met, that we shared a common concern about what was happening in the world: with our water, with our air, with our sacred fires, and with Mother Earth. Our concern is for what is going to be left for our future generations. So we decided that it was going to be our mission to travel to different parts of the world, the home place of each grandmother, and have gatherings to talk about these concerns.

We say that the Mother Earth is alive, and she has provided for us. The International Council of 13 Indigenous Grandmothers recognizes this because that is our tradition, that kind of teaching, that kind of thinking. So when we heard about the Declaration for the Rights of Mother Earth,[2] we recognized that within that declaration there are all of the principles of proper living in terms of traditional ways. Indigenous traditional ways of knowing are all incorporated in there. If we could recognize and hear throughout the whole world—not just Indigenous peoples—this basic call to consciousness, this is what the declaration is. It is a basic call to consciousness to all people, that there is a need right now to address how we are treating Mother Earth and how we are abusing her. We are so focused on the here and now, rather than what [we] are going to have ten years from now or what our future generations are going to have after we are gone.

Today with the way the multinational corporations and the countries and the governments are moving, there doesn't seem to be any consideration beyond the next ten, or maybe fifteen years. They have been given many indications, reports that are made by scientists, their own people, who are saying we are in a major crisis now in this world for our survival. Yet they keep moving forward without taking any consideration of what is happening.

Here today, here just within this region [Nagoya, Japan, 2010], just yesterday, the Grandmothers were making prayers. At the same time the Grandmothers were making prayers, calling on the powers of Mother Earth and asking for help so that our voices, our prayers, would be able to be heard, the island of Amami was receiving these major rains—this major storm—and they were saying it was the thirteenth storm that has come into this area. So when the Grandmothers heard this news, we saw that as Mother Earth knocking on our door, telling us it is time to wake up and be conscious of what she is saying, be conscious of all of the powers of natural law. Any man-made law doesn't hold water. You could make a law to try to talk about the flooding that is going on, but in the long run you are not going to stop it. No man-made law is going to stop it; these are the laws of nature that we are talking about. The laws of nature that we are talking about are for humanity to pay attention to because it is by the grace of Mother Earth that we are here. So it is very important to pay attention to that.

In the event that there is a world agreement to address protection of the world's biodiversity, then it is important for all of the nation-states and all of the corporations to really put in action their commitment that they claim to have to preserve and protect the biodiversity. We believe, the Grandmothers, that when we are talking and making these prayers, we believe it's not just the media or the people that are hearing what we are saying. This declaration for the rights of Mother Earth isn't just a world declaration. It is a declaration that is being made to the universe. And when we are making declarations to the universe, that is putting ourselves into the hands of natural law. That is beyond us as human beings. So in this way it is important that these discussions move beyond what people consider as going to give them a better-running car or a better TV to look at or any of these man-made technologies because in the long run, all these man-made technologies all dry up or become totally useless.

These are some of the concerns that we have about what is happening throughout the world for Indigenous peoples and for the protection of our lands and territories, our water, and the nature of Mother Earth.

The Council of the 13 Indigenous Grandmothers' mission is to promote peace, and part of promoting peace includes everyone having the ability to have the basic things that you need in order to survive in this world. The water, the air, the fire, the Mother Earth: we all need those things. We want to promote this concept that "we are all related," and sometimes in Western society, people don't understand that concept. So in order to create an experience that "we are all related," what I want you to do is close your eyes. Close your eyes and think about that time when you were inside your mother's womb because that is a time when you were in a very a safe, beautiful, warm environment. Everything you needed in order to develop as a human being was provided to you, and you lived inside water for three-quarters of a year. When it was time for you to come out into the world, the water came out of your mother's womb first, and you followed that water into this world. And so we call the water our first foundation of life. When we refer to the water, we call it the Holy Mother Water. And so, I was told that it was important to always give thanks to the water, to acknowledge its power and the life-giving element that it is. So this is your first foundation of life. Ever since that time, you have been relying on this water to continue to live in this world. And you can see how it is. Something really important is that when you feel the water, you can feel it, but you can't feel it. You can touch it, but you can't touch it. You can hold it, but you really can't hold it. That's this mystery of this element, this first foundation of life.

The next thing that you did when you came into this world is that you opened your mouth and you took in a breath of air. Your first breath of air. You opened your mouth and it went inside you, filled your lungs and when you let it out, you let out your first cry. You sent your voice throughout the world, all the way up into the universe and to all the spirits of the four directions. They recognized your voice, your announcement through your cry using this air. It announced your presence in this life. And so ever since then, that is what you have been doing, using this air, moving it inside of you and outside of you to make sounds. You can express yourself, your thoughts, your feelings, your emotions like that. You can express yourself, moving this air. You can sing. You can express your joy and anger. And sometimes you can hold it too. It is the second foundation of life.

Right shortly after you were born, someone in the room said, "Make this room warm for this baby. Make it bright. Light up the fire. Light up the fire bright." That's the Grandfather Fire. And then at some point in time, for the first time in your life you went outside the door of your home, maybe the place you were born. They took you outside for the first time in your life.

Grandfather Sun, this great fire in the sky, looked at you. Saw you. Put that light, that warmth upon you for the first time in your life and ever since then that's what happens every day. When you go out the door from your home in the morning, your first step you walk out there, and there it is. I'm grateful I can see it here today, like that. Beautiful sunlight was here with us. So that's the third foundation of life. We say the Grandfather, and we use it in our everyday life. Everything. Our life revolves around it.

And then somewhere along the way as you were growing up, eventually your caretaker took you, laid you down on the Mother Earth and at first you just lay there on your back. At some point you rolled over on your stomach, and you lay there on your stomach on Mother Earth. And then before too long, your caretaker took you, they sat you down on the Mother Earth, and there you sat for the first time. You got your sense of balance there using your backbone, using every bit of your being. Today it is difficult for us to sit on the floor, isn't it? We're not used to using our backbone, and so we have weak backs. But that is where you started. You sat on this Mother Earth using your backbone. And then somewhere along the way they put you back down, and you lay there on the Mother Earth. Pretty soon you got up on your hands and your knees and you started to crawl on the Mother Earth. Then next thing you know, your caretaker took you, stood you up on your two feet, and you liked how it felt. I don't know of any baby that doesn't like to feel their feet underneath them. So as a baby, as a child, you stood there with your two feet on this Mother Earth. At some point in time the caretaker let you go, and you stood there on your own two feet for the first time in your life. Have you ever noticed what a beautiful sight it is to see a child, a baby, stand for the first time in their life? That wonder. That wonder, and joy and excitement of feeling their connection to Earth. And we all did that. Then somewhere along the way, we took our first step, walking, making our path on this Mother Earth. We took our first step on this Mother Earth, started walking, and have been doing that ever since then on this Mother Earth. That's the fourth foundation of life. And every one of us has done that. So we are all related. That's the simplest way I can put it to you.

This connection that we have with these four basic foundations is not to be taken lightly. These things that Indigenous peoples talk about—called the Original Instructions, the basic call to consciousness—these four basic foundations of life are going to carry you for the rest of your life until that day, that time comes, when you are going to go back to your maker—"go back home," as we say. And that is as simple and basic as it gets. And then the other thing is that we think about our future generations. My mother told me this when I was fourteen years old: "You're not in this world for nothing. You have a purpose. You have a responsibility. You have certain things you have to do, walk and talk, in this life. What you do, what you say, how you walk, how you talk, it has an effect and impact on others around you. So pay attention to what you do." That's what she told me. She said, "It's very important for you to make your voice heard and speak up on behalf of our people." At the time when I was growing up, I didn't really feel that I was meant to do that, but as time went along, this is the path I've been walking since I was fourteen years old. So these things are really, really near and dear to my heart.

Notes

1   See http://www.grandmotherscouncil.org/. On World Water Day, March 22, 2014, the Grandmothers issued a call to women of all nations, of the four directions, to come together in prayer with the sacred life gift, water.
2   This declaration was passed at the World Peoples' Conference on Climate Change and the Rights of Mother Earth, from April 19 to 22, 2010, in Tiquipaya, Cochabamba, Bolivia, after extensive discussions. See http://therightsofnature.org/universal-declaration/.

From Our Homelands to the Tar Sands

Melina Laboucan Massimo

Only when the last tree has died
The last river been poisoned
And the last fish been caught
Will we realize we cannot eat money
—Cree proverb

I come from the community of Little Buffalo, and I am a member of the Lubicon Cree First Nation. I'm also a climate energy campaigner with Greenpeace Canada. The traditional territory of the Lubicon Cree covers approximately ten thousand square kilometres of low-lying trees, forests, rivers, plains, and wetlands (what we call muskeg) in northern Alberta. My community has dealt with three decades of massive oil and gas extraction. This exploitation of the land has been without the consent of the people and without the recognition or protection of the human rights under section 35 of the Canadian Constitution, which protects Aboriginal and treaty rights.

In the 1970s before this type of encroachment on the land happened, my father's generation engaged in sustenance living with my grandparents when they actually hunted, fished, and trapped throughout the region, throughout the traditional territory. My father was the youngest child in the family, and my *kokum* (grandmother) hid him away from the Indian agent who came to the community every fall to take away the children and force them into residential school. So he grew up on the land and did not learn English till he was ten, when they finally got him to go to school. Even into my generation, I remember going out to the traplines and going out on the horse and wagon. I was born in Peace River, where the nearest hospital was, but we lived in Little Buffalo, where my family lives, till my mom took us to Slave Lake a couple of hours away so she could find work and we could get a "good education." I remember people still living off the land. The water in the rivers, streams, and muskeg was still good to drink. But as oil and gas came through the territory, it has changed a lot.

Currently there are more than 2,600 oil and gas wells in our traditional territories.[1] Fourteen hundred square kilometres of leases have been granted for in situ oil sands extraction in Lubicon territory, and almost 70 percent of Lubicon territory has been leased for future exploitation. So what we see is an Indigenous way of life being overtaken by intensive oil and gas extraction. Where there once was self-sufficiency in the communities in the region because there was clean air, clean water, medicines, berries, and plants from the boreal forest, we now see this changing with an increased dependency on social services because families are no longer able to sustain themselves in what was once a healthy environment.

We also see health concerns: respiratory illnesses because of the noxious gases that are being released into the air and water. We see in the northern part of Alberta elevated rates of cancers and a lack of medical services. It has been calculated that almost $14 billion in revenue for the oil and gas companies have been taken out of our traditional territories,[2] yet the resources do not go back into the community. For example, we actually still have no running water in the community of Little Buffalo, where my family lives. That is ludicrous when you think about it because billions of dollars in revenue have been taken out of our traditional territory for logging, oil, and gas, and yet there is no running water and at the same time the water sources are being consumed at an alarming rate and then contaminated. This is very much a symptomatic problem that we see happening in a lot of Indigenous communities across Canada. In the few last pristine ecosystems in Canada, the communities have to deal with the increasing repercussions of contamination. What we see is our way of life being replaced by industrial landscapes, polluted and drained watersheds, and contaminated air. It is very much a crisis.

On April 29, 2011, there was a rupture in Plains Midstream Canada's Rainbow pipeline, which resulted in a massive oil spill beside the community. It was about 4.5 million litres, one of the biggest oil spills in Alberta's history. The pipeline broke and leaked. The spilled oil went down the corridor and also into the forest, but most of it got soaked up into the muskeg, which is like peatland moss and is an intricate and integral part of the ecosystem of the boreal forest. Oil spilling into the muskeg is detrimental because the muskeg is connected to all the water that is part of this ecosystem. It is not just an isolated system. It is not "stagnant" water that the government says it is. It is actually a living, breathing ecosystem that supports all the life depending on this water.

The first day of the spill, the school in the community did not know that there was an oil spill. When the children came to school that day and started to feel sick, they took the students outside the school because they thought it was a propane leak. When they got outside into the field, the principal said the children continued to be sick. They realized it was all over the community, not just inside the school. They were very concerned. The school did not receive the critical information that they should have. The community was not officially notified of the immensity of the spill until five days later, which coincidentally was after the federal election. The school had to be shut down for almost a week and a half.

The first week of the spill, community members were getting sick. Their eyes were burning. People had headaches and were feeling noxious. Officially it was stated that the air quality issues were not a problem even though Alberta Environment did not actually come on site into the community until six days after the spill. This is very problematic because the government that issues the permits for oil extraction is not taking into consideration the health and well-being of the communities in the region. They are putting the people into direct risk situations. Many people were left wondering what they should be doing—did they need to leave the community? In particular, pregnant women and small children are the most vulnerable in the community. The Rainbow Pipeline is forty-five years old, and who knows what will happen in the future for other communities along this corridor.

The same pipeline leaked in 2006, and the Energy Utility Board stated at the time that stress and corrosion factors were related to the malfunction of the pipeline's infrastructure and the spillage of a million litres. And, five years later in 2011, 4.5 million litres spilled in our traditional territory. When does it ever end? Communities will have to be on watch because of pipeline breaks like this. There are pipeline breaks all over North America. For instance, in 2010 we saw a 3-million-litre spill in Kalamazoo, Michigan. And on the west coast of British Columbia, there have been spills caused by the Kinder Morgan pipeline in 2005, 2007, 2009, and 2012.[3] People from coast to coast are very concerned about the pipeline infrastructure.

The United Nations has put forward recommendations regarding moratoriums on oil and gas in the Lubicon territory. On March 26, 1990, the UN Human Rights Committee ruled that the failure to recognize and protect Lubicon lands is an ongoing threat to our way of life and to the survival of the culture. Again in 2005, the UN Human Rights Committee cited Canada for violating the International Covenant on Civil and Political Rights. This is documented by a variety of human rights committees like Amnesty International, yet the massive extraction continues to happen.

A week and a half to two weeks after the oil spill on Lubicon homelands, huge forest fires ignited in the region, and burned out of control near the oil spill. What kind of threat does this pose to local communities if we cannot contain massive forest fires near facilities that could potentially explode and have exploded during some of these fires? What kind of danger is posed by the leaks in the pipelines we are seeing across North America because of the infrastructure needed to support the oil and gas?

The reason I work with Greenpeace is because of what is happening to my family and to my community. We see massive oil spills. We see wildlife and the ecosystems dying before our very eyes. We see a crisis in northern Alberta because of tar sands development. When I went home to deal with an oil spill, I saw how my family was being treated. They told me how they felt sick. It was utterly heartbreaking to see my family and community put in this threatened position of not knowing what their rights were or what they could do to protect themselves.

How many more communities have to be threatened, and how many more communities have to have their personal and environmental health put at risk for extreme fossil fuel extraction? Who is it really benefiting? It is not going to benefit any of us in the end. What are we leaving to future generations? We are leaving contaminated water, polluted air, a changing climate, and ecosystems that are not thriving and supporting sustainable life systems.

This type of exploitation does not have to happen. It is literally scraping the bottom of the barrel, producing the dirtiest form of oil. There are two kinds of extraction. First, the tar sands mines are as big as entire cities. When Imperial Oil's mine is finished, it will be as big as Washington, DC. The world's biggest dump trucks operate in the tar sands; they are three stories high. Second, there is what is called "in situ extraction," which is underground mining that the government says looks better because the surface of the land does not look as disturbed. However, in many cases it actually takes more water, more gas, and produces more carbon emissions. It is *not* better, but you will hear this in the media as a form of greenwashing the tar sands because it will be 80 percent of the way that they'll take out the tar sands.[4]

The Mackenzie River Basin and the Peace Athabasca delta is one of the largest and freshest intact water systems in the world. It is one-sixth of Canada's freshwater supply, yet we are seeing this water source being used by oil companies. It takes more water to extract tar sands, roughly three to five barrels of water to produce one barrel of oil, which also produces one and a half barrels of toxic by-product.[5] The source of the Athabasca River is the Athabasca Glacier, a pristine water source that is receding because of climate change.

First Nations Elders who used to go down the Athabasca in big boats now use small boats, and even so, they are hitting sandbars. The water is being drained from the Athabasca at an alarming rate. The fishermen are finding fish with tumours and crooked spines. An expert on groundwater issues, Dr. David Schindler says he is not sure if the Athabasca can withstand the demands of industry in the region.[6] When all is said and done, industry and the Canadian government would destroy 141,000 square kilometres of land, which is bigger than England and Wales combined, or bigger than the state of Florida. This is our homeland, the traditional territories of the Cree, the Dene, and the Métis.

The woodland caribou is one of the species on our homelands that is affected. It is expected that they will be extirpated or extinct in my lifetime. With the rate of tar sands expansion, local extinction of the caribou is predicted by 2040 due to the complete fragmentation and deforestation of the region.[7] The tar sands are also an international migration route for birds, hundreds of which have died in the toxic tailings ponds. My dad is a hunter—I grew up eating moose meat—and a couple of years ago he found three tumours in the carcass of a moose. The Beaver Lake Cree First Nation has a constitutional court case against the government of Canada and the province of Alberta opposing the tar sands extraction. They have also reported the same kind of findings when they hunt—that is, animals with yellow and cancerous insides.

The crisis is not only local, but also global. Even communities that do not experience elevated cancer rates and immediate toxic pollution—not just First Nations communities but communities everywhere—will still experience the effects of climate change caused by the massive carbon emissions from the tar sands, which include more floods, more drought and fire, more unpredictable and extreme weather patterns that endanger our food security and well-being.

There are solutions out there. We need to see a change in this world. We need to push for renewable energy systems that help communities to be self-sufficient and self-sustaining. We need to shift away from fossil fuel–based systems and push for a renewable energy system that can help us transition out of what we are currently facing.[8]

A landmark study published on May 9, 2011, by the United Nations Inter-governmental Panel on Climate Change shows that renewable energy could account for almost 80 percent of the world's energy supply within four decades, but only if governments pursue the policies needed to promote green power. The Canadian government gives $1.4 billion a year in tax subsidies to oil, coal, and gas companies. Much of this could be redirected to building the green infrastructure that we need for current and future generations.

First Nations are uniting in the urgent need to protect the land and water-shed, as seen in the Save the Fraser Declaration, which over 130 First Nations have signed. What people do not yet seem to understand is that when we work to protect our homelands, we protect them not only for ourselves, but also for all people on this Earth.

Notes

An earlier version of this piece is online as a photo essay at https://www.youtube.com/watch?v=qz3nSscXamI.

1 For a map of the 1,305 active wells and 1,379 capped wells as of 2009, see the Amnesty International report, *From Homeland to Oil Sands*, June 2010, http://www.amnesty.ca/sites/default/files/amr200022010enhomelandsoilsands.pdf.

2 This amount is estimated by the Lubicon Lake First Nation. See the press release on the Lubicon Lake Nation's website: "Lubicon Lake Nation Take a Stand in Alberta Oilfield," June 16, 2013, http://www.lubiconlakenation.ca/index.php/breaking-news/archived -releases-letters-and-info/407-january-16-2013-lubicon-lake-nation-take-a-stand-in -alberta-oilfield-exercise-of-jurisdiction-slows-oilfield-traffic.

3 See Forest Ethics's website, which tracks the spilling of 770,000 litres of oil from 2005 to 2012: http://forestethics.org/kinder-morgan-trans-mountain. For an infographic of oil spills, see Mychaylo Prystupa, "Kinder Morgan's Historic Oil Spills Are Double the Kalamazoo Disaster: NDP MP," *Vancouver Observer*, May 16, 2014, http://www.vancouverobserver .com/news/kinder-morgans-historic-oil-spills-are-double-kalamazoo-disaster-ndp-mp.

4 According to the Canadian Association of Petroleum Producers (CAPP) website, "80 per cent of oil sands reserves (which underlie approximately 97 per cent of the oil sands surface area) are recoverable through in situ technology, with limited surface distur- bance": http://www.capp.ca/canadaIndustry/oilSands/Energy-Economy/Pages/what-are -oilsands.aspx.

5 The range of water used depends on the technology, and the oil industry has been trying to reduce its usage to destroying three barrels of water for each barrel of oil. The most conservative estimate of water usage is found in documents like the Canadian Associa- tion of Petroleum Producers' "Water Use in Canada's Oil Sands," June 2012, http://www .capp.ca/getdoc.aspx?DocId=193756. Such industry-driven documents omit the amount of toxic waste produced, which is identified by the Pembina Institute as 1.5 barrels of toxic waste for each barrel of mined bitumen: http://www.pembina.org/oil-sands/os101/ tailings.

6 Lecture by David Schindler, "Protecting the Athabasca River from Oil Sands Development," Carleton University, April 15, 2013, https://www.youtube.com/watch?v=_wzH919TS6E.

7 See Elizabeth Shope, "Alberta Caribou herds could perish in 30 years with unchecked tar sands development," Switchboard: Natural Resources Defence Council Staff Blog, June 30, 2011. Also see Samuel K. Wasser, Jonah L. Keim, Mark L. Taper, and Subhash R. Lele, "The Influences of Wolf Predation, Habitat Loss, and Human Activity on Caribou and Moose in the Alberta Oil Sands, *Frontiers in Ecology and the Environment* 9, no. 10 (2011): 546–51, http://dx.doi.org/10.1890/100071. See also the Athabasca Chipewyan First Nation's work on caribou protection in the report, *Nih boghodi: We Are the Stewards of Our Land*, April 26, 2012, http://www.ceaa-acee.gc.ca/050/documents/p59540/83411E .pdf.

8 In the summer of 2015, Melina and her community launched the Piitapan Solar Project, a 20.8kW renewable energy installation that powers the health centre for Little Buffalo. See the blog "Building a Solar Dream in a Tar Sands Nightmare," http://www.greenpeace .org/canada/en/blog/Blogentry/building-a-solar-dream-in-a-tar-sands-nightmablog/ 54190/, as well as the Lubicon Solar website for more information about the project: http://www.lubiconsolar.ca/.

Bibliography

Amnesty International. *From Homeland to Oil Sands*. June 2010. http://www.amnesty.ca/sites/default/files/amr200022010enhomelandsoilsands.pdf.

Athabasca Chipewyan First Nation. *Nih boghodi: We Are the Stewards of Our Land*. April 26, 2012. http://www.ceaa-acee.gc.ca/050/documents/p59540/83411E.pdf.

Canadian Association of Petroleum Producers. "Water Use in Canada's Oil Sands." June 2012. http://www.capp.ca/getdoc.aspx?DocId=193756.

———. "What Are Oil Sands?" http://www.capp.ca/canadaIndustry/oilSands/Energy-Economy/Pages/what-are-oilsands.aspx.

Forest Ethics. "4 Reasons to Oppose the New Kinder Morgan Trans Mountain Tar Sands Pipeline." http://forestethics.org/kinder-morgan-trans-mountain.

Goddard, John. *The Last Stand of the Lubicon Cree*. Vancouver: Douglas and McIntyre, 1991.

Lubicon Lake First Nation. "Lubicon Lake Nation Take a Stand in Alberta Oilfield." June 16, 2013. http://www.lubiconlakenation.ca/index.php/breaking-news/archived-releases-letters-and-info/407-january-16-2013-lubicon-lake-nation-take-a-stand-in-alberta-oilfield-exercise-of-jurisdiction-slows-oilfield-traffic.

Pembina Institute. "Tailings." http://www.pembina.org/oil-sands/os101/tailings.

Prystupa, Mychaylo. "Kinder Morgan's Historic Oil Spills Are Double the Kalamazoo Disaster: NDP MP." *Vancouver Observer*, May 16, 2014. http://www.vancouverobserver.com/news/kinder-morgans-historic-oil-spills-are-double-kalamazoo-disaster-ndp-mp.

Schindler, David. "Protecting the Athabasca River from Oil Sands Development." Carleton University. April 15, 2013. https://www.youtube.com/watch?v=_wzH919TS6E.

Shope, Elizabeth. "Alberta Caribou herds could perish in 30 years with unchecked tar sands development." Switchboard: Natural Resources Defence Council Staff Blog. June 30, 2011.

Wasser, Samuel, Jonah L. Keim, Mark L. Taper, and Subhash R. Lele. "The Influences of Wolf Predation, Habitat Loss, and Human Activity on Caribou and Moose in the Alberta Oil Sands." *Frontiers in Ecology and the Environment* 9, no. 10 (2011): 546–51. http://dx.doi.org/10.1890/100071.

Keepers of the Water
Nishnaabe-kwewag Speaking for the Water
Renée Elizabeth Mzinegiizhigo-kwe Bédard

Nishnaabe-kwewag and also all women across the continent of North and South America, we have a great responsibility as women to carry that work as light keepers, carriers of the water, carriers of light.[1]

Nishnaabeg people have always lived along the water of the Great Lakes.[2] The *ziibii'ganan* (rivers), *zaagiganan* (lakes), *bog'tingoon* (rapids), *wiik-wedoon* (bays), *dkibiin* (natural springs), *biitooshk-biisenyin* (swamps), and *ziigiinsan*[3] (streams) have sustained the Nishnaabeg people on these traditional territorial lands for thousands of years. Water has been, and continues to be, critical to the health, politics, spirituality, culture, and economy of Nishnaabeg communities. Nishnaabeg people have picked medicine like *wiingaash*[4] (sweet-grass) and food like *nishnaabe-mnoomin*[5] (wild rice) along the shores of the waterways. They have cooked their food using the waters they collect from the streams and natural springs. Babies and children have always been washed in the waters of our rivers and lakes. Spiritually, it is the women who are respon-sible for praying to the water and caring for the water during ceremonies, and, as we near the end of the first decade of the twenty-first century, it is not surprising that Nishnaabeg women are standing up to protect the water. They want cleaner, non-exploited, and healthy water on the Great Lakes for their children, grandchildren, and all future generations.

In this chapter, I seek to understand the historical and contemporary significance of water to Nishnaabeg people, especially to our women. I do so by engaging with the words and wisdom of Nishnaabe-kwewag Elders Shirley Williams of Wikiwemikong Unceded First Nation and Josephine Mandamin of Thunder Bay, Ontario. I will discuss traditional Nishnaabeg knowledge about water, and the responsibilities of women in protecting water. Also, I will high-light some of the current grassroots work by the Mother Earth Water Walkers.

The Water Walkers are a group of Nishnaabeg women who are carrying water taken from the Great Lakes region as they walk around each of the Great Lakes in order to advocate for protection of the environment and Indigenous rights to clean water. It is my hope that this chapter will reinforce the importance of water to the health and well-being of Nishnaabeg people and all Indigenous peoples across North America.

French River Girl

> We are the wives, the mothers, daughters and sisters, the grandmothers, the aunties and the nieces of our community. We speak for the children and grandchildren of today, and for those yet unborn.[6]

I offer this passage because it best describes the role of Nishnaabeg women in speaking out for their responsibilities to the future generations. First and foremost, there is our responsibility to protect water and ensure that water is there for future generations. I am aware as I write this paper of my place in "all of Creation"—as a Nishnaabe-kwe. I gladly advocate for clean water and environmental awareness because I grew up along the waters of the French River, calling myself a "French River Girl." This topic, the articulation of Nishnaabeg women's responsibilities to water and the safeguarding of clean water for those "children and grandchildren of today and for those yet unborn"[7] is the core of my identity. As a French River Girl, I see the water as the lifeblood of my Mother the Earth.

I am a member of Dokis First Nation, in northern Ontario, along the French River. The French River has always been a highway of water travel and fur trading for the Nishnaabeg from the interior of northern Ontario, into the Great Lakes and beyond. The history of the French River is rich, including numerous First Nations cultures: Ojibway, Nipissing, and Omàmìwinini (Algonquin). Many French settlements and fur-trading posts were established along the edges of the waterways (rivers and lakes). Mining, lumbering, ice cutting, fishing, and hunting brought many surveyors, explorers, and industries to the region. The railway led to the development of new towns, villages, and the future city of North Bay. Steady development of this water highway brought newcomers to the region, forever interweaving the cultures and heritage of both First Nations and settler peoples. Treaties constructed the current Indian Bands of Nipissing First Nations Reserve, Garden River First Nations Reserve, and Dokis First Nations Reserve along the connected Nipissing Lake and French River area. Together, these Nishnaabeg communities formed a tight network of families, political alliances, and shared common cultural similarities defined by living on the water's edge.

The French River contains vast stretches of islands and is surrounded by diverse watersheds of marshes, forest, sand beaches, and rocky granite shore-lines. I spent my childhood catching frogs, fishing, or picking blueberries along the water's edge of the many islands that dot the French River. When I dream, I dream of the water along the French River. When I think of my ancestors, my thoughts include stories that always involve the French River. When I think of politics, it always includes the river, its people, and its history. When I think of culture and spirituality, they are grounded in traditions and teachings of that dynamic relationship that we have as Nishnaabeg people who have lived along the water's edge of the French River. The waters of the French River and Dokis First Nation represent an intimate and critical aspect of my identity as an Nishnaabe-kwe. Without water and watersheds like the French River, Nishnaabeg individuals like myself would experience a fundamental discon-nect with who we are as Nishnaabeg people. The water, along with the land, defines our identities, sustains our families and communities, and provides us with the knowledge of how to live as Nishnaabeg people.

Along the French River there are rapids. These are spaces where the waters from different channels meet and literally dance together in converging cur-rents. The water moves forward and backward, upward and downward, and from side to side. Twisting and swirling together, these converging currents are spaces where the river speaks to the world in a thundering voice to all who come across its presence. Several years ago, I wrote in my master's thesis: "The rapids seem like a dangerous place and they most definitely are, but they are also a place of life, cleansing, freedom undeterred and where the life of the River is heard above all other sounds."[8] The song of the rapids is a cleansing song, speaking of regeneration, transformation, and the health of both the water and the land. The ability to cleanse the land and river waters has always been the role of the rapids.

I am reminded of the words of (Nishnaabe) Odawa Elder Shirley Ida Williams, where she describes the cleansing power of the waters in lakes and rivers. She said to me:

> I know that the water cleans itself. When we were growing up my father used to say "It will take at least over a hundred years for the water to clean itself.... There are natural deposits in the water to help to clean itself. It's just like soap when you wash your body," he said. There are things under the water to clean itself, to purify the water itself. And, because we are putting too much dirt and other things in the water it doesn't have enough time to clean itself out, so it gets polluted. So it will take a longer time to clean itself out.[9]

Shirley's words remind me of when I was a child and we used to go to the Dokis reserve marina to do our laundry in a little shack that acted as a laundromat. I remember the sounds of the churning water in the giant metal washing machines and the smell of Sunlight soap perfuming the air. My mother, aunts, cousins, and I would spend hours at that tiny shack doing load after load of dirty laundry. I also remember the times when we used to go fishing and have afternoon shore lunches along the mouth of the rapids. The water of the rapids could be heard from far away and the smell of the water hung in the air—sunshine, pines, blueberries, and the hot granite rocks. The rapids always reminded me of the washing machine at the Dokis marina laundromat-shack. Like a washing machine, the rapids pull water into its grip and cause it to bubble and froth with oxygen, as if to clean the water and breathe life into it again. Then out the water goes, back into the river.

Similarly, the rapids are also like the heart and lungs of the human body. A heart pumps blood in; the lungs fill the blood with oxygen and cleanse the blood. Next, the heart sends that blood back out through the body, delivering essential elements to the body, while also working to remove harmful wastes. The rapids work in a similar fashion, both cleansing and feeding the river. But pollution in the waters of the French River has interfered with this sacred role. The amount of pollution being created is too much for the river waters to clean. Like a smoker or alcoholic who puts toxins into the body faster than the body can cleanse itself, the waters of our landscapes are made more unclean every year by the people living on them. As Shirley Williams warns, the increasing pollution people are putting into the water of rivers and lakes leaves no time for the water to cleanse itself.

Nishnaabeg women have always been strong proponents for the movement to clean and protect the water around the Great Lakes region. Our children have to drink the water, and we bathe our babies in those waters. As well, we feed the children wild meat and medicine taken from lands contaminated by corporate development, human refuse, and garbage. I remember a time when our women—our mothers and aunties—would take their babies down to the shoreline at sunset to wash them in the waters of the river. These beautiful women would chat about the day's goings-on, socialize, and share stories. Now, children are washed in water that has to be heated or is filled with chemicals like chlorine to kill any parasitic bacteria. Water is now bought and trucked in from outside sources, and state-of-the-art filtration technology is used to purify the water. The water is then cleaned of everything, including all life forms.

Sacred Medicine or Poison?

All that we drink and eat is stored in our bodies and can either heal or harm us. Over time, our bodies can build up both nutrients and toxins from the food and water that we ingest in a process known as bioaccumulation. To the Nishnaabeg people, this means that all that we eat or drink is stored in our organs, tissues, and cells for as long as we live. For those who live a traditional lifestyle of harvesting fish, animals, and water from the rivers, lakes, and streams in Nishnaabeg territories, there is danger in mercury poisoning, bacterial infections, and other harmful pollutants. If the deer or fish the hunter kills and consumes is tainted with toxins, then the hunter and his family will absorb those toxins into their bodies. The harmful chemicals ingested by fish, animals, plants, and birds move through the food chain until they reach people. Nishnaabekwe scholar Winona LaDuke explains this phenomenon by relating it to the sturgeon fish in the rivers of the Great Lakes:

> To the Nishnaabeg, bioaccumulation means that whatever toxins the fish has swallowed and stored in its flesh will come to be stored in our flesh as we participate in our traditional way of life based on harvesting from our lakes and streams. The disaster of mercury contamination has already impacted tribal communities throughout North America.[10]

In the past, the water we drank was considered medicine, but now it is hard to say whether it is a medicine or possibly poison we are putting in our bodies.

Now that the water in the lakes, streams, rivers, and water tables is no good to drink, Nishnaabeg people are forced to buy water. Odawa Elder Shirley Ida Williams recalls the vision her father saw for her in the future about her having to buy water one day. She tells it this way:

> When I was growing up in 1950s, my father noticed that the water wasn't as clear as it used to be. He was already aware that the water was not very clean. He said that before that you could see everything.... And he said at that time, "In your time you probably will see that the water is not going to be very clean and unhealthy to drink. And you will see the day where you will have to buy water." I think I was working in St. Catharines in 1984 and I didn't like the taste of water over there. So, I thought, "I saw bottled water in the grocery store. I think I better go get one." When I bought it a voice came into my head that said, "You are going to be buying bottle water in the future." And I thought, "Oh, how did my father know that?" And here I am I'm buying water. I was paying for the water at the cash register.[11]

Shirley's reserve of Wikwemikong Unceded First Nation now has water delivered to the homes in the community. Natural water from the rivers and lakes is no longer relied upon as a pure source of drinking water. Companies that supply water are trucking water into the community for local residents to purchase and use in their everyday lives. She adds, "When I go home the water now is being delivered to homes. Even that water doesn't taste that good. My sister, the one I stay with when I go home, she buys water. Periodically, I think many of the women boil water that they are going to drink." Due to the poor quality of water on her reserve (and on the many other reserves and reservations on both sides of the border), community members are now often opting to buy water that has been "cleaned" or "purified" by water treatment or filtration systems.

Shirley Williams worries about whether it is healthy for her community to buy water that is bottled or imported by truck to people's homes. She says, "I am concerned because when they deliver the water, how clean is the water in the water truck that is being delivered to the home? And the children drink it." Our children, who are referred to as our "future," are ingesting chemicals such as chlorine, fluoride, and the residue from the disposable plastic bottles used to store water. During a workshop at Trent University, to an audience of women, Josephine Mandamin warned about the dangers of water in the plastic bottles the women in the audience were drinking. She said:

> When I talk about the bottled water, I always think about this Elder.... even years old. I started waking up from my deep sleep of not knowing who I was an Nishnaabekwe. I had this cedar in a plastic bag and I put that down beside her. I had my little cedar and I put it down beside me. She pointed at it and said, "How long would you last if you slept in a plastic bag?" I said, "Not very long." "Well, the same thing is going to happen with your medicine. It is not going to last very long." Sure enough, I didn't take my cedar out of the bag. Two days later, it started turning brown and then the next day it started to get mouldy. It was decaying, it was dying. It was actually dying in the plastic bag! The water that you're drinking is about the same way. It is mouldy.[12]

We should be asking ourselves: Where does the water we are buying come from? Is it treated with chemicals to clean it? What is the impact of bottling water in plastic containers made of chemicals? In the end, buying water becomes a bandage on a wound that is festering beneath. Buying water does not solve the problem of a polluted environment. The land, plants, birds, and animals cannot buy "clean" water, so what do they do?

Mide-Waaboo

Traditionally, the Nishnaabeg people consider water to be our relative. Nishnaabeg believe that "all my family" includes not just our human family, but the animals, plants, birds, fish, the water, air, and the earth, which all form part of the great interdependent web of life. Even the things that are considered inanimate, we call our relatives. We call the Earth "our real Mother," the land as our "Mother's lap," and water the blood of this Mother the Earth. The calling of all Creation (including the sky, water, lands, animals, fish, and birds) into our family describes a relationship of trust, love, and faithfulness between human beings and the natural world.

Whereas colonial society views the environment as separate, the Earth consisting of raw material resources to use, exploit, and deplete, Nishnaabeg people view the land, water, plants, animals, and sky world as one unified and interdependent living system that works to sustain us all. As the land, water, sky, plants, and animals are connected, so is every aspect of life. The sacredness of water is not separate from human beings. Therefore, every act, whether throwing a pop can in a river or using chemical detergents to wash our laundry, interferes with that sacred relationship between the water and humanity. Everything has its respective place in this web of Creation, and interference with any component, no matter how small, will eventually have repercussions on all the other components.

Our traditional stories tell us that in the web of Creation, water is a sacred medicine. Shirley Williams shares that:

> From stories that I have heard they say that there is water up in the sky world somewhere in the land of plenty and that when we leave this world, this physical world and when you go into that spiritual world that there is water up there. But that there is a special place up there somewhere in the sky world where there is what they call the holy water.[13]

She explains that, "according to the traditional teachings of the Midewiwin, they refer to this water as the *mide-waaboo*, which is similar to holy water. In the Midewiwin, they also have songs for water. There are songs in particular that are given to women to sing when you pray to the water or for the water in thanksgiving for what it does."[14] She explains that because women are given these sacred prayers and songs to sing for that sacred medicine, we therefore must speak out on the water's behalf.

The Elders use water as a medicine in ceremony to both nourish and cleanse our bodies, minds, and spirits. When we come out of our fasting lodges, it is water that is there to greet us, to bring us back to the world of the living and cleanse the way for us. Water is a great gift that sustains and transforms. Water can bring life into the world, make rivers or break the great rocks over time. Water teaches us strength, the ability to endure, and patience. If water can take thousands of years to wear down, transform, and break through a rock, then we too can have the patience to do anything. Josephine Mandamin argues that water is a precious resource.

> Because water is so precious, that the only time I drink water is in the morning. First thing in the morning, that is my first drink, is that water. And I hold it up to the Creator. I hold it up to the Spirit, the Woman-Spirit who waters that water in that Third-Realm. I hold it up to her. I ask her to bring the mide-waaboo that I am going to put into my body. And I ask for blessings and I raise it four times and then I offer it to the ground or out the window or whenever I am and then I drink the water. That's the first drink. That is the most powerful drink, that is that first drink of water in the morning. Because it is that Spirit that you have called on to come to that water that you are holding in your hand, in that glass of water.[15]

The sacredness of water means that the water should be viewed as more than a mere commodity to be bought and sold. As Josephine describes, the very act of drinking water can be a ceremony that connects an individual to our relation—the water.

Water does not exist solely for use by human beings. All of life has access rights to the use of the water and its gifts. Exploiting the water to human ends will ultimately mean breaking relationships with other parts of Creation: the animals, the land, plants, the birds, land, and sky. The women of Bkejwanong Territory remind us:

> We understand that the Creator Grandfather made all that there is and breathed life into it. He made the land and the water to be pure.... Our teachings say these waters must be kept absolutely pure because these river waters are our Holy Water. By taking even the minutest chance of contaminating it, you are desecrating all that is sacred to us.[16]

The water is the birthright and a source of sustenance for our people. Each of us, therefore, has a great responsibility to protect and care for it. People were created by the Creator to act as "caretakers of the land" and all that is here. Therefore, humans should not let water be exploited, destroyed, or sold.

Keepers of the Water

Women are particularly connected to water in Nishnaabeg culture. Nishnaabeg women are often referred to as "The Keepers of the Water."[17] Josephine Mandamin calls Nishnaabeg women the "carriers of the water." She says,

> As women, we are carriers of life. Our bodies are built that way. Men are not built that way. We are special. We are very special and unique in how our bodies are made that way. And the water that we carry is that water of unity, that unites all of us. It unites all women. It unites all men. It unites all families, all nations all across the world. That little drop of water.[18]

Women have an intimate connection with water because of their ability to bring forth life. Shirley explains, "And because we are women we are the life-givers and when we have children, when it is birthing time it is the water that comes out first."[19] The birth of children marks a spiritual relationship from the time of preconception to birth where the waters of the woman's womb burst forth to cleanse the way for that new life to come forth into the world. Women are therefore held in high regard for these life-giving responsibilities and carriers of that sacred water.

Shirley Williams teaches younger women to respect their roles as life-givers, and warns that it is up to women to maintain their responsibilities to the water. She believes that all women have to protect the water as the lifeblood of Mother Earth. She supplies this perspective on the matter:

> Woman is given the responsibility of looking after the water because it is the Mother Earth, it is the woman. The woman is the Mother Earth and through the Mother Earth she has the rivers and the lakes, that's her bloodline. We in turn because we are women we are given that responsibility to help her, to clean her by praying and singing and to help her to clean herself.[20]

Josephine Mandamin says that "the main message is to walk the talk. To do what needs to be done for our Mother the Earth. She needs us!" If we are going to say we have responsibilities to water, then we have to act to carry on those traditions and fix the damage already done to the waters of our lands, lakes, and rivers.

Women's cycles, or blood time, are considered very powerful medicine for women. It is during the moon-time when women release that blood from their bodies that is most sacred. Bringing back the ceremonies of Berry Fasting and First Blood for the young girls involving their moon-time bleeding is critical to restoring the relationships and responsibilities of women to Mother the Earth as "Keepers of the Water." Those ceremonies have become a way to resist the Western culture, which does not respect the sacredness of water and women's moon-time. Josephine Mandamin feels that it is important to instill knowledge in the minds and hearts of young girls about the importance of that water we carry in us:

> Women, especially girls who are just starting their moon-time, that is the time when Mother the Earth needs that blood. She is the blood. She gives us her blood in that water. And we as women have to give her our blood, which is our precious blood. And that first blood of our young children is what she needs. So we are teaching our young girls, young women that when they first give off of their blood, give to Mother the Earth. We ask them to, don't put your blood in the sewer, don't put your blood in the garbage can. Put it in a paper bag and when you're done your first blood we'll go put it out in the bush and we'll bury it, and Mother will use that. And don't use the toilet when you're first showing your blood. Use a plastic pail or a little pail and go there. Put that water on the Earth, she needs that. Because she gives up her water, we as women have to give back the water. I remember when my grandmother used to say when somebody was on her moon-time. That very first time she would say ... now she is medicine! A woman is carrying medicine in her body, that is that powerful medicine—is her blood.[21]

As Josephine teaches in the above quote, a woman's body carries powerful medicine. During their moon-time, women's menstrual cycles are connected to the movements of Mother the Earth, but also to the moon and all Creation. Women have biological reminders of that connection with water every month when the moon-time arrives. Again, Josephine illustrates this connection:

> And when your moon-time comes, also, that is the most strongest time of your month is when you're having your period. You can actually feel the pull of the moon in your moon-time. You can actually feel in your womb, that pull when you are on your moon-time, with Mother the Earth.[22]

As Josephine describes, the moon—described as Grandmother Moon or Nokomis in Nishnaabemwin—is seen as a force that guides not just our water or our blood during moon-time, but also various other aspects of water in nature.

The moon controls the waters of lakes, rivers, oceans, and the seas. Levels of water in lakes and rivers go up and down, currents change directions, and cause storms to occur. Mother the Earth goes through cycles, just as women do. Throughout a month, weather shifts and changes just as women's bodies make ready and cleanse the womb for new life. Josephine articulates that Mother Earth goes through the same process as women:

> It's the same way when our Mother the Earth feels that full moon on Mother the Earth. If you look at the difference of the water during different times of the full moon and how that water reacts to the pull of the moon. It could be violent, it could be very gentle, it could be very peaceful, it could be all things if you watch very carefully how that water moves with the full moon. It's the same way with us women when we are in our moon-time. We go through the same cycle. We go through the same feelings. Our emotions are violent sometimes, peaceful, crying. There are different emotions we go through. Our Mother Earth goes through the same thing with her water during different times of the month. So we are told by our grandmothers when you are in your moon-time that's the most strongest time. Pray hard. Go and sit somewhere, peaceful and be with Mother Earth. And just pray for people at that time.[23]

Moon-time represents not just a reminder of a woman's responsibility to water, but of her water or blood as sacred medicine, and a time when she should think of others besides herself. Therefore, the water in nature and the water that women carry in the vessels of our wombs connects us to all of Creation—all our relations. All female creatures that live and breathe have cycles and carry that life-giving water. In this water, all female beings throughout the world—whether human, four-legged, those that fly, or those that swim—all experience the pull of the water and the drive to carry life in their wombs.

Because women have this intimate relationship with water as a sacred medicine, it makes it more tragic that the water that we should pray for, drink, and birth our babies in is now threatened. Nishnaabeg women across Nishnaabeg Territory need to stand up for our rights to clean water and to protect our traditions, culture, and identities. We are now hearing the warnings prophesized by our Elders come true. We are now forced to buy water, to watch our Mother Earth become sick with toxins, and see our four-legged animal relatives suffer or even die due to polluted water. Shirley Williams warns us all to act now before it is too late.

> We once lived in water and we are born in water. And because we have not been taught to respect our own bodies and also respect that water and what it does for us, that is why we are in this predicament today! Many women are now beginning to realize that we have to do something about the water and the pollution in water because if we don't, all of us are going to be sick at some point.[24]

Mother Earth Water Walkers

> When we hear of prophecies, we listen to those prophecies and sometimes those prophecies hit us just like that, hits you right in the heart. In the year 2000, when I was at a Sundance and an Elder was taking about the prophecy about the water, he said, "Thirty years from now ounce-per-ounce of that water is going to cost $300 per an ounce of water within the 25 years or sooner." He talked about the roles of women. How they have to start picking up their work, picking up their bundle, and doing what needs to be done about the water. And how he talked about how the Elders long time ago talked about how that water was going to be poisoned. How that beautiful water, he never believed it as a child when he heard those things. When he finished talking he looked at the crowd and said, "What are you going to do about it?" What are you going to do about it, hit me right in the heart. It seemed like he was looking straight at me when he said that. For a year-and-a-half that burned in my heart. I talked to other women about it, that we need to do something. What can we do? What are we going to do about it?[25]

The above quote by Josephine Mandamin comes from a workshop held at the Indigenous Women's Symposium at Trent University in Peterborough, Ontario, in March 2007. Josephine shared with the audience how the Mother Earth Water Walkers formed. The Water Walkers are a group of First Nations women (Nishnaabeg women and some men) who are taking action to focus public attention on the growing problems facing this world's most precious resource—water, the lifeblood of Mother Earth. So far the Water Walkers have walked around most of the Great Lakes and have only Lake Erie left to complete the circle of their journey.[26]

Josephine describes how the Water Walkers began in the winter of 2002. A group of women were sitting around, talking about traditional teachings, roles of women, and water songs.[27] She says they asked themselves the question: "What can we do to bring out, to tell people of our responsibilities as women, as keepers of life and the water, to respect our bodies as Nishnaabe-kwewag, as women?"[28] As they discussed what to do, the idea for the walk just came to them. Someone in the group simply commented:

> Well, you know we could walk around with the water and raise awareness? And somebody else said, "Yeah! A Pail of water, let's walk around with a pail of water." And somebody said, "Lake Superior." I myself live about a fifteen-minute walk from Lake Superior where we live. Then somebody else said, "I can just see Josephine walking around Lake Superior with a pail of water." And I said, "Seriously, let's do it!" And they said, "Sure, okay let's do it!" So that's how we talked about it and talked to other women that we

met. So, we did it! It's just one of those things that when the Spirit moves you, when you know that something has to be done, you don't question the Spirit, you just do it. And, that's what we did. We just did it![29]

From there, in 2003, Josephine Mandamin and other Nishnaabeg women began the circle of their journey around the entire perimeter of Lake Superior. To date, they have travelled around the perimeter of Lake Huron, Lake Ontario, Lake Michigan, and Lake Superior. Their ultimate goal has been to raise awareness of the need to protect water, the lifeblood of Mother Earth.

According to Josephine Mandamin, the Water Walk has been a "spiritual walk."[30] It has brought together women from different clans and areas surrounding the Great Lakes in both Canada and the United States, and women and men from different backgrounds. The accomplishment of the Water Walkers lies not just in their ability to raise awareness about the state of water, but also to draw women, men, children, and community together as one voice for change. The women carried water from each of the Great Lakes in a copper pot, saying prayers and singing songs of the water along the route. Josephine writes, "The water we carried in our copper pail, always reminded us of our womanly responsibilities as givers of life as Mother Earth gives us, her children."[31] The action of walking is a movement toward change for the present and the future. For many of the women participating in the Water Walk, the walk represents a chance to make a difference. In their call for the 2007 Water Walk, the organizers said, "Please join in this great and wonderful event, through walking, assisting, donating, accommodating, feasting, providing security, hosting events, and spreading the word—everything helps us all."[32] Everything does help us all when it comes to taking action to save the world's most precious resources—Nibi/water.

As one of the organizers of the Water Walk, Josephine has written in her journal log:

> This journey with the pail of water that we carry is our way of Walking the Talk. We really don't have to say anything. Just seeing us walk is enough to make a person realize that, yes, we are carriers of the water. We are carrying the water for the generations to come. Our great grandchildren and the next generation will be able to say, yes, our grandmothers and grandfathers kept this water for us!![33]

The Water Walk has enabled First Nations women from various communities to be a part of the decision-making process to protect water. In spite of a history of being exploited by government and organizations, First Nations peoples are working together in grassroots movements like the Water Walkers in order to empower their people. By just walking for the right to clean water, the Mother Earth Water Walkers are empowering themselves rather than waiting for either the government or organizations to handle the problems.

This grassroots initiative has not been funded by any government agency or organization, but by the donations of supporters along the route, fundraising efforts at local events, and the money of the Walkers themselves. Josephine notes, "We didn't have any money. We had two vehicles. We had a truck and an old Chevy Lumina that we used for the light that went around to warn people of people walking. And so we started off with donations people gathered at the ceremonies that were at the 'Send Off.'"[34] Through the help of people living along the route, friends, and family, the Water Walkers were given food, water, and support carrying the water. The overall goal has been to gather more numbers, with support from people, groups, and organizations to participate in the regional walks. With more walkers, both women and men, the Water Walkers' message becomes stronger and louder, more publicity is raised, and more First Nations women are aware of their responsibilities to the water.

Josephine has described this walk as a calling, not just for herself, but for all women. She talks about being called upon by not just her Grand Chief of the Midewiwin Lodge, but Mother the Earth herself, to take up the Water Walk around the Great Lakes. There is a spiritual calling to take action in this walk. Josephine writes in her trip journals:

> We are guided by vision and dreams, but most of all we are guided by our Spirit and Spirit Helpers. The journey with the water has become a lifetime experience, in that, the work is year round. More women and young girls are hungering for women teachings. We must feed their hunger. Elders have given advice/direction on how to proceed further. There is a concern by the Elders that First Nations in Canada are not getting the message about our concern for the water. It has been foreseen that I must walk to all the First Nation communities (reservations) along Lake Superior. How this is to be done, I cannot fathom when and how. Only the spirit will guide that journey.[35]

Josephine suggests in her logs that the message the Water Walkers are spreading through their trek around the Great Lakes is not just for First Nations women and their partners, but for all peoples in the region.[36]

The Walker Walkers walked around Lake Erie in 2007 and Lake Michigan in 2008.[37] The conclusion of the walks around all the Great Lakes does not conclude the issues raised by the women like Josephine Mandamin. The message and increased awareness of their concerns for the state of water on the Great Lakes has now been passed on to countless grandmothers, aunties, mothers, and daughters of the Nishnaabeg Nation and to many peoples living in the region. Walks have spread and been conducted along the St. Lawrence River (2009), in all four directions (2011), around Lake Nipigon, Ontario (2012), and Lake Monona, Wisconsin (2012), and Waawaasegaming (2014). As women, we have a great responsibility to the water if we plan to continue to drink and eat the foods supported by the water of the Great Lakes region. Mother the Earth and her mother, Grandmother Moon, count on us to help the water and restore balance to water—to make it clean again for the future generations.

I leave off this section with a quote by Josephine Mandamin, reporting on the Water Walks trek around the Lake Superior region. She writes this in her journal log at the end of her first walk in 2003. The quote encapsulates our responsibilities as women to Earth our Mother and, in a way, it is a vision of the role we as women must fulfill:

> The wonders of miracles and the sheer impact of what innocent prayer can bring melted our hearts and quietly marveled at the reality of what we asked for when we wished for fulfillment of our needs. Needs not wants. The wonderment of coming together of Grandmother Moon with her daughter Aki Kwe, our mother, or as science calls it, the eclipse. In this union, I was awestruck and was held in suspension with tobacco in hand as I listened to our Mother speak to her Mother about her hurts, her pains, and that she is hurting so much, that she can hardly sustain herself to provide for her children. She was telling our Grandmother how we are causing her slow destruction and causing her great pain and many illnesses. On and on she spoke, in much the same way we have spoken to our mothers when we were hurting or when we were telling on someone. Grandmother listened to all her daughter was telling her and spoke, "It's okay my girl, I will look after all things for you. There are those who are still following the teachings, doing their work, those who still keep their stories, their songs, will be recognized and acknowledged when the time comes."[38]

This quote represents a call to action for Nishnaabeg women and all women around the world. The grassroots work of the Water Walkers is an initiative that teaches us we do not need lots of money, the government, or organizations to make change in our own communities as First Nations women and men. All we need is an idea, the strength to carry it through, and the support of the community. The message I take away from the Water Walkers is that we all have our own individual responsibilities as women and men to protect Mother our Earth, not just for us, but also out of respect for our ancestors and those generations yet to come.

Nishnaabe-kwewag, Keepers of the Water

I offer some brief concluding thoughts. It is my hope that Nishnaabeg women, First Nations women, and women in general will hear the call to action in the words offered by the Elders and myself. Since we all need water to survive, is it not up to all of us to protect it? I ask that the thoughts, ideas, and words expressed here be passed on to others, so that the message of protecting this world's most precious resource—water—will reach many ears.

To finish this chapter, I wish to pass on a poem that inspired me to write this paper. The poem comes from a position paper called "Minobimaatisii-win—We Are to Care for Her" by the Women of Bkejwanong Territory (Walpole Island Unceded First Nation). The poem is named "Nibi" and goes as follows:

> **Nibi**
>
> Nishnaabekwe, the Daughters,
> You are the keepers of the water.
> I am Nibi … water … the sacred source,
> the blood of Aki, Mother Earth,
> the force, filling dry seeds to green bursting.
> I am the womb's cradle.
> I purify.
> Nibi, the lifegiver …
> forever the Circle's charge.
> I have coursed through our Mothers veins.
> Now hear my sorrow and my pain
> in the rivers rush, the rain …
> I am your grandchildren's drink.
> Listen, Daughters, always,
> You are keepers of the water.
> Hear my cry,
> For the springs flow darkly now
> through the heart of Aki … Miigwetch/We thank you.[39]

Notes

1 Josephine Mandamin, Deb McGregor, and First Nations Youth, "Women, Traditional Knowledge, and Responsibilities to Water," workshop presented at Indigenous Women: Celebrating Our Diversity, 8th Annual Indigenous Women's Symposium, Peterborough, ON, Trent University, March 16–18, 2007.

2 The Great Lakes consist of Lake Superior, Lake Michigan, Lake Huron, Lake Erie, and Lake Ontario. They sit in the eastern portion of the North American continent and straddle the border of what is now known as Canada and the United States.

3 These terms are from Shirley Ida Williams, *Gdi-nweninaa Our Sound, Our Voice* (Peterborough, ON: Neganigwane Company, 2002), 13–21.
4 Shirley Ida Williams, Native Studies 390: Immersion Spring/Summer Course, Nishinaabe-naadiwiziwin, Trent University, 2004.
5 Williams, *Gdi-nweninaa*, 310.
6 Women of Bkejwanong (Walpole Island) First Nation, "Position Paper, Minobimaatisiiwin, We Are to Care for Here, Bkejwanong—Where the Waters Divide," in Nin.Da.Waab.Jib, General Files, Walpole Island Unceded First Nation.
7 Ibid., 1.
8 Renée Elizabeth Bédard, "An Nishnaabekwe Writes History: An Alternative Understanding of Indigenous Intellectual and Historical Traditions," MA thesis, Frost Centre for Canadian and Native Studies, Trent University, 2004, 65.
9 Shirley Ida Williams, interview by Renée Elizabeth Bédard, March 7, 2007, Peterborough, ON.
10 Winona LaDuke, *Recovering the Sacred: The Power of Naming and Claiming* (Toronto, ON: Between the Lines, 2005), 234–35.
11 Shirley Ida Williams interview.
12 Mandamin et al., "Women, Traditional Knowledge."
13 Shirley Ida Williams interview.
14 Ibid.
15 Mandamin et al., "Women, Traditional Knowledge."
16 Women of Bkejwanong, "Position Paper," 2.
17 Lynn Gehl, "Science Measures, but Doesn't Prevent Water Pollution," *Anishinabek News* (October 2006): 17.
18 Mandamin et al., "Women, Traditional Knowledge."
19 Shirley Ida Williams interview.
20 Ibid.
21 Mandamin et al., "Women, Traditional Knowledge."
22 Ibid.
23 Ibid.
24 Shirley Ida Williams interview.
25 Mandamin et al., "Women, Traditional Knowledge."
26 "Aki/The Land," *Anishinabek News* (September 2006): 7, http://anishinabeknews.ca/wp-content/uploads/2013/04/2006-9.pdf; "Lake Ontario 'Pitiful': Walkers," *Anishinabek News* (July/August 2006): 23; "Nbi/Water: Lifeblood of Mother Earth," in *Anishinabek News* (April 2007): 11; "Walkers Raising Awareness About Water Issues," *Anishinabek News* (May 2005): 17, http://anishinabeknews.ca/wp-content/uploads/2013/04/2005-5.pdf; "Water Protection Spiritual," *Anishinabek News* (October 2006): 17, http://anishinabeknews.ca/wp-content/uploads/2013/04/2006-10.pdf; "Women Carry Copper Pail Around Lake Michigan to Create Awareness," *Anishinabek News* (June 2004): 17.
27 Mandamin et al., "Women, Traditional Knowledge."
28 Ibid.
29 Ibid.
30 Josephine Mandamin, Mother Earth Water Walk, Lake Huron journal entry, 2005, http://www.motherearthwaterwalk.com/?page_id=2180.
31 Josephine Mandamin, Mother Earth Water Walk, Lake Superior journal entry, 2003, http://www.motherearthwaterwalk.com/?page_id=2174.
32 "Nbi/Water: Lifeblood of Mother Earth," 1.
33 Mandamin, Lake Huron journal entry, http://www.motherearthwaterwalk.com/?page_id=2180.
34 Ibid.

35 Ibid.
36 Ibid.
37 "Nbi/Water," 1.
38 Mandamin, Lake Huron journal entry.
39 Women of Bkejwanong, "Position Paper," 5.

Bibliography

"Aki/The Land." *Anishinabek News* (September 2006): 7. http://anishinabeknews.ca/
    wp-content/uploads/2013/04/2006-9.pdf.
Bédard, Renée Elizabeth. "An Nishnaabekwe Writes History: An Alternative Understand-
    ing of Indigenous Intellectual and Historical Traditions." MA thesis, Frost Centre for
    Canadian and Native Studies, Trent University, 2004.
Gehl, Lynn. "Science Measures, But Doesn't Prevent Water Pollution." *Anishinabek News*
    (October 2006): 17.
LaDuke, Winona. *Recovering the Sacred: The Power of Naming and Claiming.* Toronto:
    Between the Lines, 2005.
"Lake Ontario 'Pitiful': Walkers," *Anishinabek News* (July/August 2006): 23. http://anish
    inabeknews.ca/wp-content/uploads/2013/04/2006-7.pdf.
Mandamin, Josephine. Mother Earth Water Walk, Lake Huron journal entry. 2005. http://
    www.motherearthwaterwalk.com/?page_id=2180.
———. Mother Earth Water Walk, Lake Superior journal entry. 2003. http://www.mother
    earthwaterwalk.com/?page_id=2174.
Mandamin, Josephine, Deb McGregor, and First Nations Youth. "Women, Traditional
    Knowledge, and Responsibilities to Water." Workshop presented at Indigenous
    Women: Celebrating Our Diversity, 8th Annual Indigenous Women's Symposium,
    Trent University, Peterborough, ON, March 16–18, 2007.
"Nbi/Water: Lifeblood of Mother Earth." *Anishinabek News* (April 2007): 11. http://
    anishinabeknews.ca/wp-content/uploads/2013/04/2007-4.pdf.
"Walkers Raising Awareness about Water Issues." *Anishinabek News* (May 2005): 17.
    http://anishinabeknews.ca/wp-content/uploads/2013/04/2005-5.pdf.
"Water Protection Spiritual." *Anishinabek News* (October 2006): 17. http://anish
    inabeknews.ca/wp-content/uploads/2013/04/2006-10.pdf.
Williams, Shirley Ida. *Gdi-nweninaa Our Sound, Our Voice*, 13–21. Peterborough, ON:
    Neganigwane Company, 2002.
———. Interview by Renée Elizabeth Bédard. March 7, 2007, Peterborough, ON.
———. Native Studies 390: Immersion Spring/Summer Course, Nishinaabe-naadiwiz-
    iwin, Trent University, Peterborough, ON, 2004.
"Women Carry Copper Pail Around Lake Michigan to Create Awareness." *Anishinabek
    News* (June 2004): 17.
Women of Bkejwanong (Walpole Island) First Nation. "Position Paper,
    Minobimaatisiiwin, We Are to Care for Here, Bkejwanong—Where the Waters
    Divide." Nin.Da.Waab.Jib, General Files, Walpole Island Unceded First Nation.

Water Walk Pedagogy

Violet Caibaiosai

Nibi—water—she is a healer,
is a life-giving force, a catalyst of spiritual and physical
holistic well-being, of renewal, purification, cleansing …
powerful … capable too of life taking

As an Anishinabe-kwe of the Sagamok Anishinabek I lived my early years along the waters of the north shore of Georgian Bay on Lake Huron. It is my great fortune that for the first six years of my life I was raised along the side of my Anishinabe family before being taken to the residential school in Spanish, Ontario, taken to a place of "higher" learning. It would be another three years before I would be set free from residential school, a place where I was broken into many pieces and in so many ways. It would be another forty years before I would recover enough to fully enjoy life again.

Forty-some years later I have finally begun my journey back to regaining a sense of identity—of being Anishinabek. I am sitting in a lodge listening to a grandmother [Josephine Mandamin] talking about walking around Lake Superior. She is there asking for other women to walk with her, stating that she is choosing to do this walk for a number of reasons. She speaks of the desire to walk and pray for water, reminding us that as Anishinabek, it is women's role to do so. At the same time the walk would also be about awareness-making, connecting intergenerationally, and engaging society at large into realizing the impact that we as human beings are having on the waters of this great land.

Sitting there in the Midewiwin teaching lodge I sometimes feel small because I struggle with the use of my original language, Ojibwemowin, and I have always wondered about my place because of that missing knowledge. But in my mind I think to myself that while I may not have my language, I do have my legs and I can walk. I agreed then to help in this walk because, I told myself, this will be easy—all I have to do is walk. Little did I know the impact that the Water Walk would have on me, how it would draw me back to the spirit not only of the land and of water, but of the essence of Creation—and in the end that it would reawaken my whole being. In a very real sense, the life-giving healing spirit of Nibi is what I would come to experience.

With these words I try to honour the beauty of our sacred Creation and the many lessons that I, as only one small perspective of life, had the wondrous opportunity to live through, though English words cannot fully translate such an experience. In doing this I wish to honour and acknowledge my relatives, those spiritual beings who came to me in my days of residential school. They are the ones who encouraged me "to go out now and travel into that other world to learn what I can and then to come home to talk about it." This is homage to a new beginning.

As Anishinabek we are taught to begin each new day by offering *asemma* (tobacco) to the Great Spirit, giving thanks to the Great Spirit, to all our relations within Creation for all that "they" do so that we Anishinabek can have life. We are told by our many Elders that *asemma* was given for us to use in our offerings of prayer; it is our connection to the spirit of all life and that whenever we have need, to use *asemma* in those times of need. In this way we remember our relationships, our interdependence with, and our dependence on Creation.

We also acknowledge Migizi, the Bald Eagle, remembering her/his act of love for us. In offering songs we are reminded of the many gifts Migizi has given so that we may remember his sacrifice. Then comes the expression of gratitude for Nibi and her life-giving spirit, again expressed in prayer, spoken or in song. These Anishinabe teachings are integral to our walk and so each day of the walk begins with an offering of *asemma*, a prayer, and songs as we welcome each new day being grateful for life.

We were given an eagle staff to carry and on that staff were attached long and colourful ribbons, each wrapped around small tobacco ties, a mix of colours that signify the clan colours of Anishinabek. The Water Walk staff was wrapped with the pelt of another of our relatives and finally the gifts of eagle feathers topped the staff, so in many ways we were never alone. All of these actions are ceremonial in nature and as such are very significant and sacred.

The morning sky is one that is known by those who rise early enough to witness the changing of the sky's colour, to hear the songs of birds as they prepare for their day, to bear witness to the first offering of water to the land. Each blade of grass, every silky thread of the spider web is made visible with moisture-laden breath of life. These I notice now because I am up early and outside within Creation.

Chi-miigwetch Gchi-manido, gizhe-manido for the life I have witnessed, to realize all that I had taken for granted before this walk. Now I have seen the smallest of beings who crawl upon the Earth, those who make their way to the tip of a blade of grass making their prayer offering to give thanks for life on each new day. In my mind I see the shimmering silvery mesh, millions of tiny water droplets blanketing all of Creation, giving just a taste of Nibi, the sacred life-giving medicine. I can only marvel at this wondrous display of Creator's work and the intangible workings of the Great Mystery and the spirit of life. I am further reminded that I, too, am comprised of water for as I stand and listen to Anishinabe-kwe singing their morning songs to us as we begin our day's journey, I am thrilled at the sight of their breath. Like vapour I could see their spirit song being lifted to Creator as their breath spiralled upward; yes, I remember, we, too, are of water. Then again on another early morning our tents glisten with the nurturing presence, a frosty crispness. I begin now to remember the many teachings that I had heard over the years that other beings in Creation remember and follow their original instructions.

As I walk I notice everything. I am reminded that I am part of Creation, and I am where I am meant to be. All of our relatives, our Elders, come to greet us along the roadside. A bird follows all along the lake, whose song echoes ahead, seemingly telling all of Creation that we are coming, praying. I start to realize that when praying for water, I am also praying for all of Creation, asking that healing will come to the land and the waters. Moose sounding in the woods, porcupine waddling on the shoulder of the road, raven soaring overhead, bear watching from a field . . . these ones show themselves perhaps to remind us that they, too, are still here. Walking awakens me to see to how our human behaviours have impacted their lives, and then I start to recognize the pattern, how all of *Anishininabe-mino-bimaadiziiyaan* (The Way of a Good Life) has been changed by the influences of a differing world view.

I notice one day that the pail is low in water, but heavy in weight and wonder if it is because of the polluted lands we are walking through, or if it is the heaviness that our Mother Earth might be feeling. We seem to have forgotten about her and all the work she does for all of life. This observation stays with me to this day, the heaviness of such a small amount of water.

We walk now through an area of new construction where trees are being cut and the land cleared for a new housing subdivision. As I walk through I witness a family of ducks as they fly off out of fear, noting that their small nesting homeland is shrinking drastically; I tell them, "I know how you feel." The sound of heavy machinery is deafening, and as I watch our Mother Earth's body being gouged open, I wonder whether *asemma* was offered first. I am thinking that it was likely not even considered. In my mind my spirit is thinking of how she is being raped, and the words of an Elder come back into my head: "If you want to know what's happening to women, look at the Earth, for what is happening to her is happening to women."

Tears course down my face, and I cannot stop them as I recognize the truth behind those words. Yes, I start now to look at my own history—of how I was "trained" in residential school to accept without question all that was happening to me; I was told not to question people in positions of authority. Being a child and not knowing the English language, I asked, "Who is authority?" The answer was "Anyone who is older than you are." My history is full of authority figures taking advantage of my physical being, of sexual molestation and assault in residential school and foster homes. The Elder's words are ringing in my ears, and the tears will not stop. Nibi, that sacred healing medicine, is finally doing her work for my spirit. For my entire growing-up life, I had put into practice the words of the nuns. I accepted what happened and I didn't tell. Now in this walk, I am free. I know that Creation knows what I have experienced and will not judge me for my history.

Another day in a string of rainy days and the blisters between my toes and on my feet have grown and are rubbing, burning. By now I had developed the habit of putting my feet inside plastic bread bags and then step into my running shoes, but Nibi—water—managed to make her way into my shoes nonetheless. The water in my water-logged shoes surrounds my toes, separating and cushioning, bringing much-needed relief to my aching feet!! How incredible a finding is this! Again, Nibi brought her healing and I could keep on walking.

It is the third year of the Water Walk (2005), and we are walking for twenty-six days, from April 30 to May 25, around Lake Huron. I am heading along the north shore of Lake Huron, the land of my childhood before and after residential school. Memories of my parents trying to raise their family in the face of the obstacles of racism, hatred, discrimination, their days of residential school, of being Anishinabek in a non-Anishinabek world, and, lastly, alcohol. I am grateful for the forgiveness I had learned by the time I reached the age of nineteen, for by then I, too, had travelled and experienced their experience and was now gaining some inkling of understanding. As I walked I shed tears, walking past the numerous foster homes where I was placed, grateful for the many lessons learned in each, both positive and negative. The gravel of the road's shoulders bear my tears as I remembered residential school days, girls running away from our school, the sorrow of my community at the death of another youth choosing to leave this physical realm rather than continue life. The memories are numerous, and these I share with the spirit of the land and of the water. As I remember a painful life story, Nibi again is doing her healing work, washing away toxic memories through my tears, lifting and re-energizing my spirit. Yes, an almost empty pail can feel so heavy!

The walk's end is near and I have been reconnected with the spirit of new beginnings. My spirit has been revitalized and now the walk is painless.

Gchi-miigwetch gakina Anishinaabe-mino- bimaadiziiyaan for all of the lessons, the teachings, the caring you have shown me. *Gchi-miigwetch Eshkagamikwe* (many great thanks to Mother Earth) for the shoulders who have borne my tears and burdens, for listening to my thoughts and prayers, and for being the greatest example of unconditional love and forgiveness that I have ever known. I am aware now there is a disconnection from our lands and teachings because of colonization. I am committed to walking a life-enhancing path and listening, abiding by the teachings, the original instructions found in our Creation stories that teach us about how to live with sustainable relationships—*biimadiziwin*—good life ways. My *dodem* (clan) is *mukwa*—the Bear—and one of our practices is working with the medicines and water; *chi-mashkiki* is a main medicine for sustainable life. Walking for water has deepened and enhanced my connection to her spirit and as such is an essential pedagogy for those of us who live downstream—we have much to learn from the medicine spirit of water.

Miigwetch gaaye Nibi for doing your work of healing, cleansing, of accepting our *asemma* each and every day, hearing and answering our prayers with the many miracles you have brought into our lives. The Water Walk for the Great Lakes began in 2003 and each summer there was a walk for each of the lakes. What was significant in this walk to me was the realization that all the teachings of our ancestors—which had been told to me about the spirit of our ancestors being within the Earth upon which we walk, for example—are so very true and very real. This spiritual element is extremely beneficial for the holistic well-being of those willing to speak with and listen to the spirit of all Creation.

The original purpose of the Water Walk had been about caring for Nibi and to encourage those of different world views to better understand why we must take better care of her; this continues to be the case with ongoing walks. We all need clean water for good life, and we all need to recognize that we can contribute toward improving the health of all Creation, not just human beings.

I am grateful to be Anishinabe, to continue to receive teachings from what is often referenced as the "spirit realm." As a child I often preferred hearing those ones as often words of encouragement and support came from there. Walking was in one sense a "fast" for Nibi, our Mother Earth, and all of Creation. When fasting anywhere, we are making spiritual connection, opening our spirit to the knowledge that is of that space. We dream at times when we are asleep, and at other times we are blessed with a dream when we are awake, like a vision. Nonetheless, it is one of the most incredible ways to receive knowledge.

Figure 9.1   Lake Superior—the "most powerful lake to walk around" (from an email by Violet Caibaiosai). (*Source:* Violet Caibaioisai)

I am grateful to those who struggled to retain and remember our ceremonies and teachings, and who continue to resist and especially to those who work to revitalize and enliven the gifts we have been given as Anishinabek!! *Mii iew!*

A Response to Pascua Lama
Cecilia Vicuña

Hearing is gold, Manquemilla, Gold Condor

The glacier is the origin of the word "cool" and the first "chill," the slow ice of an inner music that dies when no one wants to hear it.

Hollow cow they melt down letting out a lament.
An alveolus birthing its own death.

The messenger of the waters, the intermediary between the worlds, the condor is the glacier becoming extinct.

The boy/condor, guardian of the glacier was buried alive by the Incas, at the birthplace of the Mapocho river, on the summit of El Plomo, so the valley we now call "Santiago" would never lack water.

He was buried and then forgotten, only to be found 500 years later by treasure hunters. They found him to un-find him, turning him into an "archaeological object." They said: "this is the cult of the heights" and the phrase placed him in the past. Calling him the "mummy of El Plomo" they separated him from us, but the boy/condor is still asleep and his dream comes alive each time someone feels a connection with the water.

Now, the boy/condor comes back to the national consciousness at a time when the glaciers are in danger of being sold, contaminated and lost. He reappears when Chile is about to choose between hearing or not hearing the music of an ancient connection with the glacier and the land, a specificity of place, with its own particular tone.

A place is a sound, and a way of hearing it.
A web of interrelationships, an exchange between people and earth. The space of
naming.

To change the meaning of a name is to change the world.

In Alto del Carmen, in the Huasco Valley, the land of the ancestors of Gabriela
Mistral, Chile is choosing a meaning:
"Alto del Carmen" could mean "The Height of Poetry," or the place where poetry
comes to an end. Today, the Huasco Altino peoples, descendants of the Diaguitas
are the caretakers of the ancient vision of the glacier as a sacred place that
guarantees life. We have the possibility of hearing the music of place, in all its
potential, or to put a stop to life by giving away the glaciers and the mines to
the neo-colonial powers.

But, are we hearing their voice? our own forgotten inner voice, or that of the
System that says: *"Only the dollar matters" "And you, what do you know?"*
*"Now, we are the owners of the mines, and cyanide is the new guardian of the
waters."*

Water is gold
The blood of the earth
Hearing us.

The slowly moving ice is the testimony of our ancient relationship with the land,
and the ritual maintenance of its flow, our true cultural patrimony. The future
heritage of a way of being in harmony with the land, a music that sustains the
earth and human life at the same time.

In Australia, the Aboriginals have begun to recover their dignity and land through
poetry: the ritual maintenance of the landscape, their "songlines." In Chile, the
condor and the water of our stories, are our "songline." The unacknowledged
ritual of quipu making, the memory of its people, the continuity of our ancestral
world.

part iii

shared ethical and embodied practices

Moving with Water
Relationships and Responsibilities
Alannah Young Leon and Denise Marie Nadeau

The reciprocal relationship between people and water was clearly defined in Aboriginal communities of the past, for, as elder Ellen White said, "the old people always knew what the water was and what the water said and how to connect with it."[1]

Josephine (Mandamin), Anishnabe water walker, said, "our relationship with water is not just [about] our relationship with giving life; it's a relationship [based in] thinking how we live on this earth. That's really a lifelong learning."[2]

We—Alannah Young Leon and Denise Nadeau—have collaborated since the late 1990s in bringing together embodied pedagogies and water responsibilities from our respective epistemological traditions. Our intention has been to work from body wisdoms to create education tools for reconciling Indigenous and settler relationships. For Denise, this has been a journey of moving from an anthropocentric epistemology to a world view in which humans are not the centre of the universe, and where all living beings are interconnected in a web without hierarchy. With that awareness, she has learned that humans have responsibilities toward water. For Alannah, it has been one of deepening her understanding of Indigenous responsibilities and acting on them. Accordingly, we centre Indigenous traditions in our education and advocacy work as we continue to grapple with Eurocentric systems of knowledge that are both subjugating and privileged. We have developed curriculum for Indigenous front-line women, education and health institutions, and truth and reconciliation initiatives. In much of this work we combine dance/movement therapy with Indigenous traditional teachings and spiritual practices and facilitate group work that supports respectful relationship building and Indigenous resurgence.

The invitation of the Downstream Project was to consider what "creative and ethical practices offer us in this moment as we focus together on the need to respect water." We bring our reflections on the creative process and the ethical considerations we incorporated in our workshop, entitled Moving with Water, and as advisers to the Downstream planners. We consider the ethics and protocols regarding working with water in Indigenous territories, and add further reflections on how we ourselves have continued to flow with our responsibilities toward and with water. In this chapter we continue an ongoing dialogue about how we work in the interface spaces, linking our responsibilities to transformation and a deepening of our relationship with water. We each write in our separate voices and as well in a united voice, representing how the coming together from different locations and traditions has enriched our work.

We begin with our respective locations and a description of our individual creative explorations of our relationship with water. We each use what is known as the Tamalpa Life-Art Process,[3] a movement-based expressive arts practice that combines an intermodal use of dance, visual art, and creative writing to explore and access the wisdom of the mental, physical, emotional, and spiritual body. A process we use in much of our group work, it helps us get to the heart of what we want to share and keeps us fluid and embodied as we write. We then discuss how we incorporated protocols into the workshop design. In our conversation, we discuss how we interact with Indigenous knowledge teachings and describe how we engage with the corresponding responsibilities and protocol principles. We describe the Moving with Water workshop we facilitated and conclude with reflections on embodied practice with water.

Alannah

hi? ch-ka si?em̃ ?i ?u chxw?ew ?ey ?al ?e:ntha Alannah tali can ? 2X, Opaskwayak and Peguis Nations in Manitoba. To show respect for the Coast Salish–occupied territories, where I currently live and work, I introduce myself in the hən̓q̓əmin̓əm̓ language. Language is intimately connected to relationships with lands and waters and our corresponding responsibilities to them. Indigenous protocols remind me that I must acknowledge whose territories I am on and explain where my peoples are from geographically. I have been a visitor to the unceded and occupied Coast Salish territories since 1990 and remain committed to these ongoing relationships with the peoples of these nations. I do this by maintaining respectful relationships, by making space for local Indigenous voices, and by supporting local community-initiated events.

I live by the delta, where the salt waters meet the fresh waters, described as the north arm of where the Fraser River meets the Salish Sea. The physical description of the xʷməθkʷəy̓əm (Musqueam—People of the River Grass) territories and the meeting of the physical land and seascapes inform my behaviours. The physical environment is my teacher and reinforces my understanding of the Indigenous teaching "all my relatives." This phrase describes my epistemological understanding and my intention to become "a good relative" to the local communities as well as to the communities I am related to genealogically. Waters are integral to the peoples and the spiritual responsibilities I hold. I don't speak for the local territories; I speak only from my own genealogical locations and understandings.

I am a Midewiwin woman from the Anishnabe Muskekiniwak Opasqwayak Cree (Treaty #5) and Peguis Nations (Treaty #1). My understanding of the relationship with water is that it is my responsibility to take care of the water because to take care of the water is to take care of and enhance life. Water is the embodiment of the spirit of life.[4] Women take care of this responsibility through song, ceremony, and conscious intention. It is a decolonizing and resurgent activity—it is a creative process for the benefit of humans for the purpose of renewing our relationships as indicated in our constitutional narratives and laws. Anishnabe teachings tell me that we are born of, dependent on, and created in water. With this understanding I notice that I continue to follow the water, just as I did when I was born. I am expected to listen and continue to learn from the water. Nipi is the Anishnabe word for water and part of my responsibility is to sing for the water—to know the songs that continue to deepen this sacred relationship. The wisdom of the waters helps me to live a good life, teaches me how to be a good relative, and how to flow in movement from one place to another. As I continue to reflect on the Moving with Water workshop we designed for the Downstream Project, I am reminded that it is not enough to theorize; we must act. My actions are described as my work or my responsibilities. Part of the intention of this decolonizing work is to provide alternatives to binary thinking and to model multi-dimensional constitutional expressions of an ongoing creative and embodied practice.

In preparation for the workshop, I drew on paper where the Red River and the Assiniboine rivers intersect—these are the waters where I was born. One river flows north and the other east to west. The Red River has a very powerful history in terms of the Métis Rebellion and historically has been an important place of trade. Where the Red River and the Assiniboine River converge is now commonly referred to as the "Forks," or downtown Winnipeg. This is a powerful place, sometimes known as "the heart of Turtle Island." The name "Manitoba" comes from the Cree word Manitowapow or the Anishnabek word Manitopau, both meaning "the strait of the spirit," which some have described as the sound of the water meeting the rocks, is much like the sound or the description of the movement of a beating drum, and the experience of resonating the pulsation of life. It is the movement, the transformative quality that gives me hope. I translate this wish to mean that it is my responsibility to listen to the land and the waters with the intention of acting as a relative to the spirit, land, and water. The waters from the Red and the Assiniboine converge in Winnipeg, which is a Cree word describing muddy water and is the place where I was born. This place name tells me something about the roles and responsibilities I will have throughout life. The navigation of cross-currents and muddy waters describes my genealogy and in part is a resource that can inform my choices from moment to moment.

As a preparatory exercise I begin to move from south to north as the Red River does, much like arterial blood is fast and forceful. Then I consider the name of the Assiniboine River, which means the "stone water people" or the "allies." The river's movement weaves back and forth like a snake, this weaving back and forth movement I demonstrate or embody; I notice these movements are similar to the river's character and are venous-like in personality. Venous blood in the physical body has a cleansing function—the form and function of the rivers teach me to keep moving to reach for health, and the snake teaches me to use movements that rejuvenate and transform or transmute poison into healing properties. The Assiniboine River flows from east to west and merges at the Red River. The cross-current movements are like synovial fluid in the joints of my physical body, and I notice the flexibility and fluidity in my movements. I learn from the rivers' movements by mirroring their form and their functions in my own physicality. I then ask: What do these bodies of water want me to know? The explorations thus far ask that I continue to transform and to rebuild my relationship with waters, to continue to listen, to learn, and to interact responsibly, knowing the only constant is change and to respond fluidly.

In response to the question "What does water want me to know?" I also used aspects of the "life art process" as a tool to support expressions of the work. To my surprise, I drew a diagram, a creative representation of water: two hydrogen atoms, one oxygen molecule, and flowing lines representing the cross-currents. The formula H_2O represents in part the Eurocentric scientific way of looking at water. Moving from the macro movements of the watersheds to the micro movements of the molecular describes my process of increasing intimacy at the physical body level, and with the dynamic river movements. My drawing of the water molecule teaches me to continue to embody my relationship with water and to decolonize my practice and helps me to notice my habituated stances and the corresponding options for fluidity. To demonstrate this, I provide my understandings through narratives that describe my kinship genealogies. These genealogies are located within specific geographies. The place names describe the physical landscapes and points toward my corresponding responsibilities, in this case to navigate multiple streams of consciousness. Sometimes this means fluidly embodying murky cross-currents between Eurocentric knowledge and Indigenous land-based knowledge systems.

The water and Earth are my life companions—they accompany my spirit force both inside and outside my body. I contemplate and embody the grandmother principles that tell me water is responsible for supporting and enhancing all life. I know that my responsibility—my work—is to participate in creative water advocacy initiatives. This creativity is reflected in the diverse peoples and in the planet's rich biodiversity. Indigenous thought differs from colonial Eurocentric thought in the intention to remain interrelated with each other and with the non-human. Through song, ritual, and creativity, we renew and deepen our decolonization work by making commitments to enhancing life and interconnectedness. Indigenous knowledge is tied to specific places and contributes to the planet's biodiversity and to the functioning of water ecology.

I begin to move like water, I embody the water through various movements, the same water that has been here for billions of years, circulating and flowing into many forms of water, clouds, ice, mists, and torrential rains. I am flowing, iridescent, clear, cold, and in places stagnant, poisoned, life enhancing, and all knowing. I continue to be held, supported, and inspired by my relationship to the wisdom of water, and I realize that the water connects the past, present, and future just as the DNA in our blood contains this knowledge.

The Life-Art Process also includes embodied writing. From this practice I have written this poem about my exploration of moving with water.

"As long as the sun shines, grass grows and rivers flow."[5]

my blood the embodiment of water
flowing through veins and
arteries like the rivers and streams

water the embodiment of spirit
forever flowing
cycling through space and time
mirroring earth & sky

body & spirit
water shows me how we are related
through my fluid movements

pulsing, like the beating heart
of our grandmother moon—Nokomis
emanating kindness and
timeless integrity for enhancing life

water homelands—Manitowabo—
place in the narrows
flow right relationships

a stem an artery representing the responsibility of life
pumps, feeds, circulates
water the lifeblood of our homes

kinship of rivers mapping our bodies
priceless waters, like life
water dams, disrupting our natural connections

renewing our water relationships
flowing like the waters
through prayer, song & movements

Snauq calm waters resting
gathering place
water meets the shorelines

where the salt meets the fresh waters
water flows where the body systems meet the shores
showing me the paths.

Denise

My responsibilities toward water are defined by my relationship with place and ancestry. I am originally from Quebec, raised in Montreal, with family origins and ties in Gespe'gewa'gi, known as the Gaspé Coast, and the territory of the Mi'gmaq peoples. I am a twelfth-generation Quebecer of mixed French, Scottish, Irish, and English heritage. My French ancestors intermarried with the Mi'gmaq and settled in the Gaspé region. I spent all my summers there until I was eighteen. As I learn about water responsibilities, I have come to realize I have to honour the relationships and the responsibilities, defined by my ancestry, to the waters and peoples of the Gaspé region. These waters include Mawi Poqtapeg (Baie des Chaleurs) and two rivers that flow into it—the Epsegeneg Sipu (Port Daniel River) and the Gesgapegiag Sipu (Cascapedia River). The immediate threats to these waters are the prospect of oil and gas exploration in the Maqtugweg (Gulf of Saint Lawrence), rail and tanker transmission of tar sands bitumen to the port of Belledune, fracking, and overfishing of dwindling resources.

Like many from immigrant families who have moved from their homelands to other regions far away, I hold dual responsibilities. I live in the territory of the Kómoks Nation, which is on the eastern coast of Vancouver Island on the Salish Sea. I have lived on Coastal Salish territory, both in the Comox Valley and in Vancouver, for about thirty years. My immediate water engagement is with the watersheds of the Trent and Puntledge rivers, and working to protect the waters of Baynes Sound from a new form of aquaculture called "sea ranching" of sea cucumbers and geoducks clams destined for the elite market in China. In Vancouver I was involved in the actions of the xwmuthkwey'um (Musqueam—where the river grass grows) Nation to protect the ancient burial grounds of Cəsnaʔəm (right relations; the name of the place is telling us how to behave), a village site uncovered by developers who wanted to build condos near the banks of the Fraser River.

I continue to spend one-third of my life in Montreal and Gespe`gewa`gi, one-third in Coastal Salish territory, and one-third asleep and dreaming (all of us spend an average of a third of our day asleep). It is this dream world and the fluidity of water that keeps me flowing between these two place-based worlds and the multiple relationships I have in and with them. Raised in a Eurocentric tradition, for many years I saw water as outside myself, not as something to which I was intimately connected. My perspective has changed after engaging with Indigenous knowledge systems, and practising body-based therapies that moved me out of my head and into heart-centred knowing. To some extent I have been "indigenized," and I look for ways to build bridges between Indigenous teachings and post-colonial eco-feminist Christianity. This branch of Christianity is developing an ethic that challenges the anthropomorphism of colonial Christianity.[6] As well, a recent movement that is calling for "watershed discipleship" is emerging in progressive Christian circles in Canada and the United States.[7] This is a form of ecological theology that respects Indigenous teachings while uncovering within the Hebrew and Christian scriptures post-colonial readings of texts that require justice for water and for all non-human beings. I believe we need to find commonalities in all sacred teachings that address human responsibilities to non-human beings, and especially to water.

Like Alannah, I wanted this chapter to reflect the embodied and creative ways we work with and support relationships and responsibilities with water. Both individually and together we facilitate workshops around water. As well I teach about water in my university teaching. We invite people to explore water with their bodies, to draw, to sing, and to dance, so that we are moving beyond a conceptual relationship with water. To write this chapter I need to apply the Life-Art Process to move me out of the more linear way I usually fall into when writing.

I place a large piece of flipchart paper and markers before me on the floor. I spend a few minutes warming up my body, making sure that I have moved every body part, and then I begin. What is my intention in writing this article? I want to feel the sacredness and fluidity of water in my body as I write it, and to express to others the sacredness of that connection. I want to explain the process we use in workshops so that others can replicate what they can. I want to transmit my feelings about the sacredness of water and my understanding of my relationships and responsibilities around water. And lastly, I want to describe our work in a way that that does not distance the reader.

After a few minutes of prayer to help me centre in the process, I spend some time embodying through movement my intention, exploring feeling water's sacredness, reaching through my core, through the heart and out through the mouth with hands in a lotus-like shape, and then arms moving up to the sky, hands opening, and letting my arms slowly move down to the sides. I reach to the earth and tenderly cup hands around the water and offer it to the sky. I repeat, expand, and develop these moves. Then I turn to my paper to draw.

I remember Michael Blackstock's Blue Ecology image from the Downstream gathering. He complements the hydrologic cycle with the Blue Ecology cycle—adding spirit, respect, balance, harmony, and unity—and includes the Sky world (the Spirit World), the Water World, the Earth World, and the Underworld.[8] I remember his circular image, noting the moon and sun and the cycle of the salmon, which he included. Somehow all this is in my body-mind as I first draw a variation of the hydrologic cycle and then add the flow of water in and through the human form. We teach the seven fluid systems in our workshops, and I draw them in different colours: red for the venous blood system and the arterial blood system, yellow for lymph (as white would not show on the white paper), green for cellular fluid, blue for interstitial, purple for synovial, and orange for cerebral spinal. I taste my own saliva and mentally add that as it is clear and part of the glandular fluids, perhaps it is an eighth system. My drawn human form is drinking water from a blue cup, peeing yellow into the groundwater, which runs into the river, ocean, evaporates into the sky, and comes back as rain. I could add sweat, tears, womb waters, and bile, but it is clear from my drawing that our bodies are part of this cycle.

My drawing is pretty basic, but I am not happy with it. How limited is the hydrologic cycle in its understanding of interconnectedness? Where are the salmon and the rest of the spirit world? I can see my drawing is not expressing what I want, and I move to enactment—dancing my drawing. I begin to explore my fluid systems, and as I move through each of the systems and then follow the water that leaves my body and is absorbed into the earth and rain, suddenly in my mind's eye I make a breakthrough.

This time my drawing is more abstract. Blue lines flow from the base to the sky in an oval shape, then I add green for the plant life and its energetic exchange with water, and then I add yellow for the sacred energy pouring through the blue and green. This is the spirit streaming through water, plants, sunlight, and darkness. And then finally I put in the middle a swirling and curving solitary orange line that touches both the top and the bottom of the oval. I know this is it. And now I enact the drawing. I feel the fluidity of my body connecting with the water cycle and I know that this has captured what I want to explain.

To feel the sacredness of water, we humans must become fluid and feel our fluidity. We are 70 percent water, as is the planet's surface. To feel our fluidity, we must soften so we can flow like the orange line in my drawing. In order to feel and be connected, we need to be soft and fluid, not hard and muscular. We have become so individuated and brain-mind controlled that we can no longer feel a sense of interconnection. Violence, be it of the dominant culture or personal experiences of sexism, racism, colonialism, or physical violence, leaves the body armoured, contracted, with shallow breathing, a hard belly, and with no sense of the vitality of the chi energy and inner flow that connects us with the planet.

Eurocentric science records that all the water in our body is replaced seventeen times a year and that what comes in and goes out—in breath, urine, sweat, tears—is part of a larger cycle, which includes streams, rivers, oceans, rain, snow, sleet, hail, vapour, and evaporation.[9] This flow, the movement of water, transmits the constant flux that exists in the universe. Michael Blackstock's Blue Ecology cycle illustrates our interconnection through water with spirits, sun, moon, and the animal kingdom. As Indigenous teachings affirm, everything is related; we are not isolated but are part of the whole. Through water, we can enact and feel that connection. Water is both fluid and specific. We are connected in our bodies to particular watersheds and bodies of water that have become part of who are, whether we are aware of it or not.

Below is the image that has evolved from my initial drawing of our interconnection with water, an image that includes the heart as the pump of our fluids and the heart-mind open to the energy of water, land, and sky.

Figure 11.1 Moving with Spirit. (*Source:* Denise Nadeau)

Indigenous Protocols

Our first engagement with the Downstream project was in an advisory role for the program. We provided input on the protocols and design for Indigenous content and structure. These processes are decolonizing in that they help us engage with particular knowledges and peoples in relationship within specific places. This requires knowledge of local protocols. Engaging with Indigenous protocols informs both the process and product of our work. We braid them throughout to share our experience from working with local Indigenous nations. Protocols help us to facilitate a respectful relationship with our implicit knowledge of who we are, what we value, and how we engage with other nations in whose territories we are guests. They also inform how we engage in our own "homelands."

One of the first protocols is to have representation from local nations in local territories and, in this case, from the Lower Mainland of Vancouver, where the gathering took place. Opening each morning were traditional knowledge keepers who shared teachings from the local Indigenous nations: xʷməθkwəy̓əm (Musqueam), Sḵwx̱wú7mesh (Squamish), and Səl̓ílwətaʔ Selilwitulh (Tsleil-Waututh) on Coast Salish territories.

Larry Grant from Musqueam opened the first day. Welcoming us to the territory and giving teaching from the lands and waters, he used pre-contact place names to indicate long-term relationships with the lands where the conference took place. Marie/Amy George from Tsleil-Waututh explained that Snauq (the gathering place or sandbar), called False Creek by the settlers, is the name of the area where the event took place. She blessed the gathering with an ancient song from her family. Chief Bill Williams from the Squamish spoke of the local watersheds and how his community has worked to protect these waterways. Art Leon from Sts'ailes provided a welcome song about the balance required between genders and between humans and non-humans. This public song comes from his family and from the lands and waters, strengthens our relationship responsibilities to these territories, and is not intended as a form of entertainment.

In order to follow the protocol of balanced gender representation, Alannah and Violet Caibaiosai, Midewiwin water women, led an adaptation of a water ceremony from their territories. They began by singing a public water song from the Mother Earth Water Walk website. We had it available for participants to view and participate.

These are the words in Ojibwemowin and English:

> Ne-be Gee Zah- gay- e- goo
> Gee Me-gwetch -wayn ne- me – goo
> Gee Zah Wayn ne- me- goo
>
> Water, we love you.
> We thank you.
> We respect you.[10]

In order to protect the integrity of the ceremonial context, we cannot describe this water ceremony. Indigenous ceremonies have been misappropriated, misrepresented, and exploited as a common practice of colonialism. There is a need to protect the integrity of ceremony, the intention of which is renewal and regeneration. Connected to this is the protocol of not taking pictures, videos, or audio tapings of the ceremony. You are not totally present with your intentions if you are trying to save or preserve the experience for another time. This is one way we navigate away from ceremony being seen as public spectacle.

During the water ceremony someone did take a picture and did not ask if it was okay to take it. Because we had not given explicit directions to not take pictures during the ceremony, we had to interrupt the ceremony to ask people not to take photographs. In a case like this, it would have been preferable for the person who had not sought consent to delete the photos after the ceremony.[11]

These are some examples of our understandings of Indigenous ceremonial protocols that guide our work. First is collaborating with local nations in the design of the conference so as to accurately have their voices represented, as opposed to having them as an add-on or afterthought. Second is making sure to have equal representation from different local nations, third is gender balance, and fourth is protection and adaptation of ceremony appropriate for the context. In doing this, our collective work facilitates relationships so that we move beyond colonial cosmopolitanism.

Moving with Water Workshop

Creativity is one intervention we employ in both our personal, political, and professional lives. Creativity comes from an implicit place within—a unique life force we all carry. We are challenged to bring these implicit gifts found within into the world to benefit both the collective and ourselves. Dreams, like our creativity, are key indicators that help to inform our search to bring these unique gifts forward. It is a life's work in constant process.

To facilitate turning from these implicit places to explicit actions, we use expressive arts and embodiment practice within a contemporary ceremonial ritual framing as the primary tools of our work. These are decolonizing in that they engage us in a form of knowing that is different from rational linear thinking, opening us to the world of embodied spirit. Artistic knowing engages our intuition, inner wisdom, and captures our emotions through the use of symbols, shape, movement, song, music, and colour. Through the arts we can access the movements of the spirits. In expressive arts the focus is not on the creation of a piece of art or product but on the process of creativity.[12] As with ceremony, with expressive arts we are transformed and can give expression to our commitments and values in the world.

Our intention in the Moving with Water workshop was to support the exploration and experience of the interconnection with both waters within and the watersheds around us, and the responsibilities that come with both. To do this we first provided an embodied experience of where and how water functions in our bodies. We then had participants embody a water body they were related to, first through drawing it and then through movement or dancing it. Our third step was to bring participants together in a collective water ritual with movement or dance. This was a bit too ambitious for an hour-and-a-half-long session, and we share here both the strengths and weaknesses of the session and what we would now do to improve it.

We opened with Alannah singing a public water song and sharing water teachings from her Anishnabe tradition. If we were doing the workshop in an explicitly interfaith context, Denise would share water teachings from the Christian tradition. Sometimes we invite participants to sing the Water Walkers' water song, and sometimes we open with a water dance that comes from the European Gaelic sacred circle dance tradition. All these approaches affirm water as spirit.

We then do a movement exploration of the fluid systems in the body. While it is common knowledge that the body is 70 percent water, few understand exactly what that means. Drawing on Bonnie Bainbridge Cohen and Andrea Olsen's work, we invite participants to experience each of seven fluid systems in the body.[13] This is an invitation to movement and to specific movements. Each fluid system moves through the body in a different way and we ask participants to simulate the movement impulses of each fluid. This does not involve copying a leader; rather, each person is asked to explore the metaphor for each fluid in his or her own way. Denise leads the participants through each system and movement form. Arterial blood is experienced in energized, fast, interactive movement; venous blood is expressed in slow swinging, a low movement, involving release of control; lymph fluids are experienced in the pull between periphery and centre, with both focused and accurate movement aimed at a target; synovial fluids are found in the jiggling of joints in the body; cerebrospinal fluid is reflected in low, undulating movements of pelvis and spine; interstitial fluids are experienced in muscular pulsing movements throughout the entire body; cellular fluids are reflected in quiet, slow, almost meditative movement in place.

This experience allows participants to explore a range of movement that is connected to their inner being. It provides a free movement vocabulary for those who are fearful of dancing in a group. At the end of the exploration we ask participants to share in pairs about their experience and then to offer anything they might want to say to the larger group. We close this activity with a reflection on the pulsating rhythms in the body and the value of being in our fluids when we experience our body (as opposed to hardening in our muscles). The integration of fluidity in our lives allows us to consider open time, and to flow with transitions and emotional expressions. All movement supports the flow of fluids in our bodies and works against tension and holding—a decolonizing dynamic in itself. If we are fluid, we are harder to control and are less controlling.

In the second section of the session we explore embodying and listening to water bodies that are significant in our lives. There are two intentions here. One is to affirm the importance of connection to place and watersheds/water bodies. In this we are supporting the experience of water as spirit and relative. Secondly, we are inviting participants to see and listen to water bodies as living beings that have needs for their own harmony and balance. Here we challenge the colonial pattern of assuming one knows best, without consultation.

This process first involves participants working alone. They choose a body of water that is important to them, that they have some relationship with at the present moment. It may or may not be a water body that is threatened. We then ask them to do a kinetic drawing of that body of water. This is a one-minute, free-hand drawing that captures the spirit but not the details. We then ask them to write on the other side of their paper and reflect on the following questions:

- What are the characteristics of the water body—the smells, sounds, movements, and rhythms?
- For whom is this water home?
- What functions does this water have?
- What other water bodies is it connected to?

The next stage of the process is asking participants to embody the water and its characteristics—to become the body of water—exploring it with movement and voice/sound. As they do this, we ask them to hear the voice of the water, what it is saying, and whether it has a message for them. They then write the message on the back of their drawing. Each person is then asked to bring back to the group the message and a movement gesture that represents his or her body of water.

In bringing each person's message and movement/gesture back to the group, we enter into a sharing and witnessing process that is an integral part of expressive arts processes. Depending on the time available, participants first share their drawing, movement, and message with one person. This person listens respectfully, and may comment on how the other's story has affected him or her, but does not offer an interpretation. There is then a briefer sharing in the larger group—usually only the movements and messages. In the Downstream workshop we decided to do this in two groups as there was a large number of participants, and we wanted time for each group to be able to move into the third stage of the process—a collective movement piece.

We use, with music, a movement pattern called flocking, where as a group we repeat the movements that each individual offers, rather like a flock of birds flying in symmetry. So each person's water embodiment develops into a group embodiment, fluidly moving from one water body to another.

Our closing moves us into a ritual movement dance involving two large pieces of blue cloth. Each group picks up a cloth and explores moving with it as a group and then in relationship to the other group. The two pieces of cloth begin to move as one, as we come to embody spontaneously the qualities of water and to know we are connected to water and to each other.

In retrospect, we would have developed these activities differently. We did not have time to debrief the workshop in any depth. When Denise was able to do so later in a similar workshop with a Vancouver Island University First Nations Studies class, the group discussed how these explorations of water provided some insights into what decolonization meant for them. Because of time limitations we were not able to speak to the issue of place names and watershed names and the importance of each person learning the traditional names of the water bodies that he or she is relating to. Recovering place names is important for treaty and sovereignty processes, and it is important for alliance building. It shows respect for the water and for the nation in whose territory the water moves.

As we always like to move to action in our work, we fell short here in not creating a ritual that would have engaged the waters around us in the workshop. We did not enact a water ceremony with Snauq. Luckily, Alannah was present when Elder Mona Polacca, one of the thirteen grandmothers, did a small ceremony outside the building where we were gathered and directly engaged with the water.[14] Alannah noted, "She put her offering in the water and sent good intentions for a positive outcome to those who are negotiating water rights in her homeland. She teaches me something—it is not just about teaching and navigating the cross streams; it is about an embodied practice, a direct everyday ongoing minute-to-minute relationship with water."

Embodied Practice

In the opening water ceremony of the Downstream gathering Alannah and Violet adapted Midewiwin water responsibility principles to structure the ceremony. Its purpose was to re-enact women's relationship with water and acknowledge the sacredness of water and its life-enhancing properties. Other ways we flowed with water in ceremony included following the practice of the Mother Earth Water Walkers of offering tobacco to the waters. This is an offering of thanks and acknowledgement of the water. Both this and the water ceremony are embodied practices of reciprocity, giving back to the water, while bringing us back to experiencing water as spirit and relative. Water Walker Doreen Day, along with Masuru Emoto, the Japanese scientist who has photographed the changes in water molecules when they are prayed to, urge us to pray to and, at the least, to speak to water every day. These rituals keep sacredness of water alive for us as well as remind us of our responsibility to water.

Kim Anderson, a Cree/Métis educator, in her report titled "Aboriginal Women, Water and Health: Reflections from Eleven First Nations, Inuit, and Métis Grandmothers," describes how the Aboriginal Grandmothers convey the spiritual qualities of water, and the significance of the spirit of water in creating and sustaining life.[15] The Grandmother stories centre on how water is understood and related to in land-based communities, and how the central role of water in maintaining good health is dependent on how well we manage our relationships with water. If we are disrespectful or careless with this life force, we put ourselves at risk. Ceremony with water is important because it involves the intentional act of connecting, renewing, and maintaining relationship with water.

Anderson explains how in many Aboriginal cultures there are ceremonies that celebrate water, and how waters are prominent in many other ceremonies as they are associated with birth and renewal. One of the Grandmothers, Pauline Shirt, spoke about the use of water during labour and birth in her culture, illuminating how birth is understood as a ceremony. Anderson notes how Grandmother Ellen White talked about how water has always been used in Coastal Salish ceremonies, stating, "We use it in spiritual practices; we use it in the Big House; we use it in burials—we use it for everything."[16] She explains that water is used in life-transition ceremonies, such as naming ceremonies and at puberty ceremonies. Anderson quotes White as she describes the role of water in cleansing ceremonies: "We use water to cleanse certain parts of the body. It's like the knife when the doctor cuts you."[17]

The Grandmothers ask us what we are doing to foster our relationship with water, to re-establish and/or maintain a healthy relationship with water. Grandmother Josephine Mandamin, like Violet Caibaiosai, is active in the Mother Earth Water Walk. The Aki Kwe women from Bkejwanong Territory (Walpole Island) organized themselves to speak for the water to stop Imperial Chemicals from polluting the waters in their territory.[18] Like these women and other participants in the *Downstream* anthology, we engage in water practices large and small. These range from financial donations to supporting the Mother Earth Walk; to supporting and running with the Peace and Dignity runners who came through the Squamish Nation in North Vancouver on their continental run for water; to participating in monthly moon ceremonies that honour the water and singing to the water every day. We have created a collective movement piece with blue cloth for rallies and actions against the Enbridge pipeline and oil tanker proposal. Another embodied ceremonial action for water and lands is the Tar Sands Healing Walk in northern Alberta.[19]

In all of these examples we see how we can foster our lifelong relationship with water. Indigenous communities and allies are demonstrating that it is our responsibility to protect water for future generations. All these actions are embedded in ceremony. Indigenous ceremonial principles validate the water spirit as sacred and integral to life enhancement. Singing to the water is an aspect essential for an embodied relationship, so we often teach folks to sing the local Indigenous public songs in longer workshops. When water is sung for and prayed for, it becomes medicine—a life-enhancing spirit. Ceremony provides a framework for how we renew our relationships with water because it re-establishes right relationships among ourselves as humans and with the rest of the non-human beings in Creation.

The enactment of ceremony with water is neither perfunctory nor merely symbolic. A Moroccan French anthropologist, Frédérique Apffel-Marglin, who has studied the ritual behaviours of Indigenous peoples in Peru and India, illustrates how what she calls "ritual enactments" to land and water can affect these bodies. She uses the terminology of performativity in describing how rituals function in an Indigenous world view to invoke the spirit of the land or water in order to contribute to their regeneration.

> Ceremonial rituals can be understood as collective action, engaging humans, non-humans and other than humans for the purpose of generating and regenerating continuity and a livable common place…. These practices are not acts of representation; they are performances or enactments … where all are participants are called upon to jointly weave a world with a pattern in which all contribute to the outcome—a world in which the "we" is not emphatically anthropocentric.[20]

Our embodied practice emerges from this framework. Apffel–Marglin notes that in Indigenous world views, there is a continuity and flow between bodily fluids and the Earth, a moving back and forth. This differs from the notion of the biological body, a Western construct that views the body as a distinct object, separate from nature and the spirit world. This fluid body has implications for how we view the human subject and modernist assumptions about human agency and autonomy. Hence it is important in our workshop to provide an embodied experience of our fluid systems as part of the Blue Ecology cycle. In doing this we invite participants to experience the body as open and fluid. It is this ability to have fluid boundaries that supports relationship, that deep sense of connection that is possible with the spirit of water and with the human, non-human, and more-than-human worlds. It is this sense of connection, a shift in awareness so that water is seen and experienced as a living spirit and relative, which allows people to understand they have responsibilities to water.

Responsibilities and Relationship

Lee Maracle, Sto:lo/Métis writer and teacher, speaking at the Downstream gathering, used the word "obligation" to stress how responsibility is different from rights.[21] Not only is the human rights discourse that is so prevalent in

Eurocentric contexts based on the centrality of the individual to the detriment of the collective, but also its anthropocentrism distorts relationships with the non-human world. There is now a campaign for "the right to water" as a human right. Maracle challenges this, saying that we need to talk about our obligation to water as part of our circle of relationships.

This concept of our obligation to water illustrates a notion of responsibility that is grounded in Indigenous legal traditions. Before the settlers arrived, Indigenous nations on Turtle Island lived by protocols, diplomacy, and laws that were specific to each nation and linked to the land and waters on which they lived. These traditions guided governance, family life, and relationship with the land, water, and its creatures, as well as trade and relationships with other nations. Our obligations are grounded in relationships that are affirmed in these legal traditions.[22] We have a responsibility to both maintain and facilitate our relationships.

Because we are concerned with the health of the water, ceremonial ritual brings us together and holds our diverse ways of relating to water within a collective commons. We facilitate relationship building through engaging with local protocol principles. As Alannah says, "I can speak as a female Midewiwin ceremonialist, through my location here as a visitor, and because I have a commitment to be a good relative to the peoples and waters of this territory as well as that of my homelands."

Both of us have lived within xʷməθkʷəy̓əm (Musqueam) territory and have working relationships with several Musqueam people. When the xʷməθkʷəy̓əm (Musqueam) set up a peace camp in front of their ancestral village and burial site, Cəsna?əm, we both saw it as part of our responsibility to these relationships to become involved in supporting the camp and the xʷməθkʷəy̓əm (Musqueam) legal traditions that required them to assert protection of this site.

While our obligations to water may seem straightforward in the case of Cəsna?əm, sometimes there are many swirls and eddies in terms of how we maintain and facilitate relationships around water responsibilities. Denise has been engaged with a group opposed to sea ranching of sea cucumbers and geoducks in Baynes Sound and the larger Salish Sea. However, there are some members of local First Nations engaged in the shellfish industry who are interested in investing in this project. For a group of settlers to demand a moratorium on any further shellfish or seafood development in the area without consulting the local nations would only repeat a colonial pattern. The challenge for Denise is facilitating a way of finding common interests between these divergent groups who are "invested" in this water body in different ways. As in the above example, often our role is that of facilitating relationships.

To educate settlers to be good relatives takes time. There are small actions all of us can take. We can learn how to be respectful visitors on this land. Adopting the protocol of acknowledging that you are a visitor in whatever territory you may be living or working in is a first step in the complex process for settlers of re-storying our identity in this land. Lee Maracle adds that we need to get to know the land we are standing on and how the First Peoples who lived there took care of that land. "If you decide to attach yourself to the land, you need to make a commitment to it."[23]

Conclusion: Water and Resurgence

Indigenous peoples have always celebrated water, as witnessed by the ceremonies and language used to deepen and renew their relationship responsibilities. J. P. White, in the *International Journal of Indigenous of Policy Studies*, reports the following:

> Indigenous peoples have, since time immemorial, understood that water is central to the cycles of life.... Indigenous peoples have always cared for the water and followed practices that, depending on their geography, varied by season to protect and conserve fresh safe water.[24]

Colonial practices have disrupted this care and passing of knowledge in Indigenous communities. Indigenous resurgence embodies the engagement of Indigenous knowledge principles in how we live our daily lives. These principles will help us to tell future stories about the nature of our relationship with water. For White, this means "we have to look outside of Western technological solutions and come to listen to the other 'story'—the one that emanates from Indigenous Traditional Knowledge."[25]

It is this other story—the learning of traditional stories and how to insert ourselves into them—that will provide a way forward out of the nihilistic logic of Eurocentric technological solutions. Resurgence for us means engaging in daily land and water-based practices that both restore our relationships and affirm our responsibilities. These daily practices are very much part of a process that works at the economic, political, social, and cultural level. As Jeff Corntassel states, "Being Indigenous today means struggling to reclaim and regenerate one's relational, place-base existence by challenging the ongoing, destructive forces of colonization."[26]

Corntassel maintains that what will determine the health of our water/ our own health depends on how we individually and collectively address the cultural harms colonialism has caused to waters and lands. He asks us to consider questions such as: What strategies can be used to redress harms of occupation and colonialism, and protect Indigenous territories from further harm and regenerate land and water cultural practices? And ultimately, what can Indigenous nationhood tell us about sustainable relationships on Indigenous homelands? Corntassel states, "To restore the waters that have been damaged on this planet we need to centre this Indigenous framework and ask ourselves how each of us will address and answer these questions."[27] Indigenous resurgence points to Indigenous principles as guiding the future of healthy water on shared lands.

The work we offered at Downstream, both the modelling of protocols and ceremony and the Moving Water workshop, are part of these "daily acts of renewal." As is much of our work, it was done in an intercultural, interfaith context with both settlers and water protectors from many nations. In bringing together within the conference framework an embodied experience of water in the fluid systems, in connecting participants to bodies of water to which they are related and to which they can learn to listen, and in generating a collective honouring of water, we contributed to the process of facilitating our relationships with water. In demonstrating protocols that respect local nations, we modelled the importance of relationships to territories and their peoples and our responsibilities to them. Each of these steps contributes to decolonization, to moving with water and out of a static Eurocentric world view that objectifies water and our bodies. These embodied actions in a small way support Indigenous resurgence as daily practice—everyday acts of renewal of relationships and lifelong responsibilities that teach how to be a good relative living in somebody's else homelands.

Notes

1 Kim Anderson, "Aboriginal Women, Water and Health: Reflections from Eleven First Nations, Inuit, and Métis Grandmothers" (Winnipeg: Prairie Women's Health Centre of Excellence, 2010), 24, http://www.pwhce.ca/womenAndWater.htm.

2 Ibid., 27.

3 For a description of the Tamalpa Life-Art Process, see Daria Halprin, *The Expressive Body in Life, Art, and Therapy: Working with Movement, Metaphor, and Meaning* (London: Jessica-Kingsley Publishers, 2002).

4 Dorothy Christian had this statement as her email signature when she was part of organizing the Protect Our Sacred Waters event in 2007.

5 This statement is included in many treaties. I use it here because it demonstrates my genealogy and that I continue to live by these treaty responsibilities, just as they were set out by Chief Peguis in 1871, Treaty #1.

6 Elaine Wainwright, "Healing Ointment/Healing Bodies; Gift and Identification in an Ecofeminist Reading of Mark 14:3–9," in *Exploring Ecological Hermeneutics* (Atlanta, GA: Society of Biblical Literature, 2008), 131–39; Gail Yee, "Reflections on Creation and the Prophet Hosea," in *Liberating Biblical Study*, vol. 1, ed. Laurel Dykstra and Ched Myers, The Center and Library for the Bible and Social Justice series (Eugene, OR: Cascades Books, 2011), 65–79.

7 Ched Myers, "From 'Creation Care' to 'Watershed Discipleship': An Anabaptist Approach to Ecological Theology and Practice," *Conrad Grebel Review* 32, no. 3 (Fall 2014): 250–75. See also http://watersheddiscipleship.org/.

8 See Michael Blackstock, "Blue Ecology: A Cross-cultural Ecological Vision for Freshwater," in *Aboriginal Peoples and Forest Lands in Canada*, ed. D. B. Tindall et al. (Vancouver: UBC Press, 2013), 180–204.

9 Andrea Olsen, *Body and Earth: An Experiential Guide* (Lebanon: University Press of New England, 2002), 180.

10 This song was written by Doreen Day at the request of her grandson. Mother Earth Water Walk, http://www.motherearthwaterwalk.com/index.php/water/the-water-song.

11 The individual who took the photograph returned it to the organizers and deleted it from her files.

12 Christine Valters Paintner and Betsy Beckman, *Awakening the Creative Spirit: Bringing the Arts to Spiritual Direction* (New York: Morehouse Publishing, 2010), 17–18.

13 Olsen, *Body and Earth*, 171–77.

14 "Mona Polacca," the International Council of Thirteen Grandmothers, http://grand motherscouncil.org/about-us.

15 Anderson, "Aboriginal Women, Water and Health," 1–32.

16 Ibid., 21.

17 Ibid.

18 Deborah McGregor, "Anishnaabe-Kwe, Traditional Knowledge, and Water Protection," *Canadian Woman Studies* 26, no. 3–4 (Winter/Spring 2008): 26–30.

19 Rita Wong, "A Healing Walk Around the Tar Sands Dead Zone," Rabble.ca, http://rabble .ca/news/2010/08/healing-walk-around-tar-sands-dead-zone. This article describes well the integration of ceremony into this action.

20 Frédérique Apffel-Marglin, *Subversive Spiritualities: How Rituals Enact the World* (New York: Oxford, 2011), 150–51.

21 Lee Maracle, "False Creek, Real Transformations," talk presented at Downstream: Re-imagining Water, March 21–23, 2012, Vancouver, Coast Salish Territory, BC.

22 For an overview of several Indigenous legal traditions, see John Borrows, *Canada's Indigenous Constitution* (Toronto: University of Toronto Press, 2010).

23 Maracle at Downstream: Reimagining Water, March 22, 2012.

24 Jerry White, "Commentary: Water—Recognizing the Indigenous Perspective," *International Indigenous Policy Journal* 3, no. 3 (2012): 1, http://ir.lib.uwo.ca/iipj/vol3/iss3/1.

25 Ibid.

26 Jeff Corntassel, "Pathways to Indigenous Self Determination: Cultural Restoration in International Law," *Canadian Journal of Human Rights* 1, no. 1 (2012): 88, http://www .corntassel.net/culturalrestoration.pdf.

27 Ibid., 1.

Bibliography

Anderson, Kim. "Aboriginal Women, Water, and Health: Reflections from Eleven First Nations, Inuit, and Métis Grandmothers." Prairie Women's Health Centre of Excellence, Winnipeg, 2010. http://www.pwhce.ca/womenAndWater.htm.

Apffel-Marglin, Frédérique. *Subversive Spiritualities: How Rituals Enact the World*. New York: Oxford, 2011.

Blackstock, Michael. "Blue Ecology: A Cross-cultural Ecological Vision for Freshwater." In *Aboriginal Peoples and Forest Lands in Canada*, edited by D. B. Tindall, Ronald Trosper, and Pamela Perrault, 180–204. Vancouver: UBC Press, 2013.

———. "Water: A First Nations Spiritual and Ecological Perspective." *BC Journal of Ecosystems and Management* 1, no. 1 (2001): 54–66. www.forrex.org/jem/2000/vol1/no1/art7.pdf.

———. "Water-Based Ecology: A First Nations Proposal to Repair the Definition of an Ecosystem." *BC Journal of Ecosystems and Management* 2, no. 1 (2002): 7–12. www.forrex.org/jem/2002/vol2/no1/art4.pdf.

———. *Water a First Ecology.* Kamloops, BC: Wyget Books, 2008.

Borrows, John. *Canada's Indigenous Constitution.* Toronto: University of Toronto Press, 2010.

———. *Drawing Out Law: A Spirit's Guide.* Toronto: University of Toronto Press, 2010.

———. *Recovering Canada: The Resurgence of Indigenous Law.* Toronto: University of Toronto Press, 2002.

Corntassel, Jeff. "Pathways to Indigenous Self Determination: Cultural Restoration in International Law." *Canadian Journal of Human Rights* 1, no. 1 (2012). http://www.corntassel.net/culturalrestoration.pdf.

Halprin, Daria. *The Expressive Body in Life, Art, and Therapy: Working with Movement, Metaphor and Meaning.* London: Jessica-Kingsley Publishers, 2002.

McGregor, Deborah. "Anishnaabe-Kwe, Traditional Knowledge, and Water Protection." *Canadian Woman Studies* 26, no. 3–4 (Winter/Spring 2008): 26–30.

Maracle, Lee. "False Creek, Real Transformations." Conference presentation at Downstream: Reimagining Water. Vancouver, Coast Salish Territory, British Columbia, March 21–23, 2012.

McGregor, Deborah. "Anishnaabe-Kwe, Traditional Knowledge, and Water Protection." *Canadian Woman Studies* 26, no. 3–4 (Winter/Spring 2008): 26–30.

"Mona Polacca." The International Council of Thirteen Grandmothers. http://grandmotherscouncil.org/about-us.

"Mother Earth Water Walk." Mother Earth Water Walk. 2010. http://www.motherearthwaterwalk.com/.

Myers, Ched. "From 'Creation Care' to 'Watershed Discipleship': An Anabaptist Approach to Ecological Theology and Practice." *Conrad Grebel Review* 32, no. 3 (Fall 2014): 250–75.

Olsen, Andrea. *Body and Earth: An Experiential Guide.* Lebanon: University Press of New England, 2002.

Paintner, Christine Valters, and Betsy Beckman. *Awakening the Creative Spirit: Bringing the Arts to Spiritual Direction.* New York: Morehouse Publishing, 2010.

Peace and Dignity Journeys. 2012. Complex Systems Laboratory, Cecil and Ida Green Institute of Geophysics and Planetary Physics. http://complex-systems.ucsd.edu/pdj2012/node/1257.

Wainwright, Elaine. "Healing Ointment/Healing Bodies: Gift and Identification in an Ecofeminist Reading of Mark 14:3–9." In *Exploring Ecological Hermeneutics* (Atlanta, GA: Society of Biblical Literature, 2008), 131–39.

White, Jerry. "Commentary: Water—Recognizing the Indigenous Perspective." *International Indigenous Policy Journal* 3, no. 3 (2012): 1–2. http://ir.lib.uwo.ca/iipj/vol3/iss3/1.

Wong, Rita. "A Healing Walk Around the Tar Sands Dead Zone." Rabble.ca, http://rabble.ca/news/2010/08/healing-walk-around-tar-sands-dead-zone.

Yee, Gail. "Reflections on Creation and the Prophet Hosea." In *Liberating Biblical Study*, vol. 1, edited by Laurel Dykstra and Ched Myers, 65–79. The Center and Library for the Bible and Social Justice series. Eugene, OR: Cascades Books, 2011.

Bodies of Water
Meaning in Movement
Seonagh Odhiambo Horne

Dancing Water: Introduction

Asava Dance is an ensemble based in Los Angeles that has been working with participatory water ethics as part of its creative development process, most notably in the performance of *Bodies of Water*, which toured in North America 2011–12. As the founding artistic director of this ensemble, I attend to dancers' personal, political, intellectual, and embodied perceptions of questions. For example, in this piece I ask: What happens if we highlight water as central to human consciousness? Therefore, my choreography processes are not only about producing aesthetically sound works; I simultaneously engage with communities and draw attention to social concerns through dance. This is in line with a tradition of choreographers, who sometimes work in communities to map experiences and narratives as part of a creative process.[1] In addition, it is similar to many Indigenous dance traditions, including an African aesthetic, wherein dance is inseparable from the life, history, meaning, and visions of a community.

Before *Bodies of Water*, an evening-length performance at Downstream: Reimagining Water, was performed during World Water Week in Vancouver (March 2012), audiences were involved in its creation. During months prior to the performance, dancers, musicians, and I presented a series of workshops and performances in Toronto and Los Angeles that engaged communities in dialogue by using Augusto Boal's theatre techniques. Over the years, I have adapted Boalian techniques, which provide a means through which non-dancers can form movement pictures from ideas. When the dancers and I work with community members, they may see a contribution of their movement onstage. Although it will have been exaggerated for the stage by a professional dancer, there is a seed of its original in the performance. This approach weaves a fabric of connection between meaning in art, aesthetics, and engagement.

The story of making *Bodies of Water* describes a method of discovery and analysis about the nature of water that is achieved through movement studies, analysis of texts, and workshops. Within the limitations of writing as a means to communicate about dance performance, I share my narrative of founding a dance ensemble in Los Angeles, photographs that relay the water focus of our early performances, and explain how water informs the embodied participatory *somaesthetic* of the company. Our movement language, or somaesthetic, grew out of ongoing questions about water that we engaged through embodied processes. The descriptions herein cover some of the early Asava performances between 2010 and 2012, and rehearsal periods that relate to two Canadian tours involving audience participants from Toronto, Los Angeles, Vancouver, and Salt Spring Island.

The final performance in World Water Week at Downstream: Reimagining Water (2012) featured a quartet of dancers, including soloist Kimberley Michelle Smith, and a collaboration with artists Karolle Wall and Elder Florence James (Puneluxulth'). Florence blessed the dancers in the arena, aiding them to understand and carry their sacred role of transforming issues. After our performance, the dancers and I heard feedback and discussed our process. Florence and Karolle also shared their insights through the short film, *'imush q'uyatl'un*, wherein Florence's song follows the choreography of a microscopic water animal, the nudibranch.

Karolle Wall's unique footage brings attention to microscopic underwater beings such as the sea slug, and places value upon life beneath the water's surface. Dance also goes beneath the surface, which not only evokes a manner of looking under the surface of water, but also, as Karolle notes, "It bears an environmental message passed on for thousands of years: If we are to save our environment, appreciate our coastal, marine ecosystems, we must pay attention and bear witness to even the smallest of creatures."[2] Since I explored Karolle's footage in depth with the dancers during the months before making *Bodies of Water*, this performance marked a longer collaboration with both artists.

Karolle, Florence, and I had first established a connection three years earlier when Florence gave a blessing ceremony at a healing dance I created with women on Salt Spring Island (Puneluxulth' territory), where I was in residence on a Canada Council grant at the Islands Institute with Caffyn Kelley (2009–10). At that time, I developed a dance about healing St. Mary Lake with five Canadian dancers, and Karolle videotaped the choreography from underwater (www.asavadance.com). Florence James, who also offered the blessing on Salt Spring, shared many stories of her heritage and traditional teachings while on location. Magically and by chance, the spot I chose for the outdoor performance was the same location where Florence's grandfather had gone for healing water. St. Mary Lake had been a known spot for healing rituals among Puneluxulth' people, and Florence shared with me about the value of these sacred rituals to her experience. Her parents had hidden her away in a log to avoid having her taken away to residential school, an experience enforced on her contemporaries, so Florence is steeped in the teachings of her grandparents.

Karolle introduced me to the film 'imush q'uyatl'un in 2011–12 during rehearsals for Bodies of Water. The dancers and I drew inspiration from these microscopic underwater creatures for movement and character. In these ways, Karolle and Florence participated in the creative process online and at a distance. This made our experience of presenting together at World Water Week all the more meaningful. In addition, during 2011–12, the Islands Institute offered me an online artist residency, which highlighted our Asava Dance creation process.[3] This residency was invaluable as it extended the work that had been done previously on Salt Spring Island, enabling us to interact with audiences of international artists who tuned in from around the world to share movement stories about water.

Dance may be the art form that is most water-like as our bodies are made up of two-thirds water. When dance is performed onstage, it demands immediate somatic involvement and attention, which stands in contrast to writing, which can be reread once printed. The creative process of making dances is also fluid and water-like; as the dancers and I sought to embody water's insights, we conveyed our experiences or perceptions, and then the meaning of the piece evolved. Like moving water, dance is constantly in evolution. In fact, as a dancer begins to focus on staging work, with an emphasis on technical perfection that requires much repetition, the multiple foci and intelligence required of the dancer can to some degree remove her or him from the meaning. This is the subject of another essay; however, it is helpful to describe these layers as part of the dancers' experience, as part of what the audience sees. Knowing this will aid the reader in looking at quotations and photographs in the sections to follow.

As the artistic director, I wanted to establish founding principles of the company that emerged from a dance process, informed by an ethics of water. Therefore, rather than providing performance analysis and description, I emphasize our creative process, and share perceptions of an embodied ecology or engaged somaesthetics—I adapt and develop an ecologically oriented research/creative processes that could be shared with both dancers and non-dancers.

Given that meaning is derived in artistic processes through affect and absorption rather than through subject–object dialogue, the path to deepening understanding is not always straightforwardly intellectual but more through embodied experience.[4] Somaesthetics, according to Eric Mullis, is "the pragmatic discipline that explores somatic practices and ultimately demonstrates how they can lead to the attainment of fulfilling experiences."[5] This may be taken up, as Richard Shusterman argues, to improve functioning and perception, or with regard to John Dewey's emphasis on everyday origins of aesthetic experience, but either way the reference is to a meaningful aesthetic experience or "somaesthetics" that "shows how one's body can be transformed into a locus of aesthetic value.[6] For those who are interested in engaging communities further with these ideas, parts of performances or creative workshops can be observed at the Asava Dance website.

This emphasis on process rather than dance analysis suits the multi-disciplinary context of the Downstream project. Here I consider some implications of an embodied ecology that we sought to achieve through *Bodies of Water*. My goals are similar to Basia Irland, for example, whose artistic medium of ice sculpture is just as ephemeral as dance; perhaps the Asava Dance model can be replicated by others.

Implications of an Embodied Ecology

What are the implications of embracing water, lingering in it as we did, and performing embodied experiences that highlight water as central to human consciousness? *Bodies of Water* toured Canada twice, yet was created in the dustbowl of Los Angeles. In the desert we lingered beside a cement-encased Los Angeles River, which looks like a glorified storm drain, and we pondered water's insights within sight of the 210 or the 710 highways. The experience of LA River water does not always seem liquid; yet we looked beneath surfaces, drew water memories with our bodies, created sounds, and experienced our own bodies made of water. The histories of our diverse origins: Canadian and Irish, African and American, Puerto Rican and Yoruba, Russian New Yorker, Armenian, and mixed Indigenous American histories or geographies, mixed together in the studio spaces, where we listened to texts that individuals brought in, which spoke of water from different vantage points. These were the waters of our various ancestries, and included the rhythms of Martin Luther King Jr.'s speeches. Water was a means of understanding experiences that affect us and that link us to our spiritual strengths.

> And that was the fact that there was a certain kind of fire that no water
> could put out. And we went before the fire hoses; we had known water. If

we were Baptist or some other denominations, we had been immersed. If we were Methodist, and some others, we had been sprinkled, but we knew water. That couldn't stop us.[7]

Water inspirations came also from natural locations in Canada where I grew up. Plentiful, powerful waters of British Columbia created in me a filter, a way of seeing that brings nature into our bodies. Such is Karolle Wall's interpretation of the microscopic nudibranch, which the dancers embodied. And the sighs of Edgar Allan Poe's water also murmured in the dancers' breaths at times:

> For many miles on either side of the river's cozy bed is a pale desert of gigantic water lilies. They sigh one unto the other in that solitude and stretch toward the heavens their long and ghastly necks, and nod to and fro their everlasting heads. And there is an indistinct murmur which cometh out from among them like the rushing of subterrene water. And they sigh one unto the other.[8]

Poe's murmurs are about living whispers in the marsh. Likewise, dancers whisper the embodiment of water as they sigh and stretch. Karolle took us into ripples of the subterranean water.

French philosopher Gaston Bachelard likewise shared his insights into water's rippling effects, which sometimes helped us through sadness we shared in the studio process. As the Asava group became closer, Bachelard's words were meaningful. He told us, "What is heard near the river—not its voice but a sigh, the sigh of pliant plants, sad rustle of the greeneries caress ... [or] the ... world itself grows quiet, and, then, when sadness falls on the stones, the whole universe becomes mute through an inexpressible terror."[9] We read multiple writings and viewed images about water. As we entered these into the

Figure 12.1 *Dancing Rushes*, at St. Mary Lake, Salt Spring Island, BC. (*Source*: Karolle Wall)

creativity, choreographer, musicians, and dancers alike explored our emotions. The Orishas of Nigeria, particularly *Yemayá*, called to us across the ocean.

Jazz legend Bennie Maupin, who grew out of Detroit and New York's jazz scene of the 1950s and 1960s, worked in the studio alongside us, profoundly directing sound into a series of his unique compositions. He exacted precision, delicacy, and water sounds from his woodwind instruments and demanded the same precision of percussionist Angel Luis Figueroa whose own mastery carried his musical-spiritual voices to the dancers. Angel introduced us to *Yemayá,* the Orisha of motherhood and of the ocean in the Santeria religion, which originated in the Yoruba tradition from Nigeria. I drew from her strength as I directed and pooled energies of dancers. As Bennie built music, planted beside the river's flow, the melodies became recognizable and repeatable in the dance. A particular melody and instrument connected to each dancer. One appeared with the flute, another with the cajon, and another with the piano. Each dancer partook in the music development in this way, and in this sense we were all part of forming an aesthetic language.

I created water movement by using Augusto Boal's method of developing "movement pictures" from memories, as well as other techniques he developed to create "theatre of the oppressed."[10] Deriving methods from Brazilian educator Paulo Freire's writings about literacy and conscientization,[11] Boal draws from participants' personal experiences and memories to create pictured personal stories with their bodies and, in this way, he situates individuals' personal narratives into larger socio-economic or political contexts. The methods of Boal and Freire are meant to put into circulation stories that we haven't yet heard, stories beneath surfaces. This is intended to empower an oppressed community toward conscientization, or draw the awareness of a community toward issues affecting its growth and development.

The views of Freire and Boal present an engaged aesthetic in the sense that they provide communities with a sense of efficacy, a means to dialogue about concerns, and with the idea that our reality is constructed. According to Boal's aesthetic, we construct meaning just as we construct the ideas we have of one another. Freire and Boal use words as a primary tool in that construction, but as dancers we primarily use movement and symbolic gestures to construct meanings. In this case, dancers and I were sharing movement of our lives that we expanded, and personal awareness that shaped us into a larger sway of whispers in the rustling of river trees. By evolving this way musicians and dancers were part of the same waters, and so we breathed.

This way of constructing meaning in dance through movement and symbolic gestures presents a somaesthetic that is water-like. By placing water as our central influence we brought our own and communities' awareness to our dependency upon water. As we began to consider ourselves as water, the body showed us the meaning of water within, and we deepened our somatic connection to its fluidity through breath and by knowing the rhythm of our body fluids. We began to recognize various incarnations of water as powerful, rushing, trickling, dripping, and more. Water would teach us insights into our local ecology.

The movement developed as I required the dancers to soften their gestures in becoming water. Both Indigenous philosophies and perspectives of somatic healing supported the notion of softening. Somatic experience teaches us that through deep respiration our lungs participate in both the ecological rebalancing of Earth and to our own softening and fluidity of movement.

Insights from the field of somatic theory are very waterly. Denise Nadeau, similarly motivated and influenced by perspectives of Indigenous philosophies and by Bonnie Bainbridge Cohen, writes, "To feel the sacredness of water, we humans must become fluid and feel our fluidity."[12] Bainbridge Cohen, a leader in somatic theory, shows that the fluidity of our bodies can be observed much like movement under the surface of the water. Bainbridge Cohen looks under our skin and explores the microscopic movement of bodily fluid. Her research discusses the increase in cellular breathing, which allows the internal flow of fluid to pass through our tissues. In this way, our lungs become more engaged to support movement. In turn, she says, the ecological environment is affected by our breathing and awareness.[13]

In dance somatic theory, and for my purposes, experiences within the physical body are understood holistically as connected to cognitive, emotional, and spiritual aspects of embodiment. Feldenkrais practitioner Thomas Hanna coined the term "somatics" from the Greek word "soma" to describe "the body and its wholeness," which gave language to a range of theories and understandings throughout the 1970s about the therapeutic value of body wisdom and awareness.[14] As bodies are located within social, historical, cultural, and ecological environments, kinesthetic awareness also expands understanding about the larger world to which it is connected. Sondra Fraleigh contends that in the field of dance somatics has extended this "attention on self and self-awareness," which may take away from how somatic practices can help build community interactively with "the intersubjective field relative to self, others, and community ... [an] often overlooked aspect of somatics."[15] This draws further significance to the importance of collaboration between somatic theories and Indigenous philosophies, which fits with water's expansive nature. Motivated by these orientations, I instructed dancers in the art of somatic practices, especially the use of *ujaii* breath[16] and the application of breath in movement. At the same time, the composer created music in observations and sensations of movement, which produced the sounds of water.

Emergent Process: Findings Underneath Water's Surface

A few words such as "emergent," "collaborative," and "expansive" seem to characterize the creative process. I made a series of dance parts, gradually identified issues being presented, and allowed this approach to shape the questions we were asking. Similar to many artistic processes, meaning emerged rather than being assigned. That is, as we focused on the ideas of healing water, water's essence, and the concept of healing the LA River, a fluid character of water's embodiment emerged, which can be observed in the photographs in the following sections and in the videos on our website.

We were developing a means through which to collaborate with our environment, which felt healing. Music was written lovingly while dance was made; the creative process was enhanced further as artistic director and music director walked in nature near the LA River or its related streams Arroyo Seco and Gabrielino. Choreographer and composer brought collaborative water to the studio through movement and sound.

Everything beneath the surface of our daily lives came out into the open. This served me through a rupture in my life when my spouse left without warning after we had lived more than a decade together. Abandoned in the city of Los Angeles where I knew no one, the waterless range of highways and dry earth gaped back at me. I found solace when lingering in the studio at night by myself, and I created new movement within water's caresses, which I would explore with dancers and musicians the next day. A closeness and cohesion evolved within the group.

Movement creation was prayerful, meaningful, and respectful of water's complexities. I felt for the sacred mud underneath murky water, where red-legged frogs burrow; dancer participants attended to their secrets and mysteries, and to difficult pasts sometimes locked in the weeds. The movement freed us. Water gave to us the way Carl Jung describes a lake:

> Water is the commonest symbol for the unconscious. The lake in the valley
> is the unconscious.... Water is the "valley spirit," the water dragon of Tao,
> whose nature resembles water—a yang in the yin, therefore, water means
> spirit that has become unconscious. Psychologically, therefore, water
> means spirit that has become unconscious.[17]

At times, calm water gathered on the way downstream; collectively we pooled the stories of our unconscious. Sounds of piano and saxophone, flute and percussion, mingled with healing properties, wisdom, collective energy, and insight.

Water from Concrete

The words of Chief Dan George, "When she came to the city, the cement hurt her feet," in the *Ecstasy of Rita Joe* resonated as I acclimatized to the city where I had moved for a career opportunity. As a person who loves nature, I felt keenly threats posed by the dry climate. The arid desert and dry San Gabriel Valley contrasted dramatically with Vancouver, where I grew up. Amid lush rainforests and rivers in British Columbia, water is expansive and it was common, in my experience, to commune with rushing water. Just prior to moving to Los Angeles I had spent two years living a block from the beach in Hawaii, where I swam in the ocean each dawn. The contrasts to Los Angeles were deafening.

Adding to the threat of dryness, five days after I arrived in Los Angeles one of the worst forest fires in decades began to burn across acres of the San Gabriel Mountains, which were visible from my apartment. The fires lasted two months. I was struck by the lack of water, the choking air, the emphasis upon material culture, the predominant media image of Los Angeles, and the masses of freeways and cars. None of this supported a dancer's adventure to the riverbed for inspiration.

The contrasts between my Canadian experience and my new home in Los Angeles were further emphasized by a Canada Council grant in Dance I received in 2009–10, which enabled me to travel back and forth from Los Angeles to Salt Spring Island several times during the academic year to develop a piece about Healing Water. Ultimately, this resulted in a dance performance that was held beside St. Mary Lake in June 2010 and performed with four other Canadian dancers. This is where I met Florence James and Karolle Wall.

To work against my sense of alienation in Los Angeles, I began yoga classes at 6:00 a.m., which grounded me in my water body. In yoga class I met Bennie Maupin, the jazz artist with whom I would develop an important collaboration. Bennie shared a compact disc of his compositions on the second day, and his works present a perfect match to the movement I wanted to choreograph.[18] Within a month of hearing his music I had choreographed and staged a solo with dancer Kaleila Jordan, and I invited Bennie to observe this work onstage. Before long, we were working together in the studio, and I had employed several dancers with the task of healing the LA River. Bennie had a laboratory that he craved, an organic opportunity to be inspired by movement, and I was devoting my dance to the idea of water.

Water's call took me to the LA River's bed, where a river was not evident at first glance, when I was invited to a walk along dry riverbanks lined with cement, which do not suggest a natural watershed. I knew that beneath this hard concrete I needed to find healing. Even if the act of becoming water was contrary to the landscape, I knew by dancing water I would come home. Beneath cement were possibilities and hopes of a restored ecosystem.

The LA River's History: A City Trying to Find Its Heart

The Los Angeles River is a site of ongoing public dispute and activism over shared green space. Originally, the riverbed was cemented in the 1930s as an Army Corp solution to extreme flooding, and it looks like a glorified storm drain. In fact, this river was not even recognized legally as an ecosystem until recently, and it was illegal to traverse it until as late as 2010. Cementing the river was successful in terms of preventing flooding, but this was an ecological disaster. Within a few years, important native species such as yellow-billed cuckoos and red-legged frogs were largely gone. The frogs could not make their way up through concrete, and the only part of the fifty-two-mile river that remains untouched with a natural river bottom is the eleven miles of the Glendale Narrows, by Griffith Park and Atwater Village.

The 2000s was an era of increased activism and interest in the river, which resulted in some change in how the city views the river. The work of educating the public about the environment, to be more conscious of spaces around them, or of connecting them specifically to the riverbed has been undertaken both by artists and activists such as Lauren Bon, who redesigns large architectural spaces and challenges conventional conceptualizations, and Stephan Koplowitz, who brought about awareness of the river through site-specific dance performances. Their work helped educate the public, but there are still many in Los Angeles who remain unaware of the river's existence and its potentials as green or blue space.

Los Angeles is a sprawling city, a place Bon describes as "trying to find its heart."[19] Her 2006 installation, *Not a Cornfield*, was built on a forgotten industrial lot. Bon's team planted a cornfield, which became a site for dance and is now a city park. Artists like Bon ultimately help the city to come alive with greenspace and interpersonal connections. Choreographer Stephan Koplowitz developed *Taskforce* in 2008, another a site-specific consideration of Los Angeles's water resources. This important work took audiences on buses to various parts of Los Angeles where they viewed contemporary dance beside the river.

These artists focused on the LA River as an artery as they sought the heart of Los Angeles. The work is ongoing for both artists and environmental groups such as Friends of the LA River (FOLAR), a group that started with ten people cutting the fence to the river in 1986, which now runs regular, well-publicized cleanup days with several thousand participants. Various artists' missions support a connection to developing an awareness of the need for more green space. Over the last thirty years, the increased activism along the

LA River developed into an effective advocacy campaign that seeks to reverse the negative effects on the ecosystem of the city's cemented waterway, and to bring attention to this vital ecosystem as a resource and as parkland.

After the Environmental Protection Agency declared the river "a traditionally navigable waterway" in 2010 thanks to the activism of George Wolfe and others who navigated the entire length of the river effectively in kayaks during 2008, the question is not if, but how, the rebuilding and management of this river will be completed. Even so, during 2010 it was still a crime to use the river for any recreational purpose. Advocates for the river's restoration were stunned when in the fall of 2013 the Army Corps released a feasibility study that proposed the restoration of miles of habitat, the removal of concrete, and the reconnection of the main stem of river to the Verdugos and San Gabriel Mountains. Los Angeles Mayor Garcetti and others now talk about the river's improvement process, and momentum is propelling toward the implementation of a multi-million-dollar plan that further enhances eleven miles of river access and improves the quality of public experience of the river.

Asava Dance and the Rhythm of Water

Meanwhile, in 2010–12 the group of Asava Dancers was pursuing our connection to the river in natural ways through ceremony of movement and the worship of water. With the dancers and musicians in September 2010 I did ceremonial offerings of sagebrush and tobacco to the Tongva people, who are indigenous to the area (also called Gabrielino). Along the main tributaries of the Los Angeles River, the San Gabriel River, and the Arroyo Seco Stream, I spoke to the heritage of this place and asked for meaningful connection with the people of the area, so our work would honour the Elders who had given their lives and lived through horrors of colonization. This is a lifetime commitment, and the meaning of that connection continues to be revealed. On that day, making offerings to the riverbed, we felt the needs of nature.

Shortly after this time, I noticed the dancers being more inspired by nature. For example, one dancer developed a movement phrase wherein she imagined her foot caught on roots in a riverbed. With her foot stuck, she moved frantically with her upper body until she was free. Ideas like this were slowly developed into phrases of movement, and came more alive with our workshops in Toronto and Los Angeles, which provided similar inspirational movement (see asavadance.com). Our connections to one another and to the communities we met along the way grew along with a commitment to the watery movement.

Figure 12.2 Kim Smith dancing with water's inspiration. (*Source:* Keith Settle)

> In my own experience with Asava Dance, I have been emotionally involved
> with each movement that is created, so it is easier as an artist to explore
> the movements in a more personal way. Adding personal experiences and
> emotions can only enhance the "realness" of the movement and ultimately
> assists in a creative environment where movements become organic rather
> than overly rehearsed. (Kimberley Michelle Smith)

The dancers' shared commitment was demonstrated in the communication
of emotions as we learned water-inspired movement from one another. As
emotional qualities, the movement sometimes portrayed moody water.

What can be learned by attending to the body and to the fluidity of our
movement? Like lines carved by water on the mountain, lines are defined and
drawn by the water in our bodies as we trace our memories and insights. The
dancers and I learned to follow this process as we searched for insights.

The Los Angeles River is a metaphor for connectivity in the city, and the
city's unconscious, so we listened for messages from Aboriginal leaders and
healers about water. In this we heard about the responsibility "to take care of
the water because to take care of the water is to take care of and enhance life.
Water is the embodiment of the spirit of life" (Alannah Young Leon).[20]

Figure 12.3 Lindsey Lollie performs an image of still water. (*Source*: Keith Settle)

Figure 12.4 Kim Smith and composer Bennie Maupin. (*Source*: Keith Settle)

Choreography and Composition in Asava Dance

The emphasis of this chapter is dance movement. The movement presented in the photographs grew out of a process of engaging with water, and represents different time periods. Just as water's movement is expressed by dancers, photographs by Keith Settle capture movement's fluidity. However, it is impossible to discuss the dance without mentioning the profound influences of the composer and musicians we worked with.

My choreography choices are profoundly influenced by Bennie Maupin, the composer and music director of Asava Dance featured in the photographs. Bennie has been the music director of Asava Dance since its inception, and was often accompanied live by percussionist Angel Luis Figueroa, who also worked with Asava Dance from the beginning. Importantly, both of these world-class musicians participated in observing an organic process of movement development, which informs Bennie's musical compositions. As such they spent many long hours displaying water's patience. After Bennie observed dancers during the creation of the dance, he and I would also talk about the movement, about how it reflects water. Sometimes we joined in conversation beside the Los Angeles River, discussing the sound of water, and this helped us gain insight into how the dance and music join together in live collaboration. For example, the voices of different musical instruments are given a level of improvisatory freedom in Bennie's compositions just as the dancers have some level of freedom of expression that is connected to specific instruments. At the same time, the theme of water guided all of the expression and the final movement choices.

The marriage of music to dance is evident throughout the work, and each composition is an opportunity for this union. Angel Luis Figueroa performed duets with Kim under Bennie's and my direction. For example, it is important that the audience hears the body before the percussion; at other moments both are equal, but the percussion never dominates. Kim initiates the call with her body and Angel responds with his cajon. At Downstream: Reimagining Water, Kim and Angel performed an improvisation after his call to *Yemayá*, a goddess of water and the ocean. Angel also sang a song to Yemayá as a solo. This symbolizes the transformative power inherent in the ocean and the power of joining with the source of energy that we can receive from ocean water.

Angel is also an initiate of the Havana school of the Lucumí religious-folkloric tradition. The musical-spiritual voices in his background made their mark on our process in an intimate way as he introduced us to *Yemayá* in the Santeria religion. Originating in the Yoruba tradition, *Yemayá* is the Orisha of motherhood and of the ocean. She is the mother of all living things and the owner of all waters. We remained open to her influences, and her presence felt its way into the performance.

Figure 12.5 Water reflection: Kim Smith and Lindsey Lollie. (*Source*: Keith Settle)

In these ways, *Bodies of Water* presented a contact zone of meaning and bodies. The slow process revealed itself, water-like. Patient water, and its inherent ability to co-mingle, provided an avenue to join and engage with dancers and audiences.

Gaston Bachelard, in *Water and Dreams*, writes of "the river's special sigh, a sigh that comes at the time when, within us, there appears a slight, very slight sorrow, which spreads, melts away and will not be mentioned again."[21] This sigh became part of the creative process, the actions I took to channel my creative energy to overcome major loss and life rupture. I looked to the sigh of water by asking dancers to portray a sigh of wanting I had found beside the river. I recognized my sorrow in dancers' arches and reaches; the dance came to symbolize waters of my grief and letting go.

Dancers' voices and hours of movement creation mingled with my own and finally we lingered in "water's laughter." Like the red-legged frog (*grenouille*), which once hibernated by burrowing into the mud of the LA River, dancers leapt to submerge beneath concrete and rise.

The piece stimulated dialogue about water in workshops. In Toronto the dancers, musicians, and I conveyed the creative process as dance dramaturgy, discussing the meaning of water and healing with workshop participants such as Canadian dance experts Elizabeth Langley and Isaac Akrong, who discussed water as ever-present, a horizon, meditative, powerful, and ferocious. I guided them to give short movement studies, similar to those that can be observed on the Asava Dance website.[22] The Toronto audience not only discussed water's healing properties, but also the duality of water in nature, given its capacity to nurture and destroy. They pointed out the need for water in drought-stricken areas.

Water Is Transformation

We saw diverse descriptions of water highlighted in our workshops as a call to understand water's transformational power. Water taught us about transformation, and ultimately I decided to create a piece that focused on our life-changing moments, as well as moments that transform collective identities in societies. For example, during a workshop in Los Angeles we emphasized civil rights marches from Selma to Montgomery in 1965, considering this as a transformational moment for the United States. We discussed how each of us connects to a moment historically, no matter what our backgrounds, ages, and whether we are from the United States, because it was about a history of transforming human consciousness. This pivotal moment in history also clearly conveys the power of bodies. That is, in the face of brutal violence and weaponry that was used against civil rights protestors, the human body can appear frail and weak. Many people sacrificed their bodies in order that the children of the following generation would not experience the same suffering of racial violence. Human beings form the collective energy of water. Like rapid water going downstream at the end of winter, they carve away at rocks and over time create a breakthrough.

Figure 12.6 Water is transformation—Lorrin Hilton, Kimberley Smith, and Lindsey Lollie. (*Source*: Keith Settle)

Figure 12.7 Water breakthrough—Lindsey Lollie and Kim Smith. (*Source*: Keith Settle)

Conclusions: Somaesthetics, Deep Ecology, and Multi-disciplinarity

The creative process in *Bodies of Water* reveals the unique way of knowing that occurs in dance somatics when water is placed at the centre of inquiry. Water (the object of study) was not separated from the body of the dancer (researcher), and meanings or discoveries arose from within the dancing body, which is itself two-thirds water. The creative process is significant in part because dance as a field lacks discipline-specific research methodologies that account for the ways practitioners engage through embodiment. Rather than articulating peculiar dance-like means of reaching new understandings, the field sometimes appropriates or imports methodologies from other fields such as education or art, possibly to its own detriment. This perpetuates a limiting view that understands dance as either a practical tool or as an object to be analyzed. By valuing the peculiar pathway dance offers to deepened knowing through somatics, the unique knowledge of this field can be fully realized. Theories from other disciplines can then be integrated through an organic methodology.

The dance processes described here exemplify a means of building community interactively and attuning to ecological awareness that arises from within a dance process; this could inform other fields and be undertaken by non-dancers. Asava Dance practices involved both dancers and non-dancers, and drew from current somatic theorists like Bonnie Bainbridge Cohen, as well as from early writing in the field of somatics, which emerges from the Corporalist Movement with pioneers such as Laban, Bartenieff, Alexander, and Feldenkrais. Therein, the human being was understood in terms of her integration and interaction with the environment.

Dancer-researchers' refusal to legitimize a dichotomy between doing and thinking, body and mind is critical to an ecologically oriented research practice and ethics. Ciane Fernandes writes about the damaging effects of adhering to these dichotomies, particularly in the dance field where the "researcher-artist has a unique responsibility: to transform secular dichotomies into somatic and ecological manners of contemporary life."[23] The suggestion is that dance, when taught and practiced from a somatic point of view, can contribute effective and innovative means of experiencing and addressing neglected issues, such as sustainability and ecological awareness. A result of this emphasis on interaction with the environment in the field of somatics, dance aesthetics—or somaesthetics—aids those seeking an aesthetic of personal sensitization and planetary consciousness: "Ethics is the aesthetics of the future."[24]

An important emphasis of this chapter is on describing the emergent nature of knowledge in dance creative processes—the way insight arises from somatic experiences rather than from a methodology imposed from outside. The principles for research into water are emblematic of "somaesthetics," which Mullis discusses as well as "somatic-performative" research methodologies described by Ciane Fernandes. This emergent nature is vital to drawing the waterly insights dance is capable of, and "diluting barriers among fields artificially split, which hinders the flow of life, art, and research."[25]

The somatic performative process of Asava Dance follows dancers' bodily experiences of water's wisdom and insight through intuitive, embodied processes, while informed by ideas and interactions with multiple disciplines.

The presence of an ecologically oriented ethic and awareness in somatic research is clear, and may always be linked to the intuitive approach to meaning. Bennie Maupin describes water as "constantly in evolution," which refers to this intuitive aspect of water processes. Water braids our individual human consciousness as connected with a larger social consciousness.

In summary, as I directed the self-organizing creative process and built meaningful phrases of movement, Asava dancers and musicians sought to embody the various characteristics of water. In these ways, we developed a multi-disciplinary process of attunement to ecological awareness that is rooted in somatics. Asava practices could be undertaken by anyone seeking a meaningful means of embodying water because this conveys a somaesthetics of personal sensitization. Water informed our creative process and aesthetic as an ensemble, and we found ourselves opening to a planetary consciousness.

In our experiences giving Asava Dance workshops, water reflected group consciousness.

As the opening event for Downstream during World Water Week in 2012, we were grateful to participate in several workshops and talks during the following days. We considered water from the perspective of visual artists, Indigenous activists, poets, and Elders. During our interactions with other presenters at the multi-disciplinary gathering, we learned about concerns that could be incorporated into the greater consciousness. For example, Melina Laboucan Massimo's stories of individual people who were affected physically through cancers and ailments contracted due to tar sands pollution touched us profoundly. The specific movements that represent struggle and strength in our work *Exit from the Blue Room* (2012) connect to the embodiment of this consciousness, and seek to engage audiences in demanding ways. "I put all of my energy and emotion into these powerful movements and I demand an audience's attention because I invite them to actually 'feel' with me" (Kimberley Michelle Smith).

We came to know water, through our work and through this gathering, as a potent force signalling transformation of society. Through this creative method, our personal histories were revealed in familial contexts, in colonial contexts, and in geography as witnesses to water's needs. When observing the creation of movement, I became aware of emotional crevices, worn like lines carved by water on the mountain, lines defined and drawn by water in our bodies.[26] *Bodies of Water* is about intersecting painful or joyful realities that we have each experienced through a somaesthetics of water.

Notes

1 I am thinking of choreographers such as Bill T. Jones and Judith Marcuse.

2 *imush q'uyatl'un*, directed by Karolle Wall, 2009.

3 The Islands Institute is an organization based in Puneluxulth' territory, which highlights arts from the Gulf Islands, British Columbia, as well as offering international online artist residencies.

4 In *Art as Experience* (New York: Berkeley Publishing Group, 1980), John Dewey famously writes about aesthetics as an art of experience, and his philosophy conveys a process of "doing and undergoing," which can be compared to water's constant flow and changes. Dewey's major contribution to aesthetics and education was to suggest that that energies and environmental forces intermingle with the organisms that inhabit it, a fact that is well known within both Indigenous and somatic philosophies. In other words, as individuals, we know the world through our experiences, and Dewey says aesthetic experiences provide an intense distillation of meaning or an organic moment that stands out among all the others.

Dewey provided an idea of "somatic naturalism," extended by both Schusterman and Mullis as a way of striving to understand the role of the body in aesthetic experience. Richard Schusterman, "Home Alone? Self and Other in Somaesthetics and Performing Live," *Journal of Aesthetic Education* 36, no. 4 (2002): 84–92; Eric C. Mullis, "Performative

Somaesthetics: Principles and Scope," *Journal of Aesthetic Education* 40, no. 2 (2006): 104–17, http://www.jstor.org/stable/4140211.

5 Mullis, "Performative Somaesthetics," 106.

6 Ibid.

7 Martin Luther King Jr., "I've Been to the Mountaintop," Memphis, Tennessee, April 3, 1968, http://www.americanrhetoric.com/speeches/mlkivebeentothemountaintop.htm.

8 Edgar Allan Poe, "Silence—A Fable," in *The Works of Edgar Allan Poe*, The Raven Edition, Gutenburg, 2:220–21, http://www.gutenberg.org/files/2148/2148-h/2148-h .htm#link2H_4_0008.

9 Gaston Bachelard, *Water and Dreams: An Essay on the Imagination of Matter*, trans. Edith R. Farrell (Dallas: Pegasus Foundation, 1983), 67.

10 Augusto Boal, *Theatre of the Oppressed* (New York: Theatre Communications Group, 1993).

11 Paolo Freire, *Pedagogy of the Oppressed* (New York: Continuum, 1993).

12 Alannah Young Leon and Denise Marie Nadeau, "Moving with Water: Relationships and Responsibilities," in *downstream: reimagining water*, ed. D. Christian and R. Wong (Waterloo, ON: Wilfrid Laurier University Press, 2017).

13 Bonnie Bainbridge Cohen, "Fluidity of Movement in Health and Vitality," http://www .bodymindcentering.com/blogs/fluidity-of-movement-in-health-and-vitality.

14 Thomas Hanna. *Bodies in Revolt: A Primer in Somatic Thinking*. New York: Holt Reinhart, 1970.

15 Sondra Fraleigh, ed., *Moving Consciously: Somatic Transformations Through Dance, Yoga, and Touch* (Urbana: University of Illinois Press, 2015), xxii.

16 *Ujaii* breath is also called "ocean breath" in yoga.

17 Carl Jung, "Archives of the Collective Unconscious," in *Part I: Archetypes and the Collective Unconscious*, vol. 9 of *The Collected Works of CG Jung*, ed. and trans. Gerhard Adler and R. F. C. Hull (Princeton: Princeton University Press, 1980), 18–19.

18 Bennie Maupin, *Penumbra*, The Bennie Maupin Ensemble (LA: Cryptagrammaphone, 2006).

19 Lauren Bon, *Not a Cornfield*, 2006, www.notacornfield.com.

20 The statement, "Water is the embodiment of Spirit" was the email signature of Dorothy Christian when she was organizing the Protect Our Sacred Waters event in 2009.

21 Bachelard, *Water and Dreams*, 190–91.

22 *Asava Dance*, www.asavadance.com.

23 Ciane Fernandez, "Somatic-Performative Research: Attunement, Sensitivity, Integration," *art Research Journal/Revista de Pesquisa em Arte* [Brasil] 1, no. 1 (2014): 72–91.

24 Laurie Anderson, lecture, New York University 1993, quoted in Fernandes, "Somatic-Performative Research," 124–44.

25 Fernandes, "Somatic-Performative Research," 78. Fernandes carefully outlines founding principles and contextual principles of "Somatic-performative" research, including the employment of authentic movement as an axis element that guides the movement of research. She also discusses the soma of the researcher as the idea and origin that processes and studies, as well as the importance of following a pulse, or the idea of being guided by an inner pulse. Fernandes presents the ideal of interactions with multiple disciplines. Her related contextual principles suggest that: "danceability [is] applied to all beings, places, fields and contexts; Sustainability and deep ecology—dance as radical political transformation along daily basis activities in an ethics/aesthetics" (Fernandez, "Somatic-Performative Research," 73).

26 In *Sensitive Chaos: The Creation of Flowing Forms in Water and Air,* Theodor Schwenk, an engineer in Germany, was deeply concerned about the quality of water and asked how to improve its quality. In doing so, he realized that first he must understand the

"nature of water" itself on its own terms, which led to his book *Sensitive Chaos*. Schwenk describes how water flows, the subtle "movement forms" he made visible through the addition of dyes, which are observable whenever water moves. In unpolluted water, these forms appear.

Bibliography

Asava Dance. Written and sponsored by Artistic Director Seonagh Odhiambo Horne. www.asavadance.com.

Bachelard, Gaston. *Water and Dreams: An Essay on the Imagination of Matter*. Translated by Edith R. Farrell. Dallas: The Pegasus Foundation, 1983.

Bainbridge Cohen, Bonnie. "Fluidity of Movement in Health and Vitality." http://www .bodymindcentering.com/blogs/fluidity-of-movement-in-health-and-vitality.

———. *Sensing, Feeling and Action*. Northampton, MA: Contact Publishers, 2012.

Boal, Augusto. *Theatre of the Oppressed*. New York: Theatre Communications Group, 1993.

Bon, Lauren. *Not a Cornfield*. 2006. http://notacornfield.com.

Dewey, John. *Art as Experience*. New York: Berkeley Publishing Group, 1980.

Fernandes, Ciane. "Moving Studies: Somatic-Performative Research in a Wide Dance Field." Lecture Society of Dance History Scholars/Congress of Research in Dance Joint Conference, University of California–Riverside, CA, November 2013.

———. "Somatic-Performative Research: Attunement, Sensitivity, Synchronicity." *Art Research Journal/Revista de Pesquisa em Arte* [Brasil] 1, no. 1 (2014): 124–44.

Fraleigh, Sondra, ed. *Moving Consciously: Somatic Transformations through Dance, Yoga, and Touch*. Urbana: University of Illinois Press, 2015.

Freire, Paolo. *Pedagogy of the Oppressed*. New York: Continuum, 1993.

Hanna, Thomas *Bodies in Revolt: A Primer in Somatic Thinking*. New York: Holt Reinhart, 1970.

Islands Institute. http://islandsinstitute.com/.

Jung, Carl. "Archetypes of the Collective Unconscious." In *The Collected Works of CG Jung*, edited and translated by Gerhard Adler and R. F. C. Hull, 3–41. Princeton, NJ: Princeton University Press, 1980.

King, Martin Luther, Jr. "I've Been to the Mountaintop." Memphis, Tennessee, April 3, 1968. http://www.americanrhetoric.com/speeches/mlkivebeentothemountaintop .htm.

Koplowitz, Stephan. *Taskforce*. 2008. http://www.koplowitzprojects.com/taskforce/.

Maupin, Bennie. *Penumbra*. The Bennie Maupin Ensemble. Cryptagrammaphone, 2006.

Mullis, Eric C. "Performative Somaesthetics: Principles and Scope." *Journal of Aesthetic Education* 40, no. 2 (2006): 104–17. http://www.jstor.org/stable/4140211.

Odhiambo Horne, Seonagh. *Healing Water Project 2010*. http://islandsinstitute.com/ gallery/HealingWater/index.htm.

Poe, Edgar Allan, "Silence." In *The Works of Edgar Allan Poe*, 2:220–21. The Raven Edition. Gutenburg. 2008. http://www.gutenberg.org/files/2148/2148-h/2148-h .htm#link2H_4_0008.

Schusterman, Richard. "Home Alone? Self and Other in Somaesthetics and Performing Live." *Journal of Aesthetic Education* 36, no. 4 (2002): 102–15.

Schwenk, Theodor *Sensitive Chaos: The Creation of Flowing Forms in Water and Air*. Forest Row, UK: Rudolph Steiner Press, 2004.

Wall, Karolle, dir. *'imush q'uyatl'un.* 2009.

Young Leon, Alannah Young, and Denise Nadeau. "Moving with Water: Relationships and Responsibilities." *downstream: reimagining water.* Edited by D. Christian and R. Wong, 117–38. Waterloo, ON: Wilfrid Laurier University Press, 2017.

Upstream
A Conversation with Water
Cathy Stubington

As one water body speaking to another water body, dear reader, I would like to tell you about *Sawllkwa*, Runaway Moon Theatre's community performance celebrating the water that we are part of, and that is part of us. Named after the word for water in the Secwepemc language, *Sawllkwa* was presented in July 2010, following three weeks of rehearsal in Enderby, BC. These rehearsals built upon a year-long Reflection on Water through workshops in dance, music, fabric design, and ceramics that took place throughout the community. What does it look and feel like when a community expresses its gratitude to water in creative ways? Just as water carries everything along its path, *Sawllkwa* gathered energy, people, goodwill, and ideas from these and from previous community art projects.

I live on a small farm near Enderby, BC, in Secwepemc traditional territory. The farm feeds my family. I work with Runaway Moon Theatre, in the rural region surrounding the small city of Enderby adjacent to Splatsin First Nation.[1] Since 1998, Runaway Moon's community engaged art has been about, for, and with the people who live in this valley. My three children, Rosa, Leif, and Nell, have been part of Runaway Moon's projects since they were tiny; it was largely for them that I plunged into initiating our first large-scale community play, wondering how I could learn about and contribute to the place where they were to grow up. Over the course of many months, this play, *Not the Way I Heard It*, grew and grew to a cast of 163 people. Leading up to its presentation in May 1999, hundreds of people of all ages and from all walks of life were caught in its wake, making costumes, puppets, and masks; helping to organize; and sharing stories. Since then my connection to this place has been deepening through ongoing arts-based exploration,[2] which continues to draw people in, each time with a new aspect of what it means to live here.

In 2005, I was given the name Flying Spirit by the Kia7as, the Grand-mothers, of Splatsin, at a naming ceremony on the land that I am learning to connect with through this art practice. Tswum Rosalind Williams, together with the Kia7as, came up with the name "Flying Spirit." I was requested to introduce myself with this name when here in Secwepemc territory. So, I intro-duce myself as T'uctwes re S't'lcalqw as I lead you through the creation and performance of *Sawllkwa*.

The many elements that went into *Sawllkwa* were selected from things I heard during the Reflection year while talking to people about water, from conversations with Tswum Rosalind Williams, and from our initial rehearsals in which participants were invited to contribute stories about water. We wished to draw attention to and celebrate this remarkable substance that we are made of and that we touch many times each day.

Rather than take a stance on behalf of water, I prefer that *Sawllkwa* speaks for itself; the medium of community performance is already an alternative to formal discourse. So, I will take you on on the journey that you would have taken had you driven upstream from the town of Enderby on the evening of July 24, 2010, to see the performance. I am writing this guided by the forms of water, hoping to minimize the distance between experience and the telling, just as we wanted *Sawllkwa* to *be* an experience of water rather than *about* the experience of water. Many people took part, and I will introduce some of them to you. I hope you will catch a glimpse of our approach to connecting the community through art over a long period, and how this project offered many ways for people to engage with the body of water that sustains us.

We drive up the meandering road for half an hour or so to the Kingfisher Environmental Interpretive Centre. Leaving the car in a field, we cross the road and walk down a dirt lane leading to the Centre, which is a community-run salmon hatchery. The trees lining the path are strewn with dozens of small blue flags; looking closely we notice that each one is different.

The flags had been created over the previous year at public events (school field trips, the Seed Swap, Runaway Moon's annual Peony Tea, and more), where I'd set up a table again and again with scissors, cardboard, fabric, paint, and brushes. Passersby were invited to decorate small lengths of pale blue cotton with stencilled images of water. At first each person made his or her own stencil, but as these accumulated, people could either make their own or use existing ones. Over time the images passed from one hand to another, combining with other ones, just as water gathers whatever it finds along its path. Someone had hung the flags in the trees, and they became the path to the performance of *Sawllkwa*.

The path opens into a clearing in the woods, where people are gathering. A musician, Michelle, welcomes us with her accordion, and with the story of a remarkable incident that took place right here. A few years ago heavy spring rains took out a chunk of the hillside. It slid down, dislodging and carrying trees in its wake. It moved a cabin several hundred metres, leaving it right smack in the middle of the same road we drove along to get here. The owner entered his cabin to see what damage had been done. A glass of water that he had set on the table was still standing in place, its contents undisturbed. The power and the gentleness of water, Michelle marvels.

By now a crowd has gathered and Michelle, also a board member of Runaway Moon, is moving us along. The light is beginning to change. The performance has to start now so that we can see our way through before nightfall. We are ushered down a hill as if part of a descending waterfall, guided protectively by cast members lining each side of the path, who are whispering "Sawllkwa, Sawllkwa."

When staking out the path for the event, Rosalind (who is dedicated to Secwepemc language regeneration) and I listened in this very spot to water rushing through a creek further into the woods—*Sawllkwa. Sawllkwa.* We wondered if the language of this place arose from the sounds in nature. As we stood on the path, we tried saying *Sawllkwa* in many different ways. That was in the late spring, high water. Now it is midsummer and the sound of the creek is quieter. *Sawllkwa.*

Each person in our cast wears a flowing water robe. Close together in a line, catching the breeze, they become a river.

The robes had been started in fabric design workshops held throughout the past year. How can we make fabric that is like water, we wondered? Facilitators and participants experimented together, trying various techniques inspired by traditions from around the world. Our first event was a fold-and-dye workshop at the Band Hall. The second was a block-printing session in Leah's coffee shop, followed by screen printing in the basement of the United Church.

At first, people tended to make emblems, symbols, or pictures of water: umbrellas, beach scenes, riverside rocks. But how could we recreate water itself rather than a depiction of it?

Akira Hanson, a former schoolteacher and longtime Runaway Moon collaborator, discovered a spray-and-paint technique using lots of water to push around the dyes. Each person started working on a length of cotton, then moved around the room and did something to another length that someone else had started. Both process and result simulated water. Akira encouraged us to become water-like as we painted. Deb Humphries, a Runaway Moon board member and community-based artist, suggested screen printing one person's design over another's, so that the effect became multi-layered—like water—and the effort collective. In collaborative work many hands touch each piece: the fabric, the robes, the wearing of the robes, the event—all created by many hands. Our community process is cumulative: everything is made to be part of a larger whole. Just as we are all part of water.

We tried tie-dyeing with A. L. Fortune Secondary School art students. They enjoyed twisting and dying lengths of gauze cotton several times over, and seeing the ripples of water appear. Later, as the cast expanded in the final days of rehearsal, we needed more and more fabric to create more and more robes. Our practicum student from Concordia University, Jesse Orr, found herself demonstrating to the many people who showed up wanting to try tie-dye. (She was dismayed at being left in charge of something she was learning herself; the co-learning process of our fabric sessions was new to her. But tie-dye is completely generous. There is no such thing as failure; each one turns out to be a surprise.) Reams of cloth were hung outside the Enderby Drill Hall to dry, joyfully decorating the parking lot and letting people know we were there.

When dry, the fabric was made into robes by volunteers, including Rose. For each of our community projects there is at least one person who, for some reason, commits in a huge way. For this project, Rose jumped right in the deep end. A woman in her late seventies who was fairly new to Enderby, Rose told me that there had been no time for fun while growing up on a farm in the Prairies, and she was now going to make up for it. (The first Runaway Moon workshop she came to was in 2007, when we made ceramic potato noise makers with local potter Amy Huppler. Later Rose learned to do beadwork with Marie Thomas for our collaborative Apple Tree.) She came to just about every drop-in session for *Sawllkwa* (dance, music, fabric, and pottery), and apologized when she missed one. Her journey, like that of many Runaway Moon participants, was its own stream joining up with ours.

 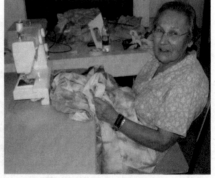

Figures 13.1 and 13.2 Runaway Moon volunteer Rose Gimlett. (*Source:* Donlea McCombs)

The water robes have travelled to other places since *Sawllkwa*: to Lillooet, where they were worn for the ceremony to release smolts into the Fraser River system, which meets with the Shuswap River on the way down to the Pacific Ocean, where salmon feast for four years before returning to their respective homes. The robes then travelled to the neighbourhood of Mount Pleasant in Vancouver, where they were worn for the unveiling of a street painting that marks an underground stream. (You can borrow them, too, if you like, to celebrate the watershed you are part of.) In working with fabric, I've felt affinities with the Kinship of Rivers project undertaken by Wang Ping, whereby they have created flags and banners about water in many contexts and joined two or more rivers/watersheds through the peoples of those watersheds. While the Kinship of Rivers project works on a much larger scale, connecting the Mississippi and Yangtze rivers, it resonates with us in its facilitation of international dialogues through close attention to the rivers that make our lives possible. Water communities work in fluid, organic ways, and our *Sawllkwa* flags have journeyed to Akonjo village, Kenya, where they were part of a water celebration there.

Down the hill we flow, hearing the word "Sawllkwa" whispered by people wearing the water robes. Hurry, we will have to crane our necks to see above the shoulders of the crowd that has gathered under the roof of the huge gazebo at the bottom of the hill. The gazebo is curtained off with thin gauze, twist-dyed so that it gives the impression of reflections on rippling water. Up close, you can detect the movement of people behind it. They appear as though they are in the water, and we are mesmerized by their underwater dance.

From up in the rafters our Kenyan guest artist Jimmy Ouma speaks the voice of Tqaltkukpi7, the Creator, declaring the parting of the waters to reveal the Earth and all of its creatures. The curtains part, revealing a group of children huddled on a rock in the centre.

Tswum Rosalind Williams, recognized as the cultural historian of Splatsin First Nation here in this corner of Secwepemc Territory, has shared cultural memory of how the Earth emerged from the water. Everyone in the cast sings a song Rosalind has written to help the children learn the Secwepemc words for thunder, lightning, rain, and torrents.

This generous sharing brings to mind the first time Rosalind and I worked together, on the Enderby and District Community Play, *Not the Way I Heard It*. That time she insisted that the whole cast of 163 people, both Native and non-Native, would be dressed in First Nations regalia to give a sense that not so long ago the Splatsin people lived here in large numbers. It was an incredible turnaround in a place where there had been little, if any, interaction between the settler and reserve communities for a long, long time. This I found out when seeking stories for the script that would represent the people of the area.

A newcomer to this reality, I could not find anyone who knew anyone on the adjacent First Nations community. After several months I met Rosalind, who agreed to work with me on the play and brought in several stories, including a re-enactment of the Creation of the Reserve. It was the beginning of improved relations here in this place.

Singing the words for water in many languages, we leave the gazebo.

This new song was created from my collection of words for water, written on a rice paper scroll seventy feet long and continuing to grow. Each word is in a different language and was written by a different person. As the scroll gets longer, it becomes more eventful to unroll it when there is a new word to add! The first words written on the scroll were *Maje*, the Kiswahili word for water, and then *Ndoh*, from Gambia. *Sawllkwa* was written in the largest letters at one of the Kia7as' [grandmothers'] meetings at Splatsin Tsm7aksaltn Teaching Centre. I have taught the song to students at UBC Okanagan, at a Runaway Moon Peony Tea, at the Downtown Eastside Arts4All Institute (Vancouver), at the third Akonjo/Kingfisher Centre Concert (Kingfisher), and at the Dance for Peace conference (Nairobi, Kenya). At the Downstream Gathering on Granville Island (Vancouver), we added the word for water in several more First Nations languages. Emil, the one-year-old son of Varrick, our theatre director, learned the first two lines of the tune; *Sawllkwa* was his very first word.

The word for water is *pi* in Dholuo, the language spoken in Jimmy Ouma's village in Kenya. Jimmy is a young actor whose community development initiatives have been supported by a number of people in our community. Three of us went to Akonjo to work with him and the youth of the village on a performance called *Pi en Ngima* (Water Is Life) in 2009. Because of this experience, we invited him to visit and be part of *Sawllkwa*. While he was here, he met with the Kia7as (grandmothers) at the Tsm7aksaltn Centre. It was eye-opening for him to meet people gathering to recollect and regenerate the Secwepemc language. This interaction has stimulated him to lead a cultural regeneration project in Akonjo on the other side of the world, where youth are gathering with the Elders to hear stories and traditions before they are lost.

Jimmy Ouma and the youth are also working on a stream rehabilitation project, which emerged from asking every home in the village about what people know about water and what they think can be done to protect it. Now there is a long-term tree-planting project in the village.

Where does a creative process begin? As time passes, these creative projects run into each other the way water trickles down a mountain and joins with other trickles coming down other slopes.

While it is the specific land community where I live that directly gives rise to the water play or water work described in this essay, my practices and perspectives resonate with others around the world in land-based communities such as the Andean world view described by Eduardo Grillo, one of the founders of PRATEC, the non-profit Andean Project for Peasant Technologies:

> All that exists in the Andean world is alive. Not only man, animals and plants but also rocks, rivers, the mountains and everything else. In the Andean world nothing is considered to be inert: everything is alive. Like ourselves, everyone and everything participates in the great celebration that is life: everyone eats, all sleep, all dance, all sing—everyone lives fully.[3]

The writings of Grillo and his colleagues have inspired me with their clear descriptions of the view that water nurtures us, and that we must reciprocate by nurturing water. Also, I learn from PRATEC of the importance in Aymara and Quechua communities of celebrating together (with water). I also acknowledge the writings of Indigenous theorists like Shawn Wilson, Joanne Archibald, and Margaret Kovach,[4] in which I have felt that the writers were talking directly to me as the reader.

I don't want to lose you along the way, so please let's return to *Sawllkwa*:

Led by the "Sun" (a role filled by my accommodating daughter Rosa), we leave the gazebo to the sound of twenty-six words for water. Six guides each lead a group of audience into the woods, where six different scenes take place concurrently so that we can all see everything. Each of the guides has developed a character with a distinct perspective on water: a sea captain, a pirate, a lanky swimmer, a man dressed up in a shower curtain. All the characters are on stilts, so it is easy to keep them in sight ahead of us in the woods.

Figure 13.3 The sun. (*Source: Salmon Arm Observer*)

Varrick Grimes first joined Runaway Moon Theatre's artistic team as director for the *Open Air* spectacle in 2006 (in which the stilt-walking "air people" protected the air from the monsters whose design was dictated by children's drawings). It was Varrick's idea that the audience, as water, would flow down a hill, opening out to a shallow pool, then separate into tributaries through the wood, later to join up again and flow out to the Shuswap River.

At the first stop in the woods we are welcomed by Neil Brooks as a Beaver. He swishes two tiny salmon puppets down a real trickle of water to the accompaniment of a young violinis hidden behind a tree. An arrangement of miniature farm animals, toy trucks, and buildings demonstrate how water is affected by everything along its path.

Neil coordinates the community-run salmon hatchery, and he will work his new beaver persona into next year's field trips for children. His miniature upstream/downstream demonstration inspired Jimmy Ouma and the youth of his village to walk along the stream looking at all of the various water collection points, noting the extent to which everything downstream is affected by what happens upstream.

Next, we are heralded by Owl, impersonated by Marlene Robbins of Splatsin, embravened by an owl mask and wings. Owl invites us into a replica of the kind of underground winter home that the Secwepemc people lived in by this river until very recently. Inside the home, it is almost dark. Coyote and Grizzly are vying for night or day, intimidating each other as they drum and dance around a fire. The boys have learned this song in their language in order to tell this stptakwela *(Creation story); today they are dancing in public for the first time.*

Figure 13.4 Beaver. (*Source*: Blair Orr)

There is still light in the woods when we leave the underground house, and we follow our guide to the next gathering spot. We are invited to sit and listen to three stories of near- drowning, a theme that came up repeatedly when we talked to local residents before the project.

One of the storytellers is Barbara, a knowledgeable and dedicated activist who has done endless research and written countless letters in defence of waterways. She laments the failure of her attempts—she hasn't been heard above the din. As they say in the Dholuo language, "Koko mar ogwal ok mon dhiang modo pi" (the squeaking of the frog cannot be heard above the slurp of the cow). For Barbara, participating in our project was like a drink of fresh water. She articulates her appreciation for our approach, which does not imply "us" and "them" but simply promotes awareness and appreciation while creating an open space for people who may not share the same views to get together. Victoria-based community artist Paula Jardine and I call this practice "oblique activism."

Runaway Moon's community-engaged work is not issue-based; our wish is to bring forward a theme in a way that allows participants and audience to see various perspectives rather than to further polarize existing attitudes. In a small community, those upstream live very near to neighbours downstream. With different opinions about water use and river traffic, the river can be something that divides. In *Sawllkwa*, we are asking people to engage, together, with a body of water—the one that nurtures us—something we all have in common. We trust that this will become reciprocal—that we will nurture the water. I believe that if we can become connected in this way to where we live, we will no longer be able to treat the Earth as merely a set of resources to use up.

A diminutive pirate on very tall stilts leads us to a bridge over a stream. He invites us to make ourselves comfy along the stream bank. Tiny replicas of traditional houses of Coastal, Interior Salish, and Plains people are nestled in the woods. Proportionately the stream becomes a river, and the undergrowth becomes trees.

We are told how long long ago Tkaltkukpi7 asked Sek'lep (Coyote) to take the salmon up the river into the interior to feed the people. A masked Coyote transforms into a tiny puppet self to meet with the residents of each miniature house. Where Coyote is shown generosity, he instructs the salmon to stay as they will be given a good home. The salmon have lived here in this place ever since.

A favourite part of *Sawllkwa* for my sister, who is from Vancouver, was watching these tiny puppets come to life in the woods. She described witnessing a deep connection between the woman manipulating the puppets and the puppets at her feet. This extraordinary connection is characteristic of community-engaged performance.

Figure 13.5 Longhouse. (*Source*: Blair Orr)

The puppeteer, Constance Christian, made the houses. She spent day after day constructing models, in intricate detail, of three traditional houses from different regions. When she had finished, she created the mask for her nephew, who danced the role of "Coyote" in the underground house. A reclusive person most of the time, when Constance decides to do something, she can't be stopped. She brings her own clear vision, and when anyone offers a suggestion, she becomes even more certain of her plan.

I first met Constance in 2004, when Runaway Moon worked with the Splatsin Health Department on a gargantuan community shadow play on the theme of addiction awareness, presented on the largest drive-in screen in North America, which happens to be on Splatsin land. (This, in turn, stimulated a community-based shadow play in the Downtown Eastside on the roots of addiction and recovery, led by Vancouver Moving Theatre—another major tributary.) At that time she had withdrawn from society.

I needed a design assistant for the shadow play, and Constance was recommended. She travelled into town every day for five weeks, and quietly and meticulously cut out shapes of shadow figures. During the performance, thirteen women from the band each spoke a single line about growing up in a home in which alcohol was a factor. (These words have become part of collective memory.) One day Constance jumped in to replace someone who was absent, and in this way became part of the performance. "It was fun," she said, "once I got my feet wet!" She has reminded me many times of this experience, crediting Runaway Moon for having brought her out of her shell. She now has a fulfilling full-time job working with children and adults in the community.

Figure 13.6 Making stuff for *Sawllkwa*. (*Source:* Cathy Stubington)

All these experiences are part of what my sister sensed when she watched the puppets make their way down the stream bank to speak to Coyote.

My daughter Nell on tall stilts, as a swimmer bragging about her Olympic medals, leads us a little further along the path, and the sound of a harp wafts through the fir branches. We see a puppet show that tells a story (brought forward by a high school student) of a Selkie, half seal, half human.

Figure 13.7 Selki story. (*Source*: Blair Orr)

New to the area, the harpist has found that being part of *Sawllkwa* has been a great way to meet people. The puppeteers are our Luo visitor Jimmy, and a brother and sister, aged six and eight, with extraordinary powers of concentration. They are one of Varrick's brilliant casting choices: the children manipulate two parents—puppets half the children's size—and gentle, large Jimmy Ouma manipulates a baby, half seal and half human.

The story ends on a haunting note as the boy/father and Jimmy Ouma/ baby leave the spot, going to meet the river, which sparkles just beyond the trees.

Further along the riverbank we encounter a puppet boot, nestled in the stones.

It was set up there by our production manager Lawrence Lee of Splatsin. Lawrence performed in the first community play in 1999 and was stage manager for *By the River* in 2005. From his experience in the bush, he has the ability to track the timing by the passage of the sun in the sky—invaluable for organizing crews to move large puppets from one place to another, or to set things to float in the current. Lawrence had taken Jimmy Ouma out into the forest to find the wood to make the puppet booth; they saw two coyotes.

The puppet show (shared by Rosalind) is about a scoundrel named Peetasah. Peetasah tricks a vain Chief with the promise of finding great riches in the underwater world. The Chief jumps into the river never to return, and Peetasah takes off with the Chief's daughter and all of his horses! The performers are my son Leif, and his honorary uncle Zompopo. Leif's lively Peetasah alongside Zompopo's dead-pan Chief is the most hilarious clown duo, and it's a wonderful way for the two to spend time together.

Figure 13.8 Peetasah. (*Source*: Blair Orr)

Wiping away tears of laughter, we make our way to some water-filled metal tanks: a halfway home for salmon smolts. Michelle is there with her accordion (bless her, she has been in every event since 1999), leading a singalong of familiar songs on the theme of Water. We take a break at this point, while we wait for the other groups to flow out of the woods. We've been on quite a journey. Perhaps you need a drink of water? Me too.

The process of putting together one of these shows, while exhilarating and liberating for participants, is exhausting for multiple reasons. One is the personal energy required, with our rigorous principle and practice of "everyone's welcome" requiring continual invitation and re-invitation over the period of a year. Another is the unpredictability: What if nobody wants to accept the invitation to participate? What if nobody can? And really, why should they? And, once they've joined in, what do we do if they drop out? We are swimming upstream against the current of electronic media, which make it easier for people to stay at home rather than be part of creating and recreating our own local culture.

And there's the time commitment. The schedule for *Sawllkwa* divided the day into morning, afternoon, and evening, and I had planned to spend two of the three sessions in the workshop space. But invariably someone wanted to come in at the exact time I was intending not to be there. Before long, I was at the workshop from early morning through to late evening. For the director Varrick it was the same. Music director Murray tried to pace himself this time, also somewhat unsuccessfully.

Two students from the Theatre in Development program of Concordia University in Montreal joined the *Sawllkwa* project for a practicum. Wanting to be sure they had a valuable experience, we arranged for them to help with two of the three sessions each day. Before long, my irreplaceable assistant Jesse was opening the workshop early each morning, and closing with us at the end of each evening, day after day. Well, it was a realistic experience of community-based arts, and of the commitment of the people who do this work. The policy "everyone's welcome" is essential to inclusivity, requiring us to push hard against the cultural currents that suggest otherwise.

Well. Our rest is over. People shoot up like a geyser from behind the containers, breaking into an intense rhythm using their palms on the water. What is the sound of water as a musical instrument? The splashing sound elaborates the percussion. Dancer Kristi Christian joyfully emerges from the centre of the container in front.

We met Kristi when she joined the first community play in 1999 and led the tiniest children in the salmon fry dance. During that project she met her husband and father of her children, who have been part of Runaway Moon for all of their lives. Kristi was the dance leader for this project, developing

Figure 13.9 Rehearsal for Fish Tank percussion. (*Source*: Blair Orr)

ideas through winter workshops open to people of all degrees of mobility, and also in movement sessions at a seniors' home in Amstrong. How do we move like water, she wondered? Both alone and collectively? She tells me that this experience still affects how she moves as a dancer.

As Kristi dips back down into the water, strange underwater creatures appear behind the tanks. They scurry to the other end and we catch sight of little puppeteers.

Children made the underwater puppets during our week-long annual *In the Shade* arts camp, where our activities and experiments led into *Sawllkwa*.

We follow the creatures around to the other end of the gazebo, where we are approached by a parade of giant water bugs: stilt-walking children, teens, and an adult, who is beaming with the excitement of her new skill. They step high, creeping and crawling to music.

How can I begin to describe the contribution Murray MacDonald has made to this community as music director of all of these Runaway Moon Theatre projects since 1998? How many people have surpassed their own expectations, singing, drumming, playing instruments, in celebration of this valley?

There is Murray under a tree, with Leif, creating a soundscape with objects. In a moment he will tear through the woods to his next position by the river, while the giant water bugs summon the audience back into the darkening woods.

Between trees we glimpse two golden water creatures dancing with a silvery sea serpent to a gentle waltz played by the string trio of sisters Amy, Hana, and little Ella.

These puppets were Jesse's special design project. (Jesse is an emerging artist interested in puppetry and community art, as well as in how art can serve environmental activism.) She imagined something really beautiful and looked forward to making the puppets. But one volunteer had an idea she wanted to try. When the puppet was complete, the creature was nothing like what Jesse had imagined. We talked about it afterwards. To what extent can the lead artist put forward his or her vision? If you don't like something someone has made, can you change it? There is no clear answer, but for sure, it is a prize to find out—at every turn—that there are many more ways of envisioning things than one's own.

The sea serpent, made by Akira, is manipulated by Becky and Hailey, two energetic high school students who, for whatever reason, decided to commit to this project. (Extensive outreach is valuable: you never know from what corner someone will appear who will become essential, and for whom it will become a lifelong memory.) Another creature is manipulated by Teresa Jensen-Christian and her daughter Emily, who joined Runaway Moon together for *By the River* in 2005 and have always been part of *In the Shade* arts camp. (It was Teresa who set me on the path to discover water with a request to help her create a water dance for a naming ceremony at Clhahl, where water is scarce.) A third puppet is brought to life by a woman who was my neighbour for thirteen years; we hardly ever spoke, but this year she jumped in, trying anything and everything—singing, dancing, puppetry. Who knows what an experience becomes in the life of each participant?

Figure 13.10 Puppeteers leading the audience to the river. (*Source*: Blair Orr)

Led again by the tiny puppet creatures, we run on a wide path in the direction of music. The trees open out to a wide sandy beach. But at this spot the audience, like a school of salmon fry swimming through a narrows, slows down. Each person is gently handed a ceramic vessel and asked to carry it carefully.

Each vessel was made by a different person in ceramic workshops over the preceeding winter. One of these took place in a back garden. Potter Stephen Plante had dug up clay from various places around Enderby. People pounded clay in buckets, sifted it, stirred it with water, and formed it. Then the vessels were baked by the side of an outdoor fire.

Little ceramic pots were made by children on field trips to Kingfisher, with the help of Dalynn Kearney, our wonderful stage manager who is everywhere and invisible, like water. She helps out at MacKenzie camp, just across the river, and she arranged for Jimmy Ouma, Zompopo, and me to go across by boat and bake the pots in the campfire one evening. While Zompopo watched over the fire, I taught the Words-for-Water song. Jimmy Ouma engaged the children and the youth in learning the vital skill of carrying buckets of water on their heads.

Some people made ceramic vessels at the Splatsin Band Hall with potter Daniel Stark. That day the hall was double-booked; we arrived to find an extended family decorating with balloons and laying out a birthday feast, but it was okay. They suggested we set up Daniel's wheel at the back of the room, and people made pots for *Sawllkwa* during the party. The grandma who was being celebrated had a great time.

Carefully carrying our ceramic vessels, we step out onto the sandy beach and along one of the pebble paths. Over to the left, water descends in a waterfall from the range forming Cooke Creek which empties here into the Shuswap River. Your eyes scan the beach and follow spirals of stones, apparently left by the swirling waters that form an eddy at the crook of the creek bend.

A group of us had placed the spirals one afternoon, discovering their shape and direction from the lay of the sandy flats and from the stones already deeply embedded. Traces of the spirals remained in the sand months later.

In the distance a motley crowd dressed in water robes is singing a lilting song about the river. They look miniscule in the wide expanse of open beach at this bend. A spiral path leads us down to the water, where a dozen or so young people dance in the eddy, dangling the long sleeves of their capes in the water, splashing it up and outward, making pinwheels of water droplets in the air. Far to the left the singing changes to a language we don't recognize: Dholuo, the language spoken on the other side of the world in Akonjo, Kenya, where the very same water flows in a stream fed from a spring beneath a big rock on a hill.

Two girls in Jimmy Ouma's village (both of whose secondary education is sponsored by friends here—another long story) spontaneously composed this

Figure 13.11 Spiral. (*Source*: Blair Orr)

song for the spectacle *Pi en Ngima* (Water Is Life) last Christmas: "Kawuono wan gi pi, Erokamano, wololore, Kawuono wan gi pi, Erokamano, wamore ahinya!" ("We have water today, thank you, today we have water, thank you, we are very happy!")

Rosalind and I had lengthy discussions on how the final section of the event could become a thank you. Her conception was that *Sawllkwa* would be a conversation between the people and the water rather than being a performance about water. We'd hoped to have hand-drummer Edna Felix and her family sing a song to the water, but they were unable to commit because of a Secwepemc gathering. Murray suggested a song about the river that had been collaboratively created in drop-in sessions for *Sawllkwa*. Loved and honoured by those who had created it, it was a song in praise of the river, but not a conversation, not a thank-you. At some point in our years of cultural exchange, Rosalind told me about an Elder who expressed thanks all day, even thanking her cooking pot. I am beginning to understand this, and to glimpse similarities between Jimmy Ouma's and Rosalind's perspectives. Recognizing this distinction between "performance about" and "thank you" became my personal research goal for the project. It is a shift from a paradigm in which we are appreciative of the environment, expressed in performance celebrating and describing water, to one in which we are part of our environment and in conversation with its elements, wherein cultural practice is the enacting of that connection. This is how I learn what it is to live in this place.

Pi en ngima. Water is life. Life is Water, water is art, art is life is water.

The crowd trickles to the water's edge. The water dancers form a line, and they begin scooping water from the river in larger ceramic vessels. You hold out the vessel you were given earlier, and it is filled. You follow the person in front of you along the pebble path, carrying the water that is yours to care for for the time being. You walk up the path toward the woods, and the sound of Erokamano *("thank you" in Dholuo) ebbs and flows further in the distance. (I run ahead, to be part of the last song!) It is almost dark in the woods, and you step carefully, feet and ears guiding you, through the woods, cradling the vessel bearing water. Yours is one of the smaller unglazed ones, made by a child and fired in the campfire; the water gradually seeps through the clay. An elderly gentleman walking next to you has a larger container with a spout, and several times he pours a little of his water into your empty one.*

It is almost pitch dark when you reach the large gazebo. It is faintly lit, and there is quiet singing emanating from it as you enter. A large circular dish is set in the middle. Written in gold in a spiral line of the dish are the words of the song that is being sung by more and more people. "As you give we will take. As you take we will give. In your likeness all things shall be reflected."

As we each approach the circular dish, we pour our water in and the water from all of our vessels becomes one. Past, present, future—we are all in water together.

Thank you to Rosalind for helping me to understand. Thank you, Murray, for jumping in on these escapades over the past twelve years. Thank you, Varrick, for helping to take each person's offering and wrestle it into a shape. Thank you, Kristi, for the joy you brought to it. Thank you, my family—Saba, Rosa, Leif, and Nell—for allowing me the time. Thank you to all the people who have participated in this journey of Reflection and of Runaway Moon. Thank You for reading this reflection. Thank you to the Elders and ancestors of the people of Splatsin for welcoming me to this Secwepemc territory. Erokamano pi, Kukwstsamc' Sawllkwa. Thank you, water, thank you.

A List of the Community Performances in Enderby and District Referred to in This Reflection

1999   Enderby and District Community Play *Not the Way I Heard It*
Enderby and District Community Play Committee/ Enderby and District Arts Council
Directed by James F. Tait and Rosalind Wiliams; written by Cathy Stubington, James F. Tait, and Rosalind Williams; designed by Ruth Howard; music direction by Murray MacDonald, Cathy Stubington, and Marion Lee

2000 *Out of the Ordinary* Community Spectacle
Enderby and District Community Play / Enderby and District Arts Council
Directed by James F. Tait, music direction by Murray MacDonald; design
led by Cathy Stubington

2001 *A Small Miracle* based on the book by Peter Collington
Runaway Moon Theatre, Enderby
Directed by Kim Collier; adapted by Lois Anderson, Molly March, and
Cathy Stubington; designed by Molly March and Cathy Stubington based
on the illustrations by Peter Collington

2004 *Enough Is Enough* Community Shadow Play
Runaway Moon Theatre and Splatsin Band Health Department, Splatsin
Written by Rosalind Williams and James F. Tait; designed by Cathy Stub-
ington and others; lighting design by Stephan Bircher; music direction by
Murray MacDonald

2005 *By the River* Community Spectacle
Runaway Moon Theatre, Enderby
Directed by James F. Tait; designed by Cathy Stubington et al.; music direc-
tion by Murray MacDonald

2006 *Open Air* Community Spectacle
Runaway Moon Theatre
Directed by Varrick Grimes; designed by Joanne Sale-Hook, Cathy Stubington, students of M. V. Beattie Elementary, and others; music direction
by Murray MacDonald

2007–8 The Food Project cycle of celebrations *A Kernel of Truth, Out in the Cold,
Planting Seeds, A Lot on Your Plate*
Runaway Moon Theatre, Grindrod and Enderby
Directed /designed by Jaci Metivier, Murray MacDonald, and Cathy Stub-
ington; *A Lot on Your Plate* directed by Varrick Grimes; music direction
by Murray MacDonald; guest artist Rene Hugo Sanchez

2009 *Pi en Ngima* Youth Spectacle
Akonjo Youth Empowerment Society / Runaway Moon Theatre, Akonjo
Kenya
Directed by Varrick Grimes and Jimmy Ouma Okello

2010 *Sawllkwa* Community Spectacle
Runaway Moon Theatre, Kingfisher
Director Varrick Grimes; cultural consultant/ co-writer Rosalind Williams;
design coordinator Cathy Stubington; music director Murray MacDonald;
choreographer Kristi Christian; guest artist Jimmy Ouma Okello

Notes

1 The Splatsin are one of the seventeen Shuswap First Nations who together make up the Secwepemc Nation.
2 Because Dorothy Christian filmed *Not the Way I Heard It*, she was invited to Nairobi, Kenya, to attend a symposium on Community-Based Peacebuilding, and she in turn invited me to go with her, which then led to Runaway Moon's collaborations with Jimmy Ouma and Akonjo village.
3 Eduardo Grillo, "Development or Decolonization in the Andes?," in *The Spirit of Regeneration: Andean Culture Confronting Western Notions of Development*, ed. Frederique Apffel-Marglin with PRATEC (London: Zed Books, 1998), 221.
4 See Jo-ann Archibald, *Indigenous Storywork: Educating the Heart, Mind, Body, and Spirit* (Vancouver: UBC Press, 2008); Margaret Kovach, *Indigenous Methodologies* (Toronto: University of Toronto Press, 2010); and Shawn Wilson, *Research Is Ceremony* (Halifax: Fernwood, 2008).

Bibliography

Archibald, Jo-ann. *Indigenous Storywork: Educating the Heart, Mind, Body, and Spirit.* Vancouver: UBC Press, 2008.
Grillo, Eduardo. "Development or Decolonization in the Andes?" *The Spirit of Regeneration: Andean Culture Confronting Western Notions of Development*, edited by Frederique Apffel-Marglin with PRATEC, 193–243. London: Zed Books, 1998.
Kovach, Margaret. *Indigenous Methodologies.* Toronto: University of Toronto Press, 2010.
Wilson, Shawn. *Research Is Ceremony.* Halifax: Fernwood, 2008.

Ice Receding/Books Reseeding

Basia Irland

Preamble

> *… each of us is quite literally air, water, soil and sunlight, and what cleanses and renews these fundamental elements of life is the web of living things on the planet.*
> —David Suzuki, *The Sacred Balance: Rediscovering Our Place in Nature*[1]

At dusk in January a beaver has just finished chewing through a willow branch to carry it to his lodge when he sees an object float by, bobbing up and down on the muddy-red water of the Río Grande near Albuquerque, New Mexico. Among the salt cedar on a small sandbar, a non-migrating Canada goose stops eating long enough to witness a carved chunk of ice go by. A tiny silvery minnow, almost extinct in this region, sees the same thing overhead through the murky current. A daughter, fishing with her father, tugs on his hand and inquires what the glistening object is that floats nearby. He says it appears to be an open book. Made of ice? Inscribed with lines of text? Another translucent volume appears, twirling in the current. With jeans rolled up, the father wades out into the shallow water, which is low at this time of year due to minimum snowpack in the mountains, and uses his fishing rod to pull the book closer to shore. Rows of seed script embedded in the ice sculpture form calligraphic paragraphs. Father and daughter look at the indecipherable text. She decides it is a language of the land, one that the birds can read from their cottonwood perches, and she speculates about where the seeds might end up. Other books appear around the edge of the sandbar island where the goose is feeding. One of the tomes gets caught in a whirlpool. Another is stuck momentarily on a protruding branch, pulls free, and begins the journey downstream as a codex of seeds slide into the river from the melting pages.

Figure 14.1 Tome II. (*Source*: Basia Irland)

4. *TOME II, DUSK.* 2009
"Text" of cottonwood seeds on the carved three-hundred-pound sculpture of ice, which slowly melts providing the necessary moisture for seed growth. The bosque beside the Rio Grande, New Mexico, has been jetty-jacked and straightened so that the river no longer floods naturally as it once did, therefore the cottonwoods struggle to get enough water and it is difficult for young ones to sprout. This book replicates the conditions needed for these native trees to thrive.

Future Cartography for Healthy Watersheds

The devastation humans have caused rivers through industrial culture is extraordinary, and the need to educate and activate local communities is vast. A green future cannot be mapped without healthy watersheds. The cartography of the next generation must include communities working together to insure clean, viable river systems, the arteries of our land. "Ice Receding/ Books Reseeding" emphasizes the necessity for communal effort, scientific knowledge, and poetic intervention to deal with the complex issues of climate disruption and watershed restoration through the release of seed-laden ephemeral ice sculptures into rivers, creeks, and streams.

This project presents a creative, lyrical way to promote positive actions that will have constructive results in helping restore streams around the world and provides a model that can be easily replicated. River water is frozen, carved into the form of a book, embedded with an "ecological language" or "riparian text" consisting of local native seeds, and placed back into the stream. The seed texts are released as the ice melts in the current. Where the seeds choose to plant themselves is serendipitous, replicating the way seeds get planted in nature. In future book launches there are plans to attach a monitoring probe (temperature, light, dissolved oxygen) and a micro-cam so we can watch the seeds progress down the river and view in real time where the current takes it and how the seeds are deposited along the banks. A GPS locator will also be installed in the ice so we can find the data logger and camera. I work with stream ecologists, river restoration biologists, and botanists to ascertain the best seeds for each specific riparian zone.

We are serving our watershed by planting native riparian seeds. When an ecosystem is restored and the plants grow along the riverbanks, they give back to us by helping sequester carbon, mitigating floods and drought, pollinating other plants, dispersing seeds, holding the banks in place (slowing erosion), creating soil regeneration and preservation, acting as filters for pollutants and debris, supplying leaf litter (for food and habitat), promoting aesthetic pleasure, and providing shelter and shade for riverside organisms, including humans.

Those who contribute to or participate in the ice book launches are determined by the location. Along the Nisqually River in Washington State, for example, Nisqually tribal members, salmon restoration specialists, musicians, fifth graders attending WaHeLut Indian School, students and professors from Evergreen State College, and forest rangers all took part. Participants in New Mexico on the Río Grande have included artists, farmers, acequia majordomos, hydrologists, Pueblo members, and hundreds of interested watershed citizens. These projects offer a way to bring many different people across historical inequities together for a common love, the river. In this way, water may be culturally healing too.

The title of this series of projects was conceived for *Weather Report*, a groundbreaking exhibition about climate change curated by art critic and author Lucy Lippard for the Museum of Contemporary Art, Boulder, Colorado. In order to call attention to melting glaciers and embed an action within the sculpture, I carved a 250-pound tome from ice and engraved it with a seed text of mountain maple (*Acer spicatum*), columbine flowers (*Aquilegia coerulea*), and Colorado blue spruce (*Picea pungens*). Four people carried the heavy book out into the current of Boulder Creek. As it rested between two large rocks, viewers could see the water flowing under the ice. One of the photographs of this piece shows three students standing in the river as they "read" the seed text on the book. Arapaho Glacier, which provides 40 percent of Boulder's drinking water, is receding rapidly due to climate disruption. When it is gone, from where will Boulder residents, both human and non-human, obtain water? These sculptures depict a problem—receding glaciers—and a suggestion for action—reseeding riparian zones—to reduce some of the effects of climate change through plants.

Recently I was asked to write a definition of the term "eco-art" for a New York University Press book, *Keywords for Environmental Studies*. The volume is edited by William Gleason, Princeton University; Joni Adamson, Arizona State University; and David N. Pellow, University of Minnesota. It seems appropriate to include the first paragraph here to help put the work I create into a wider context:

> Eco-art involves a transdisciplinary, multimedia, activist oriented process, which addresses environmental and sustainability issues. There is a shift away from art as commodity and toward new creative possibilities of art in service to communities and ecosystems. Eco-art includes artists who consider it their role to help raise awareness and create actions about important issues and natural processes; invite participation and devise innovative strategies to engage diverse communities; work directly with others to augment the knowledge associated with particular fields; produce works which inspire people to reassess the notion of commons. Eco-artists emphasize collaboration. Many of these artists work with indigenous and local community members, and specialists from a range of disciplines including media, education, architecture, performance arts, sociology, engineering, and the gamut of sciences.[2]

The ethos for this group of artists encourages the long-term flourishing of social and natural environments in which we reside and addresses the impacts humans have on ecosystems, the places we live, and the other species with whom we share these places.

The role of research about each particular location is paramount and consists of the usual web searches and head-in-book investigations, but often more informative are discussions with Elders, scientists, and river citizens. The interpersonal and relational aspects of each project are paramount and have led to long-lasting, ongoing, wonderfully warm, enriching friendships. Spending time hanging out with the river, intently listening and closely observing, is invaluable. My riparian projects are not about sitting in an armchair or classroom, but rather about connecting directly and in physical ways with the river. I used to be amazed when I would lecture to advanced undergraduate and graduate classes of 150 students in the Hydrology Department about river issues and asked how many had been to the river, which runs right through Albuquerque, and only one or two hands would go up. How was it possible that even students studying water would not go to our major local river to witness it? And these were students who specifically study water! So I would give an assignment for them to go to the Río Grande for several hours and write or draw or just be present with the flow and report back. How our universities, schools, and communities have become so disconnected from their natural surroundings is a whole other topic, but one that helps propel my work. Getting outside and getting involved with a creek or stream where one lives and knowing where water in the tap comes from are vital activities in order to reconnect with the watersheds that sustain us. Plus, it is simply invigorating to be outdoors near water.

In the book, *LAND/ART*, Malin Wilson writes:

Irland shares a legacy with intrepid 19th century naturalists, and is utterly heedless of wet, dirt and cold. Along with paddling canoes and waterproofing her hiking boots, she's handy with a microscope in the service of her art, not to mention collegial goals with biologists, botanists, and stream ecologists. She is also an irrepressible researcher, but she is transparently impassioned by water, watersheds, and the flora and fauna (including communities of people) that populate them.[3]

At each location the research and personal dialogues create new realizations and fascinating journeys. For example, before attending a water conference in Vancouver, BC, organized by Rita Wong and Dorothy Christian, I had corresponded with numerous experts about which seeds would be the most appropriate to use in the ice books I would be sculpting while there. During the conference, several scientists discussed the local problems of trying to bring back salmon to the region, including Senakw Staulk (False Creek).[4] The traditional food chain was disrupted due to lack of krill for the herring to feed upon, which in turn feed the salmon. So I made the decision to forego the use of seeds and instead create a colourful vocabulary on the ice books comprised of small bright pink krill.

The physical methodology of producing the sculptures is kept simple and low tech: first, scavenged cardboard boxes of appropriate size are found and lined with used plastic. Next, water is poured to the desired depth and placed in a freezer. (Twice, due to the size of the sculptures, I have worked with chefs so that we could access walk-in freezers and create books weighing 250–300 pounds.) After the ice is solid, it is removed from the container and carved using a variety of tools. The initial large pieces are removed with a Japanese saw. Then the book cover and pages are delicately carved with numerous attachments on a Dremel tool. Incised lines for the script are cut deep and wide enough for seeds to be inserted, after which they are spritzed with water to create a film of ice to hold them in place. (The seeds cannot soak for long periods of time in the water as it might change their molecular structure.) The work has to be done with minimal amount of melting to the sculpture. When I worked outdoors in Idaho, it was cold and dry, so with the battery-powered Dremel I could carve by the river for several hours. But in hot, damp Georgia, the books started to melt almost before I could begin to carve, so we had to stay near freezer units. In West Virginia we were given a biology lab in which to work with industrial freezers that were, during our stay, empty of specimens. (A dendritic thought: One of the miraculous attributes of frozen water is that ice floats instead of sinking.)

Although I try to keep my work as "green" as possible, I am aware that many countries, of course, do not have freezers (although books have also been sculpted from river clay), much less electricity, and that by using electricity I am adding to the carbon footprint. I also add to my footprint when I fly to foreign destinations, even when I buy carbon offsets. However, these are the dilemmas posed to those of us who try to work from an ethical standpoint.

Ephemerality and Documentation

The process of creation is as important as the sculpture, which in this case is ephemeral, remaining through documentation and plants. Part of the significance of the ice books is that they melt away. The time and energy that has gone into the carving of the books vanish in the current of a stream. Everything exists for only a finite period of time. Instead of dust to dust, here we have water to water. A marble sculpture will also eventually, over millennia, go back into the earth, but the process is speeded up drastically in melting ice. Artist and writer Harmony Hammond writes that the ice books are time-based objects, and also a vehicle for change.[5]

Ways of knowing later about an ephemeral object or event are through some type of documentation, which might be writing, film, photography, and drawing, or all of these. In the documentary film, *receding/ reseeding*, we see ice books being launched into rivers in Belgium, France, Italy, Spain, and across North America where seeds are released into spring-borne streams in Missouri or languid creeks in North Carolina or the rust-red acid mine drainage in West Virginia's Deckers Creek. The film was begun in 2007 and is updated as new projects occur.

Gallery and museum installations include thirty-inch by twenty-four-inch photographs of the books printed on canvas, with four-inch by six-inch photographs showing participants launching the sculptures into rivers. Amid the photographs is a monitor showing the video *receding/ reseeding*. The photographs include images of the books on site, either beside the water or floating in the river: We see a bridge in Paris reflected in the Canal St. Martin as an oblong book containing maple (Acer *spicatum*) seeds floats by; a rotting fish near a book with lavender (*Lavandula allardii*) in Arles, France; a frozen volume laden with snowberries (*Symphoricarpus albus*) and another one with red elderberries (*Sambucus racemosa*) riding the milky glacier melt of the Nisqually River in Washington. The scent of the wild fennel (*Foeniculum vulgare*) is almost tangible in the photograph of the small carved book that was put into the Muga River, Spain, in view of the Mediterranean, its destination. In addition to photographs and videos, museum and gallery installations have included ice books created for the opening. At eye level, on a metal grate above a trough, an ice book is placed and allowed to melt during the opening. After a week or so the seeds released into the trough during the melt sprouted in the meltwater, creating a micro- ecosystem in the gallery. The sprouts are then taken to a river to float downstream, completing a cycle.

Gifting

> *A gift is a connection.*
> —Lewis Hyde, *The Gift: Imagination and the Erotic Life of Property*[6]

Gifting is an important part of a community-based ethic across many cultures. I create physical gifts for the participants, and the ice books themselves are an offering to the river. Since I was a child, rivers have given me much pleasure, serenity, solitude, and a chance to escape urban life, and have provided opportunities for tubing, ice skating, swimming, and wading. Reciprocity matters. Participants have devoted their time and energy to making the *receding/ reseeding* projects possible, not in the physical carving of the book, which I do myself, but in gathering seeds, scouting launch locations, and taking part in the placing of the sculptures into a stream. For some of these projects, especially along the Nisqually River, the Río Grande, and the Oconee River, there have been several hundred people involved. I could not do it alone, so each person who has helped is given a gift as a commemoration, a thank you, an acknowledgement of appreciation. Usually it is a glassine envelope or small glass vial containing specific regional seeds so they can continue the planting process and become involved with the river through caretaking. Also included are minute watershed maps, lists of local and international water websites, and objects related to the specific site. Working with community members is complex, yet continuously rewarding. It provides a basis for co-operation, dialogue, and sharing information and inspiration.

Seed Language

Convince me that you have a seed there, and I am prepared to expect wonders.
—Henry David Thoreau, *Faith in a Seed*[7]

That a tiny muted bundle can transform into some enormous loud green tree or magenta flower or gnarly shrub is wondrous indeed. An individual seed is a miraculous sculptural wonder. Each is distinctive and exquisitely formed. The wispy seed of the mountain mahogany (*Cercocarpus montanus*) is a minute furry aircraft with a "tail" that corkscrews in spirals. On some of the sculptures, I utilize pods in addition to seeds, such as those of the tapering desert willow (*Chilopsis linearis*) used to form the Roman numerals on a grouping of ice manuscripts.

Today John and I were walking beside a diversion pond near the Río Grande and watched as the wind lifted millions of cattail seeds into the air. How many will actually take root to become a plant, while others decompose into soil? Will it be enough to carry on the species? Some of the seeds clung to John's flannel shirt, and when we arrived home, I got out my magnifying loupe, which I used for art slide identification in pre-digital days. There in the sunlight, enlarged by the loupe, was a multi-pronged umbrella shape without the fabric and at the end of the "handle" was a fuzzy teardrop. The entire shape was designed to hover upon dispersal, glide on the breeze, and come to rest on a piece of earth, where it could begin the whole cycle of growth again. And again.

The Latin names for plant species summon strange reverberations. Three of the seed varieties recommended by Evergreen State College botanists for restoration along the Nisqually River are black cottonwood (*Populus balsamifera ssp. trichocarpa*), snowberry (*Symphoricarpus albus*), and swamp rose (*Rosa pisocarpa*). We conjure the smell of balsam and roses. We hear symphonies. Etymological associations abound when we read such names as Apache plume (*Fallugia paradoxa*), Indian rice grass (*Oryzopsis hymenoides*), sand dropseed (*Sporobolus cryptandrus*), and stream bank wheatgrass (*Agropyron riparium*).

A Reverie of Floating Frozen Manuscripts

The seeds transcribe an international ecological text. Since it is not a specific language—neither Hindi nor Spanish, Swahili nor Russian—the ice books can be read as a cross-cultural invocation of the Earth. The tongues of the glaciers are receding, the voices of our rivers are being dammed and clogged with toxic debris. Who are the scribes writing about our waters and where are the libraries that store their moist stories?

There is something elegantly sculptural about the form of a book. When open, it looks as if it could fly right off the coffee table or shelf and out through the open window, flap its winged pages, and scatter letters to the ground. When closed, a book is a tool box, a sarcophagus waiting to be pried open, with texts on three sides deciphering some of the contents. In *Becoming Animal: An Earthly Cosmology*, David Abram describes witnessing two students holding temple wood blocks carved with ritual verses as they stood in a Nepalese river. These blocks are usually used for transferring ink onto religious pages. He writes,

> [T]he students were stamping the woodblocks over and over into the flowing surface of the river, so that the water would carry those printed prayers to the many lands through which it traveled on its long way to the Indian Ocean. Here, remarkably, was a culture wherein written letters were not used merely as a record of words once spoken, or as a score for oral speech, but as efficacious forces in their own right. The letters were not just passive sign, but energetic agents actively affecting the space around them.[8]

Just as the prayer flags I photographed strung near sacred sites and hanging from temple trees throughout Nepal and India transport blessings on the wind, the rivers of the world need all the reverence and protection each of us can provide.

Co-evolution with the *Gathering of Waters* Projects

Irland [...] takes the journey herself, swimming upstream against the currents of a society not yet convinced that our comforts are worth sacrificing for our resources.
—Lucy Lippard, art/cultural critic[9]

The ice book launchings are sometimes done in tandem with another ongoing large-scale series of mine, *The Gathering of Waters*, which facilitates co-operative relationships among people, and connects diverse cultures along the entire length of rivers, emphasizing that we all live downstream. It is imperative to work together to face our water challenges. In the increasingly arid southwestern United States, hydrologic studies show that climate change will produce earlier snowmelt and lower stream flows in rivers, resulting in the drop of groundwater levels. *A Gathering of Waters; Rio Grande, Source to Sea* took five years and on many levels continues to this day. Hundreds of participants were invited to put a small amount of river water into a canteen, write in a log book about their experience of the river, and pass these downstream to another person along the entire 1,875-mile length of the Río Grande, which begins in the San Juan Mountains of southern Colorado, flows through New Mexico, becomes the border between Texas and Mexico, and then historically enters the Gulf of Mexico at Boca Chica. Connections were made that have been lasting, and groups are working together that never would have met otherwise.

The sculptures accompanying these projects include Backpack/Repositories constructed from local materials, which contain artifacts from the *Gatherings*. They hold the scientific data, canteens, log books, maps, water samples, photographs, video documentary, and other relevant art objects and information. As with the ice book projects, each participant is presented with a handmade gift. Gatherings have occurred along the Don River, Ontario, Canada; the River Dart, Devon, England; Nisqually River, Washington State; Boulder Creek, Colorado; Deckers Creek, West Virginia; Oconee River, Georgia; and the Río Grande. Through an encompassing ethic of inclusion, we witness the diversity of life along the river being celebrated again and again as the container passes downstream, from hand to hand.

In order to participate in this project, you had to be at the river and interact with others both upstream and downstream, thereby forming a kind of human river that brings awareness to the plight of this flowing water, which is always asked to give more than it has. In the video documentary about this project, my son, Derek, stands in the middle of the Río on a small sandbar and says, "Ask not what this river can do for you, but what you can do for this river." Reciprocity is important. Rivers provide so much in myriad generous ways and it behooves us to give back to these streams and creeks in whatever ways we can in order to cultivate intergenerational perspectives and future coexistence with rivers.

Notes

1 David Suzuki, *The Sacred Balance: Rediscovering Our Place in Nature* (Vancouver: Greystone Books, 2002).

2 Basia Irland, "Eco-Art," in *Keywords for Environmental Studies*, ed. William Gleason, Joni Adamson, and David N. Pellow. New York: New York University Press, 2016.

3 Malin Wilson, *LAND/ART* (Santa Fe, NM: Radius Books, 2009), 126.

4 See Lee Maracle's essay in this volume for more on Senakw.

5 Harmony Hammond, quoted in Basia Irland's website, 2013, http://www.basiairland.com/projects/ice%20books/description.html.

6 Lewis Hyde, *The Gift: Imagination and the Erotic Life of Property* (New York: Vintage Books), 1983.

7 Henry Thoreau, *Faith in a Seed* (Washington, DC: Island Press, 1996).

8 David Abram, *Becoming Animal: An Earthly Cosmology* (New York: Vintage Books, 2010), 216.

9 Lucy Lippard, "Confluences," in *Water Library* by Basia Irland (Albuquerque: University of New Mexico Press, 2007).

Bibliography

Abram, David. *Becoming Animal: An Earthly Cosmology*. New York: Vintage Books, 2010.

Hammond, Harmony. Quoted in Basia Irland's website. 2014. http://www.basiairland .com/projects/ice%20books/description.html.

Hyde, Lewis. *The Gift: Imagination and the Erotic Life of Property*. New York: Vintage Books, 1983.

Irland, Basia. "Eco-Art." *Keywords for Environmental Studies*. Edited by William Gleason, Joni Adamson, and David N. Pellow. New York: New York University Press, 2016.

Lippard, Lucy. "Confluences." In *Water Library* by Basia Irland. Albuquerque: University of New Mexico Press, 2007.

Suzuki, David. *The Sacred Balance: Rediscovering Our Place in Nature*. Vancouver: Greystone Books, 2002.

Thoreau, Henry. *Faith in a Seed*. Washington, DC: Island Press, 1996.

Wilson, Malin. *LAND/ART*. Santa Fe, NM: Radius Books, 2009.

Tsunami Chant

Wang Ping

I'm not a singer, but please
let me sing of the peacemakers
on the streets and internet, your candles
in this darkest moment of night,
your bodies on the steps of government buildings,
your voices from the roots of grasses and trees,
from your pit of conscience.

I'm not a prayer, but please,
please give my voice to the children
in Baghdad, Basra, Afghanistan,
and every other bombed-out place on earth,
your crying out in pain and fear;
please give my hands to the mothers
raking through rubble for food, bodies;
my sight to the cities and fields in smoke;
my tears to the men and women who are brought
home in bags; and please give my ears
to those who refuse to hear the explosions,
who tune only to censored news, official words.

I'm not a citizen, but please
count my vote against the belief
that the American way is the only way,
count it against the blasphemy of freedom,
against a gang of thugs who donned crowns
on their own heads, who live for power
and power only, whose only route is

to deceive and loot, whose mouths move
only to crush, whose hands close
only into a grave.

I'm not a worshiper, but please
accept my faith in those
who refuse to believe in painted lies,
refuse to join this chorus of supreme hypocrisy,
refuse to sell out, to let their conscience sleep,
wither, die. Please accept my faith
in those who cross the bridge for peace,
only to be cursed and spat upon, but keep crossing
anyway, every Wednesday, in rain and snow,
and my faith in those who camp out night after night,
your blood thawing the frozen ground,
your tents flowers of hope in this bleak age.

I don't possess a bomb, don't know
how to shoot or thrust a sword.
All I have is a broken voice,
a heart immense with sorrow.
But please, please take them,
let them be part of this tsunami
of chanting, this chant of awakening.

part iv

a respectful coexistence in common:
water perspectives

Listening to the Elders at the Keepers of the Water Gathering

Radha D'Souza

Lac Brochet is just 7 degrees below the Arctic Circle, a small dot on the map by Lake Brochet after which it is named, a place where the horizon appears to be within walking distance, where ink-blue skies spread like a rooftop above your head, where life ambles on and follows the rhythms of nature to the extent that is humanly possible for people subjected by a New World to a new cosmology, new systems of knowledge, and new institutions for over a century and half. Lac Brochet is home to under a thousand Dene people, one of the many hundreds of Indigenous nations of Canada. Like the Adivasis of India, and many Indigenous peoples around the world, the Dene people of Canada face renewed threats to their existence as nation and people. Like canaries in coal mines, the Dene people sense impending danger to the natural environment and with it the conditions that make human life possible. That much was clear at the Keepers of the Water V gathering in Lac Brochet, Manitoba, held on August 10–14, 2011, a conference where Elder after Elder, supported by walking sticks and wheelchairs, spoke of the impending environmental and social disaster they saw coming.

"Listen to your Elders!" "Obey your Elders!" I doubt if there is any Indian who has grown up without those two imperatives. Listen I did. I sat through the conference and listened to the Elders, carefully pressing in my earplugs wired to the pocket transistor that provided the simultaneous translations from Dene to English, making sure I did not miss a word of what they said. But obey? How do I obey what the Elders said?

The Keepers of the Water movement was born from struggles against that big word with multiple meanings we call "Development." People of the Deh Cho (McKenzie) river basin became alarmed at the pollution of the river, its effects on natural and human life cycles, and the depleting waters in the watershed of the river. Environmental and social problems for Indigenous peoples of the basin were compounded by the expansion of oil and natural gas, mining, intensive commercial agribusiness, and with it infrastructure development like roads, transport, and other commercial developments further exacerbated by the unregulated use of First Nations lands as landfills and dumps. In response to these developments the Indigenous peoples of the river basin, together with local environmental groups and community organizations, convened the first Keepers of the Water gathering in Liidlii Kui, Denendeh (Fort Simpson), Northwest Territory on September 7, 2006. The issues raised by the meeting echoed the concerns of other Indigenous peoples, community organizations, and environmental groups in the region. Keepers of the Water became an annual event after that. It brings together First Nations, Métis, and Inuit peoples, environmental groups, concerned citizens, and communities affected by the deterioration in the quality of life and environment, including air, water, and land in the Arctic drainage basin in the northern reaches of Canada, including the river basins of Athabasca, Slave River, Great Slave Lake, and the Deh Cho (McKenzie) basins.

What Did the Elders Say?

There was extraordinary importance given to the Elders at the conference. They spoke on three days out of four, interspersed by the occasional official or academic. Program schedules and timetables were modified to make time for the Elders. The Elders were too preoccupied with the crisis that confronted their peoples and natures. Getting through a predetermined "conference agenda" was the last thing on their minds. The Elders were not office bearers of the band councils. They were quite simply Elders. They had travelled great distances to come to the conference. The band leaders, too, listened to them with great attention and respect. Their talk ranged over personal lives, anecdotes, historical memory, and contemporary social problems that come with modernization and change, and the foundational principles of human existence.

They reiterated certain key themes over and over again in their talks. First and foremost, we are *keepers* of water. Elder after Elder said we are guardians of water, land, flora, fauna, and everything else on Earth. They expanded on the notion of what it meant to be keepers/guardians of the water—no one can own water or land. We keep it for future generations, just as our ancestors left it for us. That is our purpose in this world, the reason why we were put on this Earth. Because our ancestors lived by this command of natural law, we could inherit this land and water and everything on it. "I foresee many difficulties for our children and grandchildren," one Elder said, referring to the pollution and depletion of water sources. "My grandfather foresaw what we are seeing today, and he did not even have an education," another said.

The second theme that came through from listening to the Elders was their articulation of rights. In their view, rights are not property rights, but rather privileges—"the grace," as one Elder put it—that flows from our covenant with our Creator. Over and over again, nearly every Elder who spoke said, "We must live by the laws of the Creator," by which they explained quite clearly they meant living by the cycles and rhythms of life. It is a primordial law that supersedes laws made by governments and states. "There are three parties to the treaty: the Indigenous peoples, the European settlers, and the Creator. To leave [out] any one of these three parties is breach of the agreement," another Elder said. To put it in the words of modern legal scholarship, the Elders were asserting a form of natural rights that they said takes precedence over constitutional rights. And this holds true for all human beings, European and Indigenous alike, as both are equal parties to the covenant with nature. To put it in the words of modern philosophers, the *relationship* between nature, society, and human life is an ontological one that inheres in Being itself. Meddling and interfering with the nature of Being, the *relationship*, is destructive. They never spoke about a "pristine nature" untouched by humans, nor about a society that was "entitled" to nature as of a right, nor about spiritual and cultural life disengaged from the ever-present concerns about food, clothing, and shelter. To live is to live in a relationship with nature, with community, and with one's inner life.

The third theme that came through the talks of the Elders is the skepticism about monetary compensation. "Money has destroyed us, it has destroyed our young people," one Elder said tearfully, remembering the alcoholism and substance abuse rampant in his community. I remembered our own Adivasis in India who accepted compensation, and within years, if not months, were destroyed by alcohol and abuse and went from being founders of Indian society—Adi-Vasi[1]—to becoming the scrap heap of modern India.

And lastly, they said in no uncertain terms, we should be wary of promises by the government. "It is amazing what is going on. They are ruling everything!" one Elder said. "The white people are not going to fix anything for us. We have to do it ourselves," a second Elder said. "Do not trust the government. When they brought us the paperwork [treaties], they said the words could not be changed, and now they are all changing it," a third Elder cautioned. I remembered the promises in the fifth schedule to the Constitution of India, promises of lands, forests, waters, and ways of life for Adivasis that are routinely reneged to make way for development projects: the dams, the mines, the factories, first by the state in the name of nation building (as if Adivasis are not part of the nation) and now in the name of "growth" and "globalization."

I understood perfectly what the Dene Elders were saying because what they said was no different from what the Adivasi Elders say, or indeed what the Indigenous Elders everywhere in the world say. Indeed, many in environmental and social justice movements, ecologists, human rights experts, and others say much the same things using their own disciplinary methods, in more scholarly languages and in more articulate ways. As I sat listening to the Elders, the question uppermost in my mind was: Can we obey the Elders?

Guardians or Stakeholders?

It seems to me that our legal resource kit does not have conceptual tools to articulate what the Elders were saying. They were saying, "We are guardians of water, land, etc." Somewhere along the way, as we move away from the communities tied to land, forests, and water, to offices of governments, politicians, policy-makers, experts, and scholars, "guardianship" translates as "stakeholders"—the word slips into our conceptual vocabulary quietly, unnoticed, without anyone realizing that the ground has shifted under our feet.

The word "stake" in English has many unfortunate associations: gambling, burning on stakes, sticks to fence off areas, assertion of property rights and such. The modern meaning of "stakeholders," however, comes from corporate managements of large transnational corporations. In the mid-1980s, against the backdrop of neo-liberal reforms following Reaganism, Thatcherism, and similar -isms, on the one hand, and, on the other, the widespread popular protests and criticism of transnational corporations for human right violations in development projects, including displacement of Indigenous peoples from traditional lands, corporate management theorists developed the concept of "stakeholders" in the company. It was a management strategy that would take into account the impacts of the management's actions on all parties who were affected by the company's activities so as to minimize "risks" to the company and maximize value for shareholders. Main stakeholders include customers, employees, local communities, suppliers and distributors, and shareholders. For the purposes of more effective management, "stakeholders" could include the media, the public in general, business partners, academics, competitors, non-governmental organizations (NGOs), activists, government, regulators, and policy-makers, either as individuals or through their associations. In this management strategy, including Indigenous peoples who were protesting against displacement by large projects as stakeholders posed no conceptual difficulties. They, too, could become one of many "stakeholders" that managers need to take into account when planning and executing company strategies. The model itself has its antecedents in the "corporatist state," a form of state that emerged nearly everywhere in the New World Order at the end of World

War II. The corporatist state was tripartite in that it included (1) the state, (2) the corporations and trade unions to represent the nation, and (3) the capital markets and the labour markets respectively. What is wrong? one might ask. The problem is that corporate managements see human and environmental rights, and the rights of Indigenous peoples as business "risks" that must be anticipated, planned for, and addressed strategically in the interests of the company's profitability so as to add value to the shareholders.

This much may not be difficult to understand even if it is unacceptable to many. What is more difficult to come to terms with is the fact that governments everywhere began to adopt the corporate model. They switched from "government" to "governance," usually without any public mandate for the shift. Government is about managing the citizen-state relations within the four corners of a constitution. Governance is about treating different sections of society as "stakeholders" in the state where the state itself becomes an "enterprise" in the global markets and international economy.

By the early 1990s, neo-liberal transformation of international organizations, including the United Nations, was well underway. The World Trade Organization was formed with a mandate to lead the transformation, euphemistically referred to as "inter-agency co-operation," to coordinate the programs and policies of other international organizations within the UN system along neo-liberal principles. International organizations like the World Bank and the International Monetary Fund made "good governance" a cornerstone of their lending policies to Third World governments, insisting they, too, must include environmental and human rights groups, Indigenous peoples, and other social groups as "stakeholders" in governance where the state is transformed into an economic enterprise in a global marketplace. Since the formation of the World Trade Organization, international organizations have met with political leaders as representatives of "economies," not citizens. NGOs and social movements suddenly found that they were being heard instead of being shunned as in the past. They embraced their role as "stakeholders" in a state that had become an economic enterprise. Some countries tweaked their constitutions for the transition to occur, while many did not. Everywhere law reforms to dismantle traditional state-citizen relationships were a big part of the neo-liberal transformation. Within social movements few understood what was actually at stake in becoming a "stakeholder."

There is a fundamental philosophical issue at stake between what the Elders at the conference said and what the policy-makers and legal actors understood. In the Elders' view, to be a guardian means the purpose of economic activities is to sustain human life and communities. *We work to live.* Provision of our needs (economic life) cannot be disengaged from social, cultural, and spiritual life, on the one hand, and our relationship with nature on the other. The purpose of "stakeholdership" is the complete opposite. The meaning of life is to sustain the economy. *We live to work.* The purpose and meaning of life is to keep the economy running. The modern-day vision of an apocalypse is the collapse of the economy, a vision that is all around us today as financial markets collapse and social and political turmoil intensifies everywhere.

For the Elders, nature is not a pie to be carved up and distributed to all according to what each deserves. "Sharing," about which they spoke at length, is not about cutting up something for distribution as goods and commodities. Sharing is about participation in the grace that nature bestows upon us. Being a stakeholder, on the contrary, is about saying "this is my share of the pie and I want it for myself to do as I please with it." Guardianship is about affirming categorically that nature, people, cultural inheritances, and future generations are not ingredients in a pie. Rather, it is about recognizing "my place" in the bigger scheme of time and space that has neither a beginning nor an end. It is about saying our social laws must be based on this universal law if they are to be meaningful.

Rights and Remedies

Turning to the concept of "rights," nearly everyone at the conference spoke about their "rights" to water and land. However, as I sat there listening to the Elders, I wondered whether the Elders used the word "rights" in the same sense as policy-makers and lawyers do? What did they mean by "right to water" and how is it different?

When they spoke about water, the Elders were clear that water could not be separated from land or people because their emphasis was on the *relationship*. Strictly speaking, therefore, they were not speaking about "right to water" at all but rather about their right to *reproduce the conditions of life*, which was neither reducible to water or land nor separable from them. The Elders were arguing for a type of natural law that is derived from the ontological conception that life is a *relationship* between nature (the material conditions for human life), society (the institutional dimension necessary for human life, including laws, norms, and such), and the psychological dimension (culture, aesthetics, and spiritual life). Laws made by state and leaders of whatever description must conform to ontological reality, failing which everything will fall apart and the reproduction of the conditions of life will become impossible. This is a very different conception of "rights" from saying "this is mine, it belongs to me."

There is one crucial feature of modern life that the Elders missed entirely, however. One problem in thinking about rights in the modern context is that modern law creates a new fictitious person called the "corporate person" and treats this person on par with the natural person.[2] The corporate person is a creature of the law and created through a legal fiction. This fictitious corporate person is in fact a monster because it does not have the most important attributes of natural persons or indeed any living being. For a start, it does not go through cycles of birth and death. It does not have a psyche, does not feel pleasure or pain, or know right from wrong. Yet like all other natural persons, the corporate person has a right to exist, and may resort to measures to survive in the same way as natural persons may adopt strategies to survive. The corporate person must, however, feed on living, pulsating people and nature by transforming them into commodities to be traded, in raw or processed forms, throughout the world in markets of one type or another to survive: labour markets, commodity markets, capital markets, land markets, and many others. Early on, corporate persons like the Hudson Bay Company in Canada and the East India Company in India created a new cosmology, new forms of knowledge and methods of social organization that transformed people and nature into a "resource," human and natural, to feed a new insatiable gargantuan monster, a new type of "person" that stands in competition with the natural person to claim the right to land, labour, and natural resources.

Modern law recognizes property rights as a fundamental human right on the same footing as right to life, liberty, and conscience. This equivalence between property rights—essential for the survival of the corporate person— and the life, liberty, and conscience essential for the survival of the natural person is seldom challenged in legal theory, let alone in legal practice, even when corporations and states are routinely challenged for their "misdeeds." Do non-discrimination laws apply in the same ways to natural and corporate persons? Can a corporate person have "responsibilities" when it possesses no psyche and is incapable, therefore, of making a judgment between right and wrong? Can corporate persons be told to "behave" as if they were human? Is corporate property to be treated on the same footing as individual ownership of the means of existence: house, tools, etc.? Should constitutions provide "affirmative actions" and "positive discrimination" to natural persons over corporate persons? One raises these questions at one's own peril at the risk of being considered quirky at best and irrational at worst.

Often when such questions are posed, the response is that the individuals who manage the corporate person are the ones who bear moral responsibilities for its "actions." This view overlooks the more important fact that the law quite explicitly affirms that a corporate person is a person in its own right, irreducible to the individuals that constitute it. A corporate person is a complex of laws. As a complex of laws, the ethical responsibilities of an individual in a corporation are circumscribed by the rules of incorporation and administration. The scope of an individual's action is limited by the specific role a person plays within the larger organization. Where individuals are dis-embedded from land and people and assigned a place within a complex of laws, i.e., re-embedded in the corporate person, they are subsumed by the corporate person, as it were. Previously the role of governments was to "keep the peace" between corporate citizens and natural citizens. Natural citizens could claim that constitutions were social contracts between them and the state, and that "governments" were bound to give priority to their claims and intervene when corporate citizens violated their constitutional rights. When states become enterprises and governance entails bringing all stakeholders together to ensure the profitability of the economy, the role of governments becomes that of facilitators. Large transnational corporations have, not surprisingly, blurred the traditional boundaries of public and private law, and neo-liberal reforms of the state have made the divide redundant at best. It is not surprising that everywhere from the United Nations to universities, from global policy-making to local governments, the name of the game today is "PPP"—public-private partnerships—where public institutions and corporate persons work in concert in service of the economy.

That a new person called the corporate person could be created through the stroke of a pen, metaphorically speaking, would be beyond the comprehension of most Elders present at the Keepers of the Water V conference and in Indigenous communities around the world. The presence of this new fictitious person leaves Indigenous peoples with only one remedy for all the wrongs: compensation. As property is life itself to the corporate person, the assumption is that corporate persons will "behave" when property is taken away in the same way as natural persons are disciplined by taking away their liberty. Compensation does not restore broken relationships between land, water, and communities, however. Once the deed is done, it has long-term intergenerational consequences that cannot be compensated by money. Fish stocks deplete, mountains are reduced to rubble, forests disappear along with rain cycles, generations are alienated from land to the extent they no longer comprehend it, and cultural wealth is lost forever, in the same way as imprisonment for murder does not bring back the dead victim. With the natural person, however, redemption is a real possibility, and through the redemption of the murderer, the community redeems itself. Corporate persons cannot, unfortunately, seek redemption. Even when punished, their punishment does not redeem the capital markets within which they exist; if anything, punishment could intensify market turmoil. To say we should have regulation and penalties for corporate persons becomes more problematic when we consider that in setting the standards of regulation and penalties, the corporate person is also a "stakeholder" and has a say in the way the law is written alongside the others.

The natural person inherits normative sensibilities that are handed down from time immemorial. The corporate person has no such inheritances and is free of the laws of time and place, nature and culture. Furthermore, there are no natural law concepts that can accommodate this new type of person and no ontological conceptions of being that provides any means of giving this person a place in the schema of nature–society–people relations.

"Don't Give UP!"

"You must never give up" was a message that was repeated by nearly every Elder who spoke. "They will never tell you what they are going to do, but you must continue to ask the right questions," another said. Through centuries of struggles they recognized that, like natural cycles, there are cycles of victories and defeats. Their historical memory could recall the struggles of the colonizers as natural persons and the recurring crises the corporate persons brought upon them. Each crisis afforded new hopes for the Elders to reassert the importance of the *relationship* between nature and people that had been ruptured. They remembered the vulnerability of the colonizers when they came to their lands and how the Indigenous peoples taught them to survive in the harsh Arctic environment. They spoke of the Great Depression and of the Europeans who fled the ravages of war and markets to seek solace in their land, water, and people. Around me it is happening again: the collapsed financial markets are blackmailing the states to bail them out, the states are bombarding their former colonies for oil and resources, and young men and women are out on the streets of Britain, Greece, Portugal, and other places, rioting. Perhaps it offers new hopes—another opportunity to embrace the first principles of life, create a new science, a new system of knowledge, new laws that can rebuild the ruptured relations between nature, society, and people.

But can we let go? Let go of that monster, the corporate person, whom we created with our laws, our knowledge, and our infinite desires? The person we created threatens to devour us now. Many of us know this. What if we are swept away by the modern apocalypse, the collapse of the economy? But if we do not let go, does the economy guarantee our survival? And the survival of land, water, forests? To let go of that monster we created ourselves requires courage. Courage is easy for the Elders, for the Indigenous peoples. They are children of Mother Earth. They have a ground beneath their feet to stand on, even if that ground has been plundered over and over again. For those of us who are children of Mother Market, long displaced and evicted from land and water, we may feel that there is no ground beneath our feet to stand on. We may see ourselves as embodiments of rules that constitute the corporate person, an embodiment of a single strand of a delegated rule in a complex of laws. We must live and die by the rules of the corporate person because there are no laws of the Creator, no third party to our covenant with the corporate person. We must live by the laws of the "invisible hand of the market" even when the command is "creative destruction." We have nowhere to fall. The edifice of the market is built on fear, fear of collapse. Was it not the sole reason for merchants to come together to create the corporate person in the first place—all those years ago when the East India Company was formed—the fear of loss?

How, then, can we obey the Elders when we are no longer able to feel the ground beneath our feet?

Neither the promises of environmental sciences nor the expansion of rights to every sphere of life—human rights, animal rights, environmental rights—provide us with the knowledge to sustain the conditions that are necessary for the reproduction of natural and human life. Can we restore our connections with nature, with our past and future, without first creating the conceptual spaces that will allow us to pose the right questions without asking the question: "How do we reconnect to and acknowledge our relationship with Mother Earth as we continue—indeed, *must* continue—to rely on her land, waters, and air, whether or not we realize it?" The ground is there, waiting for us to recognize what we are standing on, awaiting our homecoming, away from the institutional spaces we occupy within corporate persons, to the "water, forests and land,"[3] the real home, where real life can become possible once more.

Notes

1　Adi Vasi is translated as "original dwellers," that is, what would be considered "First Nations" in a Canadian context.

2　See the film *The Corporation* for a more detailed discussion of this important concept.

3　"Water, forests, land" or *Jal, Jangal, Jameen* is the slogan of the Adi Vasis in India in their struggles against corporate invasions of their lands.

Coastal Waters in Distress from Excessive Nutrients

Paul J. Harrison

Introduction

Water issues have become the most ecologically fraught question of the twenty-first century. Water serves as the seemingly silent receptacle for the toxins that we dump into our rivers and flush down our sewage system, much of which ends up in our oceans. As Astrida Neimanis outlined (Neimanis, this volume), her desire to "think with water" is guided by a sense of environmental concern and ecological urgency. Specifically, she discusses how ways of knowing through water include water as a communicator and as an archive. In a sense, the nitrogen levels in the coastal waters communicate the large-scale impact of human activity on ecosystems, and constitute an archive of our activities that is urgent for everyday people (not just scientists) to be able to read and decipher, in order to respond with solutions to the problems.

Blackstock defines "Blue Ecology" as an ecological philosophy that emerges from interweaving First Nations and Western thought, and that acknowledges water's essential rhythmical life-spirit and central functional role in generating, sustaining, receiving, and ultimately unifying life on Mother Earth. Many cultures, particularly Indigenous peoples, believe water has a spirit. It is commonly characterized as the lifeblood of the planet since water is seen as the blood flowing through the terrestrial veins of Mother Earth.[1]

Wherever one may situate one's spiritual practices and beliefs along the intercultural spectrum, we face a shared danger together. Truly pristine water in lakes and the coastal ocean that sustains life is becoming harder to find because our human impacts are pronounced and far-reaching. Beside many obvious toxins, imbalances in carbon (mainly as carbon dioxide via global warming) and nitrogen are recent human assaults to the aquatic environment.

While the concept of a carbon footprint is well known, the nitrogen footprint is relatively unknown. However, our nitrogen footprint is equally important to be aware of in terms of its potential impact on coastal and ocean waters. Excessive nitrogen concentration in our coastal waters is one of the major environmental challenges of the twenty-first century that needs to be more widely understood and managed by better government regulations.

Nitrogen (N) in the environment occurs in several forms. The most abundant form is the gas (written as N_2, this form is called "unreactive" N or molecular N), which makes up about 78 percent of the air, while oxygen (O_2) makes up nearly 21 percent. About 3 percent of our bodies is nitrogen. Nitrogen also occurs in fresh water and sea water as inorganic compounds of nitrates (NO_3), nitrites (NO_2), ammonium (NH_4), and some organic nitrogen-containing compounds such as urea, amino acids, and various gases in the atmosphere such as nitrogen oxides. All of these forms are called "reactive" nitrogen. Therefore, these reactive forms are the major concern in terms of nitrogen pollution. All biological systems need reactive nitrogen, but it is always in short supply in nature. Until the end of the nineteenth century, the main agricultural source was fixation of N_2 gas by symbiotic bacteria in the roots of legumes (e.g., beans) and even alder trees. Therefore, farmers plant leguminous crops to naturally increase the nitrogen in the soil along with manures.

By 1900 there was concern that the rapid growth of the human population would outpace the planet's natural stores of nitrogen, which were essential for food production. However, in 1908, chemists made a remarkable breakthrough and found a way to make ammonium with oxygen and nitrogen gases using the Haber-Bosch process. This was the dawn of relatively cheap nitrogen fertilizers that are now used globally by farmers. Without these man-made nitrogen fertilizers, about half of the human population would not be alive because of probable food shortages. However, the massive production of cheap nitrogen fertilizers has come with great environmental costs and impacts. This man-made nitrogen production in the last century has increased the amount of nitrogen by about ten times over the natural supplies. This means that some parts of the aquatic environment, such as lakes and coastal areas, now receive very large inputs of this man-made nitrogen, which can produce excessive algal growth, resulting in large impacts on the ecosystem natural balance and biodiversity. About 50 percent of the nitrogen in fertilizer that is added to farm fields in Europe is absorbed by crops and only 10–15 percent gets consumed by people; much of this nitrogen is released back to the environment as human waste and sewage. The other 35 or 40 percent ends up as pollution, or is wasted by conversion to N_2 gas by bacteria (i.e., a process called denitrification).[2]

Nitrogen Pollution

Chemical fertilizer use and combustion engines are the main sources of nitrogen pollution. Excessive nitrogen threatens the quality of air, soil, and water. For example, it can cycle from soils to water, to the atmosphere, and then back to soils.[3] Excess nitrogen affects ecosystems and biodiversity, the amount of excessive nitrates in drinking water, and alters the balance of greenhouse gases. Nitrogen pollution poses even greater challenges than carbon because the nitrogen element has many complex effects as it cascades through the ecosystem in many different chemical forms.[4] A recent analysis calculated that excess nitrogen in the environment and its impacts on climate change and loss of biodiversity costs the European Union about U.S.$100 billion per year. This cost is more than double the value that nitrogen fertilizers are estimated to add to European farm income (Sutton et al. 2011).

In water, excessive reactive nitrogen causes algal blooms that can kill many animals. The algal blooms can also decrease the amount of light that reaches attached seaweeds and eelgrass, which in turn reduces the protective habitat (i.e., nursery grounds) for small fish and other organisms. Many lakes are no longer suitable for recreation activities, including swimming, because of large algal blooms. Excessive nitrate in drinking water can cause human health issues, such as an increase in the risk of bowel cancer. In the air, reactive nitrogen adds to particulate matter and ground-level ozone, created when nitrous oxides react with organic compounds, causing respiratory and cardiovascular disease. In the atmosphere, nitrogen can form a greenhouse gas, nitrous oxide, which is three hundred times more potent than carbon dioxide as a greenhouse gas, and it also destroys the atmospheric ozone layer, which protects us from harmful ultraviolet radiation. In forests, ammonia pollution stimulates the growth of algal slime, which can suffocate natural tree-living plants such as mosses and lichens, thus decreasing forest biodiversity. In peat lands, nitrogen deposition decreases the storage of carbon by killing the bog-building moss *Sphagnum.* Of the total estimated cost of damage from reactive nitrogen emissions, 75 percent comes from the effects of nitrous oxides and ammonia on human health and ecosystems.[5]

Other sources and supplies of nitrogen come from the atmosphere, which originally came from land. For example, chicken and pigs produce a lot of ammonium in their manure. It is volatile and goes up into the air, where it combines with water vapour and comes back down to land and coastal areas as various nitrogen compounds that can potentially cause excessive algal growth.

These very high levels of man-made nitrogen have many negative impacts that occur in a cascade fashion.[6] Runoff from heavily fertilized farms and nitrogen from very large animal feedlots and chicken farms reach the oceans

l groundwater. This nitrogen stimulates algal blooms, which can
er various colours such as red, brown-green, and green due to
igments in the algae. These algae eventually sink and are decom-
teria. This decomposition process (i.e., bacterial respiration) uses
up large amounts of dissolved oxygen in the water and causes low oxygen
(hypoxia = less than two milligrams of O_2 per litre, or anoxia = no O_2) in the
water, which stresses animals or kills them; normal O_2 concentrations are eight
to ten milligrams of O_2 per litre). This hypoxia produces dead zones in the
coastal ocean and lakes where few organisms can live.

Dead Zones

Dead zones[7] are oxygen-depleted or oxygen-starved regions of the ocean or
lakes that are inhospitable to plants and animals (Figure 17.1).[8] Note that the
arrow for nutrient input on the right side of Figure 17.1 is much larger than
the left side, and this large nutrient input leads to an algal bloom, less fish,
and very low oxygen at the bottom. Most dead zones form annually, starting
in the spring when algal blooms occur and ending in the fall due to mixing of
the water column by winter storms. Recent studies have observed a decline in
oxygen in many regions of our oceans over the past fifty years, likely due to
global warming, which deters water column mixing, and runoff of nutrients
from our farms and cities. In 2009, it was estimated that dead zones have
increased ten times (from forty to four hundred) in the last fifty years and
the expansion was greater in the ocean than freshwater areas.[9] About half of
the 647 waterways in the United States are considered to be oxygen stressed
or hypoxic. Approximately 8 percent of the total oceanic area of our planet is
now considered to be oxygen-starved. The expansion of these oxygen-starved
regions of the ocean will have a direct effect on coastal ecosystems and the
productivity of marine fisheries due to habitat loss, a decrease in biodiversity,
and changes in nutrient cycles. The economic and food security implications
of these changes are severe. Over the past decade, dead zone outbreaks have
become more frequent and intense, mainly due to excessive nutrient inputs,
leading many to become concerned about the long-term consequences of the
decline in oxygen on ocean health.

There is a well-known dead zone at the mouth of the Mississippi River in
the Gulf of Mexico. It is the second largest in the world, after the Baltic Sea,
with a dead zone area about the size of the state of New Jersey. The Mississippi
River drains about one-third of the United States, and it transports nutrients into the Gulf. A large amount of the excessive nitrogen and phosphorus
comes from farming, especially corn and soybeans, and animal feedlots. The
watersheds that are most responsible for polluting the Gulf of Mexico are the

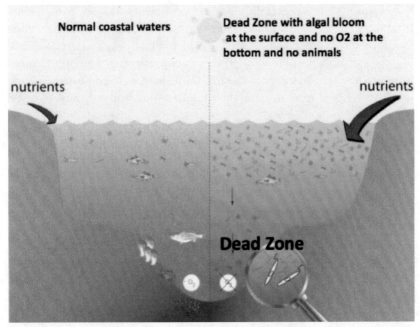

Figure 17.1 The addition of excessive nutrients causes algal blooms (green water) and the low oxygen at the bottom kills all the animals causing a "dead zone." (*Source:* Paul Harrison)

Corn Belt states of Indiana and Illinois, followed by Iowa, Ohio, Arkansas, etc.[10] About half of the corn and soy is used to feed livestock, even though soy is an excellent high-protein food source for humans. The nutrients from the farms enter the river by runoff, travel down the river, and over-fertilize a large northern section of the Gulf of Mexico up to twenty thousand square kilometres. These nutrients produce algal blooms and subsequently hypoxia in the deep water, which has a devastating economic impact on the commercial shrimp and other fish (Figure 17.1). The decomposing algae and animals on the sea floor also produce nitrogen gas and nitrous oxide, which is a potent greenhouse gas that has a heat-trapping capability three hundred times greater than the well-known greenhouse gas carbon dioxide, as mentioned earlier. The size of the Mississippi dead zone varies each year and the largest dead zone is formed when there is above-average Mississippi River discharge due to high snowfall and spring snowmelt and/or high rainfall in the spring. The high river discharge produces a light freshwater surface layer that floats on top of the more dense seawater at the mouth of the Mississippi River, and this decreases wind mixing of the water column and the subsequent transfer of the high O_2 concentrations in the air to deeper waters.

Nitrogen can also enter the marine environment from fish farms, mainly from uneaten fish food and fish excretory products. It is estimated that one metric tonne of salmon releases sixty kilograms of nitrogen and ten kilograms of phosphorus. A possible solution to reduce nutrients around fish farms is to set up a seaweed farm near the fish farm since seaweed can take up the nutrients released from fish and their uneaten food, and the seaweed could be harvested for human use.

Solutions

(1) *Personal energy consumption:* The nitrogen (and carbon) involved in energy production eventually ends up in the environment, especially in the atmosphere as nitrous oxide, which is a very potent greenhouse gas. Therefore, we need to consume less energy. This means reduced use of cars (e.g., take a bus or train), lights, heat, air conditioning, etc. These actions will reduce both the nitrogen and carbon footprints, and therefore we could make a double contribution to environmental impacts and climate change by reducing our personal energy consumption.

(2) *Food choices, especially meat:* We can reduce our nitrogen footprint or impact by simply eating less meat. There is a strong correlation between a country's wealth and its fertilizer use, and also between personal income and the per capita protein consumption.[11] Therefore, meat consumption increases with wealth and hence nitrogen pollution also increases with wealth. The agricultural production of meat is very inefficient. Of the 170 million metric tonnes of nitrogen fertilizer that is added to crops, only a small percentage actually ends up in our mouths.[12] Beef farming is even less efficient since it takes one hundred kilograms of nitrogen in corn to produce five kilograms of edible nitrogen in beef (i.e., only 5 percent is converted to beef). The remaining ninety-five kilograms of nitrogen is lost to the surrounding environment in various forms.[13] North Americans consume about 40–70 percent more protein than the recommended dietary allowance. It is possible to meet your daily protein requirement by eating just one or two cups of tofu (made from soybeans), and this also reduces the negative health effects of meat arising from animal fat. Foods fed to animals, such as corn, need very large amounts of nitrogen fertilizers to obtain high yields. Therefore, reducing meat consumption will reduce the amount of corn that is needed because from one hundred pounds of corn, we only get about ten to twenty pounds of meat and therefore eighty to ninety pounds of corn are wasted in converting grains that could be consumed by humans into animal protein, a luxury that only rich countries can afford. Therefore, the use of high nitrogen fertilizer is not about food security in North America and Europe (i.e., producing enough food for humans), but it is about human luxury consumption of animal protein. For example, if Europeans

obtained all of their protein from plants (e.g., grains, soy, corn, etc.), only 30 percent of the crop production would be needed to feed the human population, which would reduce the nitrogen fertilizer inputs and associated nitrogen pollution by 70 percent.[14] Several kinds of animal protein have been assessed to determine which meat products made the largest contribution to both our carbon and nitrogen footprints. The winner (i.e., the worst) was definitely red meat followed by dairy products.[15]

When meat production was compared to "food miles" (i.e., transport costs of the food) in terms of greenhouse gas emissions, the production phase of food contributed 83 percent versus 11 percent for the transport costs of getting the food to market.[16] Therefore, a dietary shift from meat to a plant-based diet can be much more effective way to reduce your carbon and nitrogen footprint than buying local.[17]

How to Calculate Your Nitrogen Footprint

It is possible to calculate how much you are contributing to the input of excess nitrogen into the aquatic environment and the atmosphere.[18] This calculation will provide an insight into the most important ways that you can reduce your personal nitrogen impact and how to live a more sustainable lifestyle. One of the goals of the nitrogen footprint calculator is to help people make the connection between personal nitrogen inputs and the policies used to manage and reduce these inputs. A similar calculator is being developed for farmers and other nitrogen users, as well as a tool for policy-makers that will provide regional nitrogen emission ceilings showing how much nitrogen can be released in certain regions without producing a major environmental impact.

Summary

Nitrogen pollution comes mainly from excessive use of chemical fertilizers and combustion engines. The increase in excessive amounts of nitrogen, especially from fertilizer and animal manure, is clearly linked to the increase of large algal blooms and the subsequent formation of dead zones (with little or no O_2 in the bottom water of many coastal and freshwater areas). A nitrogen footprint calculator has been developed to assess personal contributions to nitrogen inputs. The two main ways to reduce one's nitrogen footprint are to consume less energy, especially through a reduction in one's use of transportation, and to shift from meat consumption to a plant-based diet. For example, if people obtained all of their protein from plants (e.g., grains, soy, corn, etc.), then the crop production that would be needed to feed the human population would be 70 percent less since none of the crop production would be fed to animals. This would reduce the nitrogen fertilizer inputs and associated nitrogen pollution by 70 percent. While there may be cultural and psychological barriers to such a widespread shift, the signs of this shift are evident in the increasing numbers of vegetarians today. A transition may also include reducing the amount of meat one eats, even if it is not eliminated. Given that such a change in diet would be voluntary, not mandatory, this would require a much wider understanding of the environmental as well as the health benefits of a more plant-based diet to convince people to make this shift.

As mentioned in the introduction, we face a shared danger that calls for us to not only think with water, as Neimanis et al. (this volume) have suggested, but to also act with water and protect nature's life-giving and extremely valuable resource. Tracking nitrogen is one very specific and measurable way to outline constructive human interactions with water. If we each take on these actions, it would have a significant collective impact on maintaining a healthy environment. Hopefully, understanding the scientific processes that cause environmental impacts such as the excessive nitrogen problem described in this chapter will convince and compel us to make personal changes that will help to address environmental concerns that other contributors to this anthology have raised. While we have different ways of communicating in our disciplines, what brings us together in this volume is a shared value of respecting nature and preserving it for future generations.

Notes

1   Michael Blackstock, "Water-Based Ecology: A First Nations Proposal to Repair the Definition of an Ecosystem," *BC Journal of Ecosystems and Management* 2, no. 1(2002): 7–12.
2   J. N. Galloway et al., "The Nitrogen Cascade," *Bioscience* 53, no. 4 (2003): 341–56.
3   There is an excellent video on this nitrogen cascade at www.greensandbox.org/2012/07/25/when--.
4   N. Gruber and J. N. Galloway, "An Earth-System Perspective of the Global N Cycle," *Nature* 451, no. 4 (2008): 293–96.
5   J. N. Galloway et al., "The Nitrogen Cascade," *Bioscience* 53, no. 4 (2003): 341–56.
6   Ibid.
7   The Canadian film, *Revolution* (2012), by Rob Stewart visually depicts the impact of dead zones in the world's oceans.
8   For a good website on how dead zones form, see http://wfad.org/animalagribusiness/oceanpollution.htm.
9   See Galloway et al., "The Nitrogen Cascade"; Gruber and Galloway, "An Earth-System Perspective."
10. M. A. Sutton, O. Oenema, J. W. Erisman, A. Leip, H. van Grinsven, and W. Winiwarter. "Too Much of a Good Thing," *Nature* 472 (2011): 159–61.
11   S. W. Nixon, "Coastal Marine Eutrophication—a Definition, Social Causes, and Future Concerns," *Ophelia* 41 (1995): 199–219.
12   Galloway et al., "The Nitrogen Cascade," 341–56.
13   Sutton et al., "Too Much of a Good Thing."
14   Ibid.

15 Ibid.
16 C. L. Weber and H. S. Matthews, "Food-Miles and Relative Climate Change Impacts of Food Choices in the United States," *Environmental Science and Technology* 42, no. 10 (2008): 3508–13.
17 X. Xue and A. E. Landis, "Eutrophication Potential of Food Consumption Patterns," *Environmental Science and Technology* 44, no. 16 (2010): 6450–56.
18 Check out these websites on how to calculate your nitrogen footprint:
　　www.n-print.org
　　www.nitrogenNews.com
　　www.earthtimes.org/pollution/check-nitrogen-footprint/307/
　　www.sciencedaily.com/releases/2011/02/11022212251.hml
　　www.epa.gov/nutrientpollution/whatyoucando/index.html
　　www.greensandbox.com/2012/07/25/when-was-the-last-time-you

Bibliography

Blackstock, M. "Interweaving: The Transformation of Sovereign Knowledge into Collaborative Knowledge." In *downstream: reimagining water*, edited by Dorothy Christian and Rita Wong. Waterloo, ON: Wilfrid Laurier University Press, 2017.

———. "Water-Based Ecology: A First Nations Proposal to Repair the Definition of an Ecosystem." *BC Journal of Ecosystems and Management* 2, no. 1 (2002): 7–12.

Galloway, J. N., et al. "The Nitrogen Cascade." *Bioscience* 53, no. 4 (2003): 341–56.

Gruber, N., and J. N. Galloway. "An Earth-System Perspective of the Global N Cycle." *Nature* 451, no. 4 (2008): 293–96.

Neimanis, A. "Water and Knowledge." In *downstream: reimagining water*, edited by Dorothy Christian and Rita Wong. Waterloo, ON: Wilfrid Laurier University Press, 2017.

Nixon, S. W. "Coastal Marine Eutrophication—a Definition, Social Causes, and Future Concerns." *Ophelia* 41 (1995): 199–219.

Stewart, Rob. *Revolution*. 2012. Film.

Sutton, M. A., O. Oenema, J. W. Erisman, A. Leip, H. van Grinsven, and W. Winiwarter. "Too Much of a Good Thing." *Nature* 472 (2011): 159–61.

Weber, C. L., and H. S. Matthews. "Food-Miles and Relative Climate Change Impacts of Food Choices in the United States." *Environmental Science and Technology* 42, no. 10 (2008): 3508–13.

Xue, X., and A. E. Landis. "Eutrophication Potential of Food Consumption Patterns." *Environmental Science and Technology* 44 (2010): 6450–56.

Bodies of Water
Asian Canadians In/Action with Water
Janey Lew

Preface: Mobilizing In/Action

I would like to acknowledge that I wrote this chapter while living on the ancestral, unceded territories of Coast Salish peoples. The essay touches upon my observations and experiences while living on the ancestral territories of the Huchuin (Ohlone) peoples. My gratitude for the privilege of living and being a guest on these lands and waters.

An earlier version of this chapter was originally published in *Ricepaper Magazine*'s 2011 Green Issue, featuring Asian Canadians' efforts to address environmental concerns. *Ricepaper*, published by the Asian Canadian Writers' Workshop, is Canada's premier Asian Canadian arts and culture quarterly. My original plan had been to write an article about the Downstream project and to profile Asian Canadian artists, scholars, and community members involved in grassroots water projects around Vancouver. I proposed interviewing poet-scholar Rita Wong about Downstream and her recent work on water issues for the piece. I also wanted to interview Shahira Sakiyama, an activist and mother of three originally from California, who had attended the World Social Forum on water issues in Brazil in 2005, and more recently had worked with Rita on the St. George Street Rainway Project in Vancouver's Mount Pleasant neighbourhood.

As I started researching and writing the essay, I found myself asking self-reflexive questions about my own relationship to water. Having lived my entire life on the West Coast, I tended (and, to a large extent, continue) to take water for granted. At the same time, living by the ocean has attuned me to water's continuous cycles and its intense power. I was, even before writing the piece, obsessed with water-related disasters. My worries about the environment could be captured in three stock images: a polar bear clinging to a melting ice cap, cars floating on hurricane-flooded streets, and ducks covered in crude oil. Even so, working on the essay confronted me with my ignorance about water issues and water activism, both globally and locally. After interviewing Rita, I kept thinking about how not a single Chinese Canadian showed up for the 2007 Protect Our Sacred Waters event organized by Dorothy Christian and Denise Nadeau. As a scholar of Asian Canadian and Indigenous studies, my interests have moved increasingly toward questions of culture and activism in a settler-colonial context. As I worked on the essay, I couldn't shake feelings of guilt and helplessness: researching Asian Canadian water activism drew attention to my own *inaction*, the precise problem Dorothy Christian had called Chinese Canadians out on after Protect Our Sacred Waters. The essay for *Ricepaper* began taking a different shape, incorporating both personal reflection as well as reporting on Downstream, and was eventually published in the issue as two adjoining feature articles.

When Rita and Dorothy put the call out for the *Downstream* anthology, I recognized the potential to revise the piece and see it in print whole, as I had originally intended—an extended personal essay in the tradition of Phillip Lopate and Joan Didion that flows from topic to topic, personal to factual, intimate to grand scale. This form reflects the form and flow of water in the varied ways it touches our lives and the ways we interact with it. Water is both *of us* and *outside of us*. Though our interactions with water are often intimate and mundane, bodies of water and water issues can also appear distant and overwhelming. How much does the average city-dweller know about the journey water takes to arrive at the kitchen tap, or where the water that flushes down the toilet goes? What kinds of connections can we begin to make between our own watery bodies, the water we use in our homes, and the immense ocean waters or the hurricane waters that occasionally devastate communities? Moreover, the Downstream project invites us to investigate culturally sensitive approaches to water, which directs us to think about how water flows through and shapes our cultural histories. In addition to becoming more aware of our daily water uses and global water issues, what kinds of creative practices can we undertake to develop a more ethical relationship to water and, in turn, more ethical relationships with each other across cultural, racial, national, geographical, and other divides? What can we learn from how our different ancestors travelled and treated the waters that made their lives possible? How do the stories we tell about our cultural communities and water affect our water practices? While pursuing the original goal of profiling some actions taken by Asian Canadians on water issues, I continued to be provoked by these larger questions, which demanded further thinking through in writing. I started to wonder, in what ways might *writing on water* constitute a form of *action with water*? After talking with Rita, the notion of a participatory water ethic struck me as offering some answers to my questions. I also turned to Trinh Minh-ha's concept of "speaking nearby" to guide me as I explored the many flows of water that converge in my essay.

Water's ubiquity and its scope can make it an overwhelming topic to tackle. I certainly struggled with scope and scale as I drafted and revised this piece of writing. The sense of feeling overwhelmed or powerless can be a huge barrier to taking action on any issue. But changing how we think about power and action may help to unlock some of the painful inertia that comes from not knowing how or where to begin exercising our ethical responsibilities for social justice and environmental stewardship. For example, what if the principle guiding human power in relation to water was *love* instead of *control*? Likewise, recognizing the potential of creative practice to change minds and thus influence actions may redefine what constitutes activism while reminding us that imagination is a vital part of taking action.

This chapter traces changes in my thinking on water as I contemplated connections between global water disasters, local water initiatives, Asian Canadian cultural activism, and my own anxieties over inaction. I came to realize that because we interact with water so regularly and intimately in our daily lives, even when we don't think we are being active with water, we nevertheless consciously and unconsciously enact ways of thinking about and relating to water through routine water practices. Therefore, changing our consciousness about water necessarily influences our actions, which in turn can develop and take on more creative forms as we allow ourselves to define and partake in action, and perhaps activism, differently.

1. The Bleeding Gulf

Driving to and from the University of California–Berkeley campus in the summer of 2010, my attention was repeatedly caught by the radio news that tar balls were washing up almost daily on the southeastern shores of Louisiana. The BP oil spill, which had been set off by the explosion of a drilling rig in a marine oil field on April 20, 2010, had released, by the time it was capped in mid-July, just under 5 million barrels of petroleum in three months' time into the Gulf of Mexico; it was reported to be the petroleum industry's single largest accidental marine spill.[1] Tar balls are semi-solid clumps of crude oil that form through weathering in the ocean. As an oil slick spreads into the ocean, pieces of it begin to separate and disperse, aided by wind and waves. Some of the chemical components evaporate, and what remains mixes with ocean matter and undergoes further physical and chemical changes, resulting in globs of oil that eventually wash ashore onto beaches. In the months following the BP spill, tar balls appeared on beaches in all five U.S. states bordering the Gulf of Mexico: Louisiana, Alabama, Texas, Mississippi, and Florida.[2] Reporters described the tar balls as having the shape of coins, and I heard of parents in the affected states bringing their children to nearby beaches to see the tar balls.[3] I pictured these beach-going families in their cover-ups with umbrellas and plastic buckets, walking in small groups with their heads down, hunting a perverse treasure. The image of "tar coins" and the words of a pilot flying over the area above the spill, who compared the reddish streaks of the spreading oil slick to a bleeding wound,[4] came suddenly into my thoughts every so often that summer, the last I spent in Berkeley, California, as a PhD student. I waited out those last few weeks of my time in Berkeley sitting on the edge of my apartment building's swimming pool with my legs dangling in the water, reading and preparing my lectures. It calmed me to be near water.

It had been a summer of intense instability in my personal life, with the anticipation of more changes to come in the process of moving home to Vancouver. Those inner preoccupations, which at times felt so big, were unsettled and diminished by the larger events of that summer of catastrophe and contradiction, in which I keenly felt the powerlessness of witnessing, from the distance of my California pool, an environmental disaster of such great magnitude. My thoughts often drifted to the surface of the pool, rippling between calm and rough, as I grasped at my everyday routines intricately tied to complex and overwhelming urban infrastructures, and meditated on my relationship to bodies of water.

Years ago, I had read Joan Didion's essay "Holy Water," which describes in detail the immense yet intricate infrastructure required to keep water in flow around the state of California. Occasionally, when I stood over sinks in California, the words "drain Quail" would come into my head. "Quail," as Didion notes in her essay, "is a reservoir in Los Angeles County with a gross capacity of 1,636,018,000 gallons," and "draining Quail," in Didion's essay, is synecdoche for the elegance and power of a massive engineering structure (one largely buried from view in a complex system of canals, pumps, pipes, and containers) that is able to, at the press of buttons, move vast amounts of water across extensive geographical distances to sustain the quotidian habits of washing, drinking, and flushing the toilet.[5] California is the third-largest U.S. state, contains its highest populace and supports its largest economy (ranking among global economies in the top ten, with a larger gross domestic product than the entire country of Canada). Although much of the state has a Mediterranean climate, three deserts—the Mojave, the Colorado, and the Great Basin—cover 16 percent of the landmass in California. Writing in the late 1970s, Didion reflects on the regularity of the well running dry during her childhood, and notes that "[e]ven now the place is not all that hospitable to extensive settlement."[6]

Didion's essay turns on her observations about water and control. On the symbol of the ubiquitous California swimming pool, Didion writes, "a pool is misapprehended as a trapping of affluence, real or pretended, and of a kind of hedonistic attention to the body. Actually a pool is, for many of us in the West, a symbol not of affluence but of order, of control over the uncontrollable."[7] But situated in the context of Didion's 1979 essay collection *The White Album*, which meditates on the rapid and overwhelming social upheavals in the United States from the 1950s to the 1970s,[8] "Holy Water" is not so much an affirmative commentary on human control over the elements as it is a tense contemplation on the cycles of pressure and release that revolve in the management of both human and water bodies. In particular, the essay points out the intense irony of having created so many measures for control that result only in ever greater feelings of powerlessness.

"Water is important to people who do not have it," Didion writes, "and the same is true of control."[9] Didion's analogy rings true, but there is more to unpack. Water is equally significant whether there is too little or too much. Recent water-related natural disasters, like the massive tsunami that followed the 8.9-magnitude Tohoku earthquake in the northeastern Honshu Island of Japan on March 11, 2011, demonstrate that the chaos produced by flood can be as devastating as the inability to provide water during drought. If anything, the desire to control water extends deeper and projects more complex motivations than Didion's essay suggests. Water encompasses opposites. While we experience water's power daily in innumerable large and small ways, its most brutal exertions appear in its extreme ends: excess and lack. While it is, as Didion writes, "the only natural force over which we have any control ... and that only recently,"[10] recent environmental events demonstrate that human control over water is nominal and temporary at best, illusory at worst. In fact, the very opposition of humans to water is ironic, since human bodies are mostly water.[11] If we were to think of ourselves as "bodies of water," how might that change our behaviour or perceptions? How could a more integral awareness of human relationship to water affect how we think and act in our own lives and in our relationships with other people and other bodies of water? Could focusing on water help to humanize us more?

2. Humanizing the Disaster

Since 2004, there have been three major submarine earthquake and tsunami disasters in the Asia-Pacific region. The first and deadliest of the three was triggered in December 2004 by the Sumatra-Andaman earthquake, whose hypocentre was located northwest of Sumatra, Indonesia, about 160 kilometres underwater in the Indian Ocean. The 9.0-magnitude earthquake initiated a series of powerful tsunamis that amassed over 230,000 casualties in fourteen countries, including Indonesia, Thailand, India, and Sri Lanka.[12] In the months that followed the catastrophe, donations to the Canadian Red Cross alone delivered over $130 million in emergency relief funds to the affected areas.[13] Of this disaster, I recall a few things: I remember waking up the morning after Christmas that year to headlines announcing disaster; I remember making an online donation to the Red Cross in the days following the event and filing away the tax receipt; I remember taking care to avoid footage on CNN and other newscasts of the tsunami, taken in real time by panicked tourists on their cameras and cellphones.

Sitting in pajamas in my living room littered with wrapping paper and Boxing Day tinsel, I found myself disturbed by the relentless circulation of photo and video images of blurry humans clinging to trees and staggering half-naked through muddy, ruined streets. Could these images possibly humanize the disaster, or did they simply heighten the distance between the receivers of the news and the event, adding to an already false sense of security? Even as I avoided the news, my mind dwelt on the scale of destruction, turning over the phrase "hundreds of thousands of lives." These thoughts were themselves difficult to grasp; they seemed so small, like my actions, like all the accumulated details in my day, in comparison to such a large happening so far away, so forceful, so spectacular.

How do you justify thinking for a living? I was waist-deep in my graduate studies and living in Berkeley when an earthquake struck the Samoan Islands in September 2009. I caught news of it off my Facebook news feed; a few hours later, on the evening news, a precautionary tsunami warning was issued for the San Francisco Bay area, but the effects were never felt on the continent. The Samoa earthquake happened in the same week that Typhoon Ketsana passed over Southeast Asia. In total, this single week of calamity in the Pacific claimed hundreds of casualties, with many more injured and missing. Shortly afterward, I happened to be cleaning out my closet at the same time that one of my friends was collecting donations to send to the Philippines; one afternoon I met her in San Francisco and transferred two garbage bags of clothing from the trunk of my car to hers. As we parted, she thanked me and I recall being embarrassed, repeating, "It's nothing, it's nothing."

I also happened to be in California, in a hotel room at an academic conference, when the Tohoku earthquake and tsunami struck in March 2011. As with the Samoa earthquake, I first learned of the Japan disaster from my Facebook feed. I was working on my conference paper late into the night and, between paragraphs, would flip to Facebook as news rolled in, first, about the earthquake, and then the tsunami. It was an odd bricolage: rumours of the number of dead intermixed with posts announcing high scores on Farmville.

The essay I was writing was a reworking of one of my comps papers, tracing the notion of "Asian Canadian" as an academic field of study—a topic that has preoccupied scholars since the late 1990s.[14] On that trip, a few days later, a group of us gathered around the computer to watch a YouTube rant that had gone viral. A UCLA student named Alexandra Wallace had posted a video blog directed at "these hordes of Asian people that UCLA accepts … every single year."[15] Observing that the Asian students in question do not "know American manners," Wallace points to an example of students answering their cellphones in the library, noting in frustration that the students "[must be] going through their whole families, just checking on everybody from the tsunami thing."[16] One part of the video, which inspired a backlash of responses, shows Wallace mock-answering her cellphone by saying "OH! Ching chong ling long ting tong!"[17]

My students squirm when I bring up the topic of race. They like to insist that historic injustices like the head tax and internment are *simply that— historic; the multicultural world we live in is unafflicted by race.* The blatant and brazen racism exhibited by Wallace in her video diary seemed to shock and certainly to outrage many people who watched and shared the video in the ensuing weeks of the controversy before the clip had been removed from the Internet and Wallace had apologized, withdrawn from UCLA, and faded from public scrutiny. But far from being anomalous, Wallace's vitriolic contempt toward Asians is remarkable only for its ordinariness. Nothing she observes about Asian American students ventures off the established script of yellow-peril invasion, an anti-Asian trope that has circulated alongside the "Ching Chong Chinaman" refrain since at least the nineteenth century. Nor does Wallace's conflation of ethnic stereotypes, her inability to distinguish between the ching chongs and possible tsunami victims, diverge from slant-eyed generalization. "Asian" has perhaps replaced "Oriental" as the acceptable term of parlance but, in the absence of knowledge and ongoing discussion about the specific political and historical contexts that drive movements for pan-ethnic solidarity and identification, it continues to function in many of the same ways as its predecessor—othering, essentializing, objectifying, and generalizing.

For the most part, reactions to the video have disengaged Wallace's comments from the water-related disaster that prompted them. Another way of looking at it is that the event of the tsunami prompted Wallace to remove her finger from the dam, unleashing a torrent of racial anxiety that has been building in pressure against the surface of North American neo-liberal multiculturalism. What was it in the particulars of seeing Asian American faces in the library after a global environmental catastrophe that caused this young woman to respond so disconnectedly, emphasizing inherited racial hierarchies instead of raising larger questions about extreme storms in the context of climate change? Could it have been that the combined markers of Asian phenotypical difference and national presence triggered a sense of vulnerability that comes from bringing the imagined distances of Japan and natural disaster too close to home? In short, could the sight of "Asians" have disrupted Wallace's sense of political or environmental security, a security predicated on denial of responsibility for mutual human life and our global environment? And what does all this tell us about the underlying insecurity or powerlessness that prompts this form of violent outburst? These are the kinds of self-reflective questions I would expect my own students to ask about their own reactions to significant world events. While it is tempting to attack Wallace for her ignorance and antipathy, what her insulting rant demonstrates most disturbingly to me is the failure of humanistic education to get through to a political science upper-class woman enrolled at an elite public university, as well as the marked absence of any consciousness or ecological literacy in relation to climate change.

In the days that followed the Tohoku earthquake, warnings were issued about aftershocks and possible tsunami effects that extended, this time, from California to British Columbia. Back in Vancouver, I attended several earthquake-relief fundraisers, including one at Vancouver's Vivo Media Arts Centre, where Asian Canadian writers Fred Wah, Roy Miki, Proma Tagore, Lydia Kwa, and Hiromi Goto read recent work on water, Japan, and the tsunami. Again, I donated money, collecting books ("all proceeds to Japan Relief Fund") and tax receipts in return. I was wrought with familiar feelings of compassion, coupled with the numbness, helplessness, and paralysis that I had felt upon donating clothes to support the Philippine typhoon relief efforts and pouring over news about the BP oil spill. I felt dwarfed by the scale of these catastrophes, which seemed to befall so suddenly, distantly, and powerfully out of control. Technologies introduced these events with an intense immediacy into my consciousness, but also held them there transiently. Unable to grasp the direct effects of these global disasters, I offered what small gestures I could. But my own responses have left me to wonder: In what ways are my actions meaningful? What good does my thinking do?

3. Downstream

Water flows deeply through my family's history, one that reaches across the Pacific from southern Guangdong province in China, where my parents were born, to my present-day life and travels along the West Coast of Canada and the United States. Beyond the scope of my own family, water is perhaps the quintessential element symbolizing Asian migration to the Americas. Settlers of Asian descent began arriving by ship on the Indigenous lands of Turtle

Island (North America) as early as the late eighteenth century. A few historians take the origin stories back even further, locating the first contact between China and North America during Buddhist monk Hui Shen's 499 CE nautical expedition to Fusang.[18] My mother's father travelled alone by ship from Kaiping[19] county in southern Guangdong province to British Columbia in 1919. According to scholar Madeline Hsu, Chinese emigration soared from the mid-nineteenth to the early twentieth century, a large concentration of it originating from the Four Counties (Kaiping, Taishan, Xinhui, Engping) district of southern Guangdong province.[20] Rapid population growth mixed with poor agricultural conditions in the Pearl River Delta created poverty for the inhabitants of the Four Counties, which caused the area to become a major source for exporting Chinese labour. Both flood and drought are common to these areas of southeastern China, and to this day dictate agricultural output. Perhaps it was this intimate familiarity with water they carried over with them, and an acknowledgement of a vast ocean joining their two homes, that caused the earliest Chinese settlers to dub Vancouver "Saltwater City."

A trans-Pacific flow of migrant labourers, in large part, built the infrastructure of this country. Generations of Asian migrants crossed the ocean by boat to arrive and settle on this continent. The image of Asian migrants and refugees arriving by boat is a well-recognized trope in both recent and historical discussions of not only immigration, but also national identity, transnational labour, and race politics in Canada. More recently, the arrival off British Columbia's coast of nearly five hundred Tamil asylum seekers aboard the *MV Sun Sea* in the summer of 2010 sparked off another round of debates linking Pacific ocean currents, Asian bodies, and Canadian "national security." Following close behind a smaller boatload of Tamil passengers who arrived in the fall of 2009, the second group of migrants prompted Prime Minister Stephen Harper to respond that "this trend gives us significant concern."[21] Both official discourse and mainstream media have generally expressed more concern over the security of the country's marine borders than it has for the safety and well-being of those who arrive in numbers from Asia by boat. An iconic historical precedent was set during the May 1914 *Komagata Maru* incident, in which a cargo ship carrying 376 Indian passengers landed in Vancouver's Burrard Inlet. Anticipating the ship's arrival, and riding a wave of anti-Oriental sentiment already simmering in the province, British Columbia newspapers warned of "Hindu excursioners ... the forerunners of a horde of a few million."[22] The majority of the passengers aboard the *Komagata Maru*, which had been at sea for seven weeks before anchoring in Vancouver, were refused admittance to the country and detained on the ship for two months before being turned around for Asia.

With this history in mind, I sat down with Rita Wong to talk water. At the time, she was working with Dorothy Christian and others to bring together the group of artists, community workers, and scholars who would eventually contribute to the Downstream project. At the time that we spoke, Wong described Downstream as a gathering for a diverse cohort of collaborators to explore and develop a culturally sensitive poetics of water. Asked how her interest in water came about, Wong told me the story of being invited to attend a forum in 2007 called Protect Our Sacred Waters. As Wong recalls, event organizers Dorothy Christian and Denise Nadeau "were concerned about the many threats to water, including, in BC, the possibility that our rivers might be privatized."[23] The organizers, especially Christian, wanted to have a public gathering that brought together diverse cultural perspectives on water. Wong, who could not attend the event because she was out of town, forwarded notice of it to friends and members of the Chinese Canadian community at Dorothy Christian's request. Despite Wong's efforts, "[n]ot a single Chinese Canadian showed up [...] even though threats like water pollution and the privatization of rivers in BC will hurt everyone, including people of Chinese ancestry."[24] After that, Wong started to focus more deeply on water and committed to collaborating with Christian on water-related actions.

In the late 1990s, Wong was involved with a grassroots group advocating for and supporting six hundred Fujianese refugees who arrived off the British Columbia coast in four separate cargo ships during the summer of 1999. In particular, Wong connected with many of the ninety Fujianese women who, after their arrival, were detained in prison. In an open letter addressed to Storefront Orientation Services, an organization that provides services to refugee claimants, some of the Fujianese women spoke out about their experiences in the Burnaby Correctional Center for Women: "The ocean waves did not swallow our lives. But here in this civilized country, we are living in such unusual conditions. This is a prison. We long to see the world outside. We dream of being like the people outside—welcoming and celebrating the millennium."[25] Remarking on the "very racist language" surrounding the event, including local newspaper headlines that urged passengers to "Go Home!," Wong described how she wanted to bridge her theoretical analysis on systemic racism with the daily experiences of people directly affected.[26] Wong spoke with me about the irony of the Canadian government's involvement in overseas ventures that displace local populations, such as the Three Gorges dam in China,[27] and contribute to the factors that cause people to flee their home countries. This kind of global project displaces people, and when they come to Canada seeking a new home, the government refuses them entry.[28] The government justifies its irresponsible exclusions by dehumanizing people, imprisoning them, and referring to them as "boat people" and "bogus refugees."

Wong described writing as a form of commitment to embodied experience, social justice, and evolving communities: "When you write something you have to live by what you've written."[29] Writing, she contends, "changes the way you want to act because it changes the way you see and think."[30] She felt a natural progression from working with people who've journeyed by ocean to the substance of the ocean itself—the gift of water, without which people would not survive.

4. Daylighting

Water surrounds Vancouver—not only geographically on three sides of the city, but also from above and below. Six months of the year, the average monthly precipitation is above ten centimetres;[31] within those months, rain will sometimes fall every day for weeks at a time. That we are blanketed by water is an easy observation to make, but many people may not be aware that much of the city was built over water that continues to run underneath the streets in pipes. I learned this about this in June 2011 at a community design workshop hosted by a group of citizens who have been organizing to "daylight" a stream that runs beneath St. George Street in Vancouver's Mount Pleasant neighbourhood. The St. George Creek (or Rainway) project is something that Rita Wong has been involved in organizing as part of her water-related activities; the daylighting initiative has been part of the constellation of community, artistic, and scholarly activities surrounding the 2012 Downstream event, and it demonstrates the variety and scale of action and collaboration possible. Daylighting refers to the process of bringing a stream that has been culverted underground to return to surface flows. Over the last century, in the effort to develop the city, nearly all the freshwater streams in Vancouver have been buried underground. About seven hundred kilometres of these "lost" streams and creeks now flow through underground sewers.[32]

I grew up in the 1980s on the edges of Vancouver's Chinatown and the Downtown Eastside. I remember when I was elementary school–aged, walking with friends around the marshy flats of False Creek surrounding the Expo '86 site. Expo '86 sparked a massive wave of construction that included dense residential development in the areas around Science World and Yaletown in the years that followed the fair. Even now, it is hard for me to imagine living in these neighbourhoods, which I associate with chain-link fences, bogs littered with trash, and abandoned warehouses. "There is so much more to history than meets the eye," writes Lee Maracle in her essay "Goodbye Snauq."[33] The contemporary urban geography of Snauq, the area now known as False Creek, overlays a historical palimpsest of Indigenous land use, colonial occupation, industrial and urban development, and Indigenous title. Maracle's essay peels back the layers to reveal how water originally slaked the landscape "from what is now 2nd avenue in the south to just below Dunsmuir in the north," extending the shoreline as far east as "what is now Clark Drive."[34] Not only did colonial settlers have to drain the watershed to make room for the CPR railway station and to build sawmills and amenities to serve a booming forestry industry, but to do so they also had to forcibly evict Indigenous peoples by burning down the Squamish village, which had been established there since the nineteenth century. After driving out the villagers, settlers went on to drastically alter the landscape by using the basin as "a garbage dump"[35] for disposing industrial waste, in the process killing wildlife and eradicating flora. The Urban Fare that now sits the centre of the Olympic Village is a dissonant reminder that Snauq, as Maracle describes it, served as a "supermarket"[36] for Musqueam, Squamish, and Tsleil-Waututh people before the arrival of settlers. Reading Maracle's elegiaic essay, I try to hold these layers distinctly in my imagination: the industrial wasteland of my childhood, the runners and strollers populating today's steel and glass seawall, and Snauq, a social meeting ground and "common garden" that First Nations communities not only collectively drew from but also tended to.[37]

I had purposefully stayed in California during the mayhem of the 2010 Vancouver Games and was absent from the city for much of the construction of the Canada Line and the Olympic Village. In the lead-up to the Olympics, it seemed that every time I visited home, I encountered a brand-new city. Streets that I had known intimately, like Main Street and Granville Mall, were suddenly new, like boyfriends from a past life who had lost weight, gotten sexy haircuts, and developed European accents. My friends were blasé in the face of my astonishment, uttering just one word, "Olympics," as if it alone explained everything. As many people have commented, the long-term benefits of the 2010 Games have yet to be measured. The worldwide attention garnered by the Olympics has already resulted in an influx in global capital for development, and no doubt will generate investment for years to come. People heralded the 2010 Winter Games as the moment when Vancouver arrived as a world-class city.[38] But lately, as I have been walking around the city, trying to get to know the place again, I find myself gripped with inexplicable nostalgia and loss.[39]

The loss of freshwater streams around False Creek has led to the loss of habitat for wildlife that have historically depended on the watershed, including salmon that used to run in the streams that crossed the city. During the community parade, which happened on the same morning as the St. George Creek design workshop, I gathered with a large crowd of people from the neighbourhood, including many children, around a manhole cover at the corner of 6th Avenue and St. George Street and listened quietly to the sound of the water running below. Wong, who lives around the corner from the buried stream, explained to me that when she passes over St. George Street, the underground creek sounds "like it's gurgling its longing to return to daylight."[40] Earlier in the week, students from Mount Pleasant Elementary School had marked the storm drains up and down St. George Street with yellow fish and blue signs reading "Flows to St. George Creek."

Since 1985, Vancouver has been converting its combined sewer system into a separated one.[41] A system of pipes runs water in and drains water out of buildings and homes. Residential pipe systems consist of at least two, and sometimes three, different lines. One line pumps in fresh water from one of Metro Vancouver's three protected reservoirs—the Capilano Lake, Seymour River, and Coquitlam Lake reservoirs that supply Vancouver's drinking water. A second line, the sewer system, drains wastewater from our sinks and toilets and directs it to one of five treatment facilities that service Metro Vancouver. Wastewater in Vancouver is collected and treated (often inadequately) before it is released back into the Fraser River, Burrard Inlet, or the Strait of Georgia. A third line, the storm system, runs outside under the street and directs rainwater back untreated into the local water bodies. During heavy rains, combined sewer overflows cause a mix of untreated waste and storm water to be released into the natural environment. The advantage, then, of a separated system, especially in a rain-heavy city like this one, is that it takes pressure off the sewer system and allows rainwater to be more easily recycled into the watershed. The thing to keep in mind is that storm drains flow directly to natural sources, so anything deposited in a storm drain likewise gets transported into surrounding waters. The gum that you spit into a storm drain may end up in the Fraser River. The soapy runoff from washing your car in your driveway could end up in the Strait of Georgia. The effort to daylight streams and creeks not only restores an urban water feature to its more natural state, improving the riparian environment (the natural environment around the stream that, for example, helps to sustain wildlife and improve biodiversity), but daylighting also brings public awareness to our relationship with the natural water cycle, reminding us where our water comes from and how we contribute to the living watershed.[42]

I was invited to participate in the St. George's Creek parade and community design workshop by Shahira Sakiyama, an activist and organizer who has worked in the grassroots peace movement in Los Angeles and the Bay area. She moved to Vancouver in 2005 and has been involved in efforts to daylight St. George's Creek. Turning her attention away from peace movement organizing, Sakiyama sought another unifying issue on which to shift her focus; she dove into the topic of water. As Sakiyama explained to me, quoting Nigerian musician and political activist Fela Kuti, her interest in water is an extension of her interest in peace: *"water no get enemy."*[43] Her shift in focus toward water led Sakiyama to attend the World Social Forum in Brazil in January 2005, at which time she connected with a global network of people advocating for water rights. Shortly afterward, a death in her family took her to Vancouver; it was a fateful trip that had one silver lining. While in Vancouver with her family, Sakiyama met her future husband. By the end of that year, she had moved to Vancouver and, by the spring of 2006, she had given birth to her first child, a daughter. As the mother of three young children, Sakiyama identifies family as an organizing metaphor that informs her activism. She explains that her cultural background (her mother is from the Philippines, while her father's family is South Asian from Uganda) to some degree underlies and inspires her passion for global peace, justice, and environmental issues. "[K]nowing the conditions that not only some of my family live in, but that people around the world live in," Sakiyama reveals, "influences my activism."[44] But water in particular appeals to Sakiyama because it literally and metaphorically connects all humans. "Here in the West," she explains, "I feel our privileged lifestyle creates a duty to the rest of our family around the world."[45] Water, she continues, is "an 'Asian Canadian' issue because it's a human issue ... it is quite relevant for me across racial, gender, and economic lines."[46]

5. You Are Water

> [L]ie back, sink smoothly without a ripple, and assume the texture of water. Osmosis. You will not drown. You are water. And when you rise, you will take a part of that with you.[47]
> —from Hiromi Goto's "Osmosis"

Many Asian Canadian and American writers and artists have taken up the issue of water in their practice. For example, Asian American artist and architect Maya Lin, who is well known for her design of the Vietnam War Memorial in Washington, DC, has been working since 2002 on a multi-site public art project along the Columbia River. I visited several of the sites of Lin's Confluence project in the summer of 2013, which engaged with public land use, collaboration with local Pacific Northwest Indigenous communities, and histories of settler/Indigenous contact.[48] Likewise, Asian American writer Wang Ping has been drawing connections between the Mississippi and Yangtze rivers through her Kinship of Rivers project. Working with a group of collaborators, Wang has been working on an ongoing project to deliver a series of gifts to both rivers, produce multimedia exhibits, and document the process.[49] Another project engaging the theme of connected rivers, Gu Xiong's *Waterscapes* installation, opened at the Richmond Art Gallery in the fall of 2010 and considers transnational connections between the Fraser and Yangtze rivers.[50]

Zimbabwe-born, Vancouver-based multimedia artist Laiwan chose to thematically feature water at one of her public art gatherings as part of the *PDA for Your PDA (Public Displays of Affection for Your Personal Digital Assistant)* series. The resulting piece, "Ode to an Oceanic Turn," was displayed at Vancouver's Britannia Community Centre in 2011. The event invited people to contribute to a collective poem on the topic of water by texting messages to a pre-specified mobile number.[51] The *PDA for Your PDA* project explores our relationship with technology and social media, intervening in the ways we routinely engage with each other. Laiwan's work, more generally, explores concepts of mindfulness, slowing down and disrupting quotidian life. Her theoretical and critical practice of slowing down has been influential on the Downstream project, particularly in terms of developing a participatory water ethic.[52]

Having a participatory water ethic involves being conscious of the social relations one enacts through and with water in everyday choices.[53] A participatory water ethic, Wong contends, encourages you to ask yourself, "What relationship am I enacting, and do I want to enact, with water?"[54] The keys to this practice are its ethical and creative aspects that invite participation from people at the level of their everyday routines and habits. But a participatory water ethic is also about developing sensitive and inclusive cultural relationships with water. In envisioning a participatory water ethic, Wong takes her direction from water itself. As she explains, although water is to some degree constrained by certain forces that influence its "patterns and flows ... there is also infinite variation in terms of the paths that this finite amount of water can take. This teaches me that creativity is not so much limited to the individual, or ego, but involves attending to the dynamic environment that one lives in and with."[55] The invitation to imagine a participatory water ethic was a major issue on the table during the Downstream gathering at Emily Carr University in March 2012. I can attest that the process of interviewing Wong and Sakiyama for this article and participating in some of the Downstream activities opened up my own questions about how to creatively and ethically engage with water. Not only that, in observing and reflecting on Sakiyama and Wong's work on the St. George Street daylight project, as well as contributions from other Downstream participants, I came to appreciate how local issues can relate to larger global water concerns. Wong notes, "We can't control the things that are far away, that we don't see, but we can change things within our daily lives, that we're implicated in, and think about how they are connected to those larger things."[56]

A unique aspect of the Downstream project is its attention to language and the poetics of water—a theme that is reinforced in the publication of this anthology. When I asked Wong about what a poetics of water means to her, she revealed that she thinks of it as an "investigatory" process, one that brings us closer to "the roots, the anchors from which to begin to orient oneself to a watershed consciousness."[57] The idea of engaging different poetics of water interests me because of its potential to radically transform the ways we think with and relate to water. As Lee Maracle asserts in this collection, "water owns itself." We rely on water for life, borrowing it, reshaping it, and returning it eventually. The shift in perspective from thinking of water as something outside of ourselves, as an external object in need of control, to thinking of water as something constitutive of ourselves, as something that we are a part of and that draws people together in common with each other and their natural environment, is indeed a poetic shift that instigates an intellectual and political one. Disconnection and disempowerment in one's environment may be remedied by a way of thinking about water that is radically decolonial: instead of imagining water as something to be tamed for our exploitation and convenience, which separates us from consciously engaging with our natural environment in ethical and participatory ways, we can begin to think of water as what we act creatively with. The approach reminds me of Trinh Minh-ha's post-colonial practice of "speaking nearby."[58] Indeed, speaking nearby and acting with are modes of ethical engagement that move action forward while being attentive to matters of power. As Wong argues, the problem is not that people do not care about water, but rather that they feel "disempowered to act. Because people feel disempowered, they tune out."[59] Freeing ourselves from disempowerment does require us to be willing to be imaginative because, as Wong contends, "action is not easy."[60] Her advice is to "figure out what makes sense for you to do [and] to act in creative ways. Increasingly, we must take action in creative ways to be effective."[61]

Afterword: Speaking Nearby Asian Canadians and Water

In writing this chapter, I have chosen to speak nearby Asian Canadians in action with water, rather than simply reporting on Asian Canadian water activism. Speaking nearby is an ethical creative practice that attentively and humbly acknowledges the subject while also emphasizing the complicity, power, and responsibilities of the speaker. Principles of responsibility have the potential to transform creative practices from ego-driven to ethically driven acts. The interviews, events, stories, and artworks I engaged with in my research all approached water guided by principles of collaboration, creative exploration, and calls to action. Investigating some of the different actions that Asian Canadians are taking with water causes me to consider my own actions in relation to water and their meanings and impacts.

I'd like to say that writing this essay completely transformed my water practices, but the truth is much more humbling and complicated. I still take water for granted at times. For example, I have a long-standing habit of turning on the faucet about halfway through brushing my teeth and leaving it running awhile before rinsing my mouth. I noticed this when I first started working on the article for *Ricepaper* and every night it would bother me, so I began a practice of consciously turning off the tap in an effort to break the habit. It's embarrassing to admit how difficult it is to change my behaviour. After all this time, I still occasionally catch myself with the water running when I brush my teeth; other times, I manage to stop myself with my hand on the tap; and there are, of course, those mornings and nights when I'm not mindful and don't have any idea how long I may or may not have left the tap running. It's easy to beat myself up for this kind of unintentional habitual behaviour—and indeed, multiplying this example by the hundreds of quotidian interactions with water in my day—Am I taking too long in the shower? Shouldn't I be collecting rainwater for the garden? How wasteful is it to run the garbage disposal?—it would be easy to become paralyzed and despondent about my water choices and practices. But getting overwhelmed, I realized in working on this essay and reckoning with the idea of having a participatory water ethic, is *too easy*. Confronting with humility my actions with water, thinking consciously about my responsibilities in relation to water, and acting intentionally to change my water practices is more difficult, but also more rewarding and empowering.

While some activism around water is focused on securing water rights, I find it more helpful and empowering to think, as Indigenous activists and cultural teachers Toghestiy and Mel Bazil discuss, in terms of exercising our responsibilities toward water.[62] The moment at the bathroom faucet regularly reminds me of what I learned in the process of researching and writing this essay, and it reminds me that I have choices to make that respond to my knowledge (however imperfect and incomplete) about water and the actions others are taking to encourage more ethical water consciousness and relations. Acknowledging that I have responsibilities to carry out in my water practices may be humbling, but it also reminds me that while many aspects of water may be beyond my control, I still have something to do, more to learn about water, and the ability to ethically exercise my power in how I interact with and think about water. Perhaps these small changes and actions are too modest to be considered activism, but I would like to suggest that culturally sensitive water activism begins with this kind of attentiveness to the humble details in how we interact with water and the stories we carry and share about our water bodies.

Notes

1 Campbell Robertson and Clifford Krauss, "Gulf Spill Is the Largest of Its Kind, Scientists Say," *New York Times*, August 3, 2010, late edition—final, under "National Desk," http://www.lexisnexis.com.ezproxy.library.ubc.ca/hottopics/lnacademic/?verb=sr&csi=6742; Glenn Hess, "Congress Stalls on Oil-Spill Response," *Chemical and Engineering News*, August 22, 2011, 31, http://cen.acs.org.ezproxy.library.ubc.ca/magazine/89/08934.html.

2 Juan A. Lozano, "Tar Balls Hit Beach in Texas, Final Gulf State to Be Affected," *Virginian Pilot*, July 6, 2010, Virginian-Pilot edition, under "Front," http://www.lexisnexis.com.ezproxy.library.ubc.ca/hottopics/lnacademic/?verb=sr&csi=144571&r=HLEAD (Tar+balls+hit+beach+in+Texas%2C+final+Gulf+state+to+be+affected)+and date+is +July+6%2C+2010. As recently as September 2012, tar balls were found washed upon the shores of Louisiana beaches. See Daryl Lease, "The Blobs That Crashed the Party Punditry," *Virginian-Pilot*, September 8, 2012, Virginian-Pilot edition, under "Local," http://www.lexisnexis.com/hottopics/lnacademic/?verb=sr&csi=8399&sr=HLEAD(The +blobs+that+crashed+the+party+punditry)+and+date+is+September+8%2C+2012.

3 In a *New York Times* article reporting on disaster cleanup efforts, published May 10, 2010, Clifford Krauss and Jackie Calmes describe a Louisana beach "lined with coin-size tar balls attributed to oil from the BP leak." Kathi Bliss reports on July 9, 2010, in the *Lockhart Post-Register* that tar balls found on Texas beaches vary in size, but "most are coin sized."

4 In a video taken on May 7, 2010, which circulated on the Internet, pilot and environmental consultant Tom Hutchings states, "The Gulf appears to be bleeding." See John Wathen (hccreekkeeper), "BP Slick The Source 05.07.10.mov," *YouTube*, May 9, 2010, http://www.youtube.com/watch?v=uG8JHSAVYT0&list=UUw8GCcuPlEPBvI9qat3KaPA&index =51&feature=plcp. *National Public Radio* did a follow-up interview with Hutchings, where he again compares the "almost burgundy spots of oil" to blood. See Debbie Elliot, "Drilling Advocate Frustrated by Handling of Oil Spill," *NPR*, May 23, 2010, http://www.npr.org/templates/story/story.php?storyId=127057393.

5 Joan Didion, *The White Album* (New York: Simon and Schuster, 1979), 62.

6 Ibid., 64.

7 Ibid.

8 In the book's well-known title essay, Didion records in characteristic style a set of diverse and seemingly unconnected first-person observations about life around Los Angeles, California, in the 1960s. Combining notes from her own personal life with details about popular music, counterculture, the Black Panther Party, and the Manson family trial, the essay's tone ranges from anxious ambivalence to jittery awe and tackles the social and political chaos of the 1960s, setting up the collection of essays to follow.

9 Ibid., 65.

10 Ibid., 64.

11 See: Arthur C. Guyton and John E. Hall, *Textbook of Medical Physiology*, 11th ed. (Philadelphia: Elsevier Saunders, 2006), 293. Water content of the human body is referred to in medical physiology as body water. Guyton and Hall note that "In the average 70-kilogram adult human, the total body water is about 60 per cent of the body weight." Body water varies; the exact level of body water in an individual changes constantly throughout the day, and body water varies from person to person, depending on factors such as age, gender, and fat content in the body.

12 Shusaku Inoue et al., "Field Survey of Tsunami Effects in Sri Lanka Due to the Sumatra-Andaman Earthquake of December 26, 2004," *Pure and Applied Geophysics* 164, no. 2 (2007): 395.

13 Canadian Red Cross, "Tsunami Fact Sheet," April 27, 2005, http://www.redcross.ca/article .asp?id=12599&tid=001.

14 These scholars include Guy Beauregard, Iyko Day, Donald C. Goellnicht, Christopher Lee, Roy Miki, and Henry Yu, among others. Notable among these works is Miki's essay "Asiancy," which appears in his monograph *Broken Entries: Race, Subjectivity, Writing* (Toronto: Mercury, 1998). Goellnicht's "A Long Labour: The Protracted Birth of Asian Canadian Literature," *Essays on Canadian Writing* 72 (2000): 1–41, has prompted significant responses, including Lee's "The Lateness of Asian Canadian Studies," *Amerasia Journal* 33, no. 2 (2007): 1–17. Special issues of *Amerasia Journal* 33, no. 2 (2007) and *Canadian Literature* 199 (2008) have been dedicated to questions about Asian Canadian institutional development and scholarly praxis.

15 The World Monitor tv, "UCLA Student Racist Rant on Asians in the Library for Phoning," *YouTube*, March 15, 2011, http://www.youtube.com watch?v=FNuyDZevKrU&feature =fvwrel.

16 Ibid.

17 Ibid. A small sample of responses to Alexandra Wallace's video include: David So (David-SoComedy), "Vlog #4: Asians in the Library – UCLA Girl (Alexandra Wallace) Going Wild on Asians," *YouTube*, March 14, 2011, http://www.youtube.com/watch?v=lOG pGoEMu2s&feature=related; Tim Chantarangsu (TimDeLaGhetto2), "Asians in the LIBRARY?! Perspective on UCLA Girl Alexandra Wallace," *YouTube*, March 19, 2011, http://www.youtube.com/watch?v=GHyChAzTCTA&feature=related; Kate Rigg (slanty-eyedmama), "UCLA Girl's Hilarious BFF—'Asians in the Library'/Insane Response Video," *YouTube*, March 28, 2011, http://www.youtube.com/watch?v=4vq1zbT-S7A.

18 My point in bringing up theories of historical contact between China and the Americas that reach back to the fifth century is not to suggest a replacement narrative for contact or "discovery," nor do I mean to reify or legitimate essentialist connections between Asia and the Americas. Instead, my goal is to emphasize that waterways have facilitated possibilities for movement of people, goods, and ideas between Asia and the Americas in ways that may exceed hegemonic expectation. Scholarly work on the topic of Hui Shen's voyage does go back several centuries, as Charles Leland notes in the preface to *Fusang, or the Discovery of America by Chinese Buddhist Priests in the Fifth Century* (London: Trübner, 1875), v–vi. Literary scholar Lien Chao also sites Hui Shen's mission in the introduction to *Beyond Silence: Chinese Canadian Literature in English* (Toronto: Tsar, 1997), ix. Hui Shen also appears as Hoei-shin, based on the Gwoyeu Romatzyh system of romanization. For the sake of consistency, in this essay, I generally render Chinese place and proper names in *pinyin* romanization, which is based on *putonghua*, or Standard Beijing Mandarin.

19 Kaiping is pronounced "Hoiping" in its original dialect.

20 Madeline Y. Hsu, *Dreaming of Gold, Dreaming of Home: Transnationalism and Migration Between the United States and South China, 1882–1943* (Stanford: Stanford University Press, 2000), 19.

21 Daniel Leblanc, "PM Takes Hard Line on Tamil Migrants," *Globe and Mail*, August 17, 2010, under "Ottawa Notebook," http://www.theglobeandmail.com/news/politics/ottawa-notebook/pm-takes-hard-line-on-tamil-migrants/article1676011/; "Tamil Ship Could Lead to Law Change: Harper," *CBC News*, August 17, 2010, http://www.cbc.ca/news/politics/story/2010/08/17/harper-tamil-migrants.html.

22 "Hindu's Ship Can Not Show Bill of Health," *The Province*, May 22, 1914. The *Komagata Maru* and its passengers appeared as front page news almost daily in *The Province* newspaper from the time of the boat's arrival through the end of June 1914. By June 20, 1914, headlines asked, "Is it Better to Wait or Throw Hindu's Out in Quick Time?" For more on anti-Asian sentiment in British Columbia surrounding the *Komagata Maru* incident, see Chapter 5, "The *Komagata Maru* Incident," of W. Peter Ward's *White Canada Forever: Popular Attitudes and Public Policy Towards Orientals in British Columbia*, 3rd ed. (1978; Montreal: McGill-Queen's University Press, 2002), 79–93.

23 Rita Wong, email interview by Janey Lew, May 29, 2011.

24 Ibid.

25 Direct Action Against Refugee Exploitation (DAARE), "Song Written by a Fujianese Migrant Woman While Incarcerated in the Burnaby Correctional Center for Women and on Hunger Strike in November 1999 [English Translation]," Movement Across Borders: Chinese Women Migrants in Canada, April 2001, http://www.harbour.sfu.ca/freda/reports/daare.htm.

26 Rita Wong, interview by author, June 7, 2011, Vancouver, BC. On August 15, 1999, Victoria's *Times-Colonist* ran a front-page article by Cindy E. Harnett with the headline, "Go Home: We Asked You to Have Your Say about the Latest Wave of Migrants to Reach Our Shores. Your Response was Huge, the Message was Clear: Send Them Back Immediately," http://search.proquest.com.ezproxy.library.ubc.ca/canadiannews/docview/345750734/13964B7F03839009760/2?accountid=14656.

27 The dam was financially supported by Canada's Export Development Corporation after the project was turned down by the World Bank. See Ian Johnson, "Canada's Aid Seeded China Dam," *Wall Street Journal,* December 31, 2007, http://online.wsj.com/news/articles/SB119906431204358677.

28 Wong, interview.

29 Ibid.

30 Ibid.

31 Environment Canada, National Climate and Data Information Archive, "Canadian Climate Normals, 1971–2000; Vancouver City Hall," May 29, 2012, http://www.climate.weatheroffice.gc.ca/climate_normals/results_e.html?stnID=882&lang=e&dCode=0&StationName=VANCOUVER&SearchType=Contains&province=ALL&provBut=&month1=0&month2=12.

32 The *Georgia Straight's* Stephen Hui reported on July 19, 2011, about a digital mapping program developed by the University of British Columbia library, which shows the location of Vancouver's pre-development shoreline, and buried streams and creeks. The interactive map can be viewed online at: http://hss.library.ubc.ca/gis-services/oldstreams/. The False Creek Watershed Society, a non-profit organization dedicated to educating the public about the history of the watershed and environmental sustainability, also features a downloadable map and historical overview of the watershed on their website: http://www.falsecreekwatershed.org/history.html.

33 Lee Maracle, "Goodbye Snauq," *West Coast Line* 42, no. 2 (Summer 2008): 123.

34 Ibid., 118.

35 Ibid., 121.

36 Ibid., 118.

37 Ibid., 119.

38 Not unlike how Expo '86 was thought to have heralded Vancouver as a major global metropolis. Not only were the rhetorical patterns of world-class urbanization similar surrounding both events, but Expo '86 and the 2010 Olympics also wrought similar patterns of gentrification and capitalization for the city. I thank Rita Wong for urging me to clarify this point.

39 Thinking this through, I wonder, am I in the grips of what Renato Rosaldo has termed "imperialist nostalgia," a form of mourning that the colonizer adopts for that which she herself has destroyed? Rosaldo, in particular, warns writers against taking on a posture of imperialist nostalgia as a cover of innocence that occludes "complicity with often brutal domination." See Renato Rosaldo, *Culture and Truth* (Boston: Beacon, 1993), 69–70. Once confronted with imperialist nostalgia, it is not only important to acknowledge complicity (I am a settler, and I benefit from certain privileges of settler colonialism and urban development that have political and environmental effects on the territories where I live), but also to proceed with thoughtful action.

40 Wong, email interview.

41 St. George Street Parade and Community Design Workshop, June 4, 2011.

42 For more information on the False Creek watershed and daylighting efforts in Vancouver, see http://www.falsecreekwatershed.org/index.html.

43 Shahira Sakiyama, interview by Janey Lew, June 7, 2011. For information on Fela Kuti's song, see Fela Kuti, *Expensive Shit* (Editions Makossa, 1975, compact disc).

44 Sakiyama interview.

45 Ibid.

46 Ibid.

47 Hiromi Goto, *Hopeful Monsters* (Vancouver: Arsenal Pulp, 2004), 20.

48 More on the Confluence Project can be found on the project website at http://www .confluenceproject.org/.

49 More on the Kinship of Rivers project can be found on the project website at http://www .kinshipofrivers.org/home.

50 A summary of the *Waterscapes* exhibition can be found on the Richmond Art Gallery website at http://www.richmondartgallery.org/xiong.php. Like Wong, Xiong initiated a collaborative project on water (with literary scholar Christopher Lee and sociologist Jennifer Chun) funded by a SSHRC research-creation grant. Chun, Xiong, and Lee co-authored a piece for *The Capilano Review*'s Winter 2012 "ecologies" issue on the project containing Chun and Lee's field notes from a trip to China and Xiong's photographs. See Jennifer Chun, Gu Xiong, and Chris Lee, "Waterscapes: Working Notes on Globalization," *Capilano Review* 3, no. 16 (Winter 2012), 36–48.

51 Laiwan has documented the *PDA for Your PDA* project on her Wordpress blog: Laiwan, "PDA for Your PDA Series," Laiwan Recent News Blog, n.d., http://laiwan.wordpress .com/pda-for-your-pda/. Full text of the poem "Ode to an Oceanic Turn," can also be found in *West Coast Line* 71 (Fall 2011): 58–61.

52 Ibid.

53 Ibid.

54 Ibid.

55 Wong, email interview.

56 Wong, interview.

57 Wong, email interview.

58 In the opening voiceover for the film *Reassemblage*, her influential first film document-ing her ethnographic research in Senegal, West Africa, Trinh states, "I do not intend to speak about, just speak nearby." Trinh elaborates on this practice in an interview with Nancy N. Chen, by stating that speaking nearby is: "a speaking that does not objectify, does not point to an object as if it is distant from the speaking subject or absent from the speaking place. A speaking that reflects on itself and can be very close to a subject without, however, seizing or claiming it. A speaking in brief, whose closures are only moments of transition opening up to other possible moments of transition—these are forms of indirectness well understood by anyone in tune with poetic language." See Nancy N. Chen, "'Speaking Nearby:' A Conversation with Trinh T. Minh-ha," *Visual Anthropol-ogy Review* 8, no. 1 (Spring 1992): 87.

59 Wong, interview.

60 Ibid.

61 Ibid.

62 See Toghestiy and Mel Bazil, "Rights versus Responsibilities," *Vimeo* video, 3:14, posted by "BeyondBoarding," July 9, 2014, http://vimeo.com/99574930.

Bibliography

Bliss, Kathi. "Oil Spill Reaches Texas Beaches." *Lockhart Post-Register*, July 9, 2010, 6A.

Canadian Red Cross. "Tsunami Fact Sheet," April 27, 2005. http://www.redcross.ca/article.asp?id=12599&tid=001.

Chao, Lien. "Introduction." In *Beyond Silence: Chinese Canadian Literature in English.* Toronto: Tsar, 1997.

Chantarangsu, Tim (TimDeLaGhetto2). "Asians in the LIBRARY?! Perspective on UCLA Girl Alexandra Wallace." *YouTube*, March 19, 2011. http://www.youtube.com/watch?v=GHyChAzTCTA&feature=related.

Chen, Nancy N. "'Speaking Nearby:' A Conversation with Trinh T. Minh-ha." *Visual Anthropology Review* 8, no. 1 (Spring 1992): 82–91.

Chun, Jennifer, Gu Xiong, and Chris Lee. "Waterscapes: Working Notes on Globalization." *Capilano Review* 3, no. 16 (Winter 2012): 36–48.

Didion, Joan. *The White Album.* New York: Simon and Schuster, 1979.

Direct Action Against Refugee Exploitation (DAARE). "Song Written by a Fujianese Migrant Woman While Incarcerated in the Burnaby Correctional Center for Women and on Hunger Strike in November 1999 [English Translation]." Movement Across Borders: Chinese Women Migrants in Canada, April 2001. http://www.harbour.sfu.ca/freda/reports/daare.htm.

Elliot, Debbie. "Drilling Advocate Frustrated by Handling of Oil Spill." *NPR*, May 23, 2010. http://www.npr.org/templates/story/story.php?storyId=127057393.

Environment Canada, National Climate and Data Information Archive. "Canadian Climate Normals, 1971–2000; Vancouver City Hall," May 29, 2012, http://www.climate.weatheroffice.gc.ca/climate_normals/results_e.html?stnID=882&lang=e&dCode=0&StationName=VANCOUVER&SearchType=Contains&province=ALL&provBut=&month1=0&month2=12.

Goellnicht, Donald C. "A Long Labour: The Protracted Birth of Asian Canadian Literature." *Essays on Canadian Writing* 72 (2000): 1–41.

Goto, Hiromi. *Hopeful Monsters.* Vancouver: Arsenal Pulp, 2004.

Guyton, Arthur C., and John E. Hall. *Textbook of Medical Physiology,* 11th ed. Philadelphia: Elsevier Saunders, 2006.

Harnett, Cindy E. "Go Home: We Asked You to Have Your Say about the Latest Wave of Migrants to Reach Our Shores. Your Response Was Huge, the Message Was Clear: Send Them Back Immediately." *Times-Colonist*, August 15, 1999. http://search.proquest.com.ezproxy.library.ubc.ca/canadiannews/docview/345750734/13964B7F03839009760/2?accountid=14656.

Hess, Glenn. "Congress Stalls on Oil-Spill Response." *Chemical and Engineering News*, August 22, 2011, 31. http://cen.acs.org.ezproxy.library.ubc.ca/magazine/89/08934.html.

"Hindu's Ship Can Not Show Bill of Health." *The Province*, May 22, 1914.

Hsu, Madeline Y. *Dreaming of Gold, Dreaming of Home: Transnationalism and Migration Between the United States and South China, 1882–1943.* Stanford: Stanford University Press, 2000.

Inoue, Shusaku, et al. "Field Survey of Tsunami Effects in Sri Lanka due to the Sumatra-Andaman Earthquake of December 26, 2004." *Pure and Applied Geophysics* 164, no. 2 (2007): 395–411.

Johnson, Ian. "Canada's Aid Seeded China Dam." *Wall Street Journal*, December 31, 2007. http://online.wsj.com/news/articles/SB119906431204358677.

Krauss, Clifford, and Jackie Calmes. "BP Engineers Making Little Headway on Leaking Well." *New York Times*, May 10, 2010. http://www.nytimes.com/2010/05/29/us/29spill.html?pagewanted=all.

Kuti, Fela. *Expensive Shit*. Editions Makossa, 1975, compact disc.

Laiwan. "Ode to an Oceanic Turn PDA for Your PDA Public Display of Affection for your Personal Digital Assistant." *West Coast Line* 45, no. 3 (Fall 2011): 58–61.

Lease, Daryl. "The Blobs That Crashed the Party Punditry." *Virginian-Pilot*, September 8, 2012, Virginian-Pilot edition, under "Local." http://www.lexisnexis.com/hottopics/lnacademic/?verb=sr&csi=8399&sr=HLEAD(The+blobs+that+crashed+the+party+punditry)+and+date+is+ September+8%2C+2012.

Leblanc, Daniel. "PM Takes Hard Line on Tamil Migrants." *Globe and Mail*, August 17, 2010, under "Ottawa Notebook." http://www.theglobeandmail.com/news/politics/ottawa-notebook/pm-takes-hard-line-on-tamil-migrants/article1676011/.

Lee, Christopher. "The Lateness of Asian Canadian Studies." *Amerasia Journal* 33, no. 2 (2007): 1–17.

Leland, Charles. *Fusang, or the Discovery of America by Chinese Buddhist Priests in the Fifth Century*. London: Trübner, 1875.

Lozano, Juan A. "Tar Balls Hit Beach in Texas, Final Gulf State to Be Affected." *Virginian Pilot*, July 6, 2010, Virginian-Pilot edition, under "Front." http://www.lexisnexis.com.ezproxy.library.ubc.ca/hottopics/lnacademic/?verb=sr&csi=144571&sr=HLEAD(Tar+balls+hit+beach+in+Texas%2C+final+Gulf+state+to+be+affected)+and+date+is+July+6%2C+2010.

Maracle, Lee. "Goodbye Snauq." *West Coast Line* 42, no. 2 (Summer 2008): 123.

Miki, Roy. "Asiancy." In *Broken Entries: Race, Subjectivity, Writing*. Toronto: Mercury, 1998.

Rigg, Kate (slantyeyedmama). "UCLA Girl's Hilarious BFF—'Asians in the Library'/Insane Response Video." *YouTube*, March 28, 2011. http://www.youtube.com/watch?v=4vq1zbT-S7A.

Robertson, Campbell, and Clifford Krauss. "Gulf Spill Is the Largest of Its Kind, Scientists Say." *New York Times*, August 3, 2010, late edition—final, under "National Desk." http://www.lexisnexis.com.ezproxy.library.ubc.ca/hottopics/lnacademic/?verb=sr&csi=6742.

Rosaldo, Renato. *Culture and Truth: The Remaking of Social Analysis*. 1989. Boston: Beacon, 1993.

Sakiyama, Shahira. Interview by Janey Lew. June 7, 2011.

So, David (DavidSoComedy). "Vlog #4: Asians in the Library—UCLA Girl (Alexandra Wallace) Going Wild on Asians." *YouTube*, March 14, 2011. http://www.youtube.com/watch?v=lOGpGoEMu2s&feature=related.

"Tamil Ship Could Lead to Law Change: Harper." *CBC News*, August 17, 2010. http://www.cbc.ca/news/politics/story/2010/08/17/harper-tamil-migrants.html.

Toghestiy, and Mel Bazil. "Rights versus Responsibilities." *Vimeo* video, 3:14, posted by "BeyondBoarding," July 9, 2014. http://vimeo.com/99574930.

Trinh, T. Minh-ha. *Reassemblage: From the Firelight to the Screen*, DVD-R. Co-produced by Jean-Paul Bourdier. New York: Women Make Movies, 1982.

Ward, W. Peter. *White Canada Forever: Popular Attitudes and Public Policy Towards Orientals in British Columbia*, 3rd ed. 1978; Montreal: McGill-Queen's University Press, 2002.

Wathen, John (hccreekkeeper). "BP Slick The Source 05.07.10,mov." *YouTube*, May 9, 2010. http://www.youtube.com/watch?v=uG8JHSAVYT0&list=UUw8GCcuPlEPBvI9 qat3KaPA&index=51&feature=plcp.

Wong, Rita. "Decolonizasian: Reading Asian and First Nations Relations in Literature." *Canadian Literature* 199 (Winter 2008): 158–80.

———. Email interview by Janey Lew. May 29, 2011.

———. Interview by Janey Lew. June 7, 2011. Vancouver, BC

———. "seeds, streams, see/pages." *Open Letter: A Canadian Journal of Writing and Theory* 13, no. 9 (Summer 2009): 21–27.

Permeable Toronto
A Hydro-Eutopia
Janine MacLeod

One spring several years ago, I attended a Lost Rivers tour in my Toronto neighbourhood. The tour followed the course of an invisible waterway known by its colonial name, Garrison Creek. There were subtle signs of its presence here and there, depressions in the urban topography, old bridges that seemed to cross nothing. I learned that the creek was used as a dumping ground over the course of the 1800s until, by the beginning of the twentieth century, it had become an open sewer. To address this serious health hazard, the city buried the creek, incorporating it into the network of underground pipes that make up Toronto's sewer system. By 1920, the whole course of it had been filled in, with streets, buildings, and parks established over the top.[1] It now helps to carry the city's waste to the local treatment plant (or, during storm events, directly into Lake Ontario).[2]

The Lost Rivers tour was at once a volunteer-driven history lesson and a gentle political demonstration. Participants were requested to come dressed in blue; the idea was to symbolize, with our downstream-moving procession, the invisible flow of water. When we reached a deep gully in Trinity Bellwoods Park, our guide described the flocks of passenger pigeons that once would have darkened the skies overhead. In those days, she explained, you could not shoot a gun in the air without hitting a passenger pigeon, and the early settlers were not trying to miss. She told the whole story, with its familiar arc beginning in awe-inspiring abundance and ending in extinction. Then she invited us to imagine this place as it must have been in the centuries before European settlement. Garrison Creek would have hosted fish and birds, and been overhung on all sides by ancient trees—oak, locust, and pine.

Local architects have drafted a plan to daylight a portion of Garrison Creek within a public park. The creek could be excavated, separated from the sewage system, and allowed to run under the open sky again. It could be a recreational space that would also provide habitat for birds and other wildlife. Of course, the tour stoked my enthusiasm for movements to daylight buried urban waterways. As I walked home, back up the course of the invisible creek, possibilities sprang to mind. Forget about just stopping with one section. What about daylighting the whole thing? Residents could have rowboats and canoes tied up beside their front doors. I imagined living in one of these places and being able to row down Garrison Creek to go to a friend's house. I'd drift along, listening to the sounds from people's houses, until I reached one of the parks. There the banks of the creek would be bordered by woodlands and marshes. I might see beavers, muskrats, coyotes, otters, water birds, fish. Platforms along the many boardwalks would feature lounging city residents, maybe the occasional musician.

I closed my eyes, sank underground until I hit Garrison Creek, and floated with it downstream into a very different Toronto.

The gentle sounds of the creek are overlaid with dense birdsong and the honking of migratory geese overhead. There is a smell of several people sleeping in a warm room. Someone is snoring in a soft, wheezing sort of way. Although I'm perfectly relaxed and even a bit sleepy, there is at the same time a kind of sparkiness to my body, an energetic charge. My eyes open, although they are not exactly my eyes. The hand in front of my face is not exactly my hand either. The hand is a young woman's hand, and it is resting on a roughly textured pillow that seems to be stuffed with milkweed down—a bit of the silky fluff has escaped from a small tear in the fabric and she is rubbing it between her fingers. Her pinky finger is curved slightly inward like mine, a genetic trait that pops up now and again in some of the women in our family.

I have woken up as an unnoticed observer in my great-great-great-great-granddaughter's body. She is twenty-four years old, and she lives in one of the four-storey collective housing structures bordering Garrison Creek. Her name is Mouna.

Everyone else in the room is still sleeping undisturbed. Grandma is snoring on the other side of a paper screen, and Mouna's niece and nephew lie tousle-headed and open-mouthed in the next bed over. Quietly, so as not to wake anyone, my great-great-great-great-granddaughter slips into her bathing suit, finds a towel, and lifts the latch on the window by the bed. There is a little platform under the window, with a ladder that stretches down the outside of the building. The fall sunlight is brilliant and warm on the few rowboats and canoes out on the creek. Some people are fishing for breakfast, others are paddling to work. A few people wave at her as she makes her way down the four stories to ground level. There have been a series of good fall rains, so when she sits on the edge of the waterside walkway, the water is high enough for her to submerge her feet in the creek. The air is cool, almost crisp, with the warm sun bringing out all of the distinct perfumes of the creekside foliage. There is a smell of lake water, and of clear creek water, and of many different plants and trees—herbal-smelling and resinous and spicy. All of that is overlaid with a vivid smell of fall leaves, faint hints of woodsmoke, and baking.

Mouna spends some time talking quietly to the creek. She picks up some of the water in her cupped hands and lets it run away between her fingers. I can feel how content she is to be beside the creek in the sun. She admires the light on its surface, and swirls her feet around in the slow current. Leaving her towel on the edge of the stone walkway, she slips into the water and goes right under. It's not very deep, so she avoids touching the muddy bottom by stretching out parallel to the surface, moving quickly to keep warm. She imagines all her dreams from the night before washing out of her into the water, to be carried downstream to the lake.

This is the city of Toronto sometime around 2180. Toronto, Ontario, is still called Toronto, Ontario, but now everyone knows that these words mean "the place of the damp fallen torso of a great tree" and "place of the beautiful water" in Hotinonshon:ni.[3] *Both of these descriptions are apt.*

The term "utopia" is commonly understood to mean "no place," according to the Greek roots of its two syllables. However, the Greek prefix *ou-*, which means "no," can be readily interchanged with *eu-*, which means "happy," "fortunate," or "good."[4] On this latter reading, the word can be translated as "good place" and taken to mean "dreams of a better life." I am spelling the word decisively in this latter sense, both because I like to think of the imagination as its own sort of "place," and because I understand eutopias to exist entirely in the present. Although they may take place in times yet to come, these stories always depict the future as it is being imagined *now*, animated and limited by what their authors currently know and value. The story that I am telling about a possible future Toronto is shaped by what I can imagine and by what I prioritize, given my own particular situation at this moment in my life. Everyone's eutopia will look different.[5] I would like this story to be read as an invitation to collective and continuous acts of eutopian imagining, rather than as a blueprint for a perfect or finished world.

Eutopian imaginings inhabit the universe of *Should*. We *should* be able to swim in urban creeks. Everyone *should* have a safe and comfortable home. In his extensive writings on utopia, Ernst Bloch asserts that hope is not only an emotion; it is a directive force. At its best, Bloch argues, utopian thinking is not "wishful" thinking. It is "wilful" thinking. The crucial difference, for Bloch, between a vain fantasy and what he called "concrete utopia" is that the latter envisions a possible future, and thus carries hope.[6]

The ongoing, contentious act of demarcating the line between the possible and the impossible is, of course, profoundly important, and sharing eutopias might help us to open up discussions about how and where we locate the territory of the possible. I am putting some of my own eutopian imaginings into print not because I think that they are *probable* outcomes of current trends, but because I think that they are *possible* outcomes of unforeseeable events. This story carries some of my wilful thinking about water. I am imagining this hydro-eutopia as something between a prayer and a daydream, a cultivation of good wishes for unknowable descendants, and for waters themselves.

However, wishes for water are never only wishes for water. It is a substance much too thoroughly mixed with everything. Aspirations for better relationships with water are also, for me, hopes for much greater social equality, for decolonization, justice, and for the well-being of plants and non-human animals. Discussions that may seem to be about other matters entirely often have invisible aquatic dimensions. Even if waters were not key terms in struggles for justice, and even if their current despoliation were not a source of terrible grief for me, I would assert that a good eutopia needs to have some lively water around somewhere. Among its many other roles, water appears across cultures as a powerful symbol for the possibility of living a good life. Clean water helps us to think about a good world.

By the time Mouna gets dressed after her swim, breakfast is already on the table. It is warm enough this morning for everyone to eat outside in the courtyard. Some of the faces around the long table belong to members of her extended family, but there are also a number of visiting friends, housemates, neighbours from other buildings adjoining the courtyard, and a couple of strangers on compost-collection duty, who have been invited to share the meal before continuing on their rounds. There is no uniformity in this crowd, whether of appearance, or dress, or language. Gender identities, too, are stunningly diverse. As people greet one another, I recognize salutations from several different continents: "Boozhoo" ... "Hujambo" ... "Sijambo" ... "Good morning" ... "Sabah el kheir" ... "Buenos dias." Even before the conversation around the table begins, I can feel that this social dynamic is very different from what we call "multiculturalism" in the Toronto of my time. The diversity here follows generations of careful reconciliation and flourishes through real economic and political equality. This breakfast table is an exciting place to be.

Mouna sits down and helps herself to a mug of mint tea and a bowl of hot wild rice pudding with a topping of pears, fresh mint, hazelnuts, and warm cream. As it has for the past several days, conversation around the table centres on the curriculum in the local schools. Quite soon, the education meetings for the Rouge, Highland, Don, and Humber[7] watersheds will begin, and the whole city has been buzzing with a series of important issues that will be on the agenda. The relative emphasis on the skills of literacy as opposed to mastery of oral histories is a keen source of debate. And of course there is the question of language. Of all the many languages that are spoken in Toronto, which should be the primary languages of instruction in the schools? Of course everyone has free access to tutoring in any language they might wish to learn, but the question of instructional language is really the question of which ones will be common to everyone in the coming generations.

Mouna jumps in right away. "I think the best solution is to choose one verb-based language and one language of stasis."

The man next to her disagrees. "I don't know about that. I think it's time to let the languages of stasis fall into the background. Let's stick with Wyandot and Anishinabe. The lake has been used to hearing Wyandot from way back, and most people around here already speak some Anishinabe. I think most people could be comfortable with those choices. Could you pass some of those plum muffins, please?"

Mouna's aunt breaks in thoughtfully as she helps herself to some yogourt with honey. "I hear what you're saying, Min-jun. But I still think that either English or Spanish should be included. They've been spoken so widely across most of Turtle Island—you must admit that they're useful languages for that reason. We need to think about how we will carry on discussions within larger watersheds."

As the conversation becomes more animated, the smaller children wander away from the table and begin to play on some equipment in the yard. They are getting the merry-go-round going, shrieking with excitement as it picks up momentum. Other kids leap on large teeter-totters and stationary bikes that sound chimes as the wheels turn. The toys are hooked up to batteries shared by the surrounding buildings. As the kids play, they help to generate electricity for the residences. Dogs chase each other around the yard, a few cats nap in the sun, chickens peck at the grass. Songbirds are singing in the small fruit trees.

It is no accident that this foray into a hydro-eutopian Toronto began with an exercise in urban history. While the past is undoubtedly with us in the form of water's material memory, in the form of institutions, languages, habits, and traumas, it is also undeniably other. As such, it can serve as a source of inspiration for alternate futures. During the Downstream workshop, which initiated this volume, a number of speakers, including Lee Maracle, Musqueam Elder Larry Grant, and Chief Bill Williams from the Squamish Nation shared cultural memories about the abundance of Coast Salish waterways prior to colonization. Regarding Vancouver's False Creek, an inlet I know as a moderately polluted, condominium-lined urban thoroughfare, Maracle commented that "when the tide went out, our table was set." There were descriptions of the silvery flashing bodies of multitudinous herring, harvests of abalone and oysters, edible seaweeds, crab, mussels. Like the Lost Rivers tour, these stories agitate me; they remind me that False Creek *should* be teeming with marine life.

In his essay "The 10 Percent World," J. B. MacKinnon surveys the records of environmental history to provide his readers with pictures of the past abundance of global ecosystems. Many of the examples he cites concern the inhabitants of aquatic environments: the populations of Gulf of Mexico groupers, wild sponges, or Caribbean monk seals that thrived before intensive industrial fishing; teeming rock cod at the mouth of the Fraser River at the turn of the twentieth century. MacKinnon argues that we should glean a sense of possibility from these accounts. He invites his readers to imagine a coming "Age of Integration," in which humans will live in a world of abundance among restored populations of other species.[8] In a similar vein, New Zealand scuba diver and educator Wade Doak describes no-take marine reserves as "wet libraries," where school children can experience underwater environments unaffected (or at least less intensively affected) by fisheries.[9] In both cases, the written or living records are meant to inspire a particular kind of memory that unsettles the normalcy of ecological degradation and depletion.

However, there are dangers posed by these forays into the past. The stories about herring in False Creek, passenger pigeons over Toronto, or historical salmon runs on the Columbia River are heartbreaking. Given that the rapacious industrial and economic systems underlying these losses have not yet showed any signs of slowing down, the contemplation of past abundance seems as likely to bring on inconsolable depression as to invigorate hopeful action. These stories may also trap us in nostalgia, provoking an impotent longing for the past. We might become bent on finding ourselves a patch of remaining wilderness (if we have that privilege) where we as individuals might enjoy some approximation of a less thoroughly diminished more-than-human community—and abandon the rest of the world in the process. As Herbert Marcuse observes, "remembrance is no real weapon unless it is translated into historical action."[10]

It seems to me that transformative collective action is unlikely to emerge from our stories of past abundance unless we conceive of our love for the world in multi-generational terms. Although I believe that a great deal of healing and reconciliation is possible in my own lifetime, the world that I would truly like to see may take much longer to emerge. To really believe in the possibility of a good future, I need to have some faith in the visions and capacities of others who share similar dreams. I need to trust those who share this historical moment with me, as well as those who will come after me, to continue the work of transformation in their own ways.

Water helps to make intergenerational relationships palpable. All the living beings who come after us will know and touch the waters that we now know and touch—however changed those waters might be. As Astrida Neimanis and Mielle Chandler point out in their co-authored paper on water and ethics, "the materiality of water is a well of unknown futurity and facilitative capacity."[11] The generations to come are carried in water, in virtual form. We can never know what our descendants will experience in their lifetimes, but we can be fairly certain that they will emerge from a bath of amniotic fluid identical in salinity to the world's oceans. Ancestors and descendants are present—as memory or as virtuality—in the water that is always with us. A feeling for our intimacy with the dead and the unborn, and with a multitude of other creatures, may help to fend off the crippling influences of isolation and despair. The nature and depth of the political spaces we inhabit in the present may be radically altered simply by the understanding that we all inhabit a community of water-based life.

My great-great-great-great-granddaughter is eating her breakfast in a post-capital, post-oil, post-mining Toronto. On a planetary scale, it is no longer permitted to make money on money. Usury is forbidden. Markets still exist, in various forms, for a wide range of goods and services, but the age of finance capital is over. The engine that used to drive the economic growth imperative has been switched off. The vast quantities of surplus wealth, which were once concentrated among the very few, are now available to be shared. A vibrant, multi-scaled, radically participatory political culture ensures that such accumulations of wealth and influence are not permitted to re-establish themselves.

In Mouna's Toronto, food is free, and is produced in small, diverse, multi-crop organic farms. Urban wastes of many kinds are carefully incorporated into rich topsoils throughout the city and in the surrounding farmlands. Everyone has a comfortable home. Excellent health care is freely available to everyone, including various modalities of traditional medicine, massage, talk therapy, and other, as-yet-undreamed-of forms of healing. Education is also free, is available to people of all ages, and takes multiple forms—from apprenticeships to formal lectures to storytelling, songs, games, reading groups, and cultural exchanges. Libraries are enormous, well attended, and outfitted with great care and attention. People work for many different reasons in my great-great-great-great-granddaughter's Toronto, but now that everyone's basic physical and social needs are met as a matter of course, labour is no longer motivated by the threat of hunger, homelessness, or deprivation.

Mouna's Toronto is a much more permeable city than it was when I knew it, and it expresses the values and habits of a much more hydrophilic civilization. Water plays a central role in public life. Water ceremonies—practised in my time during events such as the Mother Earth Water Walk or the 2012 Freedom Train actions—have become widespread.[12] People in my great-great-great-great-grand-daughter's time talk to water. When coming upon a river or a creek, it is common practice to stop and acknowledge it in some way. Ways of doing this differ, but they all carry some measure of affection, gratitude, and care.

Access to safely treated water is now universal on a global scale. Large cities like Toronto are designed to accommodate the movements of water, and to nurture the relationships that make up vibrant watersheds. Beavers build their dams on the urban creeks. Wetlands help to filter pollutants from the rivers. All toilets are equipped to produce compost. Buildings in the city have rainwater-collection capacities and are outfitted with cisterns; if extra water is needed, treated lake water can be picked up, or delivered from, various depots around the city. Grey water is treated in ponds before being used for irrigation.

There has been a revolution in permeability. Roads, highways, sidewalks, and parking lots were all torn up following the obsolescence of automotivity, with forests, meadows, marshes, and food gardens planted or simply allowed to grow in their place. Pedestrian boardwalks are raised above the ground to avoid compacting soil unnecessarily, and to allow for the free movement of streams. Ground-level bike paths are elevated on permeable berms. Freight trains and passenger trains are designed to function in deep water to allow for periodic flooding. Climactic changes bring more frequent and intense storms to this region; the permeable construction of the city, as well as the extensive wetlands along the waterfront, allow the city to act as a sponge for high water levels, protecting the built environment from the floods. People take advantage of floodplains in the city to grow food and graze animals, allowing seasonal overflows to bring nutrients to the soil.

Several generations ago, widespread outrage over the ecological and social impacts of mining radically reshaped the production of goods. Metal objects are now constructed in modular form, so that it is easy to repair or replace parts. Alloys are produced in such a way that they can be melted down and made into something else later on. Metals previously regarded as waste are now reused and reclaimed. All but a few small-scale mines have closed down.

Likewise, the impacts of fossil fuel dependence long ago came to seem unacceptable. Extraction tapered off, and then finally ceased altogether. At the same time, nuclear power plants around the world were carefully decommissioned, as were large-scale hydroelectric dams. The production of electricity has continued, but on a far smaller scale. Wind turbines, small-scale hydro production, geothermal heating, solar and tidal power, and other renewables are commonplace. Some structures, like Toronto's bathhouses, heat with wood. Electricity is still used to power ultra-efficient trains, a number of computer-like machines, wheelchairs and other enabling devices, and lights. Hospitals have priority for electricity use.

However, with much less energy to go around, life looks very different. For one thing, it is slower. During what is known as the Age of De-acceleration, the pace of many things shifted down. With the elimination of the growth imperative, production declined dramatically, along with the number of necessary working hours. Buildings, tools, and everyday goods are now built to last. Motorized vessels have been replaced by sailboats, canoes, kayaks, and rowboats. While the electric trains are still quite fast and extensive in their networks, travel between stations relies on boats, dogsleds, horses, the occasional electric vehicle, and various forms of bicycle-powered transport.

Is this narrative getting a little boring, perhaps? Does its idyllic quality invite parody? When there are so many complex systems of injustice to unravel, does this leap into a relatively harmonious future smack of escapism? The history of the twentieth century can quite easily be read as a series of failed utopian dreams. Whether in its capitalist or state socialist forms, industrial modernity was supposed to deliver collective abundance and an end to miserable toil. Not only did these promises turn out to be vacuous for many, but the collective belief in the dreams themselves helped to support decades of terror, rampant exploitation, ecological devastation, and concentrated power.[13] As Jameson observes, there is a "general feeling that the revolutionary, Utopian, or totalizing impulse is somehow tainted from the outset and doomed to bloodshed by the very structure of its thoughts...."[14] As a result, perhaps, dystopias—from Huxley's *Brave New World* to *The Hunger Games*—are much more popular than utopias as modes of critique and agitation. Having such fresh memories of the tragic optimism that accompanied, say, the postwar American Dream, or the advent of Soviet communism, many inhabitants of the early twenty-first century are likely to find a good dose of cynicism highly welcome.

In any case, it is much easier to imagine the future going badly. As analysts from Naomi Klein to Slavoj Zizek have recently observed, contemporary capitalism seems to flourish just fine under conditions of crisis and authoritarianism.[15] Over the course of the last few decades of neo-liberalism, softening influences such as the welfare state, labour standards, and environmental regulations have been stripped from the cutting edge of capital. Increasingly, it seems as if naked exploitation backed by high-tech surveillance, terrifying military repression, and a privately run prison industry is likely to accompany the continuing rise of a global oligarchy. Water will be scarce, costly, and dangerous; rivers, lakes, and aquifers will continue to dry up as a result of over-extraction, deforestation, and climate change. The forests that I love will be clearcut, burned, or sold as luxury real estate. The ocean will continue to acidify and to collect toxic and radioactive waste. There will be more dead coral, intensifying extinctions, massive movements of desperate refugees, xenophobia, fundamentalism, sectarian violence, slavery, systemic rape.

Small wonder, then, that apocalyptic visions are so popular across the political spectrum. From evangelical Christians awaiting the Rapture to New Age hippies expecting the fulfillment of the Mayan prophecies, anticipation of The End has been feverish and widespread. These imaginaries circulate in many forms, perhaps most spectacularly in blockbuster apocalypse movies. Among the various flavours of mass destruction featured in these films, floods hold a very special place. In movies like *2012, The Day after Tomorrow,* and *Noah,* water, among other powerful forces of nature, plays a starring role as an agent of erasure, cleansing the planet of human evil. In these immensely popular narratives (the films grossed about $769 million, $543 million, and $352 million, respectively), enormous inundations sweep troubled landscapes and cityscapes. As in the biblical deluge, which these films explicitly reference, water wipes the slate clean, humanity learns to be humble, and a bright future, relatively free of ecological and social strife, can begin.

Of course, there is nothing new about anticipating, or even looking forward to, the end of the world. Apocalypse narratives come in many different forms. Taking a cue from Rachel Carson's *Silent Spring,* the environmental movement has often drawn on apocalyptic themes, playing variations on the message that "this horrible future will come to pass … unless we act now!" However, the apocalypse narratives evident in many popular films notably lack this imperative to act. In these movies (as in other apocalyptic fantasies), ecological collapse, massive climate change, or other catastrophes are inevitable and, in fact, ultimately welcome. The characters we care about always survive; even their relationship troubles usually sort themselves out in the midst of all the chaos. These narratives comfort viewers that even if the world as they know it dissolves, they, personally, and those they love, will be better off. Hope is tied to individual redemption, as opposed to collective intervention.

As responses to anxiety over untenable ecological and social conditions, these stories cultivate attitudes of radical disempowerment. They entrench Margaret Thatcher's famous dictum, "there is no alternative," in the popular imagination. That is, if it is obvious to everyone, on some level, that the living world is under immense and accelerating strain from relentless exploitation, and if it is also obvious that a demand for unending growth is the very essence of capitalism, then the absence of viable alternatives also means a certain future of mounting calamity and collapse. As Zizek once famously quipped, we are living in an historical moment where "it is easier to imagine the end of the world than the end of capitalism."[16] As such, it seems particularly imperative now to collectively envision alternative futures.

Mouna spends the morning helping to milk goats at the neighbourhood farm, and the afternoon working on the script of a play she is writing (a historical piece about the great migration of climate refugees from Somalia to Ontario during the Age of Reparation). As evening approaches, she makes her way up a spiral walkway to the bike-rail tracks at roof-level, and waits to flag down a passing vehicle. From here she can see all of the elevated walkways and bike paths in the southern half of the city. They run through the urban forest canopy and re-emerge between rooftop gardens. Here and there the paths plunge down to ground level, where they intersect with the network of flood-proof train lines.[17] Her eyes follow Garrison Creek winding down to the lake, here bordered by marshes, there bordered by buildings. As it nears the lake, the creek enters the Lakeshore Forest, where it divides into meanders and seeps through slow beds of reeds. Flocks of birds rise up above the woods, and settle again in the marsh. The lake itself is big and blue and magnificent in the fall sunshine. My great-great-great-great-granddaughter can see the ferry to St. Catharines, and the ferry to Rochester, and the one for Pickering, all moving fast under full sail.

When Mouna arrives at the storytelling tree, the audience—mostly children—is just getting settled. The new arrivals snuggle into the sheepskin mats and wool blankets that have been laid out thickly on the ground, and lean back against the wooden backrests. Someone comes around with hot rocks that have been warmed in a fire off to the side of the seating area, and tucks them in between the blankets to warm the children's hands and feet. Hot apple cider gets passed around in little clay cups, and the kids are given little cloth bags of roasted chestnuts to share. Once she sees that everyone is settled in with their drinks and snacks, my great-great-great-great-granddaughter takes her place under the tree and begins her story.

"Yesterday evening," she begins, "I told you about the Age of Endless Hunger. At that time, remember, the world was very noisy. The noise was from the sound of the Earth being chewed up and burned, and people being torn apart, and water being drained away. All over the world, the laws said that anyone who wanted any part of the Earth could only have it by making more Hunger, as fast as they possibly could.

"It was all so loud that it was difficult for people to carry on conversations with each other about what was happening, and about what they should do about it. They were always getting interrupted, or drowned out by all the sounds of chewing and tearing … even whales trying to speak together way down in the deep ocean couldn't hear each other properly.

"But the Endless Hunger did, in fact, come to an end. Does anyone remember how the change began?" A sea of little hands went up. "You in the red sweater! What do you think?"

"It was about water!" the little girl exclaimed. "People didn't think it was right for some people to have all the clean water and other people and animals and plants to have none."

"That's right!" Mouna agreed. "People saw the water being poisoned. They could see very clearly that a few people were taking all the clean water for themselves, and that the Hunger was destroying the rest. And everything seemed separate from everything else back then, and it was all moving so fast, but people could see that the water linked them together. And when they saw that the water linked them together, they felt stronger, and less lonely.

"Even then, there were good stories, in every part of the world, about how to share the world and live with kindness. Many of these stories were full of good water. There was the one about the Water of Life, that can heal any sickness and make old people young again, but only if it is given as a gift. There is the one about the cracked water pot that leaks while it is being carried down the road, leaving a bright trail of green in its wake. There is the one about the cup that is always full and running over. Who here has heard one of these stories before? All of you? That's wonderful! These are very important. You see, even back then, when people lived with all of that loud noise around them and everything moving so fast, they came up with ways to repeat these stories to one another. They talked about the ways that we are all related. They even talked about how things might be for you and I, and for everyone else who hadn't been born yet. They talked about these things the way you hear insects murmuring, or frogs. It made a sound that calmed people. Once they felt a bit calmer, they could hear each other talking about what every one of them could see, from where each of them stood, about the how the Endless Hunger was put together. And as they listened to each other they could see, more and more clearly, that the Hunger did, in fact, have an end. And that generation managed to bring about the Age of Reparation.

"Have any of you heard of the Age of Reparation?" Another sea of hands. "All of you? That's great. So what do you think happened in the Age of Reparation? OK. You up here in the front row."

"Was it how the Ojibway and the Anishinabe got their land back?"

"Excellent!" my great-great-great-great-granddaughter exclaimed. "That's right. Here on Turtle Island, lands that had been stolen from Indigenous Nations like the Anishinabe were recognized by everyone as their territories, for them to live on and to take care of in their own ways. And important wampum belts were made deciding how the lands and waters should be shared by everyone, and how decisions should be made, and a whole lot of other things. And what else happened in the Age of Reparation?"

"The people who didn't have homes got homes and the people who didn't have food got to eat nice things and lots of people moved here from far away!" said an excited kid in a purple hat.

"That's right! There were decision-making councils in those times, but they were very, very different from the ones we have today. Most of them were all tied up with feeding the Endless Hunger. They were afraid to stop, or didn't want to, or didn't know how. When the Age of Reparation came, people took over those councils, big councils and small councils and medium-sized councils, and decided together that those who had so, so much had to give back most of what they had, and the people that had a little more than a medium amount had to give some of what they had, too. People could see pretty clearly that the Hunger worked by giving a few people more than they needed, while others did not have nearly enough. And they could also see that it was time to give back some of the things that had been taken from the land and from the water.

"It was a very difficult time. Remember, the weather all over the Earth was changing very fast, and people were having to leave their homes because of floods and terrible storms and droughts and fires. Years and years of the Endless Hunger had left the rivers very weak—they couldn't even reach the ocean anymore. The forests were exhausted and so was the soil. Many birds and fish and animals had stopped breathing. So there wasn't very much to go around. The ones that had lots and lots of warm clothes and big homes and electricity and water and delicious foods and all sorts of other things were afraid of sharing them. They were afraid that if they shared what they had, they would have nothing left. They were so afraid that they were ready to hurt anyone who tried to make them share what they had.

"Now at the same time—there was so much happening all at once back then!—millions of people came to Turtle Island because their lands were under water, or because their rivers had dried up, or because people were fighting where they used to live. And the people here made them feel welcome. There used to be high, high fences crossing different parts of Turtle Island that kept people from moving around. In the Age of Reparation, these were taken down, so that people could move away from the places where the water had dried up, or where the land had been damaged or flooded. Many, many people came to find homes in Toronto. So how did we find homes for everybody? Well, first, there were lots of places where people had more room than they needed. Only one family living in a huge house. Or even sometimes only one person living in a house by themselves! So people had to move and they had to choose some other people to share with. There are lots of incredible stories from that time—about people who were used to having so much space for themselves learning to live with each other—some of them very sad and some of them very funny!

"At that time, there were wars happening all over the world because nothing made the Hunger grow faster than wars. Just like the Hunger seemed like it would never end, the wars seemed like they would never end either. So, so much Energy and so, so many metals and other precious things were being used up just *to kill and terrify people and destroy their homes on purpose! So one of the most amazing gifts that our ancestors from the Age of Reparation have given to us was the work they did to put a stop to all of those things. They had to be very careful because there were so many frightened people and dangerous machines and poisonous stories all over the place. The Peacemakers set up special shelters for everyone who had been touched by any part of those wars to come and feel safe.*

"Now, the Age of Reparation is also known as the Age of Integration[18] because people started thinking very carefully about how their lives were tied in with the lives of plants and mushrooms and insects and other animals. There was a generation back then that devoted itself to gathering up all the plastic that was floating around in the ocean, and lying around on the shores of the water everywhere—lakes, rivers, creeks. That generation pulled nets through the water, and they pulled in all the plastic, and they carefully put back all of the living things that became caught in the nets. They made those plastics into a whole lot of things that could last for ten generations or even more: raincoats, and waterproof coverings, and containers. But there were some chemicals and metals that were so restless, no one knew what to do with them. It seemed like they would just keep on giving people cancer, and making animals choke and all sorts of other horrible things.

"And that's when the Benevolent Eaters showed up to help. Do any of you help to take care of some Benevolent Eaters? Good. So you know what they look like. There are many kinds of Benevolent Eaters, but the ones we see most often in Toronto have whitish caps with grey edges, and soft white stems, and they are very pretty and also very tasty. We tap them on their caps to spread their spores. But we must never eat Benevolent Eaters who have been growing on top of plastics and other poisonous things because some of the poison might still be in them. That's why they are in separate beds where other animals can't eat them either. After another generation or two, we think that pretty much all of the poisons that were left behind by the Age of Endless Hunger will have been taken care of by the Benevolent Eaters, and then they will all be safe to eat.

"There are some poisons though, that no one—no Benevolent Eater, no bacterium, no fish or plant or lichen—can take care of for us. Does anyone know about those? No? No guesses? No, it's not mercury. There are bacteria that can make that safe for us. Any other guesses? PCBs? Not them either. No one can guess?

"Nuclear waste. It's a big mouthful, I know. Say it with me. Nuc ... lear ... waste. It's what was left over after people reached right inside the hardest metals on the Earth, and ripped the fire out of them, and used that to warm their homes and do all sorts of other things they wanted to do. It was called 'nuclear power.' Those metals had been sleeping deep in the ground, and didn't want to be disturbed. And after the fire was ripped out of the very tiniest core of them,

the metals became very angry, red-hot angry, angry enough to destroy the whole world. People had to pour cold water on those metals constantly because if they stopped for even a minute, that angry metal would burn down the building it was in, and would keep on burning until there wasn't any world left. After a while, the nuclear wastes cooled down enough for people to put them in big metal containers, where they thought they would be safe. But they weren't. Over time, water started to wear away at the containers because that's what water does. It wants to talk to everyone, even someone who is as angry as that nuclear waste. And the water would go away troubled after listening to the stuff inside the containers, and the next living creature that water touched might get sick, whether it was a cow, or an insect, or a human being, or a cat, or even a tree.

"So people knew that the nuclear waste was going to be angry for a long, long time because of what had happened to it during the Endless Hunger. And because no one could calm it down, that waste had to be kept away from water as much as possible. So a number of desert peoples around the world decided that they would guard that nuclear waste, buried in special places far from any aquifer or well. The whole world is grateful to those desert peoples. Every year, groups of people travel to those places with gifts. Some of you may want to go someday to the dry lands near the mountains, to say thank you to the people there for keeping all of us safe."

As she comes to the end of the story, Mouna sees a familiar figure smiling at her from the back of the crowd. After saying goodbye to the children and to some of the other storytellers, the two of them help to put away the mats and the blankets and the clay cups, and to snuff out the candles up in the tree. It has gotten quite dark. Both of the women have flashlights with them, but they know the way well enough to navigate by the bits of ambient light from windows filtering through the leaves. The lights of bicycles and rail-bikes, and the flashlights of other pedestrians, streak and bob through the urban forest canopy. They talk for a while, in quiet voices, about what they might make for dinner. And then my great-great-great-great-granddaughter leans her head back on her sweetheart's shoulder as they walk, to look at the stars between the tree branches. The Milky Way is exceptionally clear. The two women take turns being the one to guide the way along the trail, while the other one simply looks quietly upward.

Notes

1 Lost Rivers, "Garrison Creek," http://www.lostrivers.ca/GarrisonCreek.htm.

2 Sierra Club Ontario, *Sierra Club Ontario Deputation to the City of Toronto Public Works and Infrastructure Committee*, September 6, 2011, www.toronto.ca/legdocs/mmis/2011/.../communicationfile-24380.pdf.

3 William Raweno:kwas Woodworth, "Iroquoian Condolence Practiced on a Civic Scale," in *Alliances: Re/Envisioning Indigenous-non-Indigenous Relationships*, ed. Lynn Davis (Toronto: University of Toronto Press, 2010), 28.

4 In coining the term, Thomas More began the word "utopia" with the letter *u* to make full use of this ambiguity. Elizabeth Grosz, *Architecture from the Outside: Essays on Virtual and Real Space* (Cambridge: MIT Press, 2001), 143.

5 As Elizabeth Grosz argues, "the very acknowledgement of the multiplicity of bodies and their varying political interests and ideals implies that there are a multiplicity of idealized solutions to living arrangements…. In short, ideals need to be produced over and over again, and their proliferation and multiplication is an ongoing process…." Grosz, *Architecture from the Outside*, 149.

6 Ruth Levitas, "Educated Hope: Ernst Bloch on Abstract and Concrete Utopia," in *Not Yet: Reconsidering Ernst Bloch*, ed. Jamie Owen Daniel and Tom Moylan (London: Verso, 1997), 67.

7 All of these Toronto-area rivers have been renamed over the intervening generations, but I use their current names for easy recognition.

8 J. B. MacKinnon, "A 10 Percent World," *The Walrus*, September 2010, http://thewalrus.ca/a-10-percent-world/.

9 Kennedy Warne, "New Zealand Coastal Reserves," *National Geographic*, April 2007, http://ngm.nationalgeographic.com/2007/04/new-zealand-coast/warne-text/1.

10 Herbert Marcuse, *Eros and Civilization* (Boston: Beacon Press, 1966), 233.

11 Mielle Chandler and Astrida Neimanis, "Water and Gestationality: What Flows Beneath Ethics," in *Thinking with Water*, ed. Cecilia Chen, Janine MacLeod, and Astrida Neimanis (Montreal: McGill-Queen's University Press, 2013), 75.

12 During the 2011 Mother Earth Water Walk, for example, Indigenous walkers carried water from each of the four coasts of Turtle Island to a meeting point on the shores of Lake Superior, where they mixed them together. The Freedom Train, organized by the Yinka Dene Alliance, travelled from British Columbia to Toronto to express opposition to the proposed Enbridge Northern Gateway pipeline, as well as to the oil tankers it would bring to the Northwest Coast. Jasmine Thomas, a Saik'uz youth representative on the Freedom Train, has spoken about the water ceremonies that were carried out at various points along the way. Participants brought water from their home territories and mixed them together as a symbol of their relatedness. (Jasmine Thomas, speech at the Defend Our Coast Direct Action Training Day, October 21, 2012, Victoria, BC.)

13 See Susan Buck-Morss, *Dreamworld and Catastrophe: The Passing of Mass Utopia in East and West* (Cambridge: MIT Press, 2000).

14 Fredric Jameson, *Postmodernism, or, the Cultural Logic of Late Capitalism* (Durham: Duke University Press, 1991), 402.

15 See, for example, Naomi Klein, *The Shock Doctrine: The Rise of Disaster Capitalism* (Toronto: Vintage, 2008); and Slavoj Zizek, "How to Begin from the Beginning," in *The Idea of Communism*, ed. Costas Douzinas and Slavoj Zizek (London: Verso, 2010), 209–26.

16 In the film *Zizek!* premiered at Toronto Film Festival, 2005.

17 Many thanks to Kevin Pegg at EA Energy Alternatives for his advice on urban infrastructure design.

18 Again, this phrase is borrowed from MacKinnon, "A 10 Percent World."

Bibliography

Buck-Morss, Susan. *Dreamworld and Catastrophe: The Passing of Mass Utopia in East and West*. Cambridge: MIT Press, 2000.

Chandler, Mielle, and Astrida Neimanis. "Water and Gestationality: What Flows Beneath Ethics." In *Thinking with Water*, edited by Cecilia Chen, Janine MacLeod, and Astrida Neimanis, 61–83. Montreal: McGill-Queen's University Press, 2013.

Grosz, Elizabeth. *Architecture from the Outside: Essays on Virtual and Real Space.* Cambridge, MA: MIT Press, 2001.

Jameson, Fredric. *Postmodernism, or, the Cultural Logic of Late Capitalism.* Durham: Duke University Press, 1991.

Klein, Naomi. *The Shock Doctrine: The Rise of Disaster Capitalism.* Toronto: Vintage, 2008.

Levitas, Ruth. "Educated Hope: Ernst Bloch on Abstract and Concrete Utopia." In *Not Yet: Reconsidering Ernst Bloch,* edited by Jamie Owen Daniel and Tom Moylan, 65–79. London: Verso, 1997.

Lost Rivers. "Garrison Creek." http://www.lostrivers.ca/GarrisonCreek.htm.

MacKinnon, J. B. "A 10 Percent World." *The Walrus,* September 2010. http://thewalrus.ca/a-10-percent-world/.

Marcuse, Herbert. *Eros and Civilization.* Boston: Beacon Press, 1966.

Sierra Club Ontario. *Sierra Club Ontario Deputation to the City of Toronto Public Works and Infrastructure Committee.* September 6, 2011. www.toronto.ca/legdocs/mmis/2011/.../communicationfile-24380.pdf.

Thomas, Jasmine. Speech at the Defend Our Coast Direct Action Training Day. October 21, 2012. Victoria, BC.

Warne, Kennedy. "New Zealand Coastal Reserves." *National Geographic,* April 2007, http://ngm.nationalgeographic.com/2007/04/new-zealand-coast/warne-text/1.

Woodworth, William Raweno:kwas. "Iroquoian Condolence Practiced on a Civic Scale." In *Alliances: Re/Envisioning Indigenous-non-Indigenous Relationships,* edited by Lynn Davis, 25–41. Toronto: University of Toronto Press, 2010.

Zizek, Slavoj. "How to Begin from the Beginning." In *The Idea of Communism,* edited by Costas Douzinas and Slavoj Zizek, 209–26. London: Verso, 2010.

Saturate/Dissolve
Water for Itself, Un-Settler Responsibilities, and Radical Humility
Larissa Lai

The Importance of Indigenous Women's Leadership/Water for Itself

THE WATER OWNS ITSELF.

I start with these profound words by Lee Maracle. I read them as deep knowledge—water knowledge—but also as a poem and a translation. Lee Maracle calls us all—Indigenous peoples, Asians, settlers, thinkers, justice-oriented people—to recognize the integrity of water, its agency, its power unto itself. I see a translation across languages. I want to ask her: Is there really a word in Sto:lo for ownership in the Western sense? In English, I hear property relation, but I don't read property relation in her words. I read something like singularity, water power, the integrity of water as a sovereign, autonomous being. English won't quite sing here, and so I must listen differently to the softest trickle across the barriers of language, hegemonic English, my lost Chinese, the languages of the land I live on—Sto:lo, Musqueam, Tsleil-Waututh, Squamish, and also Blackfoot, Siksika, and Tsuu Tina. The water of itself, the water for itself, the water as a force of life that includes us, ungrateful guests, in spite of all our abuses and misapprehensions. To the water for itself I want to sing "yes," but I don't know its language. Lee Maracle reaches across land, water, language, and culture to translate: THE WATER OWNS ITSELF. The water -*ings* itself, still wings itself. The water drinks itself. Lee Maracle's essay in this volume is so important for the way it shows the negligent self-assurance of settler history and contemporary action, and also for how it teaches us a radical humility, one that does not place humans, capitalism, or non-Indigenous settlement above the self-integrity of water and our responsibilities to it.

Dorothy Christian and Rita Wong remind us that we are made up of 70 percent water—we are water, walking. The planet should be called Ocean rather than Earth. Only foolish or very ill people don't respect the self they swim in, compartmentalize it and destroy it for the sake of money, or for the sake of forms of social organization that are familiar in Europe, though unfamiliar here. And yet, as Lee Maracle reminds us, ordinary people don't fight capitalism or colonialism; they do its work. The -*licit* part of complicity, the law and licence of the father.

In talking about ordinariness in this way, Lee Maracle instructs us further on how English works. Who we understand as "ordinary" and who is placed at the centre of unmarked daily life without question are in fact those of us who are at the centre of the colonial project, though we may not like to think or ourselves in this way. Canadian citizens may be diverse in the ways we occupy that centre, but insofar as we inhabit and benefit from Canadian citizenship, we are part of it, and must carefully, thoughtfully, and creatively think through what responsibilities attend that citizenship. If the experience of Indigenous peoples were thought of as ordinary and placed at the centre of daily life, many of the structures we currently inhabit would evolve very quickly.

Paulette Regan's recent book, *Unsettling the Settler Within*, is a very useful starting point to think through how settlers can work toward both responsibility and action. This anthology, *downstream*, also does that work, specifically by helping its readers think through human relationship with water. *downstream* does not provide a clear set of instructions for how to extricate ourselves from the horrors of history. Such a thing is neither possible nor desirable. Instead, it offers a broad range of possibilities for action and engagement from multiple locations, both Indigenous and non-Indigenous. This is a more productive orientation to the past. To forget history, after all, only invites repetition. Each of us has a complex relation to the past, shaped by the specific racialized conditions of that past. Thus, each of us must relate to it differently—as survivors or as inheritors of rights, property, and privilege. Some of us inherit multiple sets of relation to the past—some of which give us strength, some of which disenfranchise, and some of which do both at once. Our thoughtful, honest self-reflection on these complex histories and our place within them must be the site of knowledge from which we begin to work.

Anishnabe Elder and Water Walker Violet Caibaiosai teaches by walking. Emerging after forty years from the horrors of residential school, she prays and walks for the water. Doing so constitutes a kind of restitching of the self back together after the fragmentation inflicted by residential school. As she step-stitches herself back together, she also step-stitches the fragmented living world back together. The restitched world is not the world it was before. The Earth and the water have been radically changed. Violet Caibaiosai understands the

Earth as a woman's body, and violence done to the Earth as violence done to the body of our mother. Western-trained literary scholars would call this a metaphor, but I suggest that to do so is another kind of translation. To understand the body of the Earth as a living being, as part of a self that is larger than the self might be to begin to understand what Indigenous peoples mean when they talk about "all my relations." So when Violet Caibaiosai talks about wrapping her water walking staff in the pelt of a relative, and adding to the top the gift of eagle feathers, she is profoundly aware of human relation to the other living creatures from which these things come. In other words, these understandings belong to an Anishnabe epistemology that does not see the living world as made up of commodities and services. The water walk heals because it is a moving relationship between the human body and the water, mediated by Anishnabe traditional understanding rather than any other cultural form. It is not a hike or a tour. It is perhaps something like a human-animal-bird connection to the land.

Like Water Walker Violet Caibaiosai, Hopi/Havasupai/Tewa Elder and Master of Social Work Mona Polacca calls us into our physical and embodied relationships, this time to the four elements: Earth, Water, Fire, and Air. Our Original Instructions, she says, are that we respect these things because they supported us from the very beginning: the waters of our mothers' wombs, the air we breathe, the fire of the sun that warms us, and the Earth that supports us when we sit and when we walk. The patriarchal culture in which we live tells us we have mastered the elements. Mona Polacca reminds us that in so doing, we take them for granted. Taking them for granted paves the way for disrespect—for objectification and fetishization—opening the possibility for commodity culture. Commodity culture cannot exist as it does without this fundamental break from the elements. She teaches us to recognize what they do for us, so we can stop pretending that the life they give is given for "free." Freedom in relation to pay is in fact no kind of freedom at all. In commodity culture, when we get something for free, often we don't respect it. We respect only those things that we have to pay for. But freedom's relation to money is the wrong kind of freedom. Polacca's work suggests that, in fact, we have our freedom only if we accept our responsibility to the elements that make it possible. We settlers and participants in capitalism have been understanding it in the wrong context.

Melina Laboucan Massimo's work shows us in very material and immediate terms all the ways in which settlers have not taken our responsibility to the elements, and particularly to water, seriously. As a Lubicon Cree climate energy campaigner, she is profoundly aware of the real material consequences that the contemporary tar extraction industry in Alberta is having on her people. In documenting the poisoning of adults, children, plants, animals, and the land itself, she queries what benefit, if any, is to be accrued by mining operations in the tar sands. Certainly, of the billions made, very little has remained in the hands of the Lubicon Cree. Even if the Lubicon Cree were to benefit financially in any way, the legacy of destruction left for future generations to suffer is so vast that one must query whether any amount of money is worth it.

For these three women leaders, teaching and action go hand in hand. To receive their teachings, one must practise in addition to listening.

The Crisis Affects Us All/Who Can "We" Be?/What Action Is Possible and in What Frames?

What is clear, then, is that we are in a state of crisis. Some Indigenous peoples, many of them women, and their allies have in recent years made a commitment to the support, preservation, and renewal of water as a living force, one to be wrested from those who perceive water as a resource to be exploited. While the need they articulate is a real one, we still live in a society in which not everyone perceives this need, and not everyone places it above other values. The drive toward the preservation of a capitalist economy, particularly in its neo-liberal form, is intense. For those of us who believe that the preservation of water is at least as necessary as the preservation of the economy, if not more so, much thinking, talking, and arguing are needed. So, too, it seems, is spiritual work, though this is complicated in our contemporary present of intensified fundamentalisms on the one hand and a brutal, neo-liberalized secularism on the other. Some of us would do away with capitalism altogether. Some of us see the need for some form of economic relation, but cannot quite see what precise form that economic relation should take. The path to another, better world is not clear, even for those who strongly desire it. What is important about the Downstream project is that it actively makes a commitment to the life of water, and actively seeks multiple pathways to its ebb and flow, its life of and for itself.

Dorothy Christian and Rita Wong, in particular, show us that the work of preserving and nurturing water begins with the self and its accountabilities. This is a complex self—70 percent water, part of the hydrological system, embedded in cities and thus in urban water systems that include reservoirs, aqueducts, sewage pipes, waste-processing plants, hydroelectric projects, and buried streams. It is a thinking self, but also an animal self. It is a raced and cultured self, a subject of history, and also one embedded in contemporary systems of governance and contemporary economic flows. From Dorothy Christian and Rita Wong, I learn to attend, then, to a set of responsibilities that accrue to me in my particularity, as the "me" that is Larissa Lai crosses through what some of the new materialists, particularly Rosi Braidotti and

William Connolly call autopoietic systems, including those that seem "natural" (like the hydrological cycle) and those that seem to be human constructions (like capitalism).

So, then, I account for myself. Reading Christian and Wong's important essay "Untapping Watershed Mind"[1] I situate myself a little differently than I do when I think of myself in relation to land.

I was born in the Los Penasquitos watershed in the town of La Jolla, California. This is the traditional territory of the Payomkowishum people. It was ground zero for Spanish colonialism in North America. The first Spanish Franciscan mission was built in San Diego, and the Mission of San Luis Rey is very close to where I was born. I grew up in the Quidi Vidi watershed, which contains the city of St. John's, Newfoundland. This is the traditional territory of the Beothuk, whom I was educated to believe were extinct, although I was told a few years ago by the Maliseet artist and Elder Shirley Bear that in fact the Beothuk are still in hiding among the M'ikmaq in Nova Scotia. My family comes from the Pearl River watershed in China, and now I live on the Treaty #7 territory of the Niitsitapi, Nakoda, and Tsuu Tina in the Bow River Basin as an uninvited guest. As a person who has been engaged in anti-racist work for the last twenty-five years or so, I would like to acknowledge the time I've spent living on the territories of the Coast Salish people—the Musqueam, Squamish, and Tseil-Waututh—in the Capilano watershed and affirm my solidarity with their anti-colonial struggle. I have an intimate relationship with both sides of the Great Divide—the side from which all rivers flow west to the Pacific Ocean, and the side from which all rivers flow east to the Atlantic Ocean.

As a contributor to the *downstream* anthology, I am answering Dorothy Christian's call for us all to reframe our identities in relation to water. In so doing, I am also walking beside Rita Wong as she listens to Dorothy's call for settler folk to learn to love the land as she does. These two women's hard work and integrity teach us how to attend to a not-so-simple ethics of being in these neo-colonial, environmentally devastating times. I want to acknowledge Dorothy Christian's expression of frustration at the need of having to work with settlers in order to save the land and water that she loves. The onus is indeed upon us un-settlers to do the work, and for her to cross that divide and to share knowledge is an act of great generosity, for which I thank her. As I watch and participate in the winning of a few Asian Canadian social justice battles for our own rights and place within the Canadian state, if the term "Asian Canadian" is to continue to have any meaning, we must continue to do social justice work, not just for ourselves but in relation to those who have suffered and withstood injustice from which we have benefited, either directly or indirectly. Especially as economic power is rising in Asia, I think people like me have a responsibility to develop analysis and response strategies around things like Sinopec's involvement in the tar sands in northern Alberta, as well as the earthquakes and tsunamis that, as Janey Lew notes, have been erupting with disturbing frequency in the Asia-Pacific region. I have been profoundly troubled by the fact that Asian Canadian struggles for justice have always occurred in the discourse of human rights, within the bounds of the state. In other words, Asian Canadian justice work, important though it is, has the unfortunate effect of reinforcing the colonial state. My homework is to figure out how to be a better ally. This is a challenge when my very being is so inextricably tied to the practices and processes of both the nation and capitalism. In recent years, some critics, as diverse as Karen Bakker, Nandita Sharma, Steve Collis, and Heather Menzies have been calling for an embrace of the concept of "the commons." We must be careful to recognize, however, that "the commons" is itself a culturally specific concept with a long, complex history, one that is not indigenous to Turtle Island, where other protocols hold. And lest this chapter seem to embrace an outdated essentialism with regard to the primacy of Indigenous peoples, I turn to Jeannette Armstrong's parsing of the name for her people, "Syilx," and Daniel Coleman's recent reading of it, to recognize Indigenous modes of naming as themselves oriented toward responsibility in action rather than as the claiming of ontological stabilities in the Western sense:

> To be *Syilx*, then, is to heed a societal imperative to twine many strands together to continuously sustain a unity of existence within the gener-ation-to-generation, year-to-year, season-to-season cycles that we are a necessary and integral part of. Like every other living thing, we have an important role to play in the health of the tmxʷulaxʷ and a specific purpose as humans in the life-force of the land, and the captikʷ ɬ of the Syilx are there to continuously rekindle the light of its truth.[2]

With a certain tentativeness actively asserted against Western scholarly norms of mastery, and attached to a culturally but not essentially Chinese value of modesty, I suggest that the taking of responsibility offered may be a more useful protocol than the assertion of a political form such as the commons. But, of course, responsibility can only be taken once it has been given, and only from those who have inherited the responsibility and understand its protocols and how to enact them. To be given responsibility is to be given a gift, which is why I understand Dorothy Christian's call to love the land as she does as a generous call. And at the same time, if responsibility has not been given, there is still a basic imperative not to destroy, break, harm, or kill.

Nevertheless, in thinking about water, it is clear that there are things we share in common. Is it possible, then, to retain a sense of life shared in (small *c*) common, without asserting a colonial, non-Indigenous cultural form of "The Commons"? It seems important to respect one's complex connections to other living and elemental beings.

For indeed, in recognizing that our bodies are 70 percent water, that water is a part of us and not something outside, and, further, that we are part of the hydrological cycle, Christian and Wong call us deeply into our relation with the Earth, the oceans, the lakes and rivers, the clouds, the sky, and with all living beings that require water, which, as far as I know, is all living beings on Earth. The work that they have embarked upon separately and together is evidence of a profound commitment to respect, love, and relate to water. Christian returns us to the importance of Indigenous protocols, which matter not only for their own sake, but also because they place us in a profound relationship with the land, the water, and one another—relationship that was so much diminished by the genocidal aggressions of the Canadian state. Wong shows us what it means to be a proper guest, by really working hard to learn and understand her own relationship with water—the watersheds, the technologized redistribution of water, what happens in the places from which water has been stolen, what happens in the relationship between waste water and sea water, and, importantly and most devastatingly, the relationship between water and mining as the ongoing colonial destruction of Turtle Island continues.

Epistemologies/Coalitions

The knowledge of human relation to and continuity with water is deeply embedded in Indigenous epistemologies. This is seen in Michael Blackstock's work, which makes a distinction between Western abiotic and Indigenous biotic ways of understanding water. Michael Blackstock does not discount Western ways of knowing, but asks for respect for water through a concept of "Blue Ecology," which combines both Western and Indigenous ways of knowing with the utmost rigour to recognize the rhythmic life spirit in water and its central role in "generating, sustaining, receiving and ultimately unifying life on Earth Mother." Our world is in desperate need of a return to balance, away from the extremes of high capital, techno-science, and greed. As both a scientist and a bearer of traditional Gitxsan knowledge, Blackstock bears the gifts of a go-between, and he clearly takes his responsibilities seriously.

I have been doing some work to try to understand the Indigenous concept of respect. While I think I have a long way yet to go in that understanding, one of the teachings I glean from the M'ikmaq educator Marie Battiste[3] is that part of the work of respect is to work to return the world to balance—a difficult thing given its extreme state of imbalance. For me, this means that we can't erase the horrors or the gifts of our colonial inheritance, but must learn to accept them and use them when we can. In the case of Blackstock's work, he takes what is useful from Western science and puts it beside Indigenous knowledge in the service of making balance. This seems to me to be the most important work any of us can do. I see this also in the work of a number of artists and writers from both Asian and Indigenous communities, and I see my work as trying to foreground the work of balance-making, and to put different balance-making practices in touch with one another.

Blackstock has described poetic expression as being like Indigenous storytelling. Such metaphors can help build alliance between Native and settler cultures. It does absolutely no good for settler folk to appropriate Indigenous practices, but if we can have our own practices that work in solidarity with Indigenous ones, then that strikes me as hugely relation-building. It is generous of Blackstock to make this opening, and I thank him for it. At the same time, I think there are still moments when settler folk just need to stand aside and exercise their listening skills.

Blackstock's visual work seems to speak to both human and non-human interlocutors. Where I in my human narrowness can glean an inkling of the continuity between his work and the natural world, it seems to me that the rivers, the fish, and the mountains might really get it.

The artist Basia Irland communicates with the non-human world of fish, rivers, and mountains through her books made of ice. She makes them in many forms and sizes, embeds them with seeds, and allows rivers to carry them, seed-texting the land. Basia Irland's work strikes me as work akin to Blackstock's. Her ice books are a communication with the river and its ecosystems, and in their solid but melting condition gesture toward the receding tongues of the glaciers. What really strikes me about Irland's work is its interspecies, inter-elemental address. The book and text form references writing culture—a form of human culture that has arguably separated those humans who engage it from the natural world. Some critics suggest that it is writing culture that instigates the nature/culture divide. Seed and water forms interact directly with what in Western Judeo-Christian terms we are accustomed to calling "nature" within a Western world view that has historically separated "nature" from "culture." Irland's work both references the divide and at the same time forces us to see the continuity between "nature" and "culture." I love the idea of seed language as an invocation to the Earth. Thinking about her Nepalese students, Irland discusses printing ritual verses on the river. Thinking about the Chinese character for "ocean," which Rita Wong gives us—as "water" + "mother," I recognize that some cultures have retained that sense of continuity with the non-human world in their practice of language. For those of us who have lost that tradition, Irland's work radically re-indexes language to land and water.

There are so many things I am taken by in her practice—her commitment to research, her call to her students to just be with the river, the ephemerality of the ice books, but also the fact that they do partake of technological culture both in their construction and in their documentation—and so there is nothing pure or self-righteous about her work, yet it is profoundly ethical. I am also taken by her committed involvement of other humans in her creative work and her commitment to the completing of cycles. She also offers us an ice book that weighs 250 pounds. It must have been a real job to make something that big and transport it back to the river. It seems to me that because of its size, there is something glacial about it. I think of her phrase "glacial tongue" and how there is an Earth/human metaphor at work there, even as humans drive back the possibility for glaciers to speak. There is a cycle here that has not yet completed. I can't quite see how to, but perhaps together we can work out some answers, however partial.

What links many of the contributors to this anthology is their engagement in epistemologies that run counter to the one that controls and constrains all of our lives, which I would call something like neo-colonial capitalism, though one might also call it the Western tradition, depending on where one is standing. Unfortunately, neo-liberal capitalism is increasingly a part of Asian tradition as well, so the idea of the "Western" becomes complicated. The problem is that the men with the guns and money aren't listening. What more can we do, together or apart, to make Blue Ecologies and Indigenous world views central and powerful? What kinds of stories and activities can cultivate the transformations we seek?

Astrida Neimanis's essay "Water and Knowledge" recognizes how deeply embedded many of us are in contemporary Western colonial systems of knowledge/power, and asks us to query this embeddedness at its root. The incitement to know—that is, the drive toward mastery for the sake of knowledge production in a capitalist and colonial economy—is a substantial barrier to our capacity for respect for water. In the face of, in particular, the Western academy's drive toward knowledge production, Neimanis calls on us to think *with* water rather than thinking *about* it. For indeed, how we imagine water and how are bodies are oriented as both part of the hydrological cycle and as specific species entities with limited capacities for perception and immersion shapes the way we think about it. We must not be so arrogant as to think that our imaginations and orientations are universal. But we do have agency in terms of how we imagine. Neimanis's concept of hydro-logics is particularly powerful for its recognition of water's multiple and unknowable capacities for transformation and movement. With Christian and Wong she recognizes that our bodies are largely bodies of water, in constant acts of exchange and transformation with other bodies of water as we eat, drink, urinate, sweat, ejaculate, weep, breastfeed, spit, snot, and shit. Even more profoundly, she recognizes that while Western knowledge is steeped in a recognition of water's capacity for flow, it does not often recognize that water has other states and other movements. Bodies transform in themselves and transform one another through complex hydro-logics. She emphasizes the gestational: we are bathed into being. She also insists we remember the archival: water dissolves and retains everything we throw into it—the plastics, the antibiotics, the tailings, and also culture, story, and history. (I think, in particular, of the Martinician critic Edouard Glissant's recognition of the Middle Passage as a site of violent gestation that produced Caribbean people.) Water, as ocean and glacier, sculpts geologically. It also differentiates, separating bodies as it holds them in relation, as currents, whorls, eddies, and weather fronts.

The issue of differentiation is an important one because it recognizes historical and embodied experience as key to how we might imagine ourselves in a more integrated and less destructive relationship with water. Neimanis recognizes her project as a feminist one, that sees how differently embodied humans (and non-humans) are impacted by colonial and capitalist violence to water. In thinking through Spivak's work on the disruption of farmers' knowledge by Western capital, she recognizes both epistemological differences among cultures as they are wetly embodied, and the destruction that can occur if the wrong (hegemonic) epistemology is the one put into action.

Neimanis's project is one of a radical humility. In asking us to embrace an epistemology of unknowing, she asks us to listen attentively to water as a response-ability we have always had, though we may not always recognize or acknowledge it.

Radical Humility, Radical Dissolution

The Downstream project is, I would suggest, a project of radical humility, but humility with intention. Recognizing the damage and destruction wrought by projects of mastery, it seeks another route. Humility involves listening, but not silence. It is not a humility for the paradoxically narcississtic purpose of self-abasement, nor is it humility as meekness. To take up the English word "humility," I might, perhaps, point to its Latin root, *humus*, or "earth." Downstream is a project that is about reconnecting to the Earth, with an emphasis on its waters. Perhaps it is better thought of as a project of radical dissolution, in which we are being called upon to see ourselves as already part of the hydrological system—"aquality"?

I want to hold English and its roots at arm's length here, recognizing that in different cultures the concept of humility functions very differently. It is not a Christian humility that the contributors to this anthology embrace. Rather, it is a complex ebb and flow of articulation and listening, speech, and silence. It is a recognition of how acts of speech and silence can differently mean and differently pressure, depending on cultural tradition, depending on the historical moment, depending on the embodiment of the speaker/writer and depending on power relations. It is an insistent humility with the Earth and its elements—Water, Fire, Earth, and Air—at the centre of its concerns. The slow drip has become an insistent tap, not on the shoulder, but from inside us.

Notes

1 In the anthology *Thinking with Water*, ed. Cecilia Chen et al. (Montreal: McGill-Queen's University Press, 2013).
2 Jeannette Armstrong, 352, quoted in Daniel Coleman, "Indigenous Place and Diaspora Space: Of Literalism and Abstraction," *Settler Colonial Studies* 5, no. 3 (2015): 11, doi: 10.1080/2202473X.2014.1000913.
3 Marie Battiste, "Nikanikinútmaqn," in *The Mi'kmaw Concordat* by James (Sakej) Youngblood Henderson (Black Point: Fernwood, 1997), 13–20.

Bibliography

Armstrong, Jeannette. "Literature of the Land—An Ethos for These Times." In *Literature for Our Times: Postcolonial Studies in the Twenty-First Century*, edited by Bill Ashcroft, Ranjini Mendes, Julie McGonegal, and Arun Mukherjee, 345–56. Amsterdam: Rodopi, 2012.
Battiste, Marie. "Nikanikinútmaqn." In *The Mi'kmaw Concordat* by James (Sakej) Youngblood Henderson, 13–20. Black Point: Fernwood, 1997.
Christian, Dorothy, and Rita Wong. "Untapping Watershed Mind." In *Thinking with Water*, edited by Cecilia Chen et al. Montreal: McGill-Queen's University Press, 2013.
Coleman, Daniel. "Indigenous Place and Diaspora Space: Of Literalism and Abstraction." *Settler Colonial Studies* 5, no. 3 (2015): 1–16. doi: 10.1080/2202473X.2014.1000913.
Regan, Paulette. *Unsettling the Settler Within*. Vancouver: UBC Press, 2011.

Bring Me Back

Janet Rogers

the influence of your confluence
birthed itself deep inside
the liquid of me
I want to embody
want to flow
want to roll
and go
freely, feeling
river power
currents
electrical correspondence
pre-occupied by how
to embody this
come to me
like personified lyrics
help me understand
river language
call my name
early and late
I want to come to you
live in your
watery heaven and
dirt burnt banks

I trust where you'll take me
just take me
make my paddle sing
once more
a grand orchestral
farewell
where clans gather under
herons' stinging stare
hawks' awesome glare
muskrats' playful games

come the rain
levels rise wide
over flow like
my joy
to be near you
can you feel
me lick your skin
we wink and flirt
in thick July sunshine
you are home and yet
not
you are your own
bold rapids of respect
wild like my knotty hair
I've learned your curves
like lessons that never leave
and I want more

keep your secrets
I have my own
you know them all
sunken love notes
never seen by my intended
and tears
the spice within
your fresh webs
hold them, heal them
sell them as cheap
crystals to the tourists
I am done
I love you
only
my Grand, Grand, Grand
bring me back
for a winter swim
my blood is filled
with your flow

About the Contributors

Renée E. Mzinegiizhigo-kwe Bédard is of Anishinaabeg ancestry and a member of Dokis First Nation. She holds a PhD from Trent University. She is currently an Assistant Professor at Nipissing University in the Department of Native Studies. Her area of publication includes work related to mothering, environmental issues, women Elders, and artistic expressions.

Michael D. Blackstock is an independent scholar who is of Gitxsan and Euro-Canadian heritage. His Gitxsan name is Ama Goodim Gyet, and he is a member of the House of Geel. Michael is a Registered Professional Forester and a Chartered Mediator. He has a Master of Arts degree in First Nations Studies and is a past member of UNESCO's Expert Advisory Panel on Water and Cultural Diversity. Michael is also a trained Northwest Coast Carver and a poet.

Violet Caibaiosai was one of the original Mother Earth Water Walkers, who collectively walked around the perimeter of all the Great Lakes to acknowledge the sacredness of water in the face of threats posed by pollution and social disregard. Caibaiosai worked as a counsellor in the community of Roseau River First Nation and an instructor at Red River College's Winkler campus, and her interests included healing communities and revitalizing indigenous knowledge systems.

Dorothy Christian, Cucw-la7, is a visual storyteller, writer, and scholar from the Secwepemc and Syilx Nations of the interior plateau region of BC. In 2017 she will defend her PhD dissertation "Gathering Knowledge: Indigenous Methodologies of Land/Place-Based Visual Storytelling & Visual Sovereignty" at UBC's Department of Educational Studies. Publications include chapters in *Thinking with Water* (2013) and *Cultivating Canada: Reconciliation Through the Lens of Cultural Diversity* (2011).

Radha D'Souza is a Reader in Law at the University of Westminster, London. Radha's research interests include global and social justice, social movements, international law and development, colonialism and imperialism, socio-legal studies, law and technology, public international law, international organizations, resource conflicts in the Third World (over water and land in particular), comparative philosophy and social theory. Radha is a social justice activist from India, where she worked in labour and democratic rights movements, first as an organizer and later as an activist lawyer.

Paul J. Harrison obtained his PhD from the University of Washington in biological oceanography. He was a Professor for thirty years in the Department of Earth & Ocean Sciences, University of British Columbia and then an Emeritus Professor. His research focused on the microscopic primary producers (the "grass of the sea") that feed the whole food chain all the way up to fish. He worked on water-quality issues such as the interaction between nutrients, red tides, and dead zones in Hong Kong for ten years. Harrison won several awards for his research and teaching.

Basia Irland is a Fulbright Scholar, author, poet, sculptor, installation artist, and activist who creates international water projects. These are featured in her books *Water Library* (University of New Mexico Press, 2007) and *Reading the River: The Ecological Activist Art of Basia Irland* (Museum De Domijnen, 2017). Irland is Professor Emerita, University of New Mexico, where she founded the Art and Ecology Program. She blogs about global rivers for National Geographic and lectures and exhibits widely. Basiairland.com

Larissa Lai is the author of two novels, *When Fox Is a Thousand* and *Salt Fish Girl*; two books of poetry, *sybil unrest* (with Rita Wong) and *Automaton Biographies*; a chapbook, *Eggs in the Basement;* and a critical book, *Slanting I, Imagining We: Asian Canadian Literary Production in the 1980s and 1990s* (WLU Press). She holds a Canada Research Chair in Creative Writing at the University of Calgary and directs The Insurgent Architects' House for Creative Writing.

Melina Laboucan Massimo is a member of Lubicon Cree First Nation (Northern Alberta) and works as a Climate and Energy Campaigner with Greenpeace in Edmonton and with the Indigenous Environmental Network internationally. She has studied and worked in Australia, Brazil, Mexico, and Canada, with a focus on Indigenous rights and culture, resource extraction, and international diplomacy. Melina's master's degree in the Indigenous Governance Program at the University of Victoria focused on renewable energy in First Nations communities. She helped her home community, Little Buffalo, complete a 20.8 kW solar installation in the heart of the tar sands.

Janey Lew is a PhD candidate (ABD) in the Department of Comparative Ethnic Studies at the University of California, Berkeley, where her research focuses on Indigenous and Asian North American literatures, intersectionality, comparative racialization, and histories of solidarity in cultural activism. She lives in Vancouver on the ancestral and unceded territories of the Musqueam, Squamish, and Tsleil-Waututh peoples, where she has taught in the English Departments at Capilano University and Douglas College and in the First Nations Studies Programs at the University of British Columbia and Simon Fraser University.

Janine MacLeod is a PhD candidate in the Faculty of Environmental Studies at York University. Along with Astrida Neimanis and Cecilia Chen, she is co-editor of *Thinking with Water*, a volume of artworks, poems, and scholarly chapters published by McGill-Queen's University Press in 2013.

Lee Maracle is the author of a number of critically acclaimed literary works and co-editor of a number of anthologies, including the award-winning *My Home as I Remember* and *Telling It: Women and Language across Culture*. She is published worldwide. Maracle was born in North Vancouver and is a member of the Sto: Loh nation. She is the mother of four and grandmother of seven. Currently Maracle is an instructor at the University of Toronto and the Traditional Teacher for First Nation's House. In 2014 she received the Ontario Premier's Award for Excellence in the Arts and is the 2016 recipient of the Ann Green Award.

Alanna Mitchell is an award-winning journalist, author, and playwright based in Toronto. She grew up on the sere Canadian prairies with a keen respect for water. She turned her book *Sea Sick: The Global Ocean in Crisis* into a one-woman play that she continues to perform internationally and is writing another play about cancer and another book about the Earth's magnetic field.

Denise Nadeau (M.Litt., M.Div., DMin.) is a theologian, somatic psychotherapist, and educator of mixed European heritage. She grew up in Quebec and still spends time in Gespe'gawa'gi and Montreal where she is an Affiliate Assistant Professor in Religion at Concordia University. She presently resides in the homelands of the K'omoks Nation on Vancouver Island. She teaches and writes in the areas of Indigenous—settler relations, Indigenous methodologies, decolonization of the body, and the deconstruction of whiteness and colonialism in Christianity.

Astrida Neimanis writes about water, bodies, weather, and other environmental matters. She is a Lecturer in Gender and Cultural Studies at the University of Sydney, on Gadigal Land, in Australia. Her book *Bodies of Water: Posthuman Feminist Phenomenology* (2017) explores the connection between our own bodies' watery constitution and our responsibility to more-than-human planetary waters.

Seonagh Odhiambo Horne explores the boundaries of community and national and global culture through dance. An Associate Editor for the *Journal of Dance, Movement and Spiritualities*, Seónagh publishes in areas of African dance history and dance pedagogy. Her research lays a foundation for a somatically oriented critical pedagogy. Currently Associate Professor at CSULA, Seónagh's choreography is performed at international festivals and residencies, and she has received grants and fellowships from Art of Engagement, Canada Council for the Arts, Fisher Center, and more. Asava Dance workshops have been offered in Hawaii, Europe, and North America.

Baco Ohama is a sensorialist, writer, text walker, and maker whose creative practice takes her over and over again to the water's edge, "to thinking about the relationships between history, language, and location." She is on faculty at Goddard College in Plainfield, Vermont, in the low-residency Undergraduate Program, and has recently moved back to Alberta to be near family and the Bow River.

Wang Ping's books include *Of Flesh and Spirit, Aching for Beauty: Footbinding in China, The Magic Whip, The Last Communist Virgin*, and more. Her multimedia exhibitions, held at locations along the Mississippi River and the Yangtze, include *Behind the Gate: After the Flood of the Three Gorges, All Roads to Lhasa: The Qinghai-Tibet Railroad*, and *We Are Water: Kinship of Rivers*. She is Professor of English at Macalester College, founder of the Kinship of Rivers project: kinshipofrivers.org.

Mona Polacca is a Tribal Liaison for cultural preservation among Native American tribes. For the past ten years she has been the Co-Secretariat of the World Indigenous Forum on Water and Peace. Her intercontinental work among Indigenous peoples includes assisting First Nations in drafting water declarations and assisting South American Indigenous Peoples in a collaborative "call for protection of the cultural and sacred waters" on the lands and territories of the Indigenous peoples of the world.

Janet Rogers is a Vancouver-born Mohawk/Tuscarora writer from the Six Nations territory. She has five published collections. *Totem Poles and Railroads* is her latest (ARP Books, 2016). Janet works in print, spoken word, performance poetry, recorded poetry, and video poetry. She is a literary descendant of E. Pauline Johnson, and understands she is continuing the work Pauline started as a Mohawk poet who found inspiration on the lands and who reported social injustices of her time.

Cathy Stubington is Artistic Director of Runaway Moon Theatre, through which she initiates large-scale community art projects that encourage community residents to creatively explore what it is to live in this place at this time. People of all ages, origins, and walks of life take part. Cathy also writes, creates, and performs with puppets, bringing alternate realities to life in different scales and settings. Her present interest includes a chorus of stiltwalkers who embody local birds. Cathy is the mother of three and lives on a vegetable farm in Secwepemc traditional territory in the British Columbia Interior.

Cecilia Vicuña is a poet, visual artist, and filmmaker born in Santiago de Chile. The author of more than twenty books of poetry, she exhibits and performs internationally. Her multi-dimensional works begin as an image that becomes a poem, a film, a song, a sculpture, or a collective performance. She calls this impermanent, participatory work "lo precario"—a series of transformative acts that bridge the gap between art and life, the ancestral and the avant-garde.

Rita Wong learns from and with water as an (un)settler living on unceded Coast Salish territories, who has responsibilities to build better relationships than colonization could imagine. She has written four books of poetry—*monkeypuzzle*, *forage*, *sybil unrest* (co-written with Larissa Lai), and *undercurrent*—and one graphic collection, *perpetual* (with Cindy Mochizuki). Wong works as an Associate Professor at Emily Carr University of Art and Design.

Alannah Young Leon is Anishnabe Midekway and Nehiy/naw Cree from Treaty One and Treaty Five territories, and currently working in unceded Salish territories. Her doctoral work documents a pedagogy of Indigenous Elders in land-based health-education programs in rural Manitoba. She is an instructor in Education Studies and Leadership at UBC and specializes in Indigenous research epistemologies, methodologies, and pedagogies. She applies her doctoral work at the xʷc̓ic̓əsəm, our place of growing together, with Indigenous Research Partnership and with the Indigenous Initiatives Health Education & Research Garden at UBC.

Index

Abram, David, 189
acidity, 30
activism, 148–49, 233; oblique activism, 169
Adamson, Joni, 184
Adivasis, 197, 199–200
air, 78, 261, 269
Akrong, Isaac, 153
Alaimo, Stacy, 51
Alberta, 13, 81–88
algal blooms, 210
alliance building, 1
Amazon, 56
Amnesty International, 83
Anderson, Kim, 14, 131
Anishnabe, 1, 107, 119, 128, 252, 261. *See also* Nishnaabeg
Appfel-Marglin, Frederique, 133
aquaculture, 123
Arapaho Glacier, 184
Archibald, Joanne, 8, 167
archive, 54
Arctic Ocean, 16, 19, 198
Arizona, 75
Armstrong, Jeannette, 14, 264
arrogance, 62
arts practice, 128
Asava Dance, 15, 139–60
Asian Canadian Writers Workshop, 217
Asian Canadians, 217–33, 263–64
Assiniboine River, 119–20
Athabasca Chipewyan, 8
Athabasca watershed, 56, 84
Atlantic Ocean, 29, 263
autonomy, 10, 259
autopoietic systems, 263

Bachelard, Gaston, 53, 143, 153
Baie des Chaleurs (Mawi Poqtapeg), 122
Bainbridge Cohen, Bonnie, 129, 145, 155
Bakker, Karen, 14, 264
Bangladeshi Flood Action Plan, 58–62
Barad, Karen, 53, 58
Barlow, Maude, 14
Barrick Gold, 13
Battiste, Marie, 265
Baynes Sound, 123, 134
Bazil, Mel, 233
Bear, Shirley, 263
Beaver Lake Cree First Nation, 85
beavers, 168, 181
Bédard, Renée, 13, 89–106
benthic zones, 56
Berman, Morris, 46
Bhopal, 51
Bill C-45, 9
binary oppositions, 52
bioaccumulation, 93
biocultural diversity, 45
Bkejwanong, 96, 104, 132
Blackfoot, 259
Blackstock, Michael, 5, 12, 39–50, 55, 58, 124, 207, 265–66
Blaney, Takaiya, 19
Bloch, Ernst, 243
blood, 34, 97–99, 114, 120, 124, 129, 273
blue ecology, 40–47, 124, 133, 207, 265
Boal, Augusto, 139, 144
bodies of water, 55, 130, 139, 221, 267
bodily fluids, 129, 145
Bon, Lauren, 148
boreal forest, 11, 82

Borrows, John, 7
bottled water, 93–94
Boulder Creek, 183
Bow River, 2, 263
BP oil spill, 219–20
Brahmaputra, 62
Braidotti, Rosi, 262
British Columbia, 83, 143, 225
Brooks, Neil, 168
Burrard Inlet, 229

Caibaiosai, Violet, v, 13, 16, 107–12, 127, 132, 260
California, 219–21, 263
Canada, 35, 82, 85
Canadian Constitution, 81
Capilano Lake, 229, 263
capitalism, 6, 17, 201, 250, 259, 263
carbon cycle, 30
caribou, 85
Carson, Rachel, 250
Cascapedia River (Gesgapegiag Sipu), 122
Census of Marine Life, 56
ceremony, 132, 136, 140
Cəsnaʔəm, 134
cetaceans, 57
Chandler, Mielle, 247
chemistry, 29
Chen, Cecilia, 14, 51
Cheslatta, 8
children, 82–83, 89
Chile, 13, 113–14
China, 56, 224, 263
Chinese, 2, 6, 11, 36, 226, 259, 266
Christian, Constance, 170
Christian, Dorothy, 1–25, 185, 218, 226, 260, 262–64
Christian, Kristi, 173–74
Christianity, 123
civil rights, 154
cleansing, 91, 96, 120
climate change, 9, 18, 46, 81, 85, 209, 224, 249
clinical depression, 31
clouds, 42, 46
Coast Salish, 1, 10, 34–37, 51, 118, 123, 126, 132, 217, 263
codfish, 40, 44
Coleman, Daniel, 264
collaboration, 12, 14, 40, 42, 44, 64, 117, 146, 163
Collis, Steve, 264

colonization, 4, 7, 8, 9, 35–37, 64, 111, 265
Colorado River, 75
Columbia River, 230, 246
combustion engines, 209
commons, 17, 134, 265
communication, 54
compensation, 204
condor, 113
confluence, 230, 271
Connolly, William, 263
contamination, 82
Coquitlam Lake, 229
Corntassel, Jeff, 135–36
corporate person, 203–5
Coulthard, Glen, 4, 17
courage, 40–41, 205
coyote, 169, 171
Creation, 95, 99, 108
creativity, 15, 128, 141, 144
Cree, 81, 85
creeks, 35, 75
crisis, 262
cultural interface, 3, 4, 5
culture, 15
curiosity, 41, 64

dams, 56, 63, 199, 226
dance, 117–18, 139–57, 173–74
Dancing at the Dead Sea, 29
Day, Doreen, 131
daylighting, 227–30
dead zones, 210–12
debt, 61
Dechinta University, 19
Declaration for the Rights of Mother Earth, 76
decolonizing, 8, 126, 128–29, 131
Deloria, Vine, 4
Dene, 85, 197–206
depression, 31
despair, 16, 31
Dewey, John, 142
Didion, Joan, 218, 220
difference, 53
differentiation, 54
dignity, 46
dissolution, 54
Doak, Wade, 246
Dokis First Nation, 90
Don River, 190
Downstream (film), 12

Downstream gathering, 5, 31, 32, 51, 124, 131, 133, 166
drinking water advisories, 9
D'Souza, Radha, 16, 197–206
Dvorak, 40

eagle, 108
earth, 5
Earth Mother, 45. *See also* Mother Earth
Eau Canada, 14
eclipse, 103
eco-art, 184
ecological urgency, 52, 207
ecology, 10, 18
Eighth Fire, 7
El Plomo, 113
elders, 1, 40, 42, 46, 84, 95, 100, 108, 117, 178, 184, 197–206, 260
Eliade, Mircea, 42
embodiment, 14, 55, 128, 131–33, 142, 269
Emoto, Masaru, 131
Enderby (BC), 5, 161, 165
energy consumption, 212
Energy Utility Board, 83
Environmental Protection Agency, 149
epistemology, 5, 40, 41, 57–59, 62, 117, 261, 265–68
ethics, 10, 15, 16, 18, 118, 123, 141, 156, 187, 190, 203, 218–19, 231, 267
European Parliament, 59
extinction, 250; mass extinction, 30–31

False Creek, 31, 34, 35, 37, 127, 185, 227–28, 245
farmers, 62–63
Fela Kuti, 229
Feldenkrais, 145, 156
feminism, 52–53, 58
Fernandes, Ciane, 156
fertilizers, 209
Figueroa, Angel Luis, 152
fire, 78–79, 83, 261, 269
First Nations oral history, 39
fish, 93, 123, 204, 212, 246, 266
fishermen, 84
flood hazards, 59–62
FLOW: For Love of Water (film), 12
fluidity, 53, 125
food, 35, 37, 212–13
Fraleigh, Sondra, 145
Fraser River, 118, 123, 165, 229–30, 246
Freeman, Victoria, 2

Freire, Paulo, 144
French River, 90–92
friendship, 9
Friends of the LA River (FOLAR), 148
frogs, 148
Fujianese women, 226

Ganges, 62
Garrison Creek, 241–42
genealogy, 120
Geographical Information Systems, 62
George, Amy (Marie), 5, 127
George, Chief Dan, 147
George, Rueben, 4–5
Georgeson, Annerose, 43
Georgian Bay, 107
Georgia Strait, 229
gestationality, 54, 57
Gibson's Landing, 29
gifting, 7, 15, 60–61, 96, 108, 187, 261, 264–65
Gimlett, Rose, 164
Gitxsan, 40, 47
glaciers, 113–14, 184
Gleason, William, 184
Glissant, Edouard, 268
global economy, 11
global warming, 15
Goddard, John, 13
Goto, Hiromi, 224, 230
governance (government), 201, 204
Grand Canyon, 75
grandmothers, 90, 102, 122, 131–32, 162. *See also* International Council of 13 Indigenous Grandmothers
Grand River, 17, 273
Grant, Larry, 5, 127, 245
gratitude, 108, 112, 177
Great Lakes, 13, 89, 90, 92–103
Green Party, 59
Greenpeace, 81, 84
Grillo, Eduardo, 167
Grimes, Varrick, 168
Guangdong province, 224
guardians, 198, 200–202
Gulf of Mexico, 16, 190, 210–11, 219–20, 246
Gulf of St. Lawrence (Maqtugweg), 122
Gu Xiong, 230

H_2Oil (film), 12
Haber-Bosch process, 208
Hammond, Harmony, 186
Hanna, Thomas, 145

Hanson, Akira, 163
Haraway, Donna, 10, 53, 57
Hardin, Garrett, 17
Harrison, Paul, 16, 30, 56, 207–16
Hawaii, 147
Health Canada, 9
hən'q'əmin'əm, 118
Hilton, Lorraine, 154
Hollow Tree, The, 33
home, 70
hope, 31, 40, 44, 46, 243
Hopi-Havasupai, 13, 75
Horne, Seonagh Odhiambo, 14, 139–60
Hsu, Madeleine, 225
Huasco Altino, 114
Huchuin (Ohlone), 217
Hui Shen, 225
human body, 92, 120
human rights, 133–34, 264
humbleness, 10, 12, 16
humility, 33, 40, 233, 268–69
Humphries, Deb, 163
Huppler, Amy, 164
Hyde, Lewis, 187
hydroelectricity, 56
hydrologic cycle, 53–55, 124, 263
hydrology, 43, 185

ice, 44, 181–87, 266–67
Idle No More, 9
Imperial Chemicals, 132
Imperial Oil, 84
India, 56, 197
Indigenous Message on Water, 19
Indigenous perspectives, 12, 43, 117–21
Indigenous resurgence, 117. *See also* resurgence
Indigenous sovereignty, 18
Indigenous Traditional Knowledge, 135
Indigenous voices, 18, 19, 75–80
inlets, 5
interdependence, 12
interfaith, 136
intergenerational relations, 10, 107, 190, 247
International Council of 13 Indigenous Grandmothers, 13, 76–78, 131
interweaving, 40, 42, 47
Irland, Basia, 14, 15, 16, 40, 181–92, 266
Iroquois Confederacy, 17

James, Florence, 140
James Bay, 56

Japan, 77
Jardine, Paula, 169
Jensen-Christian, Teresa, 175
jobs, 44–46
Johnson, Pauline, 17
Jordan, Kaleila, 147
Jung, Carl, 146

Kalamalka Lake, 1
Kalamazoo, Michigan, 83
Kearney, Dalynn, 176
Keepers of the Water, 16, 19, 97–99, 197–206
Kenya, 165
Khan, Sattar, 59–62
Khatsahlano, 34, 35
Kinder Morgan, 83
King, Martin Luther, 142–43
kinship, 120
Kinship of Rivers, 122, 165, 230
Kitsilano, 34
Klein, Naomi, 249
knowledge, 55–58, 111
Komagata Maru, 225
Komoks Nation, 123
Koplowitz, Stephan, 148
Kovach, Margaret, 167
Kwa, Lydia, 224

Laboucan-Massimo, Melina, 11, 13, 81–88, 56, 157, 261
Lac Brochet, 197
LaDuke, Winona, 93
Lai, Larissa, 6, 63, 259–70
Laiwan, 231
Lake Erie, 102
Lake Huron, 107, 110
Lake Michigan, 102
Lake Monona, 103
Lake Nipigon, 103
Lake Ontario, 241
Lake Superior, 103, 107
land, 3, 4
Land of Oil and Water (film), 12
Langley, Elizabeth, 153
Leon, Art, 127
Levi-Strauss, Claude, 46
Lew, Janey, 16, 217–240
life, 44, 46
Life-Art Process, 121, 124. *See also* Tamalpa Life-Art Process
Lin, Maya, 230

Lippard, Lucy, 183, 189
listening, 60, 269
Little Buffalo, 82
Lollie, Lindsey, 151, 153–55
Lopate, Phillip, 218
Los Angeles River, 14, 142, 146–49, 152
Lost Rivers, 241, 246
love, 219
Lubicon Cree, 2, 12, 81–88, 261
Lucumi tradition, 152

MacDonald, Murray, 174
Mackenzie River (Deh Cho), 84, 197
MacKinnon, JB, 246
MacLeod, Janine, 7, 10, 11, 51, 241–58
maje, 166
Mandamin, Josephine, 89, 94, 97–103, 107, 117, 132
Manitoba, 16, 119
Manuel, George, 4
Maracle, Lee, 1, 2, 10, 16, 41, 51, 55, 33–38, 63, 133, 135, 227, 232, 245, 259–60
Maupin, Bennie, 147, 151–52, 156
McAdam, Sylvia, 9
medicine, 93, 99, 110–11, 133
Meghna, 62
memory, 54, 69
menstrual cycles, 98–99
Menzies, Heather, 264
mercury contamination, 93
Métis, 85, 119, 133
Middle Passage, 268
Midewiwin, 95, 102, 107, 119, 131, 134
Miki, Roy, 224
M'ikmaq, 263
Miller, Howie, 7
Minh-ha, Trinh T., 219, 232
mining, 13–14, 75, 90, 113–14, 199, 262, 265
Mississippi River, 165, 210–11, 230
Mitchell, Alanna, 11, 12, 16, 29–32, 56
Mohawk, 2
Mohawk, John, 4
money, 199
Montreal, 122–23
moon, 98
moon-time, 97–99
Mother Earth, 76–79, 95, 97, 99, 103, 205–7. *See also* Earth Mother
Mother Earth Water Walk, 13, 89, 100–103, 107–12, 127, 131–32, 247, 261
Mother Market, 205

Mullis, Eric, 142
Museum of Contemporary Art (Boulder), 183
music, 146
muskeg, 81
Musqueam, 1, 34, 119, 123, 126–27, 134, 228, 259, 263
Myth of Niaslaws, 39

Nabhan, Gary Paul, 18
Nabigon, Herb, 33
Nadeau, Denise, 14, 15, 17, 117–38, 145, 218, 226
Nakata, Martin, 4
Narmada Valley, 56
natural law, 77
natural person, 204–5
Navigable Waters Protection Act, 9
ndoh, 166
Neimanis, Astrida, 6, 10, 16, 41, 51–68, 207, 247, 267
neoliberalism, 249
Newfoundland, 263
Nibi (water), 101, 104, 107, 119
Niger Delta, 56
Nigeria, 144
Nishnaabeg, 89–104. *See also* Anishnabe
Nisqually River, 183, 187–88, 190
nitrogen cycle, 30
nitrogen footprint, 16, 208–13
North Bay, 90
nudibranch, 44, 140, 143

occupation, 35
ocean, 11, 29–32, 34, 44, 56, 69–71, 207–14, 231, 247, 260, 266; acidity of, 30, 249; oxygen levels of, 30, 210; temperature of, 30
Ohama, Baco, 11, 69–71
oil and gas, 13, 81–84; oil spills, 82–85
Ojibway, 33, 90, 107, 127, 252
Oka crisis, 1
Okanagan Lake, 1
Olsen, Andrea, 129
Ominayak, Chief Bernard, 13
Ontario, 90, 107
ontology, 5, 39
orality, 75
Original Instructions, 79, 261
Orishas, 144, 152
Orr, Blair, 168, 171–72, 174–75

Orr, Jesse, 164
Ouma, Jimmy, 165, 168, 172, 176

Pacific Garbage Patch, 56
Pacific Ocean, 7, 29, 33, 165, 263
participatory water ethics, 16, 18, 139, 231
Pascua Lama gold mine, 13, 113–14
patriarchy, 53
peace, 9, 15, 19
Peace and Dignity Run, 132
Peace Athabasca Delta, 84
Peace River, 81
Pearl River, 2, 225
Peguis Nation, 119
Pellow, David, 184
performativity, 133
Permian extinction, 30
Peterborough, 100
Phare, Merrell-Ann, 14
philosophy, 43
pipelines, 13, 82–85
planetarity, 59, 63
plankton, 30
plastic, 52, 94, 268
plurality, 57
Poe, Edgar Allan, 143
poetics of water (poiesis), 7, 231–32
poetry, 69–71, 104, 113–14, 121–22, 193–94,
    271–73
poison, 93
Polacca, Mona, 10, 13, 16, 75–80, 131, 261
pollution, 16, 18, 92, 197–98, 208–13, 220
Port Daniel River (Epsegeneg Sipu), 122
Poslun, Michael, 4
poverty, 36
power, 52, 56, 60, 267, 269
PRATEC (Andean Project for Peasant Tech-
    nologies), 167
prayer, 99, 107, 122
precautionary principle, 17
property, 204
prophecies, 100
prosopopeia, 44
protocols, 126–28, 134–36, 264
public–private partnerships, 204
Puneluxulth', 140
puppets, 171–72, 175–76

Quebec, 56, 122

race, 223–24, 226, 230
rain, 34, 104
rapids, 91–92
reason, 62
reciprocity, 3, 8, 13, 190
reconciliation, 246
Red River, 119–20
Regan, Paulette, 260
relationships, 5, 6, 10, 37–38, 78, 95, 122–23,
    132–35, 189, 199, 202, 205–6, 260
relevance, 8
renewable energy, 85
residential schools, 8, 81, 107
respect, 3, 8, 9, 117, 135, 214, 265
responsibility, 3, 8, 14, 64, 79, 117, 121–23,
    133–35, 203, 233, 259, 263–65
resurgence, 117, 119, 135–36
reverence, 3, 8, 44
rice, 60, 62, 89
Ricepaper magazine, 217
rights, 199, 202–5
Rio Grande, 181, 183, 185, 187–88, 190
ritual, 133, 141
rivers, 2, 62–63, 81, 89, 91, 120, 144, 147–53,
    169, 177–78, 182–85
Robbins, Marlene, 168
Rogers, Janet, 17, 271–73
Runaway Moon Theatre, 161–79
Rusalka, 40

sacred, 95–96, 113–14, 124–25
sacrifice zones, 11
St. Catharines, 93
St. George St. Rainway Project, 217, 227–29
St. Lawrence River, 2, 103
St. Mary Lake, 140, 143, 147
Sakiyama, Shahira, 217
Salish Sea, 33, 118, 134
saliva, 124
salmon, 168
Salmon Run, 43
Salt Spring Island, 140–41, 147
Saltwater City, 225
Samaqan (TV series), 12
Sanderson, Darlene, 14
Sandford, Robert, 14
Sattar Khan, 59–62
Save the Fraser declaration, 85
Sawllkwa, 161–79

Schindler, David, 84
scientists, 1, 29, 31, 41, 43, 45, 184
Sea Sick, 11–12
Secwepemc, 1, 4, 161–63, 165, 177–78
Settle, Keith, 150–52, 154–55
sewers, 229, 241
sexuality, 54
Seymour River, 229
Sharma, Nandita, 264
shellfish, 134
Shirt, Pauline, 132
Shusterman, Richard, 142
Shuswap River, 1, 165, 168, 176
Siberian Traps, 30
Siksika, 259
silence, 60
Simpson, Leanne, 4
Sinopec, 264
Six Nations, 17
Sixties Scoop, 8
Slave Lake, 81
Smilde, Berndnaut, 42
Smith, Kimberley Michelle, 140, 150–55, 157
Snauq'w, 34–36, 122, 131, 227–28
social justice, 15, 227
somaesthetics, 140, 142, 157
somatics, 145, 156
songs, 95, 100, 119, 121–22, 127–28, 132, 166, 177
sovereignty, 40, 131, 259
Spanaxnox, 39
Spiegel, Jennifer, 51
spirit, 96, 101, 102, 109–11, 119–22, 133, 142, 146
Spivak, Gayatri, 51, 58–64, 268
Splatsin, 1, 6, 161–62, 165–66, 168, 170, 172, 178
Squamish, 1, 34, 126, 132, 228, 259, 263
stakeholders, 200–202
Stark, Daniel, 176
Sto:lo, 34, 133, 259
stories, 7, 12, 15, 18, 29, 31, 130–32, 135, 268
Stubington, Cathy, 5, 14, 15, 17, 31, 161–80
sturgeon, 93
subaltern, 58–64
submersible, 31
Sundance, 100
Suzuki, David, 181
sweat, 53

Syilx, 1, 4, 264
systemic racism, 9

Tagore, Proma, 224
Tamalpa Life-Art Process, 118
Tamil asylum seekers, 225
tar sands, 56, 81–85, 123, 157, 262
Tar Sands Healing Walk, 132
tears, 33, 35, 110, 125
technology, 10
temperature, 30
Thatcher, Margaret, 250
theory, 51
Thinking with Water, 2, 14, 19, 51–52
Third World, 58
Thomas, Kevin, 13
Thoreau, Henry David, 188
Three Gorges Dam, 56, 226
Thunder Bay, 89
tobacco, 103, 107–9
Toghestiy, 233
Tongva, 149
Toronto, 10, 241–55
toxic waste, 36, 249
toxins, 52, 93, 99
tragedy of the commons, 17
Tragedy of the Market, 17
transcendence, 40–41
transformation, 18, 40, 44, 54, 91, 118, 120, 154, 232, 246, 268
treaties, 7, 37, 90, 131
Treaty 7, 263
Trent University, 100
trickster, 47
TseKehNay, 8
Tsimshian, 39, 42
Tsleil-Waututh, 1, 5, 37, 126, 228, 259, 263
tsunami, 16, 193, 222–24, 264
Tsuu Tina, 259, 263
Txagetk, 39

umwelt, 12
UNESCO, 45
Unist'ot'en Camp, 19
United Nations, 83, 201
university system, 56
unknowability, 55, 58, 59, 63
uranium, 13, 75–76
urine, 53, 125
utopia, 243

Vancouver, 34, 126
Vancouver Moving Theatre, 170
vegetarianism, 214
Vicuna, Cecilia, 13, 113–14
violence, 125

Waawaasegaming, 103
Wah, Fred, 224
Walkem, Ardith, 14
Wall, Karolle, 140, 143
Wang Ping, 15, 165, 193–94, 230
water: as bond or relative 1, 5, 6, 15, 95, 125;
    water fountain 44; water molecule, 120;
    water use, 52
Water Is Life, 166, 177–78
Water on the Table (film), 12
watersheds, 18, 129–31, 182, 198, 210, 263
waves, 70
whales, 57
Whistler, 34
White, J. P., 135
whiteness, 8
white supremacy, 9
White Water, Black Gold (film), 12

Wikiwemikong Unceded First Nation, 89,
    94
Williams, Chief Bill, 5, 127, 245
Williams, Shirley, 89, 91–93
Williams, Tswum Rosalind, 162–63, 165–66
Wilson, Malin, 185
Wilson, Shawn, 167
Winnipeg, 119–20
Wolfe, George, 149
Wong, Rita, 1–25, 51, 185, 217, 226, 260,
    262–63, 266
World Bank, 59
World Trade Organization, 201
World Water Forum, 14
World Water Week, 141

Yangtze River, 165, 230
Yemaya, 14, 144, 152
Yoruba, 14, 152
Young Leon, Alannah, 4, 14, 15, 17, 117–38,
    150

Zamrak, Ibn, 44
Zizek, Slavoj, 249, 250

Books in the Environmental Humanities Series
Published by Wilfrid Laurier University Press

Animal Subjects: An Ethical Reader in a Posthuman World | Jodey Castricano, editor | 2008 | 324 pp. | ISBN 978-0-88920-512-3

Open Wide a Wilderness: Canadian Nature Poems | Nancy Holmes, editor | 2009 | 534 pp. | ISBN 978-1-55458-033-0

Technonatures: Environments, Technologies, Spaces, and Places in the Twenty-first Century | Damian F. White and Chris Wilbert, editors | 2009 | 282 pp. | ISBN 978-1-55458-150-4

Writing in Dust: Reading the Prairie Environmentally | Jenny Kerber | 2010 | 276 pp. | ISBN 978-1-55458-218-1 (hardcover), ISBN 978-1-55458-306-5 (paper)

Ecologies of Affect: Placing Nostalgia, Desire, and Hope | Tonya K. Davidson, Ondine Park, and Rob Shields, editors | 2011 | 360 pp. | illus. | ISBN 978-1-55458-258-7

Ornithologies of Desire: Ecocritical Essays, Avian Poetics, and Don McKay | Travis V. Mason | 2013 | 306 pp. | ISBN 978-1-55458-630-1

Ecologies of the Moving Image: Cinema, Affect, Nature | Adrian J. Ivakhiv | 2013 | 432 pp. | ISBN 978-1-55458-905-0

Avatar and Nature Spirituality | Bron Taylor, editor | 2013 | 378 pp. | ISBN 978-1-55458-843-5

Moving Environments: Affect, Emotion, Ecology, and Film Alexa Weik von Mossner, editor | 2014 | 296 pp. | ISBN 978-1-77112-002-9

Found in Alberta: Environmental Themes for the Anthropocene | Robert Boschman and Mario Trono, editors | 2014 | ISBN 978-1-55458-959-3

Sustaining the West: Cultural Responses to Western Environments, Past and Present | Liza Piper and Lisa Szabo-Jones, editors | 2015 | 380 pp. | ISBN 978-1-55458-923-4

Animal Subjects 2.0 | Jodey Castricano and Lauren Corman, editors | 2016 | 544 pp. | ISBN 978-1-77112-210-8

downstream: reimagining water | Dorothy Christian and Rita Wong, editors | 2017 | 300 pp. | ISBN 978-1-77112-213-9